BEHAVIORAL RESEARCH
a conceptual approach

Fred N. Kerlinger
University of Amsterdam

BEHAVIORAL
RESEARCH
a conceptual approach

HOLT, RINEHART AND WINSTON
New York   Chicago   San Francisco   Dallas
Montreal   Toronto   London   Sydney

Library of Congress Cataloging in Publication Data

Kerlinger, Frederich Nicholas, 1910–
  Behavioral research.
  Bibliography, p. 320.
  1. Psychological research. 2. Psychology—Philosophy
3. Psychometrics I. Title.
BF76.5.K39   150'.72   78-16793
ISBN: 0-03-013331-9

TABLE CREDITS

1.1, 10.2: from Miller, Daniel R., and Swanson, Guy E.: *Inner Conflict and Defense,* Copyright ©
1960 by Holt, Rinehart and Winston. Reprinted by permission of Holt, Rinehart and Winston.
5.2, 6.2: adapted from Clark, Carl A., Walberg, Herbert J., "The Influence of Massive Rewards
on Reading Achievement in Potential Urban School Dropouts." Copyright 1968 *American
Educational Research Journal,* Vol. 5, #3, 1968, American Educational Research Association,
Washington, D.C., pp. 305–310. 6.1: Aronson, E., and Mills, J., "The Effect of Severity of
Initiation on Liking for a Group." *Journal of Abnormal and Social Psychology,* 1959, 59, 177–181.
Copyright 1959 by the American Psychological Association. Reprinted by permission. 7.3:
Elaine Hatfield, T. Anne Cleary, and Margaret M. Clifford, "Research Note: The Effect of Race
and Sex on College Admission." *SOE,* Vol. 44, Spring 1970, data from Table 1 on p. 242. 7.4:
Berkowitz, L., "Anti-Semitism and the Displacement of Aggression." *Journal of Abnormal and
Social Psychology,* 1959, 59, 182–187. Copyright 1959 by the American Psychological Associa-
tion. Reprinted by permission. 8.1: Rokeach, Milton. *Beliefs, Attitudes, and Values.* San Fran-
cisco: Jossey-Bass Inc., Publishers. 1968. Page 170. Reprinted by permission. 10.1, 10.5: from
Communism, Conformity and Civil Liberties by Samuel A. Stouffer Copyright © 1955 by Samuel
A. Stouffer. Reprinted by permission of Doubleday & Company, Inc. 10.3: P. Lazarsfled, and
M. Rosenberg (eds.), *The Language of Social Research.* New York: Free Press, a division of
MacMillan Publishing Co., Inc. Copyright 1955. Reprinted by permission. 10.4: reprinted
from *The Enduring Effects of Education* by H. H. Hyman, C. R. Wright, and J. S. Reed by
permission of the University of Chicago Press. Copyright 1975, by the University of Chicago
Press. 11.1: from K. Marjoribanks, "Ethnic and Environmental Influences on Mental Abili-
ties." *American Journal of Sociology,* 1972, 78. Reprinted by permission of the University of
Chicago Press. Copyright 1972 by the University of Chicago Press. 12.1: reprinted from
Factorial Studies of Intelligence by L. L. Thurstone and T. G. Thurstone by permission of the
University of Chicago Press. Copyright 1941 by the University of Chicago Press. 12.8: Sontag,
Marvin, "Attitudes toward Education and Perception of Teacher Behaviors." *American Educa-
tional Research Journal,* Vol. 5, #3, pp. 395–396. Copyright 1968, American Educational Re-
search Association, Washington, D.C. 12.9: Kerlinger, F. N. "The Structure and Content of
Social Attitude Referents: A Preliminary Study." *Educational and Psychological Measurement,*
1972, 32, pp. 613–630. A.2: Whiting, J. W. M., and Child, I. L. *Child Training and Personality:
A Cross-cultural Study.* New Haven: Yale University Press, 1953. Reprinted by permission

To

William Clark Trow   Theodore M. Newcomb

Preface

The purpose of this book is to help people understand science and scientific research. Although it focuses on behavioral science and on research in psychology, sociology, and education, its central concern is the basic approach and principles of all science. Scientific disciplines differ in their content and substance, but their broad approach to inquiry is in general the same. It is this core of sameness on which the book concentrates.

One of the great needs of the time is for educated people to understand science. There is, of course, much popularization of science and scientific achievements in the media. There are also books that attempt to explain science. Most experts would probably agree, however, that much more has to be done to make science comprehensible to more people, and that scientists themselves must take some of the responsibility for such efforts.

The specific aim of *Behavioral Research: A Conceptual Approach* is to explain the abstract complexities of scientific research in a meaningful and nontechnical way without sacrificing depth and accuracy. It attempts to accomplish this by focusing on the conceptual bases of science and research and by limiting technical and methodological discussion to a few basic topics and areas. It also attempts to explain what science is and is not, what its purpose is, and how it works.

Another objective of the book is to bridge the understanding gap between the behavioral scientist and the nonscientist. The abstract nature of science and the technicalities of research can be obstacles to understanding. Moreover, they can obscure its essential simplicity and economy of purpose. It is a serious educational shortcoming that many, perhaps most, educated people know little of what an experiment is and what it is for, of measurement and its nature and purpose, or of the function and place of statistics in research. The person who has read this book attentively should have a firm conceptual grasp of behavioral science and behavioral research—from the point of view of the researcher.

A third purpose of the book is to define and explain some of the principal controversial issues associated with social scientific research. Controversies arise and flourish due to value differences and conflicts. They sometimes arise, however, from misconceptions of the problems that underlie them. What is research for? Why do it? What is objectivity? Why is it considered so important by scientists? What are basic research and applied research? Can human intelligence be measured? How do values affect science and research? Misunderstanding of such problems impedes understanding of science and research. The book therefore attempts to analyze and put these problems in perspective, if not to resolve them.

There are two main audiences for this text. The first consists of those persons who wish to learn something of the nature and problems of science and research in psychology, sociology, education, and other behavioral disciplines. What does it mean, for example, to study intelligence and prejudice scientifically? How are such enormously complex and elusive problems approached?

The second audience is advanced college undergraduate or early graduate students in almost any discipline, including nonscientific disciplines, who need to understand behavioral science and research. Students of the behavioral sciences should find the book particularly pertinent and useful. However, I have conceived it as a general text and guide for the students of many disciplines, even though its emphasis is psychological, sociological, and educational.

The book has three major parts. In the first part, Chapters 1, 2, and 3, the nature of science and scientific research is discussed. Necessary terms are defined, fundamental ideas explained and illustrated, and one or two controversial issues—objectivity, for instance—are introduced. Chapters 1 and 3 are probably the most important chapters of the book because they discuss what the goal of science is and why, and bring out the essence and purpose of scientific research problems and hypotheses. This part, then, can be called the conceptual foundations of the subject.

The second part—Chapters 4 through 13—treats what are to me the most important technical aspects of behavioral research. No one can really understand behavioral science and research without understanding at least the primary technical ideas. For example, the idea of randomness is fundamental. One cannot understand experiments or have any sort of clear idea of what research design and statistics are without understanding random processes and functions and their use in contemporary research. The coverage of this middle part is broad and diverse. It includes relations, probability, research design, measurement, and multivariate analysis. It is the technical core of the book expressed mostly in nontechnical language.

Chapter 4 lays the foundation: it examines relations and explanations and tries to show how they underlie the whole scientific enterprise. Chapter 5 offers an intuitive approach to probability and statistics. The importance of the idea of randomness, mentioned above, is strongly emphasized. Chapters 6, 7, and 8 are a unit on experimentation and research design. Research designs have the essential purpose of providing frameworks that make the answering of different research questions possible. Chapters 6 and 7 sketch the rationale of such scaffolding. Chapter 8 brings out the similarities and differences of experimental and nonexperimental research. This most important distinction is seldom thoroughly discussed in the literature. I believe it to be important enough to warrant a whole chapter. The distinction and its consequences, as treated in Chapter 8 and elsewhere in the book, can be challenged. But no matter how right or wrong the definition, distinctions, and consequences, the topic needs airing and understanding.

Measurement is the main concern of Chapter 9. Like statistics, psychological measurement is one of the major achievements of our time. While it still has far to go, a great deal is already known and some of the core of this knowledge is encapsulated in Chapter 9. While a great achievement, measurement has also been the Achilles heel of much behavioral research. The chapter helps clarify its strengths and weaknesses.

Chapter 10 seeks to describe a large and important kind of research—loosely called "sociological inquiry"—whose main characteristics are its nonexperimental nature and its measurement and modes of analysis. When, for example, researchers study mostly what can be called "sociological variables"—social class, occupational status, sex, religious and political preference, and so on—and when the predominant method of observation is counting, usually of the "sociological" characteristics of individuals, we have this kind of research. The chapter focuses on its characteristics and its use in behavioral research.

The inclusion of Chapters 11, 12, and 13 on the multivariate approach is essential in a book on contemporary behavioral research. Some individuals may think that the subject is too complex in a book of this kind. How can factor analysis, multiple regression, and discriminant analysis be explained nontechnically and accurately? A good question to which there is no ready and easy answer. The trouble is that if multivariate approaches to research and data analysis are not discussed, then a large gap is left in the reader's knowledge and understanding of behavioral research. Behavioral research is right now undergoing what is tantamount to a revolution mainly, I think, because of the multivariate approach and the modern high-speed computer. Research problems that could not in earlier years be contemplated because of inability to do the complex analyses involved are now approached almost routinely. Thus the decision was made to include the subject at a conceptual and semitechnical level. There is consequent oversimplification and ignoring of a number of important problems. The risks involved, however, are perhaps balanced by the better and more-rounded picture the reader may get. At the least, these chapters may heighten interest and open up a fascinating approach with many intriguing possibilities for creative and significant theory and research.

The third part of the book, Chapters 14, 15, and 16, discusses and probes several controversial and misunderstood problems that cause considerable trouble for science and scientists. One of these—fortunately, relatively easy to handle—is the nature and purpose of the computer. There is no doubt whatever that the computer has been and is one of the strongest influences on contemporary behavioral research. This influence is examined in the chapter. The remarkable powers of the computer are described and analyzed with the goal in mind of comprehending what the computer can do and, almost as important, what it cannot do. An attempt is also made, after this foundation is laid, to clear up one or two important misperceptions and misconceptions of the computer and its place in the research scheme of things.

The last two chapters of the book, Chapters 15 and 16, primarily probe several controversial and misunderstood problems that intrigue and perplex researchers and observers of science and research. The question of what science is for, for example, is attacked directly, and conclusions are stated that may puzzle some readers. Any complex human activity is controversial. Science is no exception. I decided, therefore, that some of the most important and troublesome misconceptions of science and research had to be addressed. There is, of course, considerable risk in doing so. It will appear that sides in a debate are taken. Actually, it is not sides that are taken so much as it is positions based on the considered nature of science. This again becomes an obstacle to understanding. For instance, many people believe that the purpose of scientific research is to enhance man's well-being. When this is flatly contradicted and it is said that the purpose of scientific research is theory, or understanding and explanation, it is not surprising that difficulties may arise. It is the aim, however, to so explain things that the reasons for statements made will be understood and at least considered. So the last two chapters of the book explore controversies and misconceptions. They attempt to put three or four of the larger partly philosophical issues of science and research into perspective.

Although the book can be considered methodological in a broad sense, it is not a methods book. No attempt is made to teach how to do research. The total emphasis is on understanding research. To be sure, it is probably not possible to understand any complex subject without actively working at it. Really to understand statistics, most people have to work at statistical problems, for example. Nevertheless, a substantial degree of understanding can be attained by a sort of vicarious working at problems. Many such "vicarious workings" are given. For instance, an important feature of the book is the description of actual research studies, usually with the theory behind the studies and the questions asked by the researchers. So the book describes the way researches have been done and is thus to some extent methodological. But it almost completely bypasses actual methods of making observations, measuring variables, analyzing data, and the like. The need for information on such topics is satisfied to some extent by the Appendix, in which types of research other than those treated in the text, certain methods of observation and data collection, and two or three common methods of statistical analysis are discussed.

I am grateful to a number of individuals for their help in reading either the draft of the whole book or of parts of it, or otherwise helping me clear up inadequate conceptions. First, my editor at Holt, Rinehart and Winston, Richard Owen, made the book possible. He not only encouraged me to tackle the project and reacted perspicaciously to all aspects of the book and saw it through to publication; he also patiently helped me overcome the many doubts and fears I had over its adequacy. (He also suffered the delays of the changed conceptions of the book, as well as of my changes of job and location.) I am grateful for his professional help and for his friendship.

Two other colleagues and friends, Professors Elazar Pedhazur and Marianne Denis-Prinzhorn, carefully and conscientiously pointed out the inadequacies of the first draft of early chapters of the book. Most important, they helped me clear away the debris of a grossly inadequate conception. I deeply appreciate their suggestions.

Some five or six readers of the whole book or parts of it have made me conscious of gaucheries, inaccuracies, and other evils. The names of three or four of these readers are unknown to me. So I thank them collectively and, as it were, anonymously. Two of the reader-critics, Professors Theodore Newcomb and Ellis Page, made highly significant and discerning critical contributions to the book. Indeed, both caused me to change direction to some extent. I cannot thank them enough for the extent and depth of their criticisms and suggestions.

Two of my University of Amsterdam colleagues, Doctors J. van Heerden and G. J. Mellenbergh, helped me clarify three or four philosophical and methodological difficulties and problems in Chapters 13, 15, and 16. I thank them for their balanced and valuable criticisms.

Work on the book would never have come to life without the intellectual stimulation of the academic communities of the University of Amsterdam and New York University. I express my appreciation of both universities in the abstract, therefore, and of my colleagues and friends at both places who, perhaps without knowing it, stimulated my interest, contributed to my thinking, and provided the kind of atmosphere that makes intellectual work possible.

Although she knows how much she has helped me, I don't think my wife really understands that she is a significant part of this book. In any case, for putting up with my frustrations and moods, disregarding what she considered to be trivial obstacles, cutting through nonsense, and giving me needed support and encouragement, I thank her.

Amsterdam, The Netherlands
June 1978   FRED N. KERLINGER

Contents

1

The nature of science and scientific research

How do we "know" the world? How can we understand people and what they do? We can read about the world and people and learn a great deal. For example, knowledge of people and their motives and behavior can be gotten from poems, novels, and psychology texts. To probe deep into people's feelings and motives, we can read Freud and Dostoevsky. A second way to learn about the world is to have others tell us about it. Parents and teachers tell children what the world is like. Politicians, newsmen, and professors constantly tell us what they think we should know. Such knowledge is derived from authority; some source we accept as authoritative gives it to us.

Observation is another important road to knowledge. We observe the world and people all our lives. We use our senses to receive and interpret information from outside ourselves. I see a car bearing down on me at great speed. I jump out of the way. I have observed the car and its speed, inferred danger, and taken action. Observation is obviously a very important source of knowledge.

Unfortunately, authority and ordinary observation are not always reliable guides. Whole populations of people will read, hear, and believe what demagogues say. And it has long been known that most people can be poor observers of even the simplest phenomena. Let two people, for example, observe an individual make gestures, and then ask them what the individual did. If they agree in their observations, it will be remark- **1** able. If they agree in their interpretation of what the individual did, it will be still more remarkable. One of the difficulties is that no events are really simple. Another is that observers interact with and affect what they observe. Thus observation is an active process that is rarely if ever simple.

Science developed partly because of the need for a method of knowing and understanding more reliable and trustworthy than the relatively uncontrolled methods of knowing generally used. An approach to knowledge capable of yielding reliable and valid information about complex phenomena, including the complex phenomenon of man himself, had to be invented. Absolutistic, metaphysical, and mythological explanations of natural phenomena had to be supplanted—or at least supplemented—by an approach that was to some extent outside man. The success of science as an approach to knowledge and understanding of natural phenomena has been remarkable. But understanding science and the approach used by scientists has been considerably less than remarkable. Indeed, it can be said that science is seriously misunderstood.

The basic purpose of this book is to help the reader understand the approach, thinking, and methods of science and scientific research. Its special focus will be research in psychology, sociology, and education. The general approach is the same, or at least basically similar, in all sciences. We will study this approach rather carefully. There are special problems and difficulties, however, in behavioral science and research, and we must to some extent know them if we are to understand such research.[1] In other words, the general approach to knowledge and understanding of physics and psychology is the same, but the details of theory and investigation are quite different. For instance, the complexity and ambiguity of human behavior, generally conceded to be more complex and ambiguous than the objects of the physical world, create major problems of reliable and valid observation and inference. To measure aspects of human behavior—aggressiveness, prejudice, political preference, and school achievement, for example—is usually more difficult than to measure the properties of physical bodies.

The need for understanding science and the scientific approach is great. The need is especially great in psychology, sociology, and education because of the human and social urgency of the problems that psychological, sociological, and educational researchers study and because of the con-

---

[1] The behavioral sciences are those sciences that study and seek to understand man, human institutions, and human actions and behaviors: sociology, psychology, anthropology, economics, political science. The term "social sciences" is also used, but "behavioral sciences" appears to be a more general, more inclusive, term. This definition is only in general correct. Although the behavioral disciplines can be fairly clearly defined, the distinctions have often been blurred in actual theory and research. Sociologists and psychologists, for instance, often borrow from each others' fields. Moreover, some behavioral scientists, despite the definition of behavioral research, study animals, sometimes with considerable impact on scientific knowledge of behavior.

troversial nature of some of the problems and methods of the behavioral sciences. This book focuses on this need.

THE GENERAL NATURE OF SCIENCE

Science is an enterprise exclusively concerned with knowledge and understanding of natural phenomena. Scientists want to know and understand things. They want to be able to say: If we do such-and-such, then so-and-so will happen. If we frustrate children, then they will probably aggress against other children, their parents, their teachers, even themselves. If we observe an organization with relatively rigid rules that severely restrict the members of the organization, say the teachers of a school, then we can expect to find considerable dissatisfaction among the members of the organization.

Scientists, then, want to "know" about phenomena. They want, among other things, to know what produces aggressive behavior in children and adults. They want to know whether frustration leads to aggression. They want to know the effects on organization members of restrictive and permissive ways of administering organizations. In short, they want to "understand" how psychological, sociological, and educational phenomena are related.

Two Research Examples

To give us something specific to work with, let us examine two research studies. One is an experiment, the other is not an experiment. For now, an experiment is a research study in which different things are done to different groups of subjects—pigeons, rats, children, adults—to see whether what is done to them produces different effects in the different groups. For instance, an educational researcher may have teachers write complimentary remarks on the completed tests of one group of high school children and nothing on the tests of another group of children (see Page, 1958).[2] Then the researcher sees how this "manipulation," as it is called, affects the performance of the two groups on subsequent tests.

In a nonexperimental study, on the other hand, there is no "manipulation," no deliberate controlled attempt to produce different effects by different manipulations. The relations among phenomena are studied with no experimental intervention. The characteristics of subjects, "as they are," are observed, and the relations among the characteristics are assessed with no attempt to change anything. For example, when sociologists study the relation between social class and school achievement, they take social class and school achievement "as they are." They measure the two "variables,"

---

[2] The references cited in this manner are given at the end of the book.

as they are called, and then study the relation between them. They do not try to change one of the variables to study the effects of the change on another variable. These ideas should become clear after reading the discussion of the two studies that follow.

AN EXPERIMENT: Massive Reward and Reading Achievement

A great deal of research has been devoted to how people and animals learn. One of the most well-documented findings is that reward enhances learning. If responses are rewarded in some way, the same or similar responses will tend to be repeated when the same or similar conditions occur again. If, for example, children are told they have done well when they spell correctly, the correct spelling will tend to be remembered and used subsequently. (The results are not so predictable if punishment is used.) The theory behind the research, called reinforcement theory, is now being applied to educational situations, sometimes with gratifying results.[3]

Clark and Walberg (1968) wondered if massive rewards might help to produce better reading achievement of potential school dropouts. They devised a simple experiment to test this notion. They used black children, 10 to 13 years old, who were one to four years behind in their school work. Two groups were set up in such a manner[4] that it could be assumed that they were approximately equal in characteristics that might affect the outcome. Intelligence, for instance, is known to affect school work like reading and arithmetic. The researchers must therefore try to make the two groups equal in intelligence before the study begins. If they do not, the outcome of the experiment may be due not to what is done in the experiment but to one group's having an average level of intelligence higher than that of the other group. In the kind of research in which two groups are used and some special treatment is given to one of the groups, this group has often been called the "experimental group." The other, to which nothing special is done, has been called the "control group."

---

[3] If the reader thinks that the positive reinforcement principle is obvious, he should bear in mind that it was not used in schools of earlier years except, of course, by insightful teachers. Rather, punishment was evidently the prime principle. Children were expected to be correct in their conduct and work and were punished if they were not. Indeed, punishment, or negative reinforcement, is still a widely used method of school motivation.

[4] They assigned the children to the two groups "at random." One way of doing this is to toss a coin for every child. If the coin is heads, assign the child to one of the groups. If the coin is tails, assign the child to the other group. The principle is that chance governs the assignment to the groups and, hopefully, nothing else. There are a number of other methods used, for example, tables of random numbers. All the methods are inspired by the same principle. The basic purpose of random assignment is to "equalize" experimental groups. Since Clark and Walberg used random assignment, they could assume that the groups were equal *before* the experiment. We discuss such chance and random matters in a later chapter.

At the beginning of the experiment *all* the pupils were praised for their work. This was used to establish reward rates for the teachers of the children. (Teachers, of course, differ in the amounts of reward they customarily use.) After six sessions the reward rates were stabilized and the experiment itself began. The teachers of the experimental group children, the children to receive the special or experimental treatment, were told to double or triple the rewards they gave, while the teachers of the control group children were told "to keep up the good work." At the end of a three-week period, the children were given a reading test.

Analysis of the test results showed that the experimental, or "massive reward," group children did better on the test than the control group children. This conclusion was inferred from a statistical test of the difference between the average reading scores of the two groups: the average of the experimental group was greater than the average of the control group. Later we will explain the principle behind such statistical tests. For now, it can be said that massive reward was effective in increasing the average score of the experimental group as compared to the average score of the control group. Whether one can say that massive rewards work with black underachieving children and should be used with them will depend on further research addressed to seeing whether the same results are obtained repeatedly—this is called replication—and testing reinforcement in general with different kinds of children. In other words, the results of one study are suggestive, certainly not conclusive. Maybe black underachieving children should be given massive reinforcement—but maybe not.

A NONEXPERIMENTAL STUDY: Social Class and Types of Upbringing

We now examine a nonexperimental study. Recall that in such a study there is no experimental manipulation; there is no differential treatment of groups of subjects. We take people and groups "the way they are" and study the presumed influences of variables on other variables, the relations between variables. ("Variable" is defined in Chapter 2. For now, it is the term used to mean some psychological or sociological concept on which people or things vary or differ, for example, sex, social class, verbal ability, achievement.) A "relation" in science always means a relation between variables. When we say that variables A and B are related, we mean that there is something common to both variables, some connection between them. Suppose we imagine that the two circles of Figure 1.1 represent the essences of whatever A and B are. That is, A represents the essence of whatever the variable A is. It is the stuff of A. The B circle, of course, represents the essence of B. Note that the A and B circles overlap and that the overlap is indicated with horizontal hatching. This indicates that some of the essences of A and B are shared. Some part of A is like some part of B, and vice versa. This shared part, indicated by the horizontally hatched area, represents the relation between A and B. A may be intelligence and B school achievement. The overlap in Figure 1.1 is the relation between

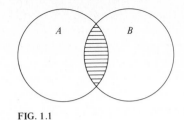

FIG. 1.1

them. What is this shared property? It is hard to say without further evidence. It may be verbal aptitude or ability; it may be what has been called general intelligence. Let us return to our example now.

Psychologists and sociologists have done a great deal of research on social class and have found it to be important in explaining different kinds of behavior: recreation, voting, and child-rearing, for example, are phenomena associated with social class. Miller and Swanson (1960) predicted, among other things, a relation between the social-class membership of parents and the time they weaned their children. A sample of 103 middle-class and working-class mothers in a large midwestern city were asked how they were bringing up their children. The result on a time of weaning question is given in Table 1.1. The numbers in the cells represent numbers of mothers who were middle class or working class and had weaned their children early or late.

Study of the numbers of cases in the cells indicates that middle-class mothers seem to wean their children at an earlier age than working-class mothers. Of the 55 middle-class mothers, 33 weaned early, whereas 22 weaned later, and of the 48 working-class mothers, 17 weaned early and 31 weaned late.[5] There is apparently a relation, though not a strong one, between social class and time of weaning. Middle-class mothers weaned their children earlier; working-class mothers weaned them later. If one calculates proportions and percentages, what has just been said becomes a bit clearer: 33/55 = .60, 22/55 = .40, 17/48 = .35, 31/48 = .65 (multiplying each of these by 100 gives percentages). These proportions are entered in the table in the lower right corners of the cells. Note that they more clearly express the relation under discussion than the frequencies (the original numbers). We can say that there is a tendency for middle-class mothers to wean early and working-class mothers to wean late. Whenever we can make an if-then statement, we have a relation. In this case, we can say, though cautiously: If middle-class mother, then early weaning, and if working-class mother, then late weaning. Naturally one cannot say that this trend is present among all middle-class and working-class mothers. This is only one sample, and the trend may or may not be present among all mothers. More research would be required to strengthen the statement and one's faith in its "truth."

[5] You should not be too concerned at this point if you do not completely grasp how to read and interpret this and other tables. The tables are being used only for illustrative purposes. Greater understanding will come later.

TABLE 1.1 Social Class and Time of Weaning, Miller and Swanson (1960) Study[a]

SOCIAL CLASS	WEANING		
	Early	Late	
Middle Class	33 (.60)	22 (.40)	55
Working Class	17 (.35)	31 (.65)	48
	50	53	103

[a] The cell entries are frequencies: numbers of mothers. The figures in parentheses are proportions, for example, 33/55 = .60. If the proportions are multiplied by 100, percentages are obtained: (33/55)(100) = (.60)(100) = 60 percent, or 60 percent of the middle-class mothers said that they weaned their children early.

These two studies have a number of features that are characteristic of behavioral research. First, one is an experimental study and the other nonexperimental. Second, they illustrate objectivity, a characteristic of scientific research that we will examine shortly. Third, their use of elementary quantitative analysis will help give us some insight into analysis and statistics. For example, in the Clark and Walberg study, averages were calculated and compared, and in the Miller and Swanson study, frequencies were tabulated and compared. These are two of the commonest modes of quantitative analysis. Fourth, the problems, relations, and methodology of both studies are simple and clear; they will be useful to illustrate points to be made in subsequent discussions.

More pertinent to the main theme of this chapter is what the studies tried to do, what their purposes were. One of the purposes of the Clark and Walberg study was to understand and explain achievement, or rather, a certain aspect of achievement, so-called underachievement. One of the purposes of the Miller and Swanson study was to explain weaning, which is, of course, an aspect of child-rearing practice. The words "understand" and "explain" have to be interpreted broadly. When we say we "understand" a phenomenon, we mean that we know its characteristics—or at least some of them—what produces it and what its relations are with other phenomena. We mean that we try to "explain" the phenomenon. We can tell what probably caused it, what influences it now, what will influence it, what it influences. It is important to note here that our understanding of a phenomenon is always incomplete, partial, and probabilistic. Indeed, much of our knowledge of the world and its phenomena, especially human and social phenomena, is partial, even shaky.

Achievement is an important phenomenon in the Western world. When we say we seek "understanding" of it, we mean, in part, that we want to know why some people achieve a great deal, while others achieve very little. Or, more ambitiously, we might want to know why some groups achieve a good deal and others little. For example, McClelland (1961), in a stimulating book, *The Achieving Society,* has described research aimed at the general question: How and why do people in different countries differ in their motivation to achieve? It is possible to go on at great length about such a rich concept as achievement. The core of the understanding and explanation idea, however, is that we explain a phenomenon by specifying what is related to it.

Clark and Walberg were interested in explaining a relatively narrow aspect of achievement. They wanted to understand and explain the reading achievement of black children who were generally deficient in school achievement. They wanted to know if massive reinforcement of achievement affected it positively. They studied, then, the relation between reinforcement and reading achievement. They were successful in showing that massive reinforcement positively affected the reading achievement of the children. They "explained" achievement to some small extent because they showed something that affected it.[6]

The phenomenon "explained" by Miller and Swanson was weaning, or perhaps more accurately, child-rearing practices, which included, among other things, disciplinary methods, types of reward used, and methods for compelling obedience. They showed, for example, that middle-class and working-class mothers differed in their weaning practices. They thus established a relation between, on the one hand, social class, and, on the other hand, weaning practice. They showed that some of the observed differences in weaning practices were due to social class, in other words. They thus to some extent "explained" differences in weaning practices.

We break off our discussion of scientific goals and purposes to discuss two highly important characteristics of science. The first, objectivity, is a methodological characteristic that is controversial and not easy to understand. The second is the empirical nature of science. After discussing these characteristics, we will be in a better position to continue the main discussion. It can be said clearly and categorically that without the "method" or "criterion" of objectivity or without the empirical approach and attitude, science as it is known in the modern world would not be possible. What does this strong statement mean? And what does it have to do with the nature of scientific research?

OBJECTIVITY AND SCIENTIFIC RESEARCH

While easy to define, objectivity is not easy to understand because of its subtlety and its complex implications. It is a most important methodological aspect of science, especially of psychological science, because its implementation makes it possible for scientists to test their ideas

---

[6] They also threw a little more light on another important phenomenon, reinforcement. They seemed to show that with some children ordinary amounts of praise and encouragement are not enough; such children evidently require a great deal of it—at least if reading achievement is to be influenced.

apart from themselves. They set up their experiments "out there." The experiments take place, so to speak, apart from themselves and their influence and predilections. Instead of being in their heads, the ideas being tested are objectified, made objects "out there," objects that have an existence, as it were, apart from their inventors. Anyone can observe an experiment and how it is done; it is quite public.

All knowledge of the world is affected, even distorted to some extent, by predispositions of observers. And the more complex the observations, the farther away they are from physical reality and the greater the inferences that must be made, the greater the probability of distortion. When the physical scientist measures weights, for instance, there is a low probability of distortion: little opportunity exists for personal views, biases, and preconceptions to enter the process. But consider the distortion possibilities in the study and measurement of authoritarianism, dogmatism, intelligence, level of aspiration, achievement, social class, anxiety, and creativity.

Take just one of these variables, creativity. Even though you and I agree that we will study and measure creativity, we may have quite different ideas of what creativity is. And these different ideas, these different perceptions, can influence our observations of, say, creativity in children. A behavioral act that to you indicates creativity may not indicate creativity to me, and these differences in perception can affect our measurements. In other words, the actual observations of creative behavior can be quite different, depending on who does the observing, unless some method to make the observations is agreed upon—and rigidly adhered to.

Objectivity is agreement among "expert" judges on what is observed or what is to be done or has been done in research. Suppose one scientist observes something and records his observation, in numerical form, say. Another scientist of equal competence independently observes the same thing and records his observation. If the procedure can be repeated with the same or similar results—that is, the scientists' observations agree— then objectivity has been achieved. In some areas of science, for example physics and chemistry, objectivity is not a severe problem because instruments of high precision, like electronic microscopes, are used to make observations. Such instruments increase the probability of agreement among judges because different judges, by using them, are more likely to obtain and report the same results. Moreover, a machine is less likely to influence the observations and to be influenced by the nature of what is observed.

The definition of objectivity as agreement among judges should not be narrowly interpreted; it is quite general. What does this mean? The main condition to satisfy the objectivity criterion is, ideally, that *any* observers with minimal competence agree in their observations. In psychology and education, for example, objective tests and scales are used. They are called "objective" because any clerks, given appropriate instructions, can score them and get the same scores (within small margins of error). Objective tests do not mean that the tests themselves are "objective." They are objective because the scores they yield are the same no matter who scores them. In contrast, the correctness of answers to essay questions depends very much on the individual judgment of the judge, whereas such judgments are virtually ruled out with objective tests. (It should be noted, however, that the scoring and assessment of essay tests can be made much more objective than they usually are.)

Let us change the perspective a bit. In the Clark and Walberg study, the measure of reading achievement was more objective than the measure of times of weaning in the Miller and Swanson study because the former was measured with an objective-type test, whereas the latter was measured through interviewing. Almost anyone scoring the reading test would get the same scores as anyone else. But different interviewers might show differences with the time-of-weaning measure, in this case for two reasons. The first is that just given: different judges can interpret interviewees' responses differently. A mother may say that she weaned her child when the child was seven to nine months old. One interviewer may be satisfied with this response and record it. But another interviewer may probe deeper and find out that the mother weaned her child at six months. The second reason is that the mother's memory may be faulty: she may simply not remember just when she weaned her child, but may say it was at ten months when it was in fact at eight months. There is no such ambiguity with objective-type measures (though they are not free from other kinds of difficulty). An objective-type reading test, for example, has explicit rules for scoring answers. The response to any item is either correct or incorrect: there is little room for scorer judgment or initiative.

The importance of objectivity requires still further explanation. While it is usually applied to scientific observations and measurement, the idea is wider. When psychologists do experiments, they strive for objectivity. This means that they do their research—they so control the experimental situation and so describe what they do—that other psychologists can repeat the experiment and get the same or similar results. In other words, objectivity helps researchers "get outside" themselves, helps them achieve publicly replicable conditions, and, hopefully, publicly ascertainable findings. Science is a public social enterprise like so many other human enterprises, but an important and unique rule of the scientific enterprise is that all procedures must be objective—so done that there is or can be agreement among expert judges. This rule gives science a distinct, almost remote nature because the greater the objectivity, the farther removed the procedure is from human characteristics—and limitations. For instance, the almost glacial objectivity of parts of the natural sciences, whose experiments are done in highly controlled laboratory situations and whose observations are made almost wholly with machines of high reliability and precision, seems very remote from people and their personal and social concerns. (This does *not* mean that the scientists doing the research and controlling the machines are, in and of themselves, immune to error.)

Compare, now, procedures in psychology and education. Physical scientists can get "outside themselves" easier than behavioral scientists because it is easier for them to set up research procedures and test hypotheses "out there" apart from their own and others' biases and predilections. This is because the procedures are more amenable to being "objectified." Once the working of a physical process is understood, it can be made to occur or be measured by most competent and knowledgeable scientists and technicians. There is, in other words, relatively high replicability.

In psychological, sociological, and educational research, however, this is true to a much lesser degree. The manipulation of psychological variables, like cohesiveness of groups, classroom atmosphere, leadership styles, and anxiety, is much more difficult to make objective because of greater complexity, range of variation, and amenability to influences other than those of the experimenter. Similarly, the measurement of behavioral variables such as intelligence, achievement, attitude, social class, and motivation is more subject to systematic and random influences, making it more difficult—though by no means impossible, as some critics say—for different observers to agree in their observations and measurements. This does *not* mean, however, that the psychologist's procedures are not objective. Indeed, they can often possess a relatively high level of objectivity. They are simply less objective than those of the physical scientist.

There is no difference whatever in principle, on the other hand, between the use of the criterion of objectivity by the physical scientist and by the behavioral scientist. The only difference is in degree of objectivity. It has been said that the behavioral sciences cannot really be scientific because they cannot use the methods of the physical sciences. This is simply not so, except in a purely literal sense. The same *approach* and similar *general* methods are used in all the sciences. So it is far from impossible to achieve objectivity in the behavioral sciences; it has been achieved successfully many times. It is just more difficult.

Objectivity and Explanation

As we proceed, we will find that objectivity, either expressed or implied, will pervade our discussion and study. This is as it should be. Without objectivity science and scientific research lose their unique and special character. Indeed, there would be no science without objectivity, as I said earlier. It must hastily be added, however, that objectivity *in and of itself* has little importance. That is, the basic purpose of science is explanation of natural phenomena; it is not simply to be objective. Objectivity is important because it can help provide more trustworthy explanations of natural phenomena. Just to be objective, however, does not mean to be scientific. A procedure can be highly objective and yield misleading observations and false conclusions. An experimenter, for example, may have succeeded in setting up a study which is a model of objectivity but whose results are misleading. He may have tested what he thought was the influ-

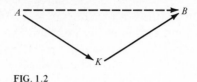

FIG. 1.2

ence of *A* on *B* and obtained results that seemed to show that *A* did indeed influence *B*. Unbeknownst to him, however, another influence, *K*, was the "true" cause of the change in *B*. The investigator's manipulation of *A* activated *K* which produced the observed change in *B*. This is shown in Figure 1.2. The broken arrow indicates the influence of *A* on *B* that the investigator was studying; he thought *A* had influenced *B*. The solid arrows indicate the real influence: *A* activated *K* which influenced *B*.

Objectivity, moreover, does not mean importance. One can often be highly objective with more trivial problems than with rich and significant problems. We may, for instance, study the relation between numbers of desks in classrooms and the verbal achievement of children. Both number of desks and verbal achievement can be measured with a high degree of objectivity. But so what? Nevertheless, objectivity is an indispensable and inseparable characteristic of science and scientific research.

Objectivity as Characteristic and as Procedure

Before leaving objectivity, we should try to clarify and correct an important misconception. Many people, even some behavioral scientists, think that objectivity refers to a quality or characteristic of persons. While it is probably true that individuals differ in degree of objectivity—considering objectivity to be a trait that individuals possess—this has little or nothing to do with objectivity in science. Objectivity in science is a procedure, a method, a way of going about one's scientific business. It does not mean that scientists are personally more objective than other people, though many of them may be.

This misconception unfortunately creates mischief. Certain critics of science aim their major criticisms at objectivity, saying, for example, that the remoteness and coldness of science destroy human values, and thus science is fundamentally harmful. This remoteness and coldness, it is said, leads to dehumanization of the scientist and the people affected by science—all of us. Scientists are even depicted as monsters, even more dangerous because they come wrapped in virtuous cloaks.

The argument is a fabric woven of nonsense. It is true—but not in the romantic way of the critics—that science is remote and perhaps cold. This follows from its goal of abstractness and from its criterion of objectivity. General laws, general statements of relations, are necessarily abstract because they must apply to many specific cases. The ideal scientific law is a mathematical equation not because scientists love mysterious and esoteric symbols and mathematics (some do, of course), but because a mathematical equation is highly abstract and general. If empirically valid, it can explain many different manifestations of the law or statement of relation. "Frustration leads to aggression" is a broad general statement of a relation. It is valuable because it covers many, if not all, manifestations of frustration and aggression.[7] It is also remote, maybe even a little cold compared to a teacher's or a therapist's description of a single aggressive boy or girl.

Abstractness, part of the power of science, is always remote from ordinary preoccupations and the warmth of human relations. This is by definition; it is part of the nature of science. Without such abstractness there is no science. So it is with objectivity. It, too, tends to make science appear remote and cold. It appears remote and cold because the testing of scientific propositions is done "out there," as much as possible away from people and their emotions, wishes, values, and attitudes, including those of the scientist. But this is precisely what must be done. One must obey the canon of objectivity—or give up science.

THE EMPIRICAL CHARACTER OF SCIENCE

The empirical character of science is considerably easier to understand than objectivity, perhaps because it is associated with what has become almost a stereotype of the scientist: as a white-coated grubber after facts. It is true that most scientists are constantly concerned with "facts," but we must try to replace stereotyped notions with understanding of the reasons for concern with factual evidence. By now the reader will know that the viewpoint of this book is strongly influenced by concern and preoccupation with theory and explanation. Nonscientists can say that they too are concerned with theory and explanation. And that is so. Philosophers seek, for example, to explain how we know things. Historians want to explain the origins of historical movements and events, for instance, the causes and consequences of the Civil War or of the Russian Revolution. Political theorists seek explanations of political movements like the influence of conservative thinking on the actions of political parties and figures.

Explanation as explanation, then, is not the sole prerogative of science. Nor is scientific emphasis on evidence an exclusive possession. Historians and political theorists, among others, invoke evidence to bolster their explanations of historical and political phenomena. What, then, is the difference? Why is science unique? To answer these questions satisfactorily will take much of this book. But we must now at least begin the explanation.

Most of modern behavioral science is characterized by a strong empirical attitude and approach. Unfortunately, the word "empirical" has been used in two ways that are quite different in meaning. In one, "empirical" means guided by practical experience and observation and not by science

[7] Such statements cannot be *too* general because, if they are, they cannot be disconfirmed. As we will see later, scientific statements must be able to be tested and be amenable to being shown to be false if they are indeed false.

and theory. This is a pragmatic view which says that if it works it is right. Never mind the reasons; what counts is that it works. This is *not* the meaning of "empirical" as used by scientists (though scientists are not unpragmatic). For the scientist "empirical" means guided by evidence obtained in systematic and controlled scientific research. Here is an example to help us understand what "empirical" means in science.

Scientific research has been directed toward determining whether it is possible for animals and people to learn to control responses of the autonomic nervous system. Can they, for example, lower their heartbeat or increase their urine secretion at will (Miller, 1971, Chs. 55, 56)? Both older and newer beliefs say that this is not possible. So, a generalization is: It is not possible for people to control responses governed by the autonomic nervous system. It so happens that the statement is probably not true: it has been found that animals (and perhaps people) can be trained to do such things as raise and lower their heartbeats, raise and lower their urine secretion, and even alter their blood pressure (Miller, 1971, Part XI). An empirically oriented statement would be: Animals can, within certain limits, control responses of the autonomic nervous system, given appropriate "instruction." Animals can be taught, for instance, to raise or lower their heartbeats and raise and lower their urine secretion. It isn't easy but it has been done. These are empirical statements since they are based on scientific evidence.

Because a statement is empirical does not necessarily mean that it is true. Since it is based on scientific research and evidence, it is more likely to be true than a statement based wholly on beliefs. Nevertheless, it may still not be true. The above statement about learning to control the autonomic nervous system to some extent, although at present supported by scientific research evidence, may turn out in the long run not to be true. It may not be possible to obtain the same results next year or the year after, or in Australia as well as in America. It is possible that the research findings supporting the statement were the result of some temporary and unrecognized cause which was characteristic only of the particular situation in which the research was done. Still, the probability of a statement based on empirical evidence being true is greater than the probability of a nonempirical statement being true. Carefully obtained empirical evidence, as we will see, is a healthy and necessary corrective of man's beliefs and a salutary means of decreasing ignorance. Nonempirical evidence, on the other hand, can and often does help perpetuate ignorance, as old proverbs do. Empirical evidence, in short, checks our frequently unbridled addiction to making assertions about the world, assertions that may or may not be true.

The word "empirical" is thus important because it indicates a way of regarding the world and people profoundly different from the traditional way which seeks explanations by appealing to authority, common sense, or reason. Is man basically selfish? We can provide quotations from the Bible, Shakespeare, or Freud; we can say that it is self-evident or obvious that man is basically selfish or not selfish; or we can carefully reason on the basis of authority and observation and conclude that man is basically selfish or not selfish. This is more or less the traditional way.

Scientists, however, are not satisfied with this way. If they think that the question is scientifically answerable—many questions cannot be answered scientifically—then they approach the problem differently. Although they may set up a theoretical explanation, in the back of their minds is always the nagging question: What will scientific evidence say? After first deciding how to define and measure selfishness, a scientist will set up a study or a series of studies to try to determine to what extent selfishness motivates human behavior and how it does so. He will then do the study under controlled conditions, and, after analyzing the results obtained, will state conclusions that seem to spring from the evidence. The evidence, then, is central to the whole process. Without it the conclusions are usually scientifically worthless.

Some readers may wonder about the importance of this distinction between empirical and nonempirical approaches. They may say that it is obvious, even self-evident, that one looks for evidence for the statements that one makes. Reasonable people will always do this. But this is just the point: they often, perhaps most often, don't. Our belief systems— religious, political, economic, educational—are indeed powerful, and *they* frequently guide our behavior, not evidence. Actually, to use empirical evidence as a practice seems to be very difficult. If it were not, many of the social problems that face us, assuming good will and adequate motivation, could be solved. To understand science and scientific research, therefore, requires a conscious and sustained effort that is not at all easy because the necessary empirical attitude requires at least temporary suspension of powerful belief systems. In other words, the first and final court of appeals in science is empirical evidence.

THE PURPOSE OF SCIENCE: THEORY AND EXPLANATION

The purpose of science has already been stated. We must now restate this purpose formally and try to dispel certain mistaken notions about its goals. *The purpose of science is theory.* Let's look closely at this bald and rather controversial statement. A theory is a systematic account of the relations among a set of variables. It is an explanation, usually of some particular though broad phenomenon. A psychologist may propose a theory of leadership of groups and organizations, or, like Freud, a theory of human motivation, or, like the influential European sociologist, Weber, a theory to account for modern capitalism, or, like the Swiss psychologist, Piaget, a theory of human knowing. Such theories are systematic attempts to "explain" the various phenomena by postulating the relations among the phenomena to be explained and a number of "explanatory variables,"

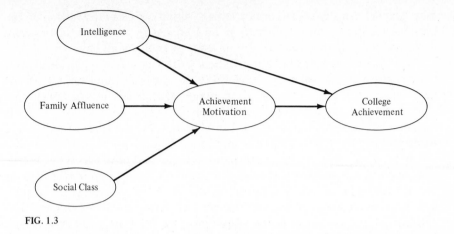

FIG. 1.3

which are themselves related in systematic ways. The basic purpose of science is to achieve theory, to invent and find valid explanations of natural phenomena.

To try to take some of the mystery from the word, let us look at a fictitious example of a "small theory" whose purpose is to explain achievement in college or the university. We relate four variables—intelligence, family affluence, social class, and achievement motivation—to college achievement in such a way that we "explain" it satisfactorily. To do so, we use the ideas of direct and indirect influences. College students differ a great deal in their success in college, and we want to explain these differences. Why do some students do well and others not so well? We assume that we are able to measure all the variables satisfactorily. The "small theory" is given diagrammatically in Figure 1.3.[8]

In the theory, two variables, intelligence and achievement motivation, are direct influences; they are both assumed to influence college achievement without going through other variables. These direct influences are shown in Figure 1.3 by the arrows from intelligence and achievement motivation to college achievement. The other two variables, family affluence and social class, are believed to have indirect influence on college achievement: they "go through" achievement motivation. For example, it is assumed that, in general, the more affluent a family, the greater the achievement motivation. Similarly, social class influences achievement motivation: middle-class young men and women have greater motive to achieve than working-class young men and women. Intelligence, in addition to its direct influence on college achievement—the greater the intelligence, the greater the achievement—has an indirect influence on college

---

[8] This example is partly realistic, partly fictitious. The reader should not take it as an "established theory." Although much is now known about college and other achievement, a great deal is still not understood. Theories in behavioral science can be viewed as attempts to chip away at our ignorance. In this sense, the example is not farfetched.

achievement through achievement motivation: the greater the intelligence, the greater the achievement motivation.

We have, then, a theory of college achievement, which may be a good theory or a poor theory depending on how well it explains college achievement. It is quite testable; all the variables are amenable to satisfactory measurement (though a theory does not necessarily have to have only variables that are measurable), and there are analytic techniques that can yield fairly clear tests of the relations specified in the theory.

Purposes of science other than theory or explanation have been proposed. We need not labor the more technical of these since they are usually deducible from theory as purpose. There is one alleged purpose of science, however, that gives much trouble and that has badly confused clear understanding of what science is about. This alleged purpose is contained in statements like the following, all of which are closely related: "The purpose of science is to improve the lot of man"; "The purpose of psychology and sociology is to help improve human society"; "The purpose of educational research is to improve educational thinking and practice." The sentiments behind such statements are indeed strong—and no wonder. It seems obvious that the purpose of science is to improve man's lot; it seems so self-evident.

The confusion has no doubt arisen because the *effects* of scientific advance have often enhanced human welfare—they have, of course, also hurt human welfare—mainly through improved technology made possible mostly by disinterested scientific research and discoveries. But this does not mean that the *purpose* of science is the enhancement of human welfare, just as its purpose is *not* to help in waging war. A more accurate interpretation is that the improvement of life can be a byproduct of science, a fortunate though not necessary outcome of scientific work and discovery.

There is a paradox here. It seems so obvious that the purpose of science is human enhancement. Yet it is a dangerous position because it leads, among other things, to distortions. The distortions result for two or three reasons. One, the mixture of strong commitment and advocacy of political and social programs, on the one hand, and scientific research into the problems of such programs, on the other hand, seem to induce bias and what has been called selective perception. This means that we see what we want or need to see rather than what is actually there. So strong is this tendency that I have almost gotten to the point of thinking that behavioral scientists should not do research on the things they passionately advocate. Or better, when they do it, they should conceive and use exceptionally elaborate safeguards against their own biases.

A second reason for distortions is that we tend to confuse the social and scientific missions, and this tends to distort what we see, to erode our objectivity, and, more important, our commitment to objectivity. The erosion of commitment to objectivity is dangerous to a scientist because, as said before, objectivity is a distinctive and indispensable scientific characteristic. Its loss destroys science itself.

To return to the main argument, science and scientific research are quite neutral. The results of scientific research can be and are used for both good and bad purposes. We make and use atomic bombs, instruments of destruction based on scientific theory and research in physics and related fields; we also use atomic discoveries for the desalinization of water, the creation of virtually limitless energy, and so on. Goodness and badness, improvement and deterioration, human happiness and human suffering, then, are the affairs of people who decide to do certain things that have good or bad consequences, that improve things or make them worse, that promote human happiness or increase human suffering. Of course, the results of science can be used to help make such decisions, and scientists as human beings can participate in the decision making, but science itself, strictly speaking, has nothing to do with the decisions. This is because the concern of science—and it is the only large-scale human activity whose concern is so disinterested—is only with understanding and explaining natural phenomena.

I strongly emphasize the purpose of science in this way because the misconception outlined above, carried to its logical extreme of setting up human welfare as the fundamental purpose of science, leads eventually to an erosion of science itself and a consequent lessening of understanding of physical and human phenomena. In the last chapter of this book we will again examine this whole problem in more detail. The reason that the purpose of science as theory has been emphasized here is that tentative acceptance of it at this point will aid our understanding of much of the content of the book. This emphasis will keep us focused on the essence and nature of science and not allow us to be distracted by what are really extraneous considerations. For instance, if we talk about the so-called underachievement of bright children, we will be able to focus on understanding achievement rather than on specific remedies for the problem. In doing so, of course, we will assume that scientific understanding of the problem may enhance the probabilities of ourselves and others finding practical solutions to the problem.

2

Behavioral scientific concepts and definitions

One of the major difficulties in approaching a new subject is its vocabulary. Not only are new words coined and used; old words are used in new and different ways. This is, of course, the case in science. We must become acquainted with terms and expressions that are used constantly in psychological, sociological, and educational research. The purpose of this short chapter is to provide this acquaintance.

Definitions are rarely interesting to readers, but they are essential because it is virtually impossible to talk intelligently about science and research—or any complex field, for that matter—without using abstract and technical terms that are unfamiliar to the reader. Behavioral scientists used such terms as "random sample," "independent variable," "experimental manipulation," and "statistical significance." While such expressions are familiar and easy to the scientist, they can be strange, annoying, and even frightening to the nonscientist. As such, they can be a formidable barrier to understanding a book like this. The usual device used to solve the problem is to define terms as one goes along. In behavioral research, however, there are just too many terms needed almost all at once. So, in addition to defining terms as we go along, this special chapter of definitions is given early in the book.

VARIABLES

The term "variable" is perhaps the most used word in behavioral scientific language. It is literally impossible to escape. For example, I intended **19** to write Chapter 1 without any technical terms. It was not possible to do so: I had to use "variable" along with one or two other technical words. The term "variable" is a concept or "construct," as psychologists say. A concept, of course, is a noun that stands for a class of objects: man, sex, aggression, verbal ability, social class, intelligence, and conformity are examples. It is easy to see that "man" stands for the many two-legged organisms who talk, write, and often display intelligence. It is not so easy to see what "aggression" stands for. To the psychologist "aggression" can mean an internal state that predisposes people to certain kinds of behavior called "aggressive." For psychological researchers, however, "aggression" means different kinds of behaviors that have the characteristic of hurting others or oneself, physically or psychologically. They must be rather specific; they must define "aggression" by somehow specifying what "aggressive" behaviors are. They do this so that they can measure or manipulate "aggression." The idea of "variable" should become clear after we examine kinds and examples of variables.

Categorical, Measured, and Manipulated Variables

When something can be classified into two or more categories, it can be a variable. "Sex" is a variable, the simplest kind of variable because there are only two categories, male and female. "Religious preference," "political preference," and "social class" are variables with more than two categories. Such variables, not surprisingly, are called *categorical variables*. They have the characteristic that all members of a category—all females, for instance—are considered the same as far as that variable is concerned. Further examples are nationality, race, occupational choice.

If a property of objects can be measured it can be a variable. "Measured" for now means that numerals can be assigned to different people or different objects on the basis of their possession of amounts of some property or characteristic. Height and weight are easy and obvious examples. But we may assign the numerals 1, 2, 3, 4, and 5 to individual children on the basis of their presumed anxiety, 5 meaning much anxiety, 4 a good deal of anxiety, and so on to 1, which means little anxiety. If we can do this, we have the variable "anxiety." In common sense terms, a variable is something that varies. Or it can be said that a variable is a property that takes on different values. A psychologist, for instance, can assign different children different values depending on their possession of different amounts of verbal ability. To do so, he may use a test of verbal ability and assign the children the numbers 10 through 50, 10 meaning a low amount of verbal ability and 50 a high amount. The variable "sex" was mentioned above: individuals can be assigned 1's and 0's depending on whether they are males or females. Even though only two numerals, 1 and 0, are assigned, sex is a variable.

In the discussion of the Clark and Walberg study in Chapter 1, reinforcement was "manipulated" as an experimental variable by giving one group of children massive reinforcement and a second group regular reinforcement. This manipulation creates, in effect, a variable. Whenever experimenters set up experimental conditions they create variables. We call such variables *experimental variables* or *manipulated variables*. They can be shown to satisfy the definition given above, though we do not do so here.

There are, then, three general kinds of variables in behavioral research: categorical variables, measured variables, and experimental or manipulated variables. Reinforcement in the Clark and Walberg study is, as said above, an experimental variable. Social class (middle class and working class), in the Miller and Swanson study on social class and child-rearing practices described in Chapter 1, is a categorical variable. Examples of measured variables are intelligence, anxiety, authoritarianism, verbal aptitude, and school achievement. They are called *measured variables* because they are "measured" with a test or other instrument that produces scores that run from low to high.

Independent and Dependent Variables

Two terms that are used a great deal in behavioral research and in this book are "independent variable" and "dependent variable." An *independent variable* is a variable that is presumed to influence another variable called a *dependent variable*. When we say, Reinforcement enhances learning, reinforcement is the independent variable and learning the dependent variable. Scientists predict *from* independent variables *to* dependent variables. They say, for instance, If teachers praise children, then the children's school work will improve.

The independent variable in a research study is the antecedent; the dependent variable is the consequent. The terms come from mathematics. Whenever a mathematical or statistical equation is written, the dependent variable is on the left of the equation and the independent variable is on the right. For example, an equation used a great deal by behavioral researchers is: $y = a + bx$. Here y is the dependent variable and x the independent variable. This is like saying, though more precisely, If x, then y. With the Clark and Walberg problem we would say If reinforcement (x), then achievement (y). (a and b in the equation are constants whose values are determined by research. Their meaning and use will be explained in a later chapter.) When graphs are drawn, as they will be later in the book, the independent variable is the horizontal axis (the abscissa) and the dependent variable is the vertical axis (the ordinate).

Miscellaneous Variables

There are certain other classifications of variables, but they are ordinarily not as important as those given above. Nevertheless, since they are used in the literature and in the conversation of behavioral researchers, readers should be familiar with them. The first of these classifications characterizes variables by the field in which they are used: psychological variables, sociological variables, economic variables, and so on. Intelligence, anxiety, and conformity are psychological variables; social class, education (number of years of schooling, for instance), and father's occupation are sociological variables; income, gross national product, and profits are economic variables. Other possibilities are political variables, anthropological variables, and physiological variables. The variables of educational research are mostly psychological, social psychological, or sociological. For example, achievement, verbal aptitude, achievement motivation, and level of aspiration are psychological; social class, parental education, educational level, and father's occupation are sociological.

Another way to distinguish variables is by disciplines within a field. In psychology, for example, one hears about personality variables (introvert-extrovert, aggressiveness, authoritarianism), physiological variables (psychogalvanic reflex, palmar sweat, heartbeat), social psychological variables (conformity, group pressure, cohesiveness), and so on. But such distinctions seem actually not to be too important. Indeed, it is sometimes difficult to classify variables in this way because they can simultaneously belong to two or three categories.

It is ordinarily not possible to study phenomena and the relations among phenomena unless variables can be defined and used. To study the school achievement of children, for instance, researchers must "create" the variable "achievement." This means that they must define and measure it; they must assign numerals to the school achievement of different children. The importance of the idea of variable and the concomitant idea of variability, variation, or variance (see below) cannot be overemphasized.

A variable, then, is a construct, a concept with a specified "constructed" meaning given it by a researcher. A variable can also be viewed as a name or a symbol to which values are assigned, the different values indicating different amounts or degrees of the variable specified by the name or the symbol. Thus, intelligence and conformity and x and y are variables if values (numerals) are systematically assigned to them.

RELATIONS

"Relation" is probably the most fundamental word in science. We will use it liberally throughout this book. Indeed, a major part of Chapter 4 will be devoted to defining the term, explaining its meaning, and giving examples of its use. For the present preliminary purpose we use an oversimplified definition. A *relation* is a "going together" of two variables: it is what the two variables have in common. The notion is comparative: a relation is a bond or connection between two phenomena, two variables. We say that there is a positive relation between, say, intelligence and school achievement, or between social class and income, or between authoritarianism and prejudice. This means that children of higher intelligence tend to do well in school, and children of lesser intelligence tend to do less well (though there are many exceptions); that the higher social classes receive greater income than the lower social classes; and that the greater the authoritarianism, the greater the prejudice. There is, then, some connection, some bond, between these three pairs of variables. In each pair, some portion of each variable is common to both of them. If you will look back at Figure 1.1 you will see the idea of the common part of the two variables depicted. Whatever is common to the two variables is shown by the hatched overlap of the circles.

STUDIES AND EXPERIMENTS

When scientists have done a piece of research, it is said that they have done a "study." *Study*, then, is a general word covering any kind of research. It is said, for example, "They did a study of intelligence and school achievement in England, France, and the United States"; "He studied the influence of anxiety on the test performance of suburban children"; "She did a study of the factors of authoritarianism and dogmatism"; "Clark and Walberg's experimental study of the effect of reinforcement on the reading achievement of black children has been severely criticized." Notice that "study" refers to both experimental and nonexperimental investigations and to different kinds of research.

Most people think they know what an experiment is: it is something researchers do in laboratories with esoteric equipment. The real nature of experiments is obscured by such vague and stereotyped notions. Although experiments are done mostly in "laboratories," they can be done anywhere—in schools, homes, factories, or even on the street. More important, a true experiment has two basic characteristics. One of these is a highly desirable characteristic that all experiments should have: random assignment of subjects to experimental groups. This means, roughly, that the subjects are assigned to experimental groups in such a way that any one subject can become a member of any one of the groups, and it is not possible to tell which group he will be in. It is still possible to have an experiment without random assignment, however, though not desirable. We postpone further consideration of random assignment until Chapter 6 because it requires rather full and detailed explanation.

The second basic characteristic of an experiment was brought out in Chapter 1—manipulation. We can now be more precise: manipulation of independent variables. (Dependent variables are almost never manipulated.) To repeat: this means that the researcher does different things to different groups of individuals. Suppose I teach four groups of fifth-grade pupils with four different methods. This is a manipulation. Suppose I want to study the effects of types of decision making on group productivity. I have a group of 90 individuals which I divide into three groups of 30 each, call them A_1, A_2, and A_3. The subjects of A_1 are given maximum opportunity to participate in the decisions of the group (part of the manipulation), the subjects of A_2 occasional opportunity to participate, and the subjects of A_3 no opportunity to participate. This, too, is a manipulation.

Experimental manipulations range from the very simple to the very complex. Clark and Walberg's independent variable manipulation was simple: two groups, one given massive reinforcement, the other regular reinforcement. So that the reader will not think that all, or even most, manipulations are limited to two groups, let's look at a slight extension of the manipulation to three groups. Aronson and Mills (1959), in an interesting social psychological experiment, tested the notion that the more difficult it is to get into a group, the more group members will value group membership. The members of one group were given a severe initiation, the members of another group were given a mild initiation, and the members of the remaining group were not required to do anything to become group members (the "control group"). (The manipulation involved having young women read aloud sexual words varying in obscenity.) It was predicted that the members of the severe group would value group membership the most, the members of the mild group would value group membership next most, and the members of the control group would value group membership least. (The expectation was supported by the results.) This, too, is a manipulation: different things were systematically done to the three groups. The virtues and other characteristics of this powerful method of obtaining knowledge will be explored later. We will also see that it is quite possible to manipulate more than one independent variable at a time.

There are several kinds of scientific studies. An experiment is only one kind. All the other kinds are nonexperimental. A survey of the opinions of the people is nonexperimental. So is any investigation of the relations among variables when there is no manipulation. The Miller and Swanson study of social class and child-rearing is an example. It was not an experiment because there was no manipulation of an independent variable. The distinction is frequently misunderstood. Studies that are not experimental are sometimes called experiments. The distinction, however, is highly important because the conclusions of a well-conducted experiment are generally stronger than the conclusions of a well-conducted study that is not an experiment. We return to the distinction in Chapter 8.

DATA

Scientists commonly use the word "data" and know pretty much what they mean.[1] Nonscientists can be confused by the word, however, because it is not always clear just what is meant by it. The word "data" means

---

[1] "Data" is one of those curious words that is really plural—the singular is "datum"—but that is sometimes treated as singular. The plural usage is usually preferable.

something given, or taken as given, from which inferences can be made. For example, I may be told that 60 percent of the people of Belgium approve of the Common Market, but that only 40 percent of the people of England approve it. I now have data that permit me to make one or two inferences, perhaps more: the people of Belgium approve the Common Market more than do the people of England (other things being equal, of course); support for the Common Market is not too strong in Belgium and England. In this example, the defined percentages are data that permit certain inferences to be made. But data are not limited to numerical or statistical results. Verbal material, like newspaper editorials or children's essays, can be considered data.

Scientists, then, usually use the word "data" to refer to results obtained from research, mostly though not always numerical or statistical results, from which they draw inferences or conclusions. They may say, "The data indicate that the more severe an initiation, the greater the value of group membership is to group members." They mean that some sort of quantitative results—for instance, the average scores of the three groups in the Aronson and Mills experiment—were such as to warrant making the statement.

Despite this rather specific use, "data" also refers to almost any evidence obtained from research studies. One can even say that "data" and "evidence" are used almost synonymously. The observations made of boards of education and recorded in some form are called "data." Computer output is called "data." Scores from tests are called "data."

MEASURES, SCORES, TESTS, SCALES

Behavioral scientists must constantly obtain quantitative estimates of the amounts of properties or characteristics that individuals or groups possess. They obtain such estimates, for one thing, so that they can assess the magnitude of the relations among variables. Raw data—people's actual answers to questions, descriptions of people's behavior from observation, and the like—must usually be converted to numbers in some way. The numbers, which presumably mirror the raw data in a reduced form, are then so operated upon that the relations among the numbers and thus among the characteristics can be studied.

Quantitative estimates of the amount of a property or characteristic that individuals or groups possess are called *measures*. When measures are obtained from tests, they are called *scores*. "Measure" is a more general word than "score," even though scores are measures.

A *test* is a systematic procedure in which individuals being tested are presented with a set of constructed stimuli, called *items*, to which they respond in one way or another. The responses enable the tester to assign individuals scores or numbers indicating the degree to which the individuals possess the property or attribute, or the degree to which they "know" the something being tested. We talk about intelligence tests, achievement tests, aptitude tests, and many other kinds of tests.

A *scale* is like a test, except that it lacks the competitive flavor of the test. The word "test" has a taste of success and failure about it; the word "scale" does not. It is an instrument so constructed that different numbers can be assigned to different individuals to indicate different amounts of some property or attribute. There are scales to measure attitudes, values, compulsivity, rigidity, interests, prejudice, and many others.

VARIATION AND VARIANCE

A fundamental statistical concept in scientific research is "variance." It is fundamental because phenomena can be compared and related only through the variations of the phenomena. What does this slightly strange-sounding statement mean? Virtually no scientific knowledge would be possible if phenomena did not vary. The psychologist could not study intelligence unless people varied in intelligence. The sociologist could not study social class and its relation to other variables if people and groups did not differ in social class. It is said that a group of people, say a fourth-grade class of school children, is highly variable in intelligence. Another way to say this is that the class' intelligence variance is large. On the other hand, the variance in intelligence of a group of university doctor's degree candidates may be small. If the reader will for now take this variation statement on faith, we will bolster the faith with reasons in a later chapter.

Although statistics will not be discussed too much in this book, it is imperative that we know some statistical terms and their general meaning. "Variance" is both a statistical and general term. It is general when it means the variability of phenomena, as discussed above. Behavioral scientists use it a great deal in this way. "Variance" is also an actual statistical measure that expresses the variability of any set of measures and thus, indirectly, of any set of individuals.[2] Behavioral scientists talk a great deal about the variance of a phenomenon or about the variance of one variable being affected by the variance of another variable. The educational researcher may ask: How much of the variance of achievement is due to variance in intelligence, to variance in motivation, to variance in home background? This is simply a brief semitechnical way of saying: Do children of high intelligence have high achievement and children of low intelligence low achievement? Do children with high motivation achieve well and children with low motivation not achieve well? Do children from favorable home environments achieve well, whereas children from unfavorable environments not achieve well?

---

[2] A general and technical discussion of the term, the ideas behind it, and how it is used can be found in Kerlinger (1973, Ch. 6).

TABLE 2.1   Three Sets of Pairs of Ranks Expressing Different
Covariances and Relations

I		II		III	
a	*b*	*a*	*b*	*a*	*b*
1	1	1	5	1	3
2	2	2	4	2	5
3	3	3	3	3	1
4	4	4	2	4	4
5	5	5	1	5	2
High		High		Low	
Positive		Negative			

All this is a way of saying that variables *covary*, vary together in systematic ways. So researchers often talk about *covariance*, a technical term that means the variance that two (or more) variables share. Look back again at Figure 1.1. The shaded part of the figure represents the covariance, or shared variance, of the two variables.

Look now at the pairs of numbers in Table 2.1. The two sets of numbers in I covary perfectly. Indeed, the two sets of numbers, *a* and *b*, are the same: for a high number in *a* there is a high number in *b;* for a low number in *a* there is a low number in *b*. There is a *high positive* relation between the two sets of numbers. The sets of numbers under II also covary perfectly—but in opposite directions: for a high number in *a* there is a low number in *b*, and for a low number in *a* there is high number in *b*. There is a *high negative* relation between *a* and *b*. Now, regard III. It is not possible to make any systematic statement about the relation between *a* and *b*. They are, it is said, unrelated. Or it is said that the relation is low, which means, in effect, not being able to say anything about the *b* numbers from knowledge of the *a* numbers. The reader should try to translate these sets of numbers into a realistic example. For instance, make statements about I, II, and III using intelligence and achievement instead of *a* and *b*

The word "variance" is used a great deal in modern behavioral science, and it will have to be used a good deal in this book. The reason is simple: it is not possible to clarify and to understand modern approaches to research and analysis without the basic general idea of variation and the more technical idea of variance.

PROBABILITY

One of the main stumbling blocks to understanding and appreciating behavioral research is what seems to be a general craving for certainty. To live with uncertainty seems to be very hard for us. Unfortunately, the craving for certainty helps demagogues, authoritarians, phony religionists, and hungry predators to thrive because they offer certainty. They give us an opportunity to escape from what is often an unbearable feeling of uneasiness and anxiety induced in us by the uncertainty of our world. They offer us a creed or a person to follow unquestioningly with promises of great rewards.

Behavioral science and research does not offer certainty. (Neither does natural science!) It does not even offer relative certainty. All it offers is probabilistic knowledge: If A is done, then B will *probably* occur. The statement used earlier, "Frustration leads to aggression," is really incorrect. A more correct statement is: "Frustration probably leads to aggression." One way of defining behavioral research might be to say that it is a way to help reduce uncertainty. Empirical research can never tell us that something is certainly so. It can, however, say something like this: The odds are about 70 to 30 that such-and-such is so.

Probability and probabilistic thinking are at the core of modern behavioral science and research. Unfortunately, probability is difficult to define satisfactorily. We take an intuitive approach, as usual, but the reader is warned that it may not suit experts. The *probability* of an event is the number of "favorable" cases divided by the total number of (equally possible) cases. ("Favorable case" means any stipulated or predicted outcome.) Let f = the number of favorable cases. Let p = the number of favorable cases divided by the total number of cases, N. Let a favorable case here be the heads of a coin toss. Then p is the proportion of heads in N coin tosses, or $p = f/N$. Since there are two possibilities in coin tossing, heads and tails, $p = 1/2$. A favorable event or case can be the 6 of a die. Then $p = 1/6$: the probability of a 6 occurring is 1/6. If there are 50 men and 50 women in a given sample of 100 people, the probability of selecting a man (or a woman) is $50/100 = 1/2$ (given an unbiased selection procedure).

This is all quite simple. But probability can be complex. Our concern here, however, is only with preliminary and intuitive understanding. In general, the reader must understand that all scientific statements are probabilistic. There is always uncertainty. The natural sciences offer greater certainty than the behavioral sciences. Nevertheless, all scientific disciplines are more or less uncertain. All statements, in other words, have an explicit or implicit p value attached to them. This is why the behavioral science literature talks so much of "trends" and "tendencies."

The reader should not worry too much if he has not thoroughly grasped all the above terms and expressions. They take getting used to. General familiarity is all that is needed at this point. Gaps will be filled in later. In any case, we now have enough definitional background to continue the main discussion.

3

Problems, hypotheses, and variables

In trying to solve a problem, one casts around for alternative solutions, for different ways of getting to the core of the problem. This process of thinking is usually inchoate, vague, even confused. One often doesn't know where to turn, what to do. One hopes for ideas, especially one really good idea. So it is in research.

To understand what a problem in scientific behavioral research is, we will first be negative. We consider problems that are really not problems in the scientific sense. They can be called value or engineering problems. Here are examples: How can integration best be achieved? What is the best way to achieve equality of educational opportunity? What is the most efficient way to build a network of roads in K County? How can we help improve the lot of the urban poor? What makes a successful teacher? How are self-actualization and maturity of personality related? The main reason why none of these is a scientific problem is that none of them, as stated, can be tested empirically.

How can integration be achieved? is an engineering problem. The questioner wants to know how to do something. The road-building and the urban poor questions are also engineering questions. Science cannot answer them because their form and substance are such as not to be testable: they neither state nor imply relations between variables. They ask, rather, how to do things. Science can provide hints and inferences about possible answers, but can never directly answer such questions. The **29** equality of educational opportunity question is a mixture of a value question and an engineering question: What is the best way to achieve equality of educational opportunity?

Whereas an engineering question asks how to do something, a value question asks which of two or more things is better or worse than other things, or whether something under consideration is good, bad, desirable, undesirable, or morally right or wrong. Value questions contain words like "good," "bad," "better," "best," "desirable," "must," "should." They ask for judgments about the things being valued. "What is the *best* (most efficient, most desirable, and so forth.) way to do so-and-so?" is a value question. So is, "Is Method A *better* than Method B to achieve equality of educational opportunity?" Value propositions or statements are similar except that they are declarative rather than interrogative sentences. Examples are: "Student evaluation of professors will help to improve teaching"; "It is wrong to discriminate against minorities"; "Thou shalt not kill"; "Teachers must understand children's needs." The judging quality and the moral imperatives involved in these statements are obvious. More important for our purpose, there is no way to test such statements empirically. The statement, "It is wrong to discriminate against minorities," for example, states no relation or implication of a relation between variables that can be tested; it states a moral judgment about a social practice.

Science, as science, then, can give no answers to engineering and value questions because it cannot test such propositions and show them to be correct or incorrect. When you tell me that religion is a good thing, all I can do is agree or disagree with you—and love or hate you, have peace with you, or fight you. I cannot, as a scientist, subject the statement to an empirical test, mainly because a human judgment is involved—something is "good"—and science is and will always be dumb on judgments of any kind.

It can be said, for now, that testable propositions contain variables that can be measured or manipulated, or they imply such variable measurement and manipulation. Here are three testable propositions, one of them quite familiar: "Frustration produces aggression"; "The greater the cohesiveness of groups, the more influence they have on their members"; "Slum conditions produce delinquency." Observe that these statements have variables that can be measured or manipulated: frustration, aggression, group cohesiveness, influence, slum conditions, delinquency. When it is said that these statements are testable, it is not implied that they are "good" statements that lead to "good" scientific research. All that is meant is that they are somehow capable of being shown by evidence to be correct or incorrect.

Value and engineering propositions, then, are not scientifically testable. There are other kinds of propositions that are not testable and that are hard to categorize. Their common characteristic seems to be vagueness and a sort of virtue. Here are a few examples: "Disease is a manifestation of God's will"; "Democratic institutions and practices are peculiarly suited to the ethos of the American people"; "Racial harmony depends on mutual understanding"; "Human maturity depends upon self-actualization." To the scientist such statements have little or no meaning. They do, of course, have meaning to ministers, politicians, parents, teachers, and novelists, but they are beyond the grasp of science.

Such questions, *as stated*, are not testable either because they lack the form of testable questions or propositions (to be discussed later) or because the language in which they are expressed is so vague as to be scientifically unmanageable. Here is another example from education. This is a problem that, although it has intrigued and plagued educational researchers for half a century, is virtually unanswerable scientifically, at least as stated: What makes a successful teacher? To many educators, this may not seem like a problem. They think they know the answer; they think they know what a successful teacher is. Until now, however, the problem has not been solved—in a scientific sense.

There are several reasons why it has not been solved. For one, the question is hopeless because there is no statement of a relation between variables. It can therefore not be tested and answered scientifically. (In all fairness, it may never be answered.) For another, the problem is extremely complex: it has a number of facets that are not immediately apparent and that make it difficult to deal with. For example, what is meant by "successful"? Successful in getting children to learn, we would think. Learn what? What does "learn" mean? Is "success" tied to certain personal and professional characteristics of teachers? what teachers actually do in classrooms? their attitudes? "Successful" also implies "unsuccessful." What does it mean if a teacher is unsuccessful? Does "unsuccessful" mean the opposite of "successful"? Or is it just different? Or is "unsuccessful" as complex an idea as "successful"?

In short, we have here a complex issue whose difficulty has not been realized. Is it any wonder, then, that it has not been solved?

PROBLEMS

In a general sense, a problem is a question that states a situation needing discussion, inquiry, decision, or solution. While this general definition conveys a meaning that most of us can understand, it is unsatisfactory for scientific purposes because it is not definite enough. It does not say or imply what researchers must do to answer the question the problem states. A more satisfactory definition is: A *problem* is a question that asks how variables are related.

In the Clark and Walberg study outlined in Chapter 1, the research problem can be stated: Does massive reinforcement enhance the reading achievement of black underachievers? The general problem of the Miller and Swanson study may be stated: Do mothers of different social classes use different types of upbringing? A more specific problem (see Table 1.1) is: Does time of weaning children differ in middle and working classes? These problems are rather specific; they can, of course, be stated more generally.

Many years ago Hurlock (1925) asked the question, What are the effects on pupil performance of different types of incentives? This problem is more general. Here is another general problem (Etzioni, 1964): Does conflict enhance or impede the efficiency of organizations? An interesting social psychological problem was proposed by Frederiksen, Jensen, and Beaton (1968): How does organizational climate affect administrative performance? Berkowitz (1959) asked the following significant question: Under conditions of hostility arousal, how does anti-Semitism influence displacement of aggression? Or, When frustrated, do highly anti-Semitic persons exhibit more aggressive behavior toward other people than do persons low in anti-Semitism? In her highly significant cross-cultural work on "natural categories" of cognition, Rosch (1973) asked the following question: Do natural prototypes of color and form facilitate the learning of categories of color and form?[1]

To repeat, a scientific research problem is first a question, a sentence in interrogative form. Second, it is a question that usually asks something about the relations among phenomena or variables. The answer to the question is sought in the research. Clark and Walberg, on the basis of their findings, were able to say that massive reinforcement enhanced the reading of the black underachieving children of their study. Miller and Swanson were able to say that their middle-class mothers tended to wean their children earlier than did working-class mothers.

Three criteria of good research problems and problem statements may help us understand research problems. First, the problem should express a relation between two or more variables. It asks questions like: Is A related to B? How are A and B related to C? Although there are exceptions to this criterion, they are rare. Second, the problem should be stated in question form. Questions have the virtue of posing problems directly. In the Hurlock example given above, the problem is directly stated by the question on the relation between incentives and performance.

The third criterion is more complex. It demands that the problem be such as to *imply* possibilities of empirical testing. (See "The Empirical Character of Science" in Chapter 1.) Empirical testing means that actual evidence is obtained on the relation stated by the problem. To obtain evidence on Hurlock's incentives-performance question means to manipulate (or measure) incentives, to measure pupil performance, and to assess the presumed effect of the incentives on performance. Admittedly, it is often difficult to say clearly that a problem has empirical testing implications. Nevertheless, the distinction must be made if the research is to have any chance of success. The key difficulties with untestable questions are that they are either not statements of relations ("What is knowledge?"

---

[1] These problem statements are not always given in the words of the original authors.

"How should reading be taught?"), or their constructs or variables are difficult or impossible to define in such a way that they can be manipulated or measured. This is generally true of moral questions and value questions, questions that ask about the rightness or wrongness of things, or their goodness or badness, or their desirability or undesirability. Let's concentrate on value statements again. Take such statements as "Democracy is the best of all possible governmental systems"; "Equality is just as important as freedom"; and "Marriage is good." These are value statements; they are not scientifically testable. The untestability of value statements was discussed earlier, but the distinction between value statements and empirical or testable statements is so important we must examine it again a bit more analytically.

To say something is good or bad, better or worse, or best or worst is to pronounce a human judgment. Only people can say that something is good or bad—and that's the end of it. No scientific procedure can yield an answer about the relative desirability of anything. Scientific statements simply say, in effect, If this is true, then that will probably occur; If you frustrate people, then they will probably aggress against others, against objects, or against themselves. Such statements make no commitment to goodness or badness, desirability or undesirability, or moral worth or lack of moral worth. Nor can they make such commitments. To be sure, scientists as people can pronounce such judgments—and they can be wise or as silly as other people in doing so—but when they do they step out of their scientific role.

It is in this sense that science is neutral. It is not neutral because there is some special virtue in being neutral. It is just the nature of science, which inheres in testing empirical relations among phenomena or variables—and to do this requires that the phenomena be such as to be observed, manipulated, or measured. While scientists can study values, as values, and their relations to other phenomena—for example, they can study how the holding of certain economic values influences the way people vote ("Capitalism is good"; "Private property is sacred")—they cannot study statements that pronounce ethical, moral, and other judgments. There is just no way to get at the empirical referents of words like "should," "ought," "good," "bad," and "must."

HYPOTHESES

A *hypothesis* is a conjectural statement of the relations between two or more variables. Hypotheses are declarative sentences, and they relate in some way variables to variables.[2] They are statements of relations, and,

---

[2] As mentioned before, there are exceptions to the relation requirement. For instance, some research seeks to discover the dimensions or factors underlying many variables. Relational hypotheses may not be used in such research.

like problems, must imply the testing of the stated relations. Problems and hypotheses are similar. They both state relations, except that problems are interrogative sentences, and hypotheses are declarative sentences. Sometimes they are almost identical in substance. An important difference, however, is that hypotheses are usually more specific than problems; they are usually closer to actual research operations and testing. Many examples throughout the book will make this distinction clear, even though hard and fast rules are not easy to spell out.

Here are some hypotheses from research: The greater the cohesiveness of a group, the greater its influence on its members (Schachter, Ellertson, McBride, & Gregory, 1951); Learning new material interferes with remembering older learned material (Lindsay & Norman, 1977, pp. 320–324); Early deprivation produces later mental deficit (Bennett, Diamond, Krech, & Rosenzweig, 1964). Note that all three hypotheses are relations and that empirical testing of them is clearly implied because the variables can either be manipulated (interference, group cohesiveness, even early deprivation) or measured (influence, recall of material, mental deficit), or both.

Take the last of these hypotheses: Early deprivation produces later mental deficit. "Early deprivation" is the independent variable. It can mean lack of food and nourishment in early years. It can mean lack of love and affection in early years. Or it can mean early lack of adequate stimulation—talk, toys, other people or other animals, and so on. Notice that it can be a manipulated variable: animals can be systematically deprived of food, affection, or stimulation. It can also be a measured variable: we somehow determine, for instance, the amount of deprivation a child or adult has had in his early years, perhaps by questioning him and his parents. Clearly, "early deprivation" is empirically available. "Mental deficit" is also empirically available. It can be measured with one or more of the many tests of mental ability or mental deficit that are available. There may, of course, be a difficult problem to decide just what is and what is not "deficit." Nevertheless, the point here is that the variable is capable of being measured.

The hypothesis, Early deprivation produces later mental deficit, then, is a hypothesis because it states a conjectural relation between variables that can be manipulated or measured. The relation is expressed by the word "produces." A relation word or expression connects variables with each other in some way: "produces," "is positively related to," "is a function of," and the like. A better way to conceive almost all such statements, however, is to translate them to if-then statements. While there are no fixed rules on how to write hypotheses—there are several kinds, all legitimate and useful—most of them can be put into if-then form: If p, then q, p and q being constructs or variables. "If frustration, then aggression"; "If early deprivation, then later deficiency in school achievement"; "If reinforcement, then enhanced learning." In all these statements two variables are related to each other with the words "if" and "then." Very simply put, a hypothesis is almost always a statement of a relation, the nature of the relation being specified to some extent by the if-then structure of the statement.

We have considered hypotheses with only two variables. In modern behavioral research, however, it is more likely than not that there will be more than two variables. Hypotheses will be more like: If p, then q, under conditions r and s. If positive incentive (p), then enhanced learning (q), given female (r) and middle class (s). Note that another way to symbolize this hypothesis is: If p_1 and p_2 and p_3, then q: If positive incentive (p_1) and female (p_2) and middle class (p_3), then enhanced learning (q). We return to multivariable, or "multivariate," problems later in the book. They are very important.

In sum, hypotheses are *tentative* statements of relations, and it is these tentative statements that are tested in research. Let's now see why hypotheses are important.

Virtues of Hypotheses

Hypotheses are much more important in scientific research than they would appear to be just by knowing what they are and how they are constructed. They have the deep and highly significant purpose of taking man out of himself, so to speak. That is, their appropriate formulation and use enable man to test aspects of reality with minimal distortion by his own predilections. They are part of the methodology of science associated with the criterion of objectivity discussed in Chapter 1. This means that hypotheses are powerful tools for the advancement of knowledge, because, although formulated by man, they can be tested and shown to be probably correct or incorrect apart from man's values and beliefs. Naturally, scientists want their ideas of reality to agree with "reality."

A social psychologist, for instance, may believe that a method for dealing with prejudice he has devised, call it method K, is more effective than other methods in reducing prejudice. He thinks that if K were used systematically in high schools and colleges, it would help to reduce prejudice against minority groups wherever it is used. He is saying that method K is more effective than other methods and more effective than doing nothing. If he is to test his belief scientifically, he must have some way of getting outside his belief, getting outside himself. Hypotheses help to do this. The social psychologist can set up a hypothesis that method K, after sufficient use, will produce greater decrements in prejudice than will, say, methods L and M (and, perhaps, other methods, or no method).

The hypothesis is now a statement "out there" independent of the researcher. It is "outside him" in the sense that, no matter what his personal beliefs, predilections, and biases—his dislike of prejudice, for example—it can be tested apart from the beliefs, predilections, and biases. While he may personally favor method K, his belief that method K is superior cannot affect the hypothesis testing and its outcome. Thus, hypotheses are a particularly potent means of objectively bridging the gap between one's beliefs and empirical reality. They are tools for testing reality and can be shown to be probably correct or incorrect independent of the investigator.

Hypotheses have other virtues. One of these is that they can be, and often are, deduced from theory. Any theory of import will have a number of empirical implications that can be deduced from it. A whole book, for example, has been written (Dollard, Doob, Miller, Mowrer, & Sears, 1939) on the implications of the general hypothesis that frustration produces aggression. Actually, this general hypothesis is broad enough to be a basic statement of a theory, a theory of aggression. And it has empirical implications. For instance, if you frustrate children, they will aggress against other children, against adults, even against themselves. Dollard and his colleagues even pointed out that one can deduce Marxist implications from the general hypothesis: If working people are exploited (paid low wages, made to work long hours, and so forth), then they will be frustrated. If frustrated over a long period, they will finally rise up and destroy their frustrators, the bourgeoisie. The point is that any theory, if it is really a theory, will have many implications for testing; it will generate (with help, of course) many testable hypotheses. Indeed, this is how theories are tested.

Hypotheses and Testability

This line of thought leads us nicely to another important idea about hypotheses. In order to be scientifically useful, they must be testable, or at least have implications for testing. A hypothesis that is untestable has no scientific use. That is, one must be able to spell out the variables of a hypothesis—or one must be able to deduce its implications in variable form—and then have some operational way of manipulating or measuring the variables so as to study the relations between them. The frustration-aggression hypothesis is a particularly good example: we have already given two or three testing possibilities—and there are many more. Reinforcement theory, much of which concentrates on reward, or positive reinforcement, generates many hypotheses in different fields and with different kinds of organisms. One such example was given in discussing the Clark and Walberg study in Chapter 1. Recall that the relative effects of massive reinforcement and regular reinforcement on reading achievement were tested. Theories of attitude change, theories of group process, theories of learning, and theories of occupational status have all generated testable hypotheses.

Some theories and theoretical statements, on the other hand, are untestable—at least with the means at our disposal today. As such, they are beyond a scientific approach. A classic case is some Freudian theory. For example, Freud's theory of anxiety is untestable, at least as Freud stated it, in part because it includes the construct of repression. By repression Freud meant the forcing of unacceptable ideas deep into the unconscious. Empirical deductions from the theory will, of course, have to include the construct of repression, which is tied to the construct of the unconscious. While one can state relations among the variables of anxiety theory, defining the constructs of repression (as Freud meant it) and the unconscious in order to measure them is extremely difficult, if not impossible.

To use a construct in the testing of a hypothesis, one must deduce, at least to some extent, the empirical implications or meaning of the construct. When one does so, one has the makings of a so-called operational definition, an idea explained in detail later in this chapter. In the case of the construct of repression, this is difficult to do because the behavioral manifestations of repression are elusive. Freud himself gives several. A famous one is slips of the tongue. But does every slip of the tongue indicate repression? And how can we measure them, assuming they do indicate repression? While the matter is far more complex than this, I hope that a little of the essence of the difficulty has been conveyed.

The relations of the theory, then, cannot be satisfactorily tested, at least at present, because the constructs entering the relations, the p's and q's of the if p, then q statements, cannot be brought to the level of empirical operation. This does not mean, as some have said, that Freud's ideas are unscientific. Such a view is oversimplified. One can deduce many testable hypotheses from Freudian theory. And perhaps even the more difficult Freudian concepts will eventually yield to scientific ingenuity.

Examples of Problems and Hypotheses

The discussion so far has been mostly *about* problems and hypotheses. It may be wise to give more examples. Recall, first, that problems are questions about relations among variables. Does practice in a mental function improve future learning in the mental function (Gates & Taylor, 1925)? This is an old and well-known problem. If you practice memorizing, can you improve your memory and your future memorizing? (The answer seems to be discouraging.) Does forced compliance induce change in belief? This is an important problem. After World War II, the Allies occupied Japan. The Japanese were forced—though the word was rarely used—to comply with Allied orders. Did this compliance change Japanese beliefs? The authorities were ordered to conduct their political and economic affairs in a democratic manner, for example. Did they become more democratic? (The answer seems to be Yes.) The Soviets and the Chinese, among others, have long used forced compliance to change belief structures. Does it work? (Again, the answer seems to be Yes.)

Are women who are "hard to get" more desirable to men than women eager for alliance (Walster, Walster, Piliavin, & Schmidt, 1973)? This problem springs from folklore about women: those who are relatively inacessible are more desirable. The variables are inaccessibility, "hard-to-getness," and desirability. The problem is particularly interesting because the research done on it by Walster and her colleagues seems to upset an old myth. Walster et al. started out testing the hypothesis that men prefer hard-to-get women. They even derived a rather elaborate and clever theoretical rationale to explain the relation. But four experiments failed to support the hypothesis. In a classic statement, the authors said, "Did we give up our hypothesis? Heavens no. After all, it had only been disconfirmed four times" (Walster et al., 1973, p. 115). We will give the answer to the problem later.

Is similarity of belief more influential than race in accepting others (Rokeach & Mezei, 1966)? This highly controversial problem asks, in effect, whether likeness of belief is more powerful than likeness (and difference) of race in influencing people to accept others. If a white agrees with a black's beliefs, will he accept him more than he will accept a white with whose beliefs he disagrees? If one is a conservative, for example, will one in general accept black conservatives more than one will accept white liberals? These are fascinating questions, but not easy to answer. Here we have a problem that is stated in implied quantitative terms since "more" is used. (The answer to the question appears to be Yes, belief is more important than race, but not in all circumstances.)

Earlier it was said that many, perhaps most, behavioral research problems have more than one independent variable. Here is a problem statement with three independent variables: How do academic aptitude, high school achievement, and level of aspiration influence academic achievement (Worell, 1959)? Such multivariable problems are closer to psychological and social reality: they more accurately mirror the complex causal structure of phenomena, in this case of academic achievement.

Here is a hypothesis derived from the first problem given above: Practice in a mental function has no effect on the future learning of that mental function (Gates & Taylor, 1925). Note the if p, then q structure of the hypothesis: If practice in a mental function, then (no) future learning of the mental function. Note, too, the negative form of the hypothesis: practice has no effect. This is unusual. Most hypotheses specify some sort of direction of effect. (The hypothesis was supported.)

A more conventional hypothesis is: Individuals having the same or similar occupational roles will hold similar attitudes toward things significantly related to the occupational role. This means, for example, that physicians will hold similar beliefs and attitudes toward medical matters. If the hypothesis is supported by evidence, we would expect most physicians to think alike about Medicare.

Our final hypothesis is a kind of hypothesis that is increasingly being tested in contemporary behavioral research: Anti-Semitic people will displace aggression on to others when their hostility is aroused (Berkowitz, 1959). Here there are two variables—anti-Semitism and hostility arousal—that lead to displaced aggression. The hypothesis says that anti-Semitism will "produce" displaced aggression only under the circumstance of hostility arousal. That is, the structure of the argument is: If p,

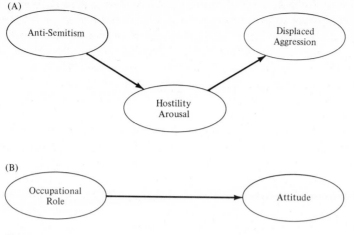

FIG. 3.1

then *q*, given *r*; or, If anti-Semitism, then displaced aggression, given hostility arousal. The argument is depicted in Figure 3.1(A). Also given in the figure (B) is the simpler argument of the immediately preceding hypothesis on occupational role and attitude. We see that in (B) occupational role operates directly on attitude. In (A), however, anti-Semitism produces displaced aggression only when hostility is aroused. This is called an *interaction*, which means that two (or more) variables operate together; they interact to produce an effect. We will take up this interesting phenomenon in more detail in a later chapter.

VARIABLES

One of the key words in the literature of the behavioral sciences is "variable." While we have earlier given a definition and many examples, it is now necessary to be more systematic and precise about the term and its definition. It is to be hoped that the precision will have the virtue of getting rid of most of the ambiguity that often accompanies the word and its use.

General Definition of Variable

A variable is obviously something that varies, that has different values. We measure, we say, the level of aspiration of a group of children. For each child we obtain a score, some kind of number. We say we have measured the variable, "level of aspiration." While intuitively appealing, even instructive, this definition is not really a definition. And it is not accurate.

A *variable* is a symbol to which numerals are assigned. Examples of such symbols are *A*, *x*, *M*, or intelligence, level of aspiration, anxiety. The variable x can take on a set of numerical values, for example, scores yielded by an intelligence test or a reading test. The variable A can take the values a_1, a_2, a_3, and so on, which may stand for the numerical values yielded by an attitude measure with a seven-point scale. We may have the attitude scores of four individuals: $a_1 = 6, a_2 = 3, a_3 = 5, a_4 = 4$. A is a variable. If we wish, we can name it Attitudes toward Women.

This definition of variable is simple and general, although a little removed from common sense. It is general because it covers all conceivable cases and kinds of variables. And, although not a common-sense kind of definition—it may even be a bit strange at first—it is quite uncomplicated and easy to grasp. There are symbols, which can be letters of any kind in the alphabet, or words or short expressions: X, Y, A, K, intelligence, attitudes toward women, anxiety, social class, level of aspiration, retention, religious preference, income, and so on. Clearly, variables are properties that take on different values. Some variables can have many values, even an infinite number (theoretically); on the other hand, variables can have as few as two values.[3] Intelligence, retention, and attitudes toward women have many values. Sex has only two values, usually 1 and 0, 1 being assigned to one sex and 0 to the other sex. Alive-dead and employed-unemployed are also two-value, or dichotomous, variables. Social class ordinarily has two, three, or four values. Religious preference is somewhat different. Although a so-called nominal or categorical variable (see below), the values assigned to it are invariably 1's and 0's, but we will not now show how this is done.

Before changing the subject, it should be pointed out that variables are also concepts or constructs. A concept is, of course, a general term that expresses the presumed central idea behind a set of related particulars. Scientists, when talking about the concepts used in their work, often call them "constructs." "Construct" is a useful term because it indicates the synthetic nature of psychological and sociological variables. It expresses the idea that scientists often use terms in accordance with the needs and demands of their theories and research. Intelligence, aptitude, anxiety, locus of control, aggression, authoritarianism, social class, sex, and achievement are all constructs. If the definition of "variable" given above can be satisfied—that is, if numerals can be assigned to objects according to rules—then we can call a construct a variable. The reader will often encounter these terms in the literature of psychology and education, but they will not always be used precisely. Nevertheless, it should be remembered that there are differences between them. For example, it is good to know that although it is theoretically possible to make most constructs variables, it is not always practically feasible to do so. An example, Freud's repression, was given earlier.

---

[3] It is possible, by definition, for a variable to have only one value. It is then called a *constant*. We deal almost exclusively with variables that have two or more values.

Operational Definitions

There are two kinds of definitions: constitutive and operational. A *constitutive definition* defines words with other words: "weight" is the "heaviness of objects"; "anxiety" is "apprehension or vague fear." Constitutive definitions are dictionary definitions and, of course, have to be used by everyone, including scientists. They are, however, insufficient for scientific purposes. Suppose we define "intelligence" as "mental acuity," "the ability to think abstractly," and the like. Notice that we are using other concepts or conceptual expressions in lieu of "intelligence." There is, of course, no escaping the necessity of using such definitions in and out of science. But scientists must go further. They must define the variables they use in hypotheses *so that the hypotheses can be tested.* They do this by using what are known as operational definitions.

Operational definitions have arisen from a new way of thinking: instead of thinking only constitutively, scientists also think operationally. An operational definition is a bridge from concepts to observations. This is a radically different way of thinking and operating, a way that has revolutionized behavioral research, particularly research in psychology and education.

An *operational definition* assigns meaning to a construct or variable by specifying the activities or "operations" necessary to measure it or to manipulate it. An operational definition, alternatively, specifies the activities of the researcher in measuring a variable or in manipulating it. It is like a manual of instructions to the researcher: It says, in effect, "Do such-and-such in so-and-so manner." A well-known though rather extreme example is: Intelligence (anxiety, achievement, and so forth) is scores on X intelligence test, or intelligence is what X intelligence test measures. This definition tells us what to do to measure intelligence. It tells the researcher to use X intelligence test. Achievement may be defined by citing a standardized achievement test, a teacher-made achievement test, or grades assigned by teachers. We here have three distinctly different ways of operationally defining the same construct. The reader should not let this multiplicity of operational definitions bother him; it is part of their flexibility and strength. After all, a construct like achievement has many facets, and researchers can be interested in different facets at different times. Consider even the obvious examples of different subject-matter achievement: reading, arithmetic, art, and so on.

Take a more difficult example. Suppose we wish to define the variable "consideration." It can be defined operationally by listing behaviors of children that are presumably considerate behaviors and then having teachers observe and rate the children's behavior on a five-point scale. Such behaviors might be: when the children say to each other, "Excuse me" or "I'm sorry"; when one child yields a toy to another on request; or when one child helps another with a task.

The kind of definition just discussed can be called a *measured* operational definition. It tells the researcher how to measure (and observe) a variable. Recall the Miller and Swanson variables, social class and time of weaning. There are also *experimental* operational definitions that tell the researcher how to manipulate a variable. For example, reinforcement can be operationally defined by giving the details of how subjects are to be reinforced—as Clark and Walberg did. In the study of the effects of different incentives on pupil arithmetic performance mentioned earlier, Hurlock (1925) praised some children, blamed some, and ignored others. Frustration can be defined as prevention from reaching a goal, a constitutive definition with clear implications for experimental manipulation. This was nicely realized by Barker, Dembo, and Lewin (1943), who operationally defined frustration by describing children in a playroom with "a number of highly attractive, *but inaccessible*, toys." (The toys were put behind a wire-net partition; the children could see them but not touch them.)

Like other ideas presented in this book, the operational definition is a remarkable invention. As said at the beginning of the section, it bridges the gap between concepts or constructs and actual observations, behaviors, and activities. To clarify this, look at Figure 3.2. The figure depicts the two levels on which the scientist operates: the level of constructs and hypotheses (I) and the level of observation and manipulation (II). The two levels are connected by an operational definition. When the psychological researcher says, "Frustration produces aggression," he operates at level I. In order to test the hypothesis, he must work on level II: he must actually manipulate (or observe or measure) frustration and measure aggression. To work on level II, he must first provide a means of getting there. This means is the operational definition, which furnishes the bridge from the construct-hypothesis level to the observation level. Researchers, then, shuttle back and forth between the two levels. The views of scientists as people who spin abstruse theories divorced from the real world (level I), or who only manipulate things, make observations, and measure things (level II), are both stereotypes that distort scientific reality. Virtually all scientists operate at both levels.

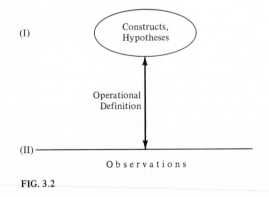

(I)   Constructs, Hypotheses

Operational Definition

(II) —————————————————————————

Observations

FIG. 3.2

The following two examples of operational definitions may help to solidify the ideas being presented. In research on secondary and higher education "achievement" is often operationally defined as grade-point average, or GPA. Holtzman and Brown (1968), in a study of the presumed effect of study habits and attitudes on the achievement of high-school students, defined it as follows: "The criterion of school achievement, grade-point average . . . was generally obtained by assigning weights of 4, 3, 2, 1, and 0 to grades of A, B, C, D, and F, respectively." In other words, numerals were assigned to teacher grades. This is an operational definition of achievement: it assigned a specific and concrete "meaning" to the construct "achievement." Note, however, that there are other ways to define achievement operationally. One such way would be to ask teachers to rate their students' overall achievement by assigning a numeral from some set of numerals (or letters for categories) to each student. The two operational definitions, however, may yield different results. If they are both "good" operational definitions, they should agree rather well.

In an interesting study considered earlier, Walster et al. (1973) defined one of their main variables quite ingeniously. In their research they tried to find an answer to an old question: Are women who are "hard-to-get" more attractive to men than women who are not hard-to-get? Men subjects were handed five folders containing information on a woman. Three of the folders had "date selection forms," which contained the woman's presumed reactions to five men who were possible dates. These reactions were recorded as checks made by the woman on a scale ranging from "definitely want to date." That is, each "woman" had presumably made five checks on five folders, and these checks indicated whether she was hard-to-get or easy-to-get. For example, if she checked all five scales toward the "definitely want to date" end, she was easy-to-get. If, on the other hand, she was not enthusiastic about any of the men, she was hard-to-get. The most interesting and crucial category was the woman who was selectively hard-to-get: she didn't want any of the men but you (one of the folders was that of the man subject). This procedure, then, was the operational definition of "hard-to-getness," a most ingenious "definition."

In the above examples, notice that the operational definition spells out in considerable detail what the researcher must do to measure the variables. Holtzman and Brown specifically told how grade-point average was to be measured, and Walster et al. detailed the procedure to obtain measures of "hard-to-getness." Similarly, in experimental situations, operational definitions specify what experimenters do to manipulate one or more independent variables. They literally give the operations involved.

Nothing whatever has been said about the quality of operational definitions. Like constitutive definitions, they can be good or bad, well-conceived or poorly conceived. There have been criticisms of operational definitions (and the philosophy of operationism that inspired them) that have really missed the point. It has been said, for example, that no operational definition can ever express the full meaning and richness of concepts like aggression, repression, anxiety, authoritarianism, learning, achievement, and so on. Precisely. They can never do this. Nor, for that matter, can constitutive definitions! Operational definitions are limited definitions, often severely limited, whose purpose is to enable the researcher to get at aspects of behavioral "reality." There is always the danger of so fractionating a concept that there is little relevance to its "real" meaning. This does not imply, however, that it is impossible to invent and use operational definitions that approximate significant *aspects* of conceptual "reality." Difficult, but not impossible. Indeed, scientific success in inventing and using such limited definitions has been gratifying. As we proceed with our study, we will see more and more worthy examples of operational definitions and the shuttling back and forth between the two levels of scientific operation.

Relations and explanations

4

Suppose I am a social scientist interested in minority group problems. In my research I have been studying various relations in an attempt to get deeper understanding of minority group problems and problems of prejudice and discrimination. One of these relations is between discrimination against minority groups and proneness to violence of the minority groups. I believe, for instance, that the more a group is discriminated against, the more likely its members are to resort to violence. I have collected data on eight minority groups and can rank them on two variables: *discrimination* and *violence*. Experts have ranked the eight groups on the degree of discrimination practiced against them, 1 meaning greatest discrimination and 8 the least discrimination. I have also obtained statistics on the amount of violence that has characterized the eight groups in the past five years. (Let's not worry now about how this was done.) From these statistics I have ranked the eight groups from high to low in violence, 1 meaning high violence and 8 low violence.

The two sets of ranks I obtained are given in Figure 4.1. The figure expresses a "relation." It does this because it shows two sets of numbers that have been systematically paired: the first minority group, which had been discriminated against the most and thus had the rank 1, had a rank of 2 on violence. The second minority group, the group discriminated against next most (rank of 2), had the third rank (3) on violence, and so on for the remaining groups. In short, the two sets of ranks put into relation to each other as in Figure 4.1 expresses a relation. **45**

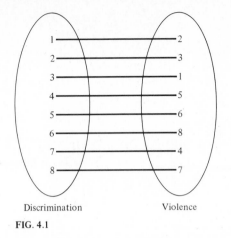

Discrimination   Violence

FIG. 4.1

Calling the two sets of numbers a "relation" may seem a bit odd. It really is not. Indeed, it is quite precise and unambiguous, as we will see. All relations can be expressed in some such way, although numbers do not always have to be used. The point is that the two sets of numbers, taken together and as they are in Figure 4.1, *are* a relation. Later, we will see that relations have direction and magnitude. In the present case the direction is positive: both sets of numbers "go along" with each other: low ranks in discrimination tend to be paired with low ranks in violence, and high ranks with high ranks. The magnitude of the relation will be discussed later in the chapter.

In Chapter 2 we said that "relation" is probably the most fundamental term in science. This is so because understanding and explaining phenomena is the basic aim of science, and phenomena can be understood only through their relations with other phenomena. There is no such thing as "knowing" anything absolutely and in and of itself. We cannot contemplate and study, say, delinquency by itself. We can understand and explain it only by studying what is related to it, what psychological and sociological variables influence it. Then we may have some clues as to why and how delinquency occurs.

But what is a relation? When people talk about relations, they take it for granted that they know what they are talking about: one thing is related to another thing. But this is hopelessly vague; it tells us nothing really of what relations are. Even a dictionary definition is unsatisfactory. Such a definition might be: "A relation is a bond, a connection, between people or things; it is a logical, natural, or synthetic association between phenomena." Unfortunately, this is not very helpful. While we may get some idea of what a relation is from such a definition, it is too vague for science. Fortunately, it is easy to define relations unambiguously and precisely provided we have some elementary background in set theory. We diverge briefly, then, to examine sets.

SETS

A *set* is a well-defined collection of objects or elements (Kemeny, Snell, & Thompson, 1966, p. 58). "Well-defined" means that it must be possible to tell when a given object, among a collection of objects under discussion, does or does not belong to the set. Terms like "group," "class," "flock," and "family" indicate sets.

There are two ways to define a set. First, we can list all the members of the set. Then it is easily possible to determine whether any given object belongs to the set. For instance, suppose we have a list of the names of the countries that are members of the United Nations. To determine whether a given country is a member of the set United Nations, we simply check the list of all member countries. The list itself is the definition of the set. It is quite precise and unambiguous, but not always useful in research. Lists of members of sets are often too large to be practical—the residents of Madrid, for example—are not available, or impossible to obtain, or, even when obtainable, may change by the time we go through the whole list.

The second and more useful way to define sets is to give a rule that tells us when any given object or individual does or does not belong to a given set. Many "rule definitions," as they are called, are easy. For example, in defining the variable political preference the rule can be: registered Republican or registered Democrat. Another simple though perhaps more fallible rule is: Ask any given individual whether he is Republican or Democrat. The "rules" for most variables in the behavioral science, however, are more complex. In much, perhaps most, behavioral research rule definitions are used to define the sets of objects—people, pigeons, groups, numbers, words—under study.

RELATIONS

In Figure 4.2, two sets are given. They are enclosed with ovals to indicate that they are sets. The first, call it *A*, is a set of five children, three boys

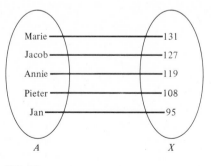

FIG. 4.2

and two girls. We assume that the children have been chosen in some systematic way for a research purpose. For example, suppose they are a sample of five sixth-grade children in K school in Amsterdam, The Netherlands. The second set, labeled X, is a set of five intelligence test scores obtained by testing the five children. The lines connecting the names to the scores simply indicate that, on the basis of the test, Marie was assigned 131, Jacob was assigned 127, and so on. We have, then, two sets, one of five names representing five children and one of five numbers representing the children's scores on an intelligence test.

Maybe we can make the example a little more interesting. Study Figure 4.3. The set of five intelligence test scores, X, is on the left. The set on the right, S (for "sex"), has two members, M and F, meaning male and female. The members of the two sets, X and S, are connected with lines as follows: If an X score is that of a boy, then draw the line to M; if a score is a girl's, draw the line to F. In this way we have stated a relation between the scores and the letters M and F, or, more generally, a relation between intelligence and sex. We may believe that girls (in this sample, maybe in Amsterdam) are more intelligent than boys. To test this notion we can average the scores of boys and of girls and compare the averages. The averages (means) are 125 for girls and 110 for boys. We may conclude that girls are more intelligent than boys, a risky conclusion indeed! The point now is not the adequacy of the conclusion but the underlying use of sets to study a relation.

This rather obvious discussion of sets can be extended to greater numbers of cases and more complex variables. No matter how many cases and how complex the variables, however, the basic principles and rules are the same. More to the point, we have defined a relation, a relation between intelligence and sex. How? We simply connect the members of one set, X, to the members of another set, S, using the simple rule for drawing the lines given above. Now we give an abstract definition of "relation" that is completely general and will apply in all cases.

A relation is a set of ordered pairs. An *ordered pair* is two objects of any kind in which there is a fixed order for the objects to appear or to be placed. In Figure 4.2, (Marie, 131) is an ordered pair. The set of ordered pairs is the two sets in Figure 4.2 taken together, the names listed first and the scores

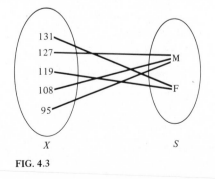

FIG. 4.3

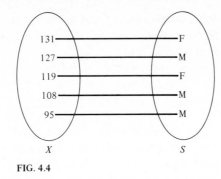

FIG. 4.4

second: {(Marie, 131), (Jacob, 127), (Annie, 119), (Pieter, 108), (Jan, 95)}. In other words, "ordered" means always taking the members of one of the sets first and the members of the other set second. The set of pairs just named *is* a relation. It may not be interesting or significant or even meaningful but it *is* a relation.

A relation was also given in Figure 4.3, though it is a bit harder to see. If we give the relation in another way, as in Figure 4.4, it is easier to see. Again, we have a set of ordered pairs: {(131, F), (127, M), (119, F), (108, M), (95, M)}. This is then a relation by definition. In this case, however, it is a little more meaningful: the set of ordered pairs expresses a relation between the intelligence test scores and the sex of the subjects, or, more simply, between intelligence and sex.

The definition of relations as sets of ordered pairs is completely general, quite unambiguous, and highly useful. With it we have broken away from the ambiguity of dictionary definitions. Notice that the definition says nothing whatever about the interest, significance, or worth of a relation. It states only what a relation is. And that is a lot, because we know that if science is largely study of relations then it is largely study of sets of ordered

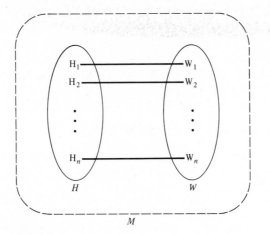

FIG. 4.5

pairs. Moreover, it permits us to study and learn the substance, direction, and magnitude of relations. Before going into these ideas, let us look at an ubiquitous relation, marriage.

If marriage is a relation, then it must be a set of ordered pairs. This may be a curious way to think of marriage, but it is useful in research. Take all the husbands and wives in a community in pairs, with husbands (or wives) always placed first in each pair. This is shown in Figure 4.5 where husbands $H_1, H_2, \ldots, H_n$ are given in the set labeled H, and wives $W_1, W_2, \ldots, W_n$ are given in the set labeled W.[1] The ordered pairs, with H's always first, are joined by lines, yielding a new set of pairs, indicated by the broken lines drawn around both sets and labeled M. This is a relation, by definition. We call it "marriage."

RELATIONS IN BEHAVIORAL RESEARCH

The definition of relations as sets of ordered pairs is conceptually both simple and powerful, but a little arid for the nonscientist. We can now consider what may be more interesting: the use of relations in scientific behavioral research. Before doing so, however, we should know that there are aspects of science and research in which relations seem not to be studied. For instance, a good deal of research has taxonomic and descriptive functions. A study may seek only to describe the characteristics of a particular population or sample: the relative incidence of births, deaths, suicides, marriages, and so on, in San Francisco. Little or no attempt may be made to relate variables to each other. Such work is legitimate and often important.

Similarly, researchers often group observations of characteristics of people and things into categories. This is *taxonomy*, the activity of classifying things into natural or synthetic groupings. A great deal of psychological work, for example, has been aimed at classifying individuals into categories: introvert and extrovert; dominant and submissive; inner-directed and other-directed; independent and dependent; and so on. While important and essential, taxonomic and descriptive work, strictly speaking, is supplementary to the study of relations. In any case, the greatest part of the discussion in this book will view science as being preoccupied with the study of relations. We approach a little closer to such study by first examining the direction and magnitude of relations.

The Direction and Magnitude of Relations

Let us assume, again, that I am studying discrimination and violence and that during a particular study I obtained the two sets of ranks given in

---

[1] The symbols H_1, H_2, and H_n and W_1, W_2, and W_n mean husband 1, husband 2, and husband n and wife 1, wife 2, and wife n. n is the last husband and last wife. The numerals in this symbolism are called subscripts; they simply define the number of an individual or a pair in a set.

Figure 4.1. Let us also assume that I am testing the hypothesis that discrimination against minority groups is associated with violence. The hypothesis can be quantitatively expressed: The greater the discrimination against minority groups, the greater the violence of the minority groups. (We assume that discrimination and violence are adequately defined and measured.) We ask the question: Do the data in Figure 4.1 support the hypothesis? To answer the question we need to know the direction and magnitude of the relation expressed by the two sets of ranks.

The direction is easily determined. We simply inspect the ranks to see if they seem to "go together" and how they go together. The ranks in the left set (Discrimination) vary from 1 through 8 in perfect order. The ranks on the right (Violence) do not follow this perfect order. Do they, however, generally follow the order of the ranks on the left? That is, are high ranks on Discrimination accompanied, in general, by high ranks on Violence, and similarly for low ranks? If so, then the direction of the relation is positive. In this case, the answer is Yes: high ranks in Discrimination are in general accompanied by high ranks in Violence, and low ranks in Discrimination are accompanied by low ranks in Violence. The relation is positive.

But what is the magnitude of the relation? We know the relation is positive, but we do not know the extent to which there is agreement between the pairs of ranks. There are a number of ways to assess the magnitude of relations, and we will examine three or four of them, even though we wish to avoid technical complexity in our pursuit of conceptual clarity. First, we make a graph of the relations of Figure 4.1. The graph is given in Figure 4.6. The horizontal axis is usually called X and the vertical axis Y. X is the independent variable, Y the dependent variable, or X = Discrimination and Y = Violence. The eight ranks have been indicated on each axis, and the eight pairs of ranks plotted as indicated: (1,2), (2,3), . . . , (8,7). For example, the Discrimination value of 1 in Figure 4.1 is referred to the X or Discrimination axis of Figure 4.6, and the Violence value of 2 is referred to the Y or Violence axis of the figure. A cross is placed

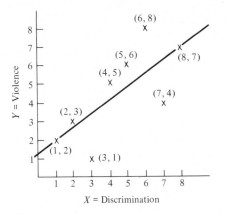

FIG. 4.6

at the juncture of the two values and is marked (1,2). The remaining values of Figure 4.1 are similarly plotted. A line has been drawn through the plotted points so as to be as close as possible to all of them simultaneously. This line expresses the relation just as the plotted points do. It is called a "regression line," though we might call it a "relation line." We will return to such highly useful lines later when we will see that they express relations clearly and succinctly.

Do the plotted points and the regression line indicate that the hypothesis is supported by these "data"? The answer is Yes, they do. The plotted points indicate that large values of X, Discrimination, are accompanied by large values of Y, Violence, medium values of X by medium values of Y, and low values of X by low values of Y. The statement, If discrimination, then violence, seems to be correct. Specifically, those minority groups who have suffered the most discrimination have been the most violent, and those minority groups who have suffered the least discrimination have been the least violent. The relation is not perfect—there are exceptions, for example (3,1) and (7,4) on the graph—but it holds up in general.

But we still have not directly discussed the magnitude of the relation. We have said that large values of Y "go along" with large values of X, and smaller values of Y "go along" with smaller values of X. This is, of course, a statement of magnitude, but we want to be more precise. We want to know how "strong" or how "weak" the relation is. If the direction of the regression line is from the lower left to the upper right of the graph and all the points are precisely on the line, the relation is "perfect" and positive. Such perfect relations almost never occur in behavioral research, however. Sometimes the plotted points all come close to the line. If they do, the relation is "strong." If they do not, if they are scattered relatively far from the line, the relation is "weak," or even near zero. (In the latter case, the line itself would be horizontal or nearly horizontal. We explain this later.)

There are still more precise ways to express the direction and magnitude of relations. One highly useful way is through correlation and the so-called coefficient of correlation. "Correlation" means just what the word sounds like: the co-relation among two sets of values, or the varying together of the X and Y values, as explained above. "Correlation coefficient," a term used a great deal in research, is a measure of the interdependence, the varying together, the simultaneous increase or decrease of two sets of numerical values. Because of their great importance in research, let us go into the ideas of relation, correlation, direction, and magnitude more deeply.

While it is correct from a definitional point of view to say that a relation is a set of ordered pairs, such a definition only clarifies the idea of a relation. It does not help the scientists to draw conclusions from data. They want to know the direction and magnitude of relations, as said earlier. The *direction* of a relation is whether it is positive or negative (or more complex). If the two sets of measures of a set of ordered pairs vary together—

TABLE 4.1   Three Sets of Ordered Pairs Showing Different
Directions of Relations

(A)		(B)		(C)	
X	Y	X	Y	X	Y
1	2	1	8	1	4
2	4	2	6	2	8
3	5	3	5	3	5
4	6	4	4	4	2
5	8	5	2	5	6

researchers say "covary"—in the same direction, the relation is positive. If
they vary together in opposite directions, the relation is negative.

Three sets of ordered pairs are given in Table 4.1. In set A, the scores of
X and Y have the same rank order.[2] In set B, on the other hand, the rank
orders of the two sets of scores are opposite, that is, the high scores of X are
accompanied by the low scores of Y [for example, (5,2), (4,4)], and the low
scores of X are accompanied by the high scores of Y [for example, (1,8),
(2,6)]. The pairs of the set of ordered pairs shown in C have no discernible
direction; the two sets show no systematic tendency to vary one way or the
other. The set has been included in the table to illustrate the case of "no
relation," or, more precisely, zero relation, and to contrast it to sets A and
B.

The *magnitude* of a relation is the extent to which two sets of measures
vary together (covary) positively or negatively. In set A of Table 4.1, the
magnitude of the relation is high because the rank orders of X and Y are
identical. Similarly, the magnitude of the relation of B is high because the
rank orders are completely opposite. Nevertheless, the two sets of numbers
vary together: the lower numbers of Y go with the higher numbers of X,
and the higher numbers of Y go with the lower numbers of X. In set C,
however, no systematic varying together of the two sets of numbers can be
discerned. It is as though the numbers of the second set were inserted at
random (which they were). In such cases, it is often said that there is "no
relation" between the sets. That this is a somewhat inaccurate way of
talking is obvious because *any* set of ordered pairs *is* a relation. Nevertheless, in ordinary research discourse the ordered pairs of set C would be
said to show no relation. The correct expression is "zero relation."

Is it possible to be more precise about the magnitudes of the relations of
the sets of measures of Table 4.1? Fortunately, it is. One highly useful
measure of the magnitude of relations is the coefficient of correlation,
which was mentioned and briefly described a little while ago. This is
simply an index, in decimal form, that indicates the direction and mag-

[2] The scores of Table 4.1 are not ranks. Nevertheless, they can be easily converted to
ranks; for example, the ranks of the Y scores in A are 5, 4, 3, 2, 1.

nitude of the covarying of two sets of scores.[3] Such indices vary from −1.00 through 0 to +1.00. +1.00 indicates a perfect positive relation—the two sets of scores have exactly the same rank order, for example, as in A of Table 4.1—and −1.00 indicates a perfect negative relation as in B of the table. 0 (zero), of course, indicates "no relation" or "zero relation." All decimal fractions between −1.00 and +1.00 are possible: −.78, −.51, −.08, .12, .42, .83, and so on. Many such coefficients or indices of relation are used in the behavioral sciences, but in this book we are concerned mainly with understanding and interpreting such indices and not with their calculation.[4]

Graphing Relations

In Figure 4.6 we graphed the relation between the ranks of Figure 4.1. To get a deeper intuitive grasp of quantitative relations, let us draw graphs of the three relations of Table 4.1. These are given in Figure 4.7. The X scores are indicated by the X axis and the Y scores by the Y axis. The pairs—(1,2), (2,4), (5,8), and so on—are indicated by the crosses: the cross for the pair (4,6) in A, for example, is placed at the point of intersection 4 units out on X and 6 units up on Y. It is circled. Lines have been drawn through the points so that they run as close as possible to all the points. In discussing Figure 4.6 we said such lines are called regression lines, that they are drawn so that they are as close as possible to all the plotted points, and that they express the relation between the X scores and the Y scores. Note that the lines drawn in A and B come very close to all the points. The line drawn in C, however, cannot come close to all the points. Indeed, the best one can do is to draw a nearly horizontal line that is close to the mean (arithmetic average) of the Y scores.

Perhaps the most important interpretation of the three situations is as follows. In A, the high positive relation means that as the X scores get larger so do the Y scores. The high negative relation of B, on the other hand, means that as the X scores get larger the Y scores get smaller. It is not possible to make any such systematic assertion in C: one cannot predict the magnitude of the Y scores from the magnitude of the X scores. In advanced sciences like physics—and often in psychology and education—one can make more precise magnitude statements; for instance, as X increases 1

---

[3] An *index* is a number used to characterize a set of numbers and is usually calculated with a formula from two or more other numbers. A mean, or arithmetic average, is an index; it indicates the central tendency of a set of numbers. The range, the highest number minus the lowest number, is an index. IQ's (intelligence quotients) are indices: mental age (calculated from a test) divided by chronological age. The coefficient of correlation is a rather complex index that sensitively expresses the "going togetherness" of two sets of scores. It is an ubiquitous statistic because of its descriptive power and because sets of correlation coefficients can themselves be analyzed with powerful methods.

[4] The interested reader may wish to consult an elementary statistics book for detailed directions on how to calculate such indices. See, for example, Edwards (1973).

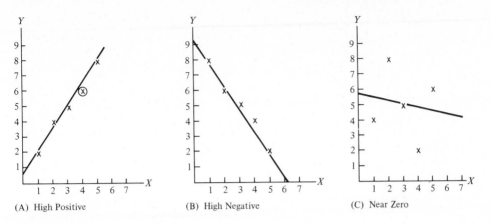

(A) High Positive   (B) High Negative   (C) Near Zero

FIG. 4.7

unit, Y increases 2 units, or as X increases 1 unit, Y decreases one-half a unit.

It may help the reader if we drape these bare relations and the graphs with variable clothing. In A of Figure 4.7, imagine X to be education, or years of education, and Y income. The relation of A, then, would mean that as education increases, so does income. This happens to be so, but the relation is not nearly as high as the graph indicates. Using the same variables in B gives us an unlikely relation that research evidence does not support: as education increases, income decreases. In C, no systematic prediction from education to income is possible. Knowing amount of education does not enable us to say that income increases or decreases systematically. But let us take a somewhat more interesting example.

An Example of Direction and Magnitude of a Relation

Suppose a researcher suspected that prejudice against minority groups was in part due to authoritarianism.[5] It has been found, say, that some people have a kind of personality called authoritarian. Some of the characteristics of authoritarians are aggressiveness, a tendency to be punitive, conventionality, uncritical submission to authority and leaders, and generalized hostility toward groups different from their own. The researcher reasons, on the basis of a theory of prejudice, that these characteristics combine to produce prejudice toward minority group members.

There are a number of ways the researcher can find out how correct he is. Suppose he constructs a scale to measure the extent to which individuals possess the characteristics given above. Call this scale the A Scale. He also uses another scale, the AS Scale, that has been shown in previous research to measure anti-Semitism, or prejudice against Jews. He is study-

---

[5] This is a famous hypothesis for which there is considerable evidence (Adorno, Frenkel-Brunswick, Levinson, & Sanford, 1950).

ing, then, one aspect of the relation between authoritarianism and anti-Semitism. He could, of course, have measured the subjects' attitudes toward blacks, foreigners, Indians, and other minority groups. Among the many individuals to whom the two scales were administered, suppose that 10 were selected to represent the whole group to whom he administered the scales, and that the 10 pairs of scores are those in Table 4.2. (Ten sets of ordered pairs are hardly enough to assess a relation reliably. Behavioral scientists customarily use many more. The principle is the same, however, whether 10 or 10,000 sets of pairs are used.)

The researcher wants to know the direction of the relation and its magnitude: its sign, positive or negative, and to what extent the two sets of scores covary. First, the two sets of scores, with authoritarianism scores always coming first and anti-Semitism scores second, are a set of ordered pairs and thus a relation. It is easy to see the direction of the relation: it is positive because there is a marked tendency for high A scores to be accompanied by high AS scores—for example, (6.2, 5.7), (5.9, 5.3)—and similarly for low A and AS scores—for example, (3.5, 4.0), (3.9, 3.5).

It is not as easy to assess the magnitude of the relation, that is, just how pronounced is the tendency for the A and AS scores to "go together": high with high, medium with medium, and low with low. Inspection of the set of ordered pairs seems to indicate that the covarying of the scores, their "going togetherness," is pronounced. To see this more clearly, the ranks of the scores, ranks 1 through 10, with 1 indicating the highest score and 10 the lowest, have been entered in Table 4.2 beside the A and AS scores (in parentheses). Note that in general the ranks go together: the low-numbered ranks of A are matched by the low-numbered ranks of AS, and similarly for the medium- and high-numbered ranks. In sum, the relation between authoritarianism and anti-Semitism, in this sample, is positive and "substantial." How large is "substantial"? It is possible and desirable

TABLE 4.2   Ten Fictitious Authoritarianism and Anti-Semitism Scores Selected from a Large Group of Such Scores, with Rank Values of the Scores[a]

Authoritarianism (A)	Anti-Semitism (AS)
6.2 (1)	5.7 (2)
5.9 (2)	5.3 (3)
5.7 (3)	4.7 (5)
5.1 (4)	5.8 (1)
4.8 (5)	4.4 (7)
4.5 (6)	4.5 (6)
4.2 (7)	3.9 (9)
4.1 (8)	4.8 (4)
3.9 (9)	3.5 (10)
3.5 (10)	4.0 (8)

[a] The numbers in parentheses are the rank values of the scores, with 1 being high and 10 low.

to calculate indices of the magnitude of relations. Such indices are called coefficients of correlation, as pointed out earlier.[6]

EXAMPLES OF DIFFERENT KINDS OF RELATIONS

The description and discussion of the Clark and Walberg and the Miller and Swanson studies in Chapter 1 and the above description of the relation between authoritarianism and anti-Semitism should have given us a little of the flavor of contemporary psychological and educational research and of the nature of relations. Now we need to be more specific. To do so, we briefly outline a hypothetical relation between intelligence and school achievement, and then study three different kinds or forms of relation, again using hypothetical examples.

Intelligence and School Achievement: A Hypothetical Example

When there is a relation between two phenomena, two variables, they vary together. Put it this way: If there is a relation between two variables, when one of them changes the other also changes. Suppose we have some way to measure, say, both intelligence and school achievement, and we observe the values of both of these measures in a sample of children. To the extent that the values of one of them varies with, or "goes along with," the values of the other, to this extent the two are related. To the extent that the observed values of the school achievement measure change when the observed values of the intelligence measure change, to this extent the two are related. This is called *concomitant variation*.

Study the graph of Figure 4.8, which depicts a hypothetical relation between intelligence and school achievement. A number of joint scores have been plotted in the graph. The first pair of scores (to the extreme left) are (1,2), that is, one child's intelligence score is 1 and his achievement score is 2. The next child's scores are (2,2). The last child's pair of scores is (5,4). The principle is: As the intelligence scores vary, so do the achievement scores. The two sets of scores in general vary together—in this case they increase together. A line has been drawn through the plotted points so as to be as close as possible to all of them. It indicates the direction of the relation: positive, because low scores on intelligence are accompanied by low achievement scores, while high intelligence scores are accompanied by high achievement scores.

[6] For the curious reader, the coefficient of correlation of the A and AS scores of Table 4.2 is .77, which indicates that the relation is substantial.

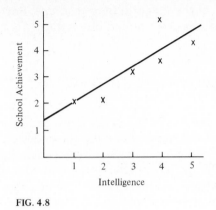

FIG. 4.8

Hypothetical Examples of Relations with Different Directions and Magnitudes

Suppose a teacher has the intelligence test scores (in the form of IQ's) and the achievement test scores of seven pupils and wants to know something about the relation between the two sets of scores. The scores are:

IQ	Achievement
145	51
125	57
118	60
110	48
100	54
97	35
90	32

The teacher plots the scores on a graph, as in Figure 4.9. He wants to know the direction and approximate magnitude of the relation.

It is obvious that the relation is positive: In general, higher IQ's tend to be accompanied by higher achievement scores and lower IQ's to be accompanied by lower achievement scores. The magnitude of the relation is harder to grasp from the graph. But we can see that it is substantial. If the relation were as high as possible, the little circles would all lie on a straight line running from lower left to upper right. The more they depart from a straight line, the lower the relation. While the seven points by no means lie on a straight line that runs as close as possible to all the points simultaneously—the line drawn on the graph—they are fairly close to it. (Recall that this line is called a regression line.) Another way to get a rough idea of the magnitude of the relation is to compare the ranks of the two sets of scores, as we did earlier. This is left to the reader as an exercise.

Now suppose we take a relation with a negative direction and considerably less in magnitude. Such a relation is shown in the graph of Figure

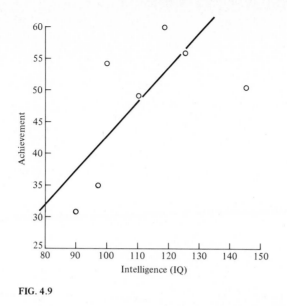

FIG. 4.9

4.10. Suppose this depicts the relation between affluence of neighborhoods and delinquency. We again have seven scores. This time, however, they are more scattered: they are farther away from the line drawn as close as possible to all the points. Moreover, the direction of the line, which now runs from the upper left to the lower right of the graph, is different. It indicates that the relation is negative: as neighborhoods become more affluent, there is less delinquency. But the relation is now much weaker than it was in Figure 4.9, where the plotted pairs of scores were rather close to the regression line. Note that four of the plotted points (the little circles) are quite far from the line. In sum, the relation is negative and it is not strong.

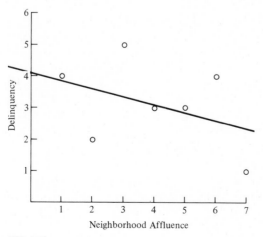

FIG. 4.10

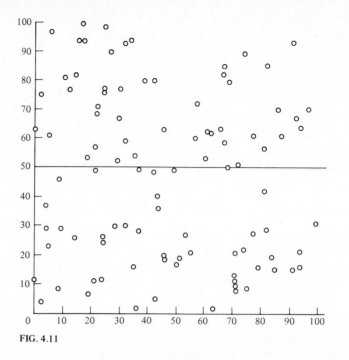

FIG. 4.11

Many variables, of course, are not at all related, except by chance: their relation is zero or close to zero. This means that knowledge of one variable yields no knowledge of another variable. One cannot say, for instance, that as one variable increases the other variable increases or decreases. Such a situation is depicted in Figure 4.11, where 100 pairs of numbers between the numbers 0 and 100 have been plotted. The numbers were obtained from two columns of one- or two-digit random numbers in a larger table of such numbers (Kerlinger, 1973, pp. 715 and 717, last two columns of two-digit numbers.)[7] Randomness and random numbers, an enormously important scientific and technical modern development, will be explained in Chapter 5. Suffice it to say here that random numbers are like the results obtained from tossing a coin or rolling dice: there is no known or detectable order of any kind in the numbers. One cannot predict in the present case—since both sets of numbers are random—any number from any other number. If a 90 turns up in one column, one cannot say a high number is likely to accompany it in the other column, and similarly for low and middle numbers. In ordinary language use, the numbers of the pairs are all jumbled: all possible combinations can occur, but one can't predict one number from another.

Compare Figure 4.11 with Figures 4.9 and 4.10. In the latter two figures there was systematic "going together" of the numbers, even though there was considerably less "going together" in Figure 4.10 than in 4.9. But it

---

[7] These numbers were generated with a special program on a large computer.

can be seen that the plotted points of Figure 4.11 are all over the graph, and, most important, there is no discernible order or "going together." This is a state of zero relation.

We will have more to say about relations throughout the book. They are the stuff and core of science. To understand that the main business of science is explanation and that explanation comes mostly from study of relations is to understand the foundation of much science. Now, let's try to tie up the ideas of explanation and relations and, while we're at it, bring in the highly important notion of theory.

SCIENTIFIC EXPLANATION, THEORY, AND RELATIONS

Although relation, theory, and explanation were discussed in Chapter 1, their importance demands deeper examination. Science is constantly preoccupied with explaining things. To "explain" something means to tell what the something is. But it is virtually impossible, in this world at least, to tell directly what something is. We can never get at the full "essence" of anything (though mystics tell us otherwise). In science we want to explain natural phenomena. For instance, we want to explain "prejudice," which means that we tell how it arises, why it arises, how it keeps going, what affects it, what it affects, and so on.

To explain something, at least satisfactorily, is certainly one of the most difficult tasks we can set for ourselves. Moreover, it is literally impossible to explain everything about any phenomenon, or about any sets of phenomena. To explain everything about prejudice, for example, is simply not possible, especially if we demand that a good part of our explanation be backed up by empirical evidence. In other words, absolute "truth" is forever impossible. But reasonable approximations to explanations of natural phenomena can be given in a scientifically satisfying manner.

The only way to explain anything, then, is to determine how that thing relates to other things. Thus explanation of prejudice means to find out how prejudice is related to other natural phenomena. If we were interested only in the development of prejudice in children, we would at least want to know at what ages children become aware of "other groups." The relation would be between age and knowledge or awareness of other groups.

We said earlier that science deals only with natural phenomena and "natural" explanations of such phenomena. To explain prejudice, for example, by saying that it is part of human nature, that all individuals are "naturally" prejudiced against groups different from their own groups, is not an explanation in the scientific sense because it invokes a term, "human nature," that is so vague as to be unamenable to scientific observation. Where do we find "human nature"? How do we measure it? Or it may be said, "God made different groups different, and differences lead to hostility." This, too, is not explanation in the scientific sense. Invoking God as the cause of differences removes the statement from scientific concern. Moreover, one can easily retort that God made all people alike. And to say that differences lead to hostility, while a better statement because it at least implies the possibility of observation, is still too vague for scientific observation. All group differences? Just some? What kind? What sort of hostility? Under what circumstances? And so on.

There are, of course, many such "explanations" of human behavior and phenomena. "Illness is a punishment for sin"; "Economic depressions are due to the Jews"; "Blacks are innately musical." Such "explanations" are scientifically hopeless because, as stated, they are not amenable to scientific investigation and testing. Indeed, a major contribution to science is its rejection of "explanations" that really explain nothing. Explanation can be only of natural phenomena, and "natural phenomena" mean occurrences in the observable world. Any phenomenon, to be a natural phenomenon, must be observable or potentially measurable or manipulable. It is not necessary that it be directly seen. But there must be some evidence of its manifestations in the empirical world. "Prejudice," in this sense, implies behavior of a certain kind.

How, then, does science explain prejudice—or any other natural phenomenon? To repeat, it can be explained only by relating it to other phenomena. And such explanations are necessarily always partial and incomplete. It has been found, for example, that authoritarianism is positively related to prejudice (Adorno et al., 1950): People who are highly authoritarian tend also to be prejudiced against Jews, blacks, and foreigners. It has also been found that if most people in a defined group of people hold stereotyped beliefs (relatively rigid and fixed beliefs) about the members of another group, then they will also tend to have negative attitudes toward the members of the other group. It has also been said—and supported by some evidence (Dollard et al., 1939)—that frustration leads to aggression, that many people are socially and economically frustrated and focus the resulting hostility on other groups. We have here, then, three phenomena related to prejudice: authoritarianism, stereotypy, and frustration. We thus have a partial explanation of prejudice.

Prejudice is a rather difficult concept or construct. Let us take an equally complex phenomenon or variable, but one perhaps more readily illustrated, achievement, and synthesize an explanation of it. In so doing we use an example of a theoretical explanation similar to that given toward the end of Chapter 1. The importance of the ideas justify the additional example. Suppose we wish to know why certain pupils do not do well in school. It is already known that intelligence is one explanatory variable: Children below a certain intelligence level tend not to do well in school.[8] But many

---

[8] Because the nature of our task in this book is to clarify science and scientific research, no attempt is made to discuss the controversial aspects of concepts like intelligence. We assume, when using a variable like intelligence, that it is measured validly. This assumption may of course not be correct.

such children do do well —and many children of higher measured intelligence do not do well. Intelligence alone, then, is only a partial explanation. It is also known that many children of lower social class do not do well in school compared to children of middle-class status. It has also long been thought, though not strongly supported by evidence, that motivation—wanting or not wanting to do well—is an important variable influencing school achievement.

Now, let us set up an "explanation" of school achievement with the three variables just mentioned. Bear in mind that this example is oversimplified. School achievement is a complex phenomenon whose explanation still eludes scientists and educators. We are here giving only a limited and partial explanation for pedagogical purposes. In any case, the "explanation" is depicted in Figure 4.12. The arrows indicate relations or influence. A single-headed unbroken arrow indicates "influence"; a double-headed broken arrow indicates a mutual influence, or simply a relation. ("Influence" usually implies a one-way effect; "relation" implies that the influence may be one way or the other, or both ways.)

The explanation as depicted indicates that intelligence and motivation directly influence school achievement. The more intelligent children tend to do better schoolwork, and the children who are more interested in schoolwork and more desirous of doing schoolwork do better work. Intelligence and social class and intelligence and motivation mutually influence each other. Middle-class children, for example, have on the average higher intelligence test scores, and the more highly motivated children are on the average the children of higher intelligence. Motivation is directly influenced by social class. Working-class children are not as interested in schoolwork as middle-class children, presumably because the less affluent environment is not conducive to enthusiastic acceptance of learning and study. (Besides, the American school *is* a middle-class institution.) Social class exerts no direct effect on school achievement, then. It influences achievement only indirectly through intelligence and motivation.

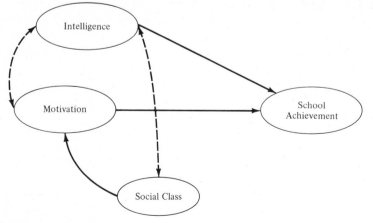

FIG. 4.12

The point of this example is not its adequacy or validity. Rather, the point is to show what a behavioral scientific explanation of a phenomenon is like and how relations are the stuff of such an explanation. The phenomenon of school achievement is "explained" by the relations between, on the one hand, intelligence, motivation, and social class and, on the other hand, school achievement—and also by the relations among intelligence, motivation, and social class.

The whole set of variables and the specified relations among them can be called a "theory." Of course, this would have to be called a "small theory," or an embryo theory, because a highly complex phenomenon like school achievement can hardly be explained by three variables. Nevertheless, most scientific theories consist of just such systematic relations among variables. A *theory*, then, is a set of interrelated constructs (variables), definitions, and propositions that presents a systematic view of phenomena by specifying relations among variables, with the purpose of explaining natural phenomena.

This discussion of "explanation" in science has been necessary to try to take the mystery out of scientific explanation and theory. All explanation, of course, uses relations. The difference between scientific explanations and nonscientific explanations of phenomena, however, is profound. It inheres in the word "systematic," "controlled," and "empirical." The difference should become clearer as we enlarge our discussion.

5

statistics

...obabilistic world. In it there is almost nothing
...ents are relatively certain, of course. It will al-
...York or Amsterdam during the next 30 days.
...rtainly make love in California tomorrow! But
...assured. There are ranges of certainties: some
..., like those just mentioned. Other things are
...ill other things are far from certain. We talk
..., though we often live as though the events of
...ists, however, not only talk probabilistically;
they live probabilistically in their research worlds.

One of the main differences between different branches of science is
degree of certainty of events and relations. The degree of certainty in the
natural sciences, for example, is often very high. A physicist can state a
physical law and can put high dependence in behavior of physical bodies
and events. Indeed, many relations in physics are called "laws" partly
because of the high degree of certainty associated with them. Nevertheless,
there are always margins of error, even though popular literature and
people seem to have complete faith in physical laws and the behavior of
physical objects and events.

The events and relations of the behavioral sciences are much less certain. Chemists can say that if a certain amount of chemical A is added to a   **65**

certain amount of chemical B, an explosion will occur. The statement is probabilistic, even though the probability is very high (in most cases) that it is correct. Psychologists, on the other hand, can say that if children are frustrated they will exhibit aggression, but the probability is not nearly as high that the statement is correct. When political scientists say, "If conservative, then vote Republican," the statement is empirically valid because people with conservative leanings more often than not vote Republican. But the statement has rather low probability for particular cases. *On the average*, political scientists will *probably* be correct. If they try to predict the votes of particular individuals, however, they will often be wrong.

Despite differences in degree of certainty, it is important to understand that all sciences are probabilistic. The thinking of scientists in all fields is fundamentally the same. Scientists differ radically, however, in the *levels* of probability that are customarily associated with the phenomena and relations they work with. It is also important, if we are to understand sciences like psychology and sociology, to be able to think and live comfortably with probabilistic assertions. We must know clearly that every assertion, every statement of relation, has a probabilistic tag on it. Whenever we say "If p, then q," we really mean "If p, then probably q." What is so in life generally is so in science: certainty is a myth; it is forever beyond our reach.

Statistics is a child of probability. It is in part a tool for telling scientists how dependable their research results are—and thus how dependable their assertions are. Clark and Walberg's main result, the average difference between the reading achievement of their experimental and control groups, told them whether the hypothesis about the effect of massive reinforcement on the reading achievement of underachieving black children was "empirically valid." ("Empirically valid" means that research evidence supports an assertion about a relation.) The only way, as far as we know today, that they could have assessed the empirical validity of the statement was by using statistical and probabilistic reasoning and statistical methods of assessment. What does this mean?

When a research result is obtained, we want to know whether it is a result we can depend on. If we do the same experiment again and again and again, will we get pretty much the same results each time we do it? If so, the results are dependable. Is the difference between the average reading scores of Clark and Walberg's experimental and control groups dependable? Can we be reasonably confident that if Clark and Walberg had done the same or a similar experiment three, four, or more times they would have gotten the same or similar results: the same or similar differences between the average reading scores of the experimental and control groups? A statistical test of their results can answer this question. While the scope of this book forbids going into the details of such statistical tests, we need to understand generally how statistics and probability "work," how they use the ideas of chance and randomness to help scientists reach conclusions about research results.

Probability and statistics are interesting, intriguing, and even fascinating subjects. And despite the misconceptions associated with their nature and use, they are close to reality because they resemble the nature and pattern of our lives and reach into the essence of our thinking and behavior. Take our decision making. We constantly make decisions about what to do. Almost invariably we have to weigh the odds and consequences of what we do. And the outcomes, of course, are never certain. We are, then, almost statistical and probabilistic calculators—even though many people would be upset by the idea that their lives and decisions are statistical in nature. After all, statistics works with numbers, and my life is not based on numbers! But our lives *are* based on numbers, explicitly or implicitly. There are always numerical probabilities associated with the outcomes of our acts and decisions, though we can rarely know what they are.

Here is a paradox. Statistics and probability deal essentially with uncertainties; yet in research they help us become more certain of the results we obtain! This does not mean that we can be certain of the results themselves but that we can rather accurately assess the degree of certainty of the results. If I have done an experiment using an experimental group and a control group, for instance, and have obtained a difference between the two groups in the predicted direction, how certain can I be that this difference is large enough to warrant my confidence that it is a "real difference"? Will I be able to say something like: "The probability that the difference between the average scores of the two groups is not fortuitous, or is not due to chance, is high. There is only one chance in a hundred that the difference is a chance result." Though probabilistic, this is a strong statement.

PROBABILITY

Probability and randomness are two of the most powerful notions yet invented to help account for both the order and the confusion of the world. But they are also frustrating notions because we do not quite know what we are talking about when we discuss them. This sounds peculiar. It seems to be true, however, of most seemingly simple ideas that upon careful examination they turn out to be bafflingly complex. Probability and randomness are good examples. They are both hard to define. For our purpose, fortunately, there is no great problem. It is well known how probability and random procedures work—and some of this knowledge will serve our purpose.

Probability: A Definition

Although "probability" was defined in Chapter 2, we now need to expand and elucidate the earlier discussion. The *probability* (p) of an event is the number of "favorable" cases of the event divided by the total number of (equally possible) cases. ("Favorable" means favorable to an event whose probability we are assessing.) This is expressed by the equation:

$$p \text{ (event)} = \frac{\text{number of favorable cases}}{\text{total number of possible cases}}$$

This is a theoretical, or so-called *a priori*, definition.[1] Toss a coin once. The probability of a head is 1/2 because there are two possibilities: {H, T}. Now toss the coin twice. What is the probability of two heads? We must be careful. There are four possibilities. On the first toss, either a head or a tail turns up. On the second toss, either a head or a tail turns up. The total number of possible outcomes is 4: {(H$_1$, H$_2$), (H$_1$, T$_2$), (T$_1$, H$_2$), (T$_1$, T$_2$)}, where H$_1$ = head on first toss, T$_2$ = tail on second toss, and so on. The denominator of the probability fraction is 4. Since there is only one possibility of two heads, (H$_1$, H$_2$), the probability of two heads in two tosses is 1/4.

Let's change and extend the problem a bit. What is the probability of obtaining three heads in three tosses? The possibilities are given in the tree of Figure 5.1. The possibilities in the above problem of two tosses are given in the first two stages of the tree, labeled "First toss" and "Second toss." The probabilities of the outcomes are also labeled: they are all 1/2. The third toss merely adds possibilities. To list all the possible outcomes of three tosses, just find them along the branches of the tree: {(H$_1$, H$_2$, H$_3$), (H$_1$, H$_2$, T$_3$), . . . , (T$_1$, T$_2$, T$_3$)}. There are eight such outcomes, so the denominator of the probability fraction is 8. Therefore, the probability of 3 heads in three tosses is 1/8, since there is only one case of 3 heads: (H$_1$, H$_2$, H$_3$).

The probabilities of other events—any single defined outcome is called an *event*—can be easily determined. The denominator is always 8. What is the probability of 2 heads and 1 tail? It is 3/8, because there are three such events in the tree. (Count them; they are checked in Figure 5.1.) One can also calculate the probability of any single event by multiplying the probabilities along any one of the branches of the tree. For instance, the probability of 3 heads is: $1/2 \cdot 1/2 \cdot 1/2 = 1/8$. The probability of H$_1T_2T_3$ is $1/2 \cdot 1/2 \cdot 1/2 = 1/8$. In this example, the probability along any one branch is the same, because the probability of H or T is always 1/2. In many problems, however, there will be different probabilities, and the calculation is not so simple. In the next example to be studied, the probabilities are not 1/2.

---

[1] Another well-known definition is called the *a posteriori*, or *frequency definition*. It says that, in an actual series of trials, probability is the ratio of the number of times an event occurs to the total number of trials. Here one performs a number of tests, counting the number of times a defined event occurs and then calculating the ratio. The result of the calculation is the probability of the defined event. We use both kinds of definitions, but mostly the *a priori* kind.

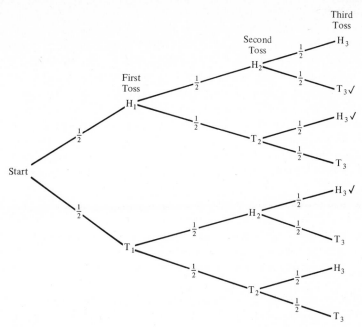

FIG. 5.1

The main problem in probability calculations is to determine the total number of possibilities, after carefully conceptualizing the problem. But why labor this rather trivial example of coin tossing? We do so because the thinking and the method are similar in most probability problems. Of course, other complexities enter real problems. For example, in the coin problem the probabilities of heads and tails are assumed to be equal. In real problems this may not be so. Moreover, there are invariably many more possibilities. Nevertheless, the same ideas pervade most probability problems.

Take a more realistic example. Suppose we have a sample of 100 voters, 60 Democrats and 40 Republicans. If we put the 100 voter names (on slips of paper) into a bowl, mix them thoroughly, and draw one, what is the probability that a Republican will be drawn? It is 40/100 = .40. (It is customary to express probabilities in decimal form.) This is obvious and needs no elaboration. But suppose in a research study we need 30 subjects. How many Democrats and how many Republicans should we get if we draw 30 slips from the bowl? We should get 60/100 × 30 = 18 Democrats and 40/100 × 30 = 12 Republicans. Will we get these numbers exactly? Probably not. But we should get numbers close to them if we thoroughly mix up the slips after each draw. They should be something like: (18, 12), (19, 11), (20, 10), (17, 13), (16, 14), and so on. These are the most likely possibilities. If we drew 10 Democrats and 20 Republicans, or 1 Democrat and 29 Republicans, we would be quite surprised. The first combination is unlikely, the second highly unlikely.

Randomness

We must break the flow of the discussion to introduce a basic idea behind modern statistics and statistical thinking: randomness. Unfortunately, it does not seem possible to define randomness in an unambiguous way. A dictionary definition—haphazard, accidental, without aim or direction—does not help us much. Indeed, scientists are quite systematic about randomness: they carefully select random samples and plan random procedures in experiments.

Suppose an omniscient being has a huge encyclopedic book. Every event and every detail of every event—for the past, for tomorrow, for the next day, and so on and on—are carefully inscribed in the book. There is nothing unknown. Of course, there is no randomness because if one knows everything there can be no randomness. It is possible to take the position that nothing happens at random, that for any event there is a cause. The only reason that one uses the word "random" is that human beings do not know enough. In this view, randomness is ignorance, as it were.

Taking a cue from this argument, we can define randomness in a backhanded way: events are random if we cannot predict their outcomes. For instance, there is no known way to win a penny-tossing game. If there is no system for playing a game that ensures our winning or losing, then the outcomes of the game are random. More formally put, *randomness* means that there is no known law, capable of being expressed in language, that correctly describes or predicts events and their outcomes (Kemeny, 1959, pp. 68–75).

A set of 100 numbers, 0 through 9, is given in Table 5.1 in sets of 10 each. These numbers were taken from a very large set of such random numbers. (Disregard the last line of the table for the time being.) Study the numbers. You will be hard put to find any form of regularity or system in them. There are no successively recurring odd or even numbers; there are

TABLE 5.1   Set of 100 Random Numbers, 0 through 9, and Means Calculated from Subsets of the Numbers

	1	2	3	4	5	6	7	8	9	10
	9	0	8	0	4	6	0	7	7	8
	7	2	7	4	9	4	7	8	7	7
	6	2	8	1	9	3	6	0	3	9
	7	9	9	1	6	4	9	4	7	7
	3	3	1	1	4	1	0	3	9	4
	8	9	2	1	3	9	6	7	7	3
	4	8	3	0	9	2	7	2	3	2
	1	4	3	0	0	2	6	9	7	5
	3	1	8	8	4	5	2	1	0	3
	2	1	4	8	9	2	9	3	0	1
Mean:	5.0	3.9	5.3	2.4	5.7	3.8	5.2	4.4	5.0	4.9. Total mean = 4.56.

no regular sequences of numbers. They are, in effect, unpredictable. (If one searches long enough, perhaps, one can always find something!)

In short, when events are random, we cannot predict them individually. Oddly enough, however, we can predict them quite successfully in the aggregate. That is, we can predict the outcomes of large numbers of events. While we cannot predict whether a tossed coin will be head or tail, we can, if we toss it 1,000 times, predict with considerable accuracy the total numbers of heads and tails. If we draw a sample of 100 from a population of 400 children, 200 boys and 200 girls, we cannot predict whether any single child will be a boy or a girl, but we can quite accurately predict the total numbers of boys and girls in our sample—in this case 50 boys and 50 girls—provided the sampling is random and the sample is large.

An important manifestation of the reliability of the statistical prediction of the behavior of large sets of numbers is given at the bottom of Table 5.1. These numbers are means, or arithmetic averages. Each mean is calculated from 10 individual random numbers. We can always predict with considerable accuracy that the values of these means will be close to the "theoretical value" of the mean of the numbers 0 through 9. This theoretical mean is $(0 + 1 + . . . + 9)/10 = 4.5$. Observe that six of the 10 means are above 4.5 and four are below 4.5. Only one, the fourth, 2.4, departs much from 4.5. The more numbers used to calculate means, the closer the means will probably be to the theoretical mean. If, for example, we calculate the mean of all 100 numbers in Table 5.1, we get 4.56, quite close to 4.5. Such regularly predictable behavior of large sets of numbers is most useful in research. It gives scientists a framework for assessing results in the sense that they can check obtained results against results to be expected "theoretically" or on the basis of chance.

Probability, Randomness, and Behavioral Research

It may seem like a large leap from coin-tossing and random numbers to the use of probability theory in actual research. And it is from one point of view: the "events" of actual research are much more complex. But the basic notions are the same, or at least quite similar. We will try to show this with a hypothetical example inspired by a well-known psychological experiment.[2] We will then reinforce the ideas by returning to the idea of randomness.

Suppose I do an experiment with three groups of young people. I want to know, if I can, whether increasing the difficulty of getting into a group enhances the attractiveness and value of the group. The hypothesis is that difficulty of initiation into a group enhances the value of the group in the

[2] The idea for this hypothetical experiment has been taken from a real experiment by Aronson and Mills (1959) in which the above hypothesis was tested. I follow Aronson and Mills' design closely, but fabricate results for the present probability purposes.

eyes of group members. Suppose certain suburbanites want to belong to a country club. The thinking behind the experiment is that the more difficult it is to get into the club—high initiation fee, high annual dues, a long wait between being put up for membership and being considered, the "right" skin color, the "right" religion, the "right" set of social beliefs, for example—the more the members will value the club and their membership in it.

To test the hypothesis, I decided to have three groups of individuals undergo three different degrees of difficulty to belong to a group. Let's assume that this was done under carefully controlled conditions; the members of one group, A_1, underwent a severe hardship to enter the group, those of another group, A_2, a mild hardship, and those of the third group, A_3, no hardship. At the end of the experiment I had all the experimental subjects respond to an instrument that measured the perceived desirability of belonging to the group. Suppose the averages of the three groups on this measure were $A_1 = 5.2$, $A_2 = 4.7$, $A_3 = 3.5$. (The scores reflect a scale with 7 points, 1 meaning very low perceived desirability of group membership, and 7 meaning very high perceived desirability.)

These averages support the hypothesis. Or do they? A_1, the severe-condition group, has the highest average; A_2, the mild-condition group, has the next highest average; and A_3, the no-hardship group, the lowest average. But suppose somebody objects and tells me that this result is a chance one, one that could easily have happened if the members of the group had picked scores out of a hat, or—in effect the same thing—had responded to the desirability instrument simply by writing any answers to the questions. How can I know that these three averages are not one of the many results that can easily happen by chance? How can I "test" the three means for their presumed departure from such chance expectations?

To allay the reader's curiosity momentarily but perhaps not satisfactorily, a statistical technique known as the analysis of variance can be used to test quite precisely the results and their departure from chance expectation. Suppose, however, that I know nothing about analysis of variance. Can I still test the hypothesis? Yes, but not as well. Let's now invent a test. While not the best test, perhaps it is better than no test and has the virtue of showing in a simple way how probability theory works and is applied.

The hypothesis stated above implies a rank order of the three experimental group averages. It predicts, in effect, that the members of A_1, the severe-hardship group, will find the group most desirable; that the members of A_2, the mild-hardship group, will find the group desirable but will not value it as highly as A_1; and that the members of A_3, the no-hardship group, will value the group least. So a group rank order is predicted by hypothesis: A_1 scores will be on the average greater than A_2 scores, and A_2 scores will be greater than A_3 scores. If we accept the averages of the groups as indicative of the groups' assessment of group membership and let A_1, A_2, and A_3 stand for the averages, then the hypothesis can be written symbolically: $A_1 > A_2 > A_3$, where ">" means "greater than." This rank order is, then: 1   2   3. Since the three obtained averages are $A_1 = 5.2$, $A_2 = 4.7$, and $A_3 = 3.5$, the hypothesis seems supported, as indicated earlier. But maybe this is a result that could have happened by chance.

Apply probability theory. What are the possibilities? We want to test the hypothesis with a fraction, the denominator of which will have a number that expresses all the possibilities. How many possible rank orders of three averages can occur? List them:

1	2	3
1	3	2
2	1	3
2	3	1
3	1	2
3	2	1

There are six possible rank orders. So the denominator of the probability fraction is 6. The obtained, 1   2   3, is one of these. What is the probability that it could have occurred by chance? What is the probability, to look at it another way, that this particular rank order, which reflects the hypothesized rank order, can occur simply as one of the deals of a card game where people are dealt cards with 1, 2, and 3 on them?

After all, we have no way of knowing for sure that the rank order of the three averages really reflects the influence of the varying degrees of hardship the experimental subjects underwent. All we can do, if the rank order of the averages comes out as we say it will, is to infer that the hypothesis is correct. And the way to do this is to assess the obtained experimental results by comparing them to results that could have happened by chance—by dealing cards from a well-shuffled deck, for example.

The result from our hypothetical experiment, 1   2   3, agrees with the hypothesis. By chance this result can occur one time in six, since it is one of the six possible rank orders. Therefore, the probability of the rank order of the averages, 1   2   3, is $1/6 = .17$. One interpretation of this result is that if I did the same experiment 100 times *and the experimental manipulation had no effect*—that is, the hardship conditions had no influence on the perceived desirability of membership in the groups—the rank order 1   2   3 would occur about 17 times. On this basis, can we say that the experimental manipulation has had an effect and that the hypothesis is supported? Hardly. After all, one would not be very assured when the chances are 1 in 6, or 17 in 100, of getting such a result by chance alone. Still, it *is* a statistical test and tells me something about my results.

This test is not a very good one, then. If I had had four groups and predicted the rank order of averages as 1   2   3   4, and this is what happened in the experiment, then I would have considerably greater confidence in the empirical validity of the hypothesis. This is because with four averages there would be 24 possible rank orders of the averages: 1 2 3 4;   1 2 4 3;   1 3 2 4;   1 3 4 2; and so on through 4 3 2 1. Thus, the probability of obtaining 1 2 3 4 is

$1/24 = .04$, which means that there are about 4 chances in 100 of obtaining 1 2 3 4 by chance alone—and these are good odds. If I say that my hypothesis is 1 2 3 4, and this is what I get, I can be fairly certain that my result is not a chance one and that the hardship condition has indeed influenced perception of the desirability of group membership. (It is suggested that the reader lay out all the possible rank orders to see the validity of this reasoning.)

This is still not a very good test, however. It has been used here to illustrate with a realistic example the probability reasoning involved. Nevertheless, more powerful statistical tests are based on similar reasoning. As we proceed, we will try to bring out the reasoning behind such tests, even though we will not describe how to do the tests.

A Probabilistic Misconception and Independence

There is an utterly erroneous and misleading common-sense notion of the probabilities of events. It is usually contained in the expression "the law of averages," which says something to the effect that if there is a large number of occurrences of an event, then the probability of that event on the next trial is smaller. Suppose a coin has been tossed five times and five heads have turned up. The common-sense notion of the "law of averages" would lead one to believe that there is a greater chance of getting tails on the next toss—or, conversely, a smaller chance of getting heads. Not so. The probability of heads on the next toss is the same as it was on all the previous tosses: 1/2. The probabilities do not change, no matter what the earlier outcomes were. Each event is said to be independent.

What bearing does this misconception have on understanding research, the way researchers operate, and on statistical results and their interpretation? In order to apply probability theory ideas to research data, it must often be assumed that observations and the data resulting from observations are independent. *Independence* means that the occurrence of one event, A, in no way affects the occurrence of another event, B. This means that the probability of B is not affected by A. "Event" should be interpreted broadly. It can mean any kind of defined occurrence: the toss of a coin, the occurrence of heads, a rat's choice of a path in a maze, a child's verbal or written response to a test item, an experimenter's manipulation of a variable.

Independence is not easy to demonstrate, partly because lack of independence can be quite subtle. Take the common example of a researcher in an experiment manipulating two variables at the same time to study their separate and possibly joint effects on a dependent variable. Suppose an educational researcher has reason to believe that different methods of teaching reading work differently with different kinds of reading materials. The two variables must be so handled or manipulated that the actual handling of one does not influence the other because of the handling or manipulation or because of the nature of the variables. Suppose that the researcher used two methods, of teaching reading, A_1 and A_2, and two kinds of reading materials, B_1 and B_2, corresponding to difficult materials and easy materials. Suppose, too, that method A_1 takes considerably longer to use than method A_2, and that length of time spent in teaching reduces the difficulty of any reading materials. Then there would be lack of independence because method A_1 contains within itself, so to speak, an extraneous factor related to difficulty of materials (variable B). In other words, method A_1 will tend to work better with more difficult reading materials, not because of the nature of the method but simply because it takes more teaching time than method A_2. There is then lack of independence between variables A and B, since an extraneous aspect of variable A, amount of teaching time, is related to variable B, difficulty of material.

Another example of lack of independence is in measurement. If, say, we give a 10-item test to a number of children and then add each child's scores on the 10 items to get a total score on the test—a common procedure—we are assuming that the 10 items are independent and the responses to them independent. This assumption is reasonably well satisfied with many tests and measures, and the procedure is useful and valid. But suppose we asked the children to rank order the 10 items according to their importance (or some other criterion). The items and the responses to them are no longer independent, because before the first item is chosen to be ranked 1, the most important, there are 10 choices. After the first choice is made, there are then nine items left to be chosen. After the first nine items are ranked, there is only one left—and no choice. The responses to later items, in other words, are affected by the responses to earlier choices. This is systematic lack of independence. Such lack of independence affects statistics and the interpretation of statistics. This does not mean that rank order and similar methods cannot be handled probabilistically and statistically. Indeed, we showed a little earlier how a simple rank order problem could be solved using probability theory. It simply illustrates lack of independence. In sum, many statistical techniques assume independence, and their use and interpretation with nonindependent phenomena or procedures can be misleading.

This excursion into independence was undertaken to try to clarify the probabilistic misconception outlined earlier. The outcomes of earlier chance events do not affect the outcomes of subsequent events—or perhaps we ought to say that they should not affect the outcomes of subsequent events. If the probability of getting heads on the first toss of a coin is 1/2, then it is 1/2 on the tenth, twentieth, or fiftieth toss, no matter what the earlier outcomes were. This is so unless, of course, something was done to change the coin or the tossing, or there was some extrinsic influence at work, as in the methods experiment.

Randomness and Research

We should now be in a better position to study randomness and its connection to actual research. Why is the idea of randomness important in research? How is it used? How is it helpful to researchers? Part of the answer was given earlier, but we need to go further. The results of experiments, for example, have to be assessed. Researchers have to ask: Do the results support the hypothesis? Suppose I obtain means, in an experiment with two groups of subjects, of 52.40 and 42.25 and they are in the hypothesized direction. I must also have some way of assessing how "large" the difference between them is. After all, this difference might be one of the many differences that could have occurred by chance. One hardly wants to base scientific conclusions on chance or random results!

Conceive of what would probably happen under purely chance conditions. This means that there is no certainty at all; there are no systematic influences at work, or if there are systematic influences, they are all so mixed up that they cancel each other out, so to speak. All is a hodgepodge. If there had been no systematic influence at work in the Clark and Walberg experiment, then the reading score averages in repetitions (replications) of the experiment would have fluctuated in unpredictable ways. Such averages might look like those in Table 5.2, which displays experimental and control group averages from five hypothetical replications of the experiment, together with the actual averages obtained by Clark and Walberg (last line of the table). The averages in the first five data lines of the table were made up to resemble averages calculated from random numbers whose magnitudes were like the magnitudes of the Clark and Walberg averages.

In experiments 1, 2, and 5, the averages of the experimental groups are higher than those of the control group, but in experiments 3 and 4 they are lower. Moreover, the averages do not differ much from each other. The lack of systematic results and the smallness of the differences between the averages are shown in the column labeled "Difference." Such results are characteristic of results obtained on a chance, or random, basis. Contrast them with the actual Clark and Walberg averages and the difference between them (+4.76). Statistics, then, helps us to determine or assess whether obtained results "really" differ from "results" that would be obtained under chance or random conditions.

TABLE 5.2   Reading Score Averages of Five Hypothetical
             Replications of Clark and Walberg Experiment
             under Chance Conditions—and Actual
             Obtained Averages

EXPERIMENT	EXPERIMENTAL GROUP	CONTROL GROUP	DIFFERENCE
1	27.42	26.50	+ .92
2	28.10	26.95	+2.15
3	26.18	27.05	− .87
4	27.41	28.56	−1.15
5	28.64	27.90	+ .74
Clark and Walberg	31.62	26.86	+4.76

TABLE 5.3   Twenty Pairs of Random Means and the
Differences between Means

M_1	M_2	DIFFER-ENCE	M_1	M_2	DIFFER-ENCE[a]
51.84	50.06	1.78	48.87	48.52	.35
46.20	53.95	− 7.75	53.08	52.94	.14
47.69	53.61	− 5.92	56.51	46.79	9.72
51.83	49.31	2.52	47.99	48.33	− .34
53.21	49.16	4.05	49.37	47.29	2.08
48.87	50.22	− 1.35	49.02	55.51	−6.49
49.64	58.36	− 8.72	45.68	52.39	−6.71
51.37	49.57	1.80	47.04	49.95	−2.91
45.07	55.44	−10.37	53.51	46.00	7.51
49.28	49.43	− .15	52.74	47.65	5.09

[a] The last three columns are simply a continuation of the first three columns.

A Little Study of Random Differences

Let's explore randomness a bit more, continuing the idea of random group differences. We are still talking about a random base for assessing the results of data obtained in research. A set of 20 pairs of means and the differences between the means is given in Table 5.3. These means were obtained by a random process. A computer was made to generate 4,000 random numbers 0 through 100. Then the means of 40 sets of 100 numbers each were calculated. These means were paired by putting the first mean with the twenty-first mean, the second mean with the twenty-second mean, and so on.[3] The differences, under the column labeled "Difference," were calculated by subtracting in each pair the second mean from the first mean.

Concentrate on the 20 differences. They range from −10.37 to 9.72. There are nine positive differences and 11 negative differences. This is close to chance expectation, since with random numbers we expect approximately equal numbers of plus and minus differences. (We ignore plus and minus signs henceforth to simplify the discussion.)

Suppose that we had done an experiment with two groups and actually obtained means of 52.40 and 42.25. The difference between these means is $52.40 − 42.25 = 10.15$. Using the differences between means of Table 5.3 as a random base, we want to assess what is called the "statistical significance" of the difference of 10.15. A "statistically significant" result is one that departs "sufficiently" from chance expectation or a random base. Does the obtained 10.15 so differ from chance? Is it a statistically significant result?

Return to the differences of Table 5.3. The two largest differences are 10.37 and 9.72. This means that 10 percent $(2/20 = .10)$ of the 20 differences

[3] The full set of 4,000 numbers and the 40 means are given in Kerlinger (1973, pp. 714–718).

are greater than 9. If we are willing to accept about a 10 percent risk of being wrong, we can say that the difference obtained in the experiment, 52.40 − 42.25, or 10.15, exceeds the chance expectation. (If we had taken account of the signs of the differences, the risk would be lower. Why?)

Suppose, however, we are not satisfied with a 10 percent risk. We want to be more sure that our experimental difference of 10.15 is a "real" departure from chance expectation. We want, in other words, to decrease the probability of making a mistake and accepting what is really a chance difference as a "real" difference. So we say that the probability must be .05, or 5 percent, rather than .10, or 10 percent. Five percent of 20 is 1: $20 \times .05 = 1$. In this case we take only one difference, the highest one, 10.37. According to the differences given in Table 5.3, there is one chance in 20, or 5 percent—the probability is .05—of obtaining a mean of 10.37 or greater *by chance*. Our obtained difference is 10.15. Since there is only one difference in the table this large, we can say that the obtained experimental result, the difference between the experimental and control group means, is probably not a chance result. There is, in other words, only about 1 chance in 20, or a probability of $1/20 = .05$, that our difference is a chance difference. We then conclude that the experimental group mean is statistically greater than the control group mean. We say that the difference between the means is "statistically significant."

The reader should know that this procedure—called a Monte Carlo procedure—is not the way researchers ordinarily assess the statistical significance of their results. The demonstration was done only to show the nature of the thinking, to manufacture, so to speak, a random base against which to assess a particular experimental result. But the idea behind the more sophisticated methods actually used is highly similar. Another shortcoming of our demonstration was that only 20 pairs of means were used. A better Monte Carlo procedure would be to use 2,000 or 20,000 means and to have the computer pair the means at random. Nevertheless, the essence of the idea was present: an experimental result was assessed against a random base.

POPULATIONS, SAMPLES, STATISTICS

Until now the discussion has been mostly focused on the use of probability and statistics to assess the reliability of research results. Intelligent reading and understanding of behavioral research literature, however, require learning related but different applications of statistical ideas. We consider, therefore, definition and explanation of certain important concepts used in most contemporary behavioral research, starting with "statistics" itself.

Statistics is the theory and method of analyzing quantitative data obtained from samples of observations in order to summarize data and to accept or reject hypothesized relations among variables. This definition suggests two purposes of statistics: to reduce large quantities of data to manageable form and to aid in making reliable inferences from quantitative data. The first purpose is illustrated with the following example. A mean, say, is calculated from 100 scores. With the help of an appropriate measure of variability—a measure that expresses the scatter, or the range, of the scores—this mean expresses the central tendency of the 100 scores. It "describes" one aspect of the scores, in other words. The first purpose, then, is description. We have little interest in it in this book. The second purpose is comparative and inferential. The mean can be compared to the means of other groups. Means of different groups, then, can be compared in order to test hypotheses and infer if the hypotheses are or are not supported. Other statistics can, of course, be similarly compared.

A *statistic* is a measure calculated from a sample, as indicated earlier. A statistic is a summary measure: it summarizes, or expresses in summary form, some aspect of a sample. The mean expresses the central tendency of the scores, their general level. This property has great usefulness, especially in experimental research where the central tendencies of groups of scores are often compared. Recall comparing the means of the massive reinforcement and regular reinforcement groups in the Clark and Walberg study. The so-called standard deviation, another statistic, expresses the variability of a set of scores; it is a summary expression of how heterogeneous the set of scores is. Using it one can, among other things, assess the homogeneity or heterogeneity of different sets of scores.

A *population* is a set of all the objects or elements under consideration. All eight-year-old children in Geneva, Switzerland, are a population. All the men in an army are a population. A *sample* is a portion of a population usually taken as representative of the population. To study and test a hypothesis of Piaget about an aspect of the thinking of eight-year-old children, we might somehow draw a sample of 100 such children from the population of eight-year-old children in Geneva. A measure calculated from the scores of all the members of a population is called a *population value*. If we calculate a mean from all the intelligence test scores of all the eight-year old children of Geneva, the mean is a population value. If, however, we calculate a mean from the sample of 100 children drawn from the population, the mean is a statistic. There are many statistics, some few of which we will study.

The ideas of population values and statistics and of population and sample seem to confuse people, partly, I suspect, because the difference between them is often arbitrary, a matter of definition. This is particularly true in behavioral research because populations are often inaccessible—even the United States census cannot cover all Americans—and because samples can be treated as populations for the purposes of research. A simple example is sex. Males and females are samples of all human beings. The population is all human beings in San Francisco, say. San Francisco males and San Francisco females are samples of this population. But a researcher may for good reason—his problem may involve only women—

study the characteristics and behavior of females. San Francisco females, then, become the population. Now, suppose the researcher administers a psychological instrument designed to measure attitudes toward women to all the women living in San Francisco. He calculates the mean and standard deviation from the attitude scores of all these women. The mean and standard deviation are population values.

It is highly unlikely, however, that even the most zealous researcher can or will study all the women of any city. It is much more likely that he will study a sample of women selected from the population. Suppose in this case that the sample consists of 700 San Francisco women. If the researcher administers the attitude scale to the 700 women and calculates a mean and a standard deviation, these will be statistics, since they were calculated from samples.

The second purpose of statistics, to aid in making reliable inferences from observational data, centers in the words "inference" and "reliable." An *inference* is a proposition or generalization derived by reasoning from other propositions, or from evidence. In statistics, inferences can be drawn from tests of what are called statistical hypotheses. From the difference between the experimental and control group means of the Clark and Walberg study, the appropriate use of a statistical test, and reasoning, we "conclude" that the experimental group mean is greater than the control group mean. That is, we have two statistics, two means, calculated from the experimental group and the control group scores. We subtract one mean from the other, in this case the control group mean from the experimental group mean. If this difference is "sufficiently large," which means larger than some values that is conceived to be a chance expectation, we conclude that the experimental group obtained higher reading scores on the average.

Such inferential use of statistics is the core of statistics in contemporary behavioral research. The word "reliable" in the above-stated purpose of statistics refers to the stability of obtained results and thus the stability of the inferences made from the results. If we obtain a certain difference between the means of two groups, will the same or similar difference appear again and again if the experiment is repeated again and again? If we have a certain set of frequencies in a crossbreak or cross tabulation, as in the Miller and Swanson example of Chapter 1, will we get similar patterns of frequencies—and similar departures from chance expectations—if the study is repeated? Statistics helps us answer such questions, thus providing us with a potent means of assessing the stability and empirical validity of our inferences from data.

MISCONCEPTION OF STATISTICS

Misconception of statistics is common. Many people also find the subject distasteful. Educated people will be heard to say, "I simply can't understand statistics"; "I can handle words well enough, but when it comes to statistics . . ." Expressions like these often show a deep-seated alienation from numbers and quantitative concepts. It is probably true that some individuals cannot handle mathematical and statistical concepts easily. But most educated people can and should be able to handle statistical ideas and operations—given motivation and effort. They can learn to be interested, even excited, by the power and beauty of the analytic methods used in the behavioral sciences. Certainly the day has come when teachers and educated laymen can no longer afford to ignore or escape the necessity for understanding the basic ideas behind probability, statistics, and modern methods of analysis.

Statistical study without understanding basic ideas is a dispensable trial to the spirit—a bore and chore. Twenty to 30 years ago, there was good reason to avoid statistical study. The emphasis in teaching statistics and in statistics books was on calculations, derivations, or both. Today, however, the picture has changed. Statistics books and much instruction emphasize the ideas and reasoning behind statistical thinking and calculation. This has not made the subject easier. I won't try to gull the reader by saying statistics is easy. But it is not nearly as hard as many people think it is. It can be learned and learned well enough for practical use. More important, if properly learned with a constant emphasis on basic ideas, it can be an exciting preoccupation.

Unfortunately, there is a more serious misconception of statistics, which, if held strongly enough, is completely debilitating. Good teachers, can bring most fearful people around to a point of functional competence. They can do little or nothing, however, with the present misconception, which is difficult to describe, perhaps because it has several facets and also something of a religious fervor. Its core seems to be that statistics has little or no relation and relevance to "reality." It is said that researchers perform complex and abstruse operations with numbers derived in mysterious ways from what people say and do, and then come out with conclusions that are distortions of "reality." For example, a researcher administers tests of intelligence and achievement to children, calculates averages of the tests, compares them to national averages, and finds the obtained averages to be higher or lower as the case may be. But these averages, it is said, have little correspondence to reality, the complexity and individuality of actual children. They are abstractions that mean nothing as far as any individual child is concerned. Thus the whole procedure is irrelevant to the intelligence and achievement of real children. Similar arguments apply to the whole range of statistical operations.

It is clear that this misconception is based on imperfect notions of the purposes and uses of statistics. All statistics *are* abstractions. Any particular statistic may not correspond to the scores of any single individual. But it is not supposed to! Its purposes are quite different. Holders of the misconception seem to want statistics to mirror "real reality," to do something magical, in short. Like all human technical devices, they can do only what they are designed to do, and this is always limited to special aspects of a total "reality." A statistical average is only a statistical average, nothing more. It is not meant to be "like" any individual. But it can have considerable, even great, explanatory power when properly used and interpreted.

The purpose of statistics, then, is not to mirror any so-called reality or to reflect the idiosyncrasies of individuals. Rather, its main purpose is to help researchers get at the meaning of sets of data. It is thus an indispensable aid in the interpretation of data. One can say that statistics disciplines data by so operating on the data that reliable inferences from empirical observations can be made. Indeed, one would be hard put to conceive of modern behavioral research without it. Naturally, there are dangers in its use. One can have inadequate data and lull oneself into a feeling of spurious adequacy by plunging into statistical operations and calculations. One can generalize beyond one's data and use statistics to make oneself and others believe that such generalization is appropriate and correct when, in fact, it is inappropriate and incorrect. Despite the dangers and difficulties, statistics, the probability theory behind it, and the fundamental and fruitful notion of randomness are powerful and useful tools whose great value it is our task to appreciate.

6

The design
of experimental
research
one-variable designs

The plan and structure of research are often called the design of research. The word "design," as used here, focuses on the manner in which a research problem is conceptualized and put into a structure that is a guide for experimentation and for data collection and analysis. We define *research design,* then, as the plan and structure of investigation conceived so as to obtain answers to research questions.

EXPERIMENTAL RESEARCH

Modern conceptions of the design of research are founded in experimental research, which was described earlier, though not in depth. The essential characteristics of experiments were not systematically defined, nor were different designs of experiments discussed. In this chapter and the next, therefore, we focus on the major characteristics of experimental research and the principal kinds of designs used in experiments.

An *experiment* is a research study in which one or more independent variables are manipulated and subjects are assigned at random to experimental groups. Some experts may quarrel with this definition, saying, among other things, that random assignment is not an absolutely necessary condition in an experiment. They are right, in one sense. One *can* do an experiment without assigning subjects to experimental groups at random. But it will be a much weaker experiment than one with random assignment. In any case, we keep the definition as it is because in a strict sense random assignment *is* a necessary aspect of experiments. (The meaning of "random assignment" will be discussed later.)

Suppose research is to be done to test the notion that early deprivation affects later mental development. Assume that there are two experimental conditions and 40 rats. The rats are assigned at random to the two groups. One way of doing this is to toss a coin as each rat is considered. If head turns up, assign the rat to the first group; if tail turns up, assign the rat to the second group. To one of the two groups so formed one experimental treatment, say "deprivation," is assigned, also at random. The other group will experience "no deprivation." The definition of an experiment is satisfied. There will be an experimental manipulation, and the subjects are assigned to the experimental groups at random.

In principle it makes no difference how and where the experiment is done. Many people think that all or most experiments are done in laboratories. Many *are,* but many are not. It is even possible, though difficult, to do an experiment over a large geographical area. Many behavioral research experiments are so-called field experiments. This simply means done outside the laboratory "in the field." While there are important differences between laboratory experiments and field experiments, their essential conception is the same.

ONE-WAY DESIGNS

The Aronson and Mills experiment described in Chapter 5 is a "one-way" design. This means that there is only one independent variable. Subjects were assigned at random to three experimental groups, A_1, A_2, and A_3. The subjects assigned to experimental group A_1 were given a severe initiation in order to join a hypothetical group, the subjects assigned to A_2 a mild initiation, and the subjects assigned to A_3 no initiation. The manipulated variable, then, was initiation, or severity of initiation. (Recall that "manipulation" means to do different things to different groups.[1])

The design of the experiment would look like the "design" given in Table 6.1 A design of this kind simply shows the conditions or manipulations of the independent variable or variables. It is borrowed from a scheme of data analysis. That is, it is convenient to enter the data of an

---

[1] A common misconception about psychological experimentation is that people are manipulated—a highly distorted and mischievous idea that has caused and is still causing difficulties for psychological researchers. While it is possible that people can be manipulated in experiments, this has nothing to do with the nature of experiments in which *variables* are manipulated. Manipulation in experiments simply and always means doing different things to different groups; the manipulation reflects one or more independent variables.

TABLE 6.1   Design of Aronson and Mills (1959) Experiment

SEVERITY OF INITIATION		
A_1	A_2	A_3
Severe	Mild	None
Scores on dependent variable (perceptions of group's value)		

experiment in a table like that of Table 6.1. In this case there would be 20 scores in each of the experimental conditions, the three implied columns of the table. Such a scheme clearly shows the general design of the research and also suggests the data analysis. (For convenience and clarity the dependent variables scores have been suggested in the table.)

The design of the Clark and Walberg experiment is given in Table 6.2. It is a little simpler than the Aronson and Mills design because there are only two experimental conditions, massive reinforcement and regular reinforcement. The two designs have the same conceptual base, however.

The designs of Tables 6.1 and 6.2 can be called one-way designs since there is only one independent variable. (Actually, the name is borrowed from a statistical method associated with such designs: one-way analysis of variance.) They are not limited to two or three experimental conditions: there may in fact be any number of experimental conditions. This is expressed in Table 6.3, where k independent variables are suggested. There would be k groups of subjects and thus k columns of dependent variable scores in the table. Statistical analysis of the data would test hypothesized (and other) differences among the k groups.

If a psychologist were to do the experiment implied in Table 6.1, he would choose suitable subjects and assign them to the three experimental groups at random. One effective though laborious way to do this is to use a table of random numbers. Suppose there is a total of 60 subjects. Assign a number from 1 through 60 to each of the 60 subjects (in any arbitrary way). The psychologist then enters a table of random numbers at any page and at any point—raising a pencil in the air and dropping the arm so that the pencil points to one of the random numbers will do—and reads off and copies down the 60 numbers without repetitions. The first 20 numbers form one group, the second 20 another group, and the third 20 still another group. The numbers are then assigned to the subjects in any convenient way (see below). We have, then, three experimental groups consisting of

TABLE 6.2   Design of Clark and Walberg (1968) Experiment

TYPES OF REINFORCEMENT	
A_1	A_2
Massive	Regular
Scores on dependent variable (reading achievement)	

TABLE 6.3   Generalized One-Way Experimental Design

EXPERIMENTAL CONDITIONS			
A_1	A_2	A_3 . . . . A_k	
Scores on dependent variable			

subjects who have been assigned to the groups at random. The highly important reasons for doing things this way will be discussed shortly.

The psychologist now assigns the three experimental treatments at random to the three groups of subjects. This is an added precaution in the procedure. It avoids possible bias of the experimenter in assigning experimental treatments to groups. The whole procedure is called "randomization." After this the researcher does the experiment. In this case he "manipulates" the independent variable, severity of initiation, by having the members of A_1 undergo severe initiation and the members of A_2 mild initiation. The members of A_3 are a control group whose members do not experience any form of severity of initiation; they engage in some different activity unrelated to initiation. They may be asked to read passages of poetry, for example. (Why bother to have them do anything?)

After the experimental manipulation, the psychologist in some way measures the dependent variable, the perceptions of all the group members of the desirability of belonging to the group. Finally, he analyzes the data, the measures of the dependent variable, and draws appropriate conclusions from the data. We examined how this is done in Chapter 5: he determines whether the averages of the three groups are as predicted by the hypothesis.

THE DESIGN OF AN EXPERIMENT AND RANDOMIZATION

We need to go deeper into the potent ideas of design and random assignment. The above description of an experiment was only an outline of the whole procedure. In what follows, we focus on random assignment and the principal reason for using it. In Chapter 5, random differences between groups were discussed and illustrated. In that discussion we tried to bring out the nature of random differences contrasted to experimentally obtained differences. We now use the same ideas but specifically to highlight the relation between the design of experiments and random assignment of subjects to experimental groups.

All experiments have one fundamental idea behind them: to test the effect of one or more independent variables on a dependent variable.[2]

---

[2] It is possible to have more than one dependent variable in experiments. In this book, however, we consider mainly research with one dependent variable. Nevertheless, in a later chapter we will discuss multivariate research and analysis because of its increasing importance in the behavioral disciplines.

Experimenters test the implications of if p, then q statements. Take, again, the simplest possible case. Suppose an educational researcher wants to test the relative efficacy of two methods of teaching certain arithmetic operations. The independent variable is methods of teaching and the dependent variable arithmetic achievement. The experimenter has, say, a good test of arithmetic achievement, the measure of the dependent variable. He carefully specifies what he will do with the two methods of teaching—call the two methods A_1 and A_2. That is, he operationally defines Y, the measure of arithmetic achievement and the experimental conditions, A_1 and A_2. None of this is new to us.

Now, however, he must somehow set up two groups of pupils, and he must do it in such a way that he can assume that before the experiment starts the groups are statistically "equal" in all possible variables that can affect the dependent variable, arithmetic achievement. If he cannot assume that his groups are equal *before* he starts the experiment, then the conclusions he reaches after the experiment are questionable. If the groups are not equal, then the final results may be due to some influence or influences other than the manipulation of the independent variable. Suppose that intelligence affects arithmetic achievement—and it, of course, does—and one of the two groups, unbeknownst to the researcher, has children who are on the average more intelligent than the children of the other group. Then, after the experiment is done, suppose the arithmetic achievement mean of the first group is greater than the mean of the second group. This higher mean may be due to the superior intelligence of the group and not due to the experimental manipulation. Such extraneous unwanted effects must be controlled if researchers are to have confidence in their results.

Suppose, further, that intelligence and sex affect arithmetic achievement. One way that was used to "equalize" experimental groups, to control unwanted effects, was to "equalize" the groups by systematically assigning subjects to them so that the unwanted variables were equally distributed between the groups. In this particular case of intelligence and sex, for example, the researcher can measure the children's intelligence with an intelligence test and assign children of comparable intelligence to the two groups equally. If he has a total of six children (far too few, of course) and their IQ's are 121, 119, 106, 109, 94, and 95, he can assign the children with IQ's of 121, 106, and 94 to A_1 and those with IQ's of 119, 109, and 95 to A_2. This will make the groups approximately equal in intelligence (as measured). Then he can assign boys and girls equally to the two groups. If he has four boys and two girls, he can assign two boys and one girl to each group. Naturally he may have to change his earlier intelligence assignment, since it is quite possible that the higher intelligence scores were those of girls (or boys), making impossible balanced assignment to the two groups on the basis of *both* variables.

This method of assignment of subjects to groups is rightfully dying out because of a severe limitation: it controls only the two variables intelligence and sex. How about other variables that can conceivably affect arithmetic achievement: numerical aptitutde, social class, attitude, and so on? Such other variables remain uncontrolled. What can one do?

Random Assignment and Randomization

The method of assigning subjects to experimental groups that (theoretically, at least) avoids the difficulties just discussed is random assignment. If there are only two groups, one can toss a coin for the assignment of each subject: If heads, then assign to A_1; if tails, assign to A_2. This should work well enough if the coin-tossing is done properly. But the method of using random numbers discussed earlier works with two, three, or any number of groups. Tables of random numbers are widely available and, in fact, have become indispensable to many research operations.[3] Random numbers have the essential characteristic of being unpredictable: if they are random, there is no known way to predict their sequence, their oddness or evenness, their magnitude, and so on. Thus they are used by scientists for a number of purposes, which, as discussed in Chpater 5, almost all boil down to providing a chance or random basis against which to compare obtained results or any sort of observed phenomena.

The basic principle behind statistical tests, as said earlier, is: *Compare obtained results to those expected by chance.* The use of random numbers to assign subjects to experimental groups at random is based on the same general principle, except that the random numbers are used to assign subjects to groups. Another example should make this clear.

Suppose I want to do an experiment in which I test three methods of teaching, A_1, A_2, and A_3. A_1 might be a recitation method, A_2 a discussion method, and A_3 a combined recitation and discussion method. I have 30 children and know their intelligence test scores and their sex. I believe that intelligence and sex may, in and of themselves, affect the outcome—the outcome, or dependent variable, say, is some form of problem solving. So I want to be assured that the possible influences of these two variables, and other possible influential variables, are controlled. In Table 6.4, the 30 scores and indications of sex, male (M) and female (F), are given. The intelligence scores are given in rank order, from high to low. The numbers 1 through 30 have been assigned to the children and are also given in the table (left column).

I want to be able to assume that the three groups are statistically equal in all possible independent variables that may affect problem solving. So I assign the children to the three groups at random using a table of random numbers. This is like considering the 30 children as a population and drawing three samples of 10 each at random from the population. *Random sampling* is that method of drawing a portion, or sample, of a population so that all possible samples of size n have the same probability of being

---

[3] Tables of random numbers are available in several texts. For example, see Snedecor and Cochran (1967, pp. 543–546).

TABLE 6.4   Intelligence Test Scores (Ranked) and Sex of 30
Children, with Random Numbers Assigned
to All Children

NUM-BER	INTELLI-GENCE SCORE	SEX	RANDOM NUMBER	NUM-BER	INTELLI-GENCE SCORE	SEX	RANDOM NUMBER
1	147	F	26	16	108	F	3
2	141	F	13	17	104	M	22
3	137	M	29	18	104	M	23
4	136	F	11	19	103	M	21
5	132	M	19	20	102	M	19
6	128	M	14	21	101	F	5
7	128	M	10	22	101	M	17
8	126	F	27	23	99	F	24
9	125	F	4	24	95	F	8
10	122	M	6	25	94	M	12
11	118	M	30	26	92	F	18
12	115	F	7	27	90	F	16
13	115	M	2	28	90	M	20
14	110	F	28	29	89	M	25
15	109	F	15	30	87	F	1

selected. There are very many possible samples of size 10 that can be drawn from the population of 30 (some 30 million!), and they all have an equal probability of being selected—if the sampling is random. In random assignment, we use the same idea and, in effect, draw three samples of 10 each. The first 10 are assigned to one group, the second 10 to another group, and the third 10 to still another group.

I drew the 30 random numbers from a table of random numbers, restricting my choices to the numbers 1 through 30 and ignoring any numbers greater than 30. A simpler and less laborious way would be to instruct a computer to generate the 30 random numbers. (A person would take about 20–30 minutes, perhaps more, to do this. A computer takes a second or two! Of course, a computer program must be written to tell the computer what to do. This takes considerably longer, but it can be used for other similar problems.) The numbers I drew from the table, in the order in which they were drawn, are given in the left-hand column of Table 6.5 (30, 13, 16, . . .; 4, 25, 2, . . .; 19, 17, 18, . . .). The three experimental groups are labeled A_1, A_2, and A_3. The IQ and sex designations of each subject are given beside the random numbers. For instance, the first subject in Table 6.5 was the thirtieth subject of Table 6.4 A glance at the latter table shows that this subject had an IQ of 87 and was female. The second subject in Table 6.5 was number 13 in Table 6.4 and had an IQ of 115 and was male. The 30 subjects, then, have been randomly assigned to three groups, together with their IQ's and sex designations.

Did I succeed in thoroughly mixing the subjects so that I can assume that the groups are statistically "equal"? I will never know completely, but

TABLE 6.5   Data of Table 6.4 Rearranged in Random Order

	A_1			A_2			A_3		
Number	IQ	Sex	Number	IQ	Sex	Number	IQ	Sex	
30	87	F	4	136	F	19	103	M	
13	115	M	25	94	M	17	104	M	
16	108	F	2	141	F	18	104	M	
9	125	F	6	128	M	23	99	F	
21	101	F	15	109	F	29	89	M	
10	122	M	27	90	F	1	147	F	
12	115	F	22	101	M	8	126	F	
24	95	F	26	92	F	14	110	F	
5	132	M	20	102	M	3	137	M	
7	128	M	28	90	M	11	118	M	
$M_{No.}$ 14.7			17.5			14.3			
M_{IQ}	112.80			108.30			113.70		$M_t = 111.67$
Male		4			5			6	15
Female		6			5			4	15

I can check to some extent. First, I calculate the means of the subject numbers in each of the groups. These means are given at the bottom of Table 6.5. They are 14.7, 17.5, 14.3. The mean of the numbers 1 through 30 is 15.5. The discrepancies are relatively small: −.8, 2.0, −1.2. (If I had 50 or 100 numbers in each group, they would probably be smaller. Why?) Second, I calculate the means of the IQ's, an important calculation because I want very much to "equalize" intelligence in the three groups. The mean of all 30 IQ's is 111.67. This, then, is the expectation for each group. The calculated group means are 112.80, 108.30, 113.70. The discrepancies from expectation are −1.13, −3.37, 2.03; they are small. Finally, I count the males (M) and females (F) in the groups. The numbers are given at the bottom of the table. Again, the discrepancies are small. Therefore, the randomization has "succeeded": the groups are fairly "equal" in intelligence and sex. I also assume they are "equal" in other possible influential variables.

This process of randomly assigning subjects to experimental groups is one important aspect of randomization. Here is a rather formal and slightly stiff definition of what has just been illustrated. *Randomization* is the assignment of objects (subjects, treatments, groups) of a universe to subsets of the universe in such a way that, for any given assignment to a subset, every member of the universe has an equal probability of being chosen for the assignment. There is no complete guarantee that randomization will "equalize" groups, but the probability is relatively high that it will do so.

There is another way to express the idea: by stating a functional principle, the *principle of randomization:* Since, in random procedures, every member of a population has an equal chance of being selected, members with certain distinguishing characteristics—male or female, high or low intelligence, Republican or Democrat, dogmatic or not dogmatic, and so on—will, if selected, probably be counterbalanced in the long run by the selection of other members of the population with the "opposite" quantity or quality of the characteristic. This is not a law of nature. It is simply a statement of what most often happens when random procedures are used.

Aronson and Mills Revisited

To pull together the ideas discussed and illustrated so far in this chapter and in Chapter 5, we return to the Aronson and Mills experiment. Now, however, we report the actual experiment and some of its results. The hypothesis tested was that difficulty of initiation into a group enhances the values of the group in the eyes of the group members. For example, many organizations impose difficulties and barriers to membership. Does undergoing such hardships enhance the value of the groups in the eyes of their members?

This interesting and perhaps humanly perverse hypothesis was tested in an ingenious way.[4] Three groups of 21 young women each—the 63 women were assigned to the groups at random—were subjected to three experimental conditions: (1) *severe condition*, in which the subjects were asked to read obscene words and vivid descriptions of sexual activity; (2) *mild condition*, in which the subjects read words related to sex but not obscene; and (3) *control condition*, in which the subjects were not required to do anything.

An elaborate procedure was used. Part of its intent was to make actual membership in the group not too attractive. All subjects were required to listen to a presumed discussion of present members of the group, who "in general conducted one of the most worthless and uninteresting discussions imaginable" (Aronson & Mills, 1959, p. 179). The dependent variable was the young women's ratings of the discussion and the participants in the discussion (presumably present group members). Aronson and Mills believed that the subjects of the three groups would rate the discussion and the participants differently: the severe condition most favorably, the mild condition next most favorably, and the control condition least favorably (and realistically). If we can accept the validity of Aronson and Mills' implied reasoning that the higher the ratings of the dull discussion and the discussion participants the more the subjects valued membership in the group, then the hypothesis derived from the theory of cognitive dissonance (see footnote 4) was supported by the experimental evidence.

The means of the combined ratings of the discussion and the participants were: severe condition: 195.3; mild condition: 171.1; control: 166.7. The results seem to support the hypothesis: the severe-condition subjects rated the discussion and the participants most favorably, the mild-

---

[4] The hypothesis was derived from the theory of cognitive dissonance (due to Festinger), which says, in brief, that when ideas or behaviors cause conflict in an individual, he will strive to restore balance to reduce "cognitive dissonance." The reader will see the dissonance produced in the subjects of the experiment.

condition subjects rated them next most favorably, and the control-group subjects least favorably. Since the subjects were assigned to the three groups at random, the researchers could assume that the groups were "equal" statistically before the experiment, and that differences between them after it were due to the manipulation, the different conditions. But we ask, as always, could the three means and the differences between them have risen by chance? A statistical test that assessed the statistical significance of the differences showed that the obtained means and the differences between them could probably not have arisen by chance. According to one such test, differences as large as those reported could have occurred by chance less than once in 100 times. This is good evidence for the empirical validity of the hypothesis.

The basic design discussed in this chapter has many applications in behavioral research, though it must be confessed that it has not been used much except in its two-condition form. Behavioral researchers, especially psychologists, seem to have a strong preference for the kind of design discussed in the next chapter. Whenever two or more experimental conditions of one independent variable need to be compared and studied, as in the Aronson and Mills study and in the Clark and Walberg study, and one can assume that the experimental conditions work under many or most circumstances or have strong effects, the one-way design is appropriate and useful.

The one-way design has a rather severe limitation, however. If the experimental variable works only in conjunction with one or more other independent variables, then the design is inappropriate. In the next chapter, where we will consider experimental research in which there is more than one independent variable, we will see why and when the one-way design can be inappropriate.

Perhaps the most important learning the reader should carry away from this chapter is the applicability and power of random procedures. One of the great strengths of experiments is that randomization can be used. It is the only defensible method invented to increase the probability of the validity of experiments and the inferences made from them by increasing the probability of "equality" of experimental groups in all possible independent variables. Its use gives the researcher great strength in making inferences from data and coming to conclusions about theories and hypotheses.

7

The design
of experimental
research
factorial designs

Research design is data discipline. Its implicit purpose is to impose controlled restrictions on observations of natural phenomena. A research design tells an investigator, in effect: Do this and that; don't do that or that; be careful with this; ignore that; and so on. It is, in short, a blueprint of the research. If a design is well conceived, the ultimate research product has a greater chance of being empirically valid and worthy of serious scientific attention. Without content—good theory, good problems, good hypotheses—the design of any research is empty. But without form, without structure adequately conceived and created for the research purpose, little of value can be accomplished.

The elegance and strength of modern research design and the idea that design is data discipline become much more apparent in factorial designs, the kind of design we study in this chapter. Their elegance should become apparent as we study examples. Their strength springs from the two main purposes of research: to provide answers to research questions and to control sources of influence.

Most experiments in the behavioral disciplines early in the century used only one independent variable and only two experimental conditions. This was the "classic design" of research, one group often being called an experimental group and the other a control group. Moreover, subjects were not assigned to the groups at random. We have already seen that the idea of two experimental conditions can be easily expanded to **93** more than two conditions. This is still one independent variable, however. Only the experimental conditions have been increased, not the variables. In the Aronson and Mills experiment, for example, three experimental conditions were used, but these experimental conditions constituted only one independent variable.

In the 1930s, a revolution in the conceptualization of research design and statistical analysis began. More than one independent variable was introduced. Many such designs were eventually called factorial designs.[1] They consist essentially of experimental designs in which two, three, or more independent variables are simultaneously used to study their independent and joint effects on a dependent variable. This was truly a remarkable breakthrough in behavioral research because complex research problems and hypotheses could be studied. Such designs had several advantages, the three most important of which are: more sophisticated theory could be formulated and tested; more realistic problems could be investigated; and the joint influence of variables could be studied.

AN EXAMPLE OF A FACTORIAL DESIGN[2]

A group of social psychologists are concerned about the problem of handling prejudice. What do you do when someone, say a friend or professional or business colleague, makes a bigoted remark about Jews (or Catholics, or Protestants, or blacks, or Italians, or any group)? Do you remonstrate with him, tell him he's wrong, give him a moral lecture? Or, perhaps, do you do nothing? It is likely that if you do nothing, you are supporting or reinforcing prejudice, because you are in effect affirming by your silence the norms that support prejudice in American society. Let's agree, then, that you have to say something. What should it be? What will have the most effect?

For a long time religious and moral appeals have been used, especially by ministers, priests, and rabbis. "It is un-Christian to say things like that"; "It is inconsistent with Jewish morality to be prejudiced"; and so on. On the other hand, there is a school of thought that thinks religious-moral appeals are ineffectual. After all, they do not seem to have worked very well in the past. People who espouse this school of thought think, rather, that a more pragmatic approach may help. For example, point out to the person who makes a prejudiced remark how prejudice hurts all of us, how it can be turned against any group, how it impedes democracy, and so on.

To test which of these kinds of appeal will work better, in the sense of persuading or convincing people not to make prejudiced statements, the social psychologists can, of course, set up an experiment like the Clark and Walberg experiment. They decide to call one appeal "Moral Appeal." In-

---

[1] Factorial designs should not be confused with factor analysis. We will examine factor analysis later.

[2] The idea for this example was derived from an experiment by Citron, Chein, and Harding (1950).

stead of being limited to religious appeals, moral appeal will include other moral arguments, for instance, "It is wrong to talk that way about Jews (blacks, Catholics, and so on)"; "We must treat others as ourselves." They call the other appeal described above "Pragmatic Appeal."

This is the bare minimum for an experiment. Subjects can be assigned to two groups at random and somehow be made to experience the two kinds of appeal. Their reactions to stereotypes of minority group members can then be obtained, and the difference between the means of the two groups can be assessed for statistical significance. The paradigm of this experiment looks like the left top of Table 7.1 (A in the table). It is the familiar two-group design.

But suppose the social psychologists have reason to believe—on theoretical or experiential grounds—that the mode of expression used in making such appeals makes a difference. That is, they believe that an impassioned appeal is more effective than a calm and more objective appeal. They can, of course, test the belief or hypothesis in a separate experiment. The paradigm of such an experiment is the same as that of the first experiment, Table 7.1(A). It is given in the top right of the table (B in the table).

It is possible, of course, that each of these experiments can be done. And they may yield significant differences between the means. The social psychologists, however, are not really intrigued by the idea of separate experiments. They have a much more interesting idea: Why not do the two experiments at the same time and study the separate effects of appeals and mode of expression and also study and assess their joint effect on the dependent variable? So they do. The paradigm, or model of the design of

TABLE 7.1   Construction of a Two-by-Two Factorial Design

such an experiment is given in the lower part of Table 7.1 (C in the table). This design will yield three tests from one experiment. The first test assesses the *Appeals,* Moral and Pragmatic. The second assesses the *Modes of Expression* Impassioned and Calm. That is, these two tests have the same form. It is as if two separate experiments were done and the differences between the groups in each experiment assessed.

The third test is more interesting. What it does in effect is to assess the interaction, the mutual working, of the two independent variables in their joint effect on the dependent variable. This means assessing the effect of variable *A* at different levels of variable *B*. It is possible, for example, that the moral appeal may be more effective than the pragmatic appeal only when given in an impassioned manner. Or it may be that the pragmatic appeal is more effective than the moral appeal when given in a calm manner. When an independent variable has different effects at different levels or aspects of another independent variable, this differential effect is called *interaction*. It is said that the two variables *interact* to affect a dependent variable. Factorial designs can have more than two independent variables, and therefore it is possible to study more than one interaction, but we restrict ourselves for the most part to two independent variables.

The notion of testing several hypotheses in one experiment, and the use of the kind of design shown in Table 7.1(C) to do it, have strongly influenced behavioral scientific research. And no wonder! It is an efficient, powerful, and elegant way to do things. We must look at it very carefully, then. In doing so, let us remember that the principles we have discussed to this point are the same here: randomization and random assignment, the assessment of the effects of independent variables on dependent variables, and the solution of research problems using research designs and statistical tests. Let us return to our hypothetical experiment to illustrate the basic ideas.

The social psychologists assigned 15 individuals at random to each cell of Table 7.1(C), a total of 60 subjects. Each subject received the appropriate experimental treatment. There were, of course, four of these corresponding to the four cells of Table 7.1(C). To expedite talking about the experiment and to emphasize the "double function" of each cell of the table, the appropriate *A* and *B* designations have been inserted in the corners of Table 7.1: A_1B_1, A_2B_1, A_1B_2, A_2B_2. *A*, of course, stands for the variable *Appeals,* and *B* for *Mode of Expression*. A_1 and A_2 and B_1 and B_2 stand for the categories of *A* and *B*. A_1 and A_2 are Moral Appeal and Pragmatic Appeal; B_1 and B_2 are Impassioned Mode of Expression and Calm Mode of Expression. We are more interested, however, in the joint designations.

A_1B_1 is the juncture, or intersection, of the *A* and *B* variables at the A_1 and B_1 point, namely, the upper left cell labeled A_1B_1.[3] A_2B_1 is the juncture

---

[3] For the reader who knows some set theory, A_1 and A_2 can be conceived as partitions of the set *A*, and B_1 and B_2 partitions of the set *B*. A_1B_1, A_1B_2, and so on, are intersections of the sets *A* and *B*, or, in general, $A \cap B$. A_1B_1 can be written $A_1 \cap B_1$, A_2B_1 can be written $A_2 \cap B_1$, and similarly for the other two subsets. These subsets can be thought of as cross partitions.

of the A and B variables at the A_2B_1 point, the upper right cell. The other two cells, similarly, are the remaining two junctures of A and B. Let's suppose the experiment has been done. The experimenters had the subjects in each group observe two people who discussed Jews. One of the individuals made disparaging remarks about Jews. The other individual answered him and tried to point out why he should not talk as he did. The remarks the second individual made differed, however, in four ways, and each way corresponded to one of the four cells of Table 7.1(C). The subjects assigned to the upper left cell, A_1B_1, heard him use a moral appeal delivered in an impassioned manner, and those in the lower left cell, A_1B_2, heard him use a moral appeal delivered in a calm manner. Those subjects in the upper right cell, A_2B_1, heard him use a pragmatic appeal delivered in an impassioned manner, and, finally, those in the lower right cell, A_2B_2, heard him use a pragmatic appeal delivered in a calm manner. Two days after the experiment was done, the subjects' attitudes toward Jews were measured. (Further experimental details used in the experiment and how the attitudes were measured need not concern us.)

Three important points need to be made about this experiment and about factorial designs in general. First, two experiments are included in one. One of these tests the relation between appeals and the dependent variable, and the other the relation between mode of presentation and the dependent variable. Second, with the random assignment of subjects to the four groups (the four cells) and care in doing the experiment, it can be assumed that the two treatments, appeals and mode of presentation, are independent of each other. Although independence was discussed at some length in Chapter 5, its importance warrants further elucidation. The two variables are what is called *orthogonal* to each other. "Orthogonal" means right-angled, and this means independence of the two variables, which justifies conceiving the one experiment as two experiments. It is not always easy to understand this point, and it is important to do so. When two variables are independent of each other, they are uncorrelated. If we could calculate the correlation between them, it would be zero or close to zero. This means that the effects of each of them on the dependent variable can be considered and assessed separately. If the correlation between them were not zero, if, for instance, it was .50, then they are not independent; some part of the effect of one of them on the dependent variable might be due to the other one.

The third point is the most interesting. If, in reality, the two independent variables somehow work together to affect the dependent variable, this effect can be studied and assessed. Suppose that the social psychologists are not really interested in the independent variables separately. They think that it is not the appeals alone that have an effect, but rather the appeals in combination with the modes of presentation. Specifically, they think that the moral appeal works only when presented in an impassioned manner, that presenting a moral appeal in a calm rational manner is fruitless; it requires high emotion to carry conviction. (Witness the success of fundamentalist preachers and demagogic politicians.) Conversely, they believe that the pragmatic appeal requires a calm and rational mode of presentation to be effective. This is a more interesting and, of course, complex line of reasoning. They are espousing what is called an interaction hypothesis: the two variables interact to affect the dependent variable.

Let us fabricate some results to illustrate different possible outcomes of the experiment. And then we will see how the research questions can be answered by the data obtained in the experiment. Table 7.2 contains four outcomes of the many that are possible. The numerical entries are means. We assume that the dependent variable, attitude toward Jews, was measured on a seven-point scale, with 7 indicating a highly positive attitude and 1 a highly negative attitude. If means are italicized, they are significantly different. For instance, in (I), 6 and 4 are italicized, which means the M_{A_1} is significantly greater than M_{A_2} (indicated at the bottom of the data by $A_1 > A_2$, A_1 is greater than A_2). The differences between the A means or the B means, considered separately, are called *main effects*. If, for example, M_{A_1} is compared to M_{A_2}, this is a main effect—of the variable A.

The four setups, or subtables, are not crossbreaks, which were studied earlier when we examined the Miller and Swanson frequency and percent-

TABLE 7.2   Four Sets of Possible Outcomes Obtained in a
Fictitious Factorial Design Experiment (Means)[a]

(I)

	MORAL A_1	PRAGMATIC A_2	
IMPASSIONED B_1	A_1B_1 6	A_2B_1 4	5
CALM B_2	6 A_1B_2	4 A_2B_2	5
	6	4	

$A_1 > A_2$

(II)

	MORAL A_1	PRAGMATIC A_2	
IMPASSIONED B_1	A_1B_1 6	A_2B_2 6	6
CALM B_2	4 A_1B_2	4 A_2B_2	4
	5	5	

$B_1 > B_2$

(III)

	MORAL A_1	PRAGMATIC A_2	
IMPASSIONED B_1	A_1B_1 6	A_2B_1 4	5
CALM B_2	5 A_1B_2	5 A_2B_2	5
	5.5	4.5	

$A_1B_1 > A_2B_1$

(IV)

	MORAL A_1	PRAGMATIC A_2	
IMPASSIONED B_1	A_1B_1 6	A_2B_1 4	5
CALM B_2	4 A_1B_2	6 A_2B_2	5
	5	5	

$A_1B_1 > A_2B_1$
$A_2B_2 > A_1B_2$

[a] Entries in the cells and on the margins are means. Italicized means indicate significant differences.

age data. They simply show a convenient way to present the design and data of a factorial study and analysis. The 6 in the A_1B_1 cell of (I) is a mean calculated from the attitude scores of the 15 subjects in the cell. The 4 at the bottom of the table is a mean calculated from the 30 subjects in the A_2 column. The other means were calculated similarly. Factorial design data are often presented in this convenient and readily interpretable way. The effects of the separate variables—in this case, appeals and modes of presentation, or A and B—as well as the joint effects can be seen rather clearly by setting the variables against each other like this.

The data in (I) indicate that the moral appeal, A_1, was significantly greater than the pragmatic appeal, A_2. There was obviously no difference between the mode of presentation means (5 and 5) and thus no difference between B_1 and B_2. The data in (II), on the other hand, indicate a significant difference between impassioned presentation and calm presentation, B_1 and B_2, and no difference between moral appeal and pragmatic appeal, A_1 and A_2. These data would indicate, in the first case, that moral appeal is more effective than pragmatic appeal in influencing attitudes toward Jews, no matter what the mode of presentation. In the second case, the impassioned mode of presentation was more effective than the calm mode, no matter what the kind of appeal. The examples are, of course, unrealistic. The means are not likely to be round numbers like these, and they are highly unlikely to be equal [the means of 5 and 5 in (I) and (II)]. Nevertheless, they illustrate the essential points.

The data in (III) are more interesting. They indicate that the moral and pragmatic appeals differ significantly only when presented in an impassioned way. The two appeals are alike with the calm mode of presentation. This is the phenomenon of interaction, mentioned earlier. Recall that interaction occurs when the effects of an independent variable are different at different levels of another independent variable. In this case, the independent variables A and B "interact" because it is not simply a case of A affecting the dependent variable, as in (I), but because A affects the dependent variable depending on what level of B it is at. In other words, the effect of A depends on B; A must interact with B to be effective. There are many examples of interaction in life. The success of some men seems to depend on the women they marry. But for other men it doesn't matter: they succeed no matter whom they marry. Prejudice against Jews, though widely prevalent, manifests itself, only, say, in times of crisis. Prejudice and kind of social situation interact, then.

The example of (IV) is in some ways the most interesting. The data indicate that moral and pragmatic appeals are significantly different with both approaches, impassioned and calm, but in opposite directions. The moral appeal, A_1, is more effective than the pragmatic appeal, A_2, with an impassioned mode of presentation, B_1, but the pragmatic appeal, A_2, is more effective than the moral appeal, A_1, with a calm mode of presentation, B_2.

It should be obvious to the reader that we are here dealing with much more complex situations than those of the one-way designs and analysis of the last chapter. Two or more main effects are tested, and possible interactions of independent variables are also tested. It should also be obvious that the factorial approach is a formidable one. One can more closely approximate in experiments the actual complexity of real situations. This is a major intellectual breakthrough in research and analysis.

Factorial designs have many forms, some of which can be very complex indeed. It is possible, in addition to the relatively simple 2×2 design we have already discussed, to have designs with two independent variables but with more experimental conditions. ("2×2" means "two conditions by two conditions," or variables A and B each has two experimental conditions.) For example, two conditions by four conditions, or three conditions by five conditions. These are succinctly expressed in the literature as 2×3 and 3×5 (read "two by three"; "three by five"). Such designs are frequently used, especially in psychological and educational research.

Three or more independent variables are possible in factorial designs. One can have, for instance, two conditions by two conditions by four conditions, or $2 \times 2 \times 4$. The simplest of such designs, $2 \times 2 \times 2$, is often used in psychological experiments. While potent and highly interesting, such designs are not our concern. It should be noted, however, that with three independent variables and a factorial design seven tests are possible: the three main effects and four interaction effects! If the reader intends to read the research literature, some knowledge of such designs and their analysis may be necessary. It is recommended, therefore, that a good statistics-design text be studied (for example, Edwards, 1972).

There are a substantial number of other experimental designs used in the behavioral sciences. We do not study them in this book, not because they are not important but because of our emphasis on basic conceptual ideas and deemphasis on technical complexities. The reader will find the good though somewhat difficult discussion of Campbell and Stanley (1963) helpful.

RESEARCH EXAMPLES OF FACTORIAL DESIGN

We now try to put more life into the subject by citing three research studies in which the power of factorial design and analysis is nicely illustrated. While it is often difficult to find good examples of certain other techniques, it is not at all difficult to find good to excellent uses of factorial design, especially in psychological research. Psychologists have been quick to seize on the virtues—and perhaps the aesthetic quality—of factorial design to further their theoretical and experimental ends.[4]

[4] Part of the reason for the extensive use in psychology of factorial design is the emphasis on experiments and experimentation. Social psychology is a good example: modern social psychology is virtually experimental social psychology. There are, of course, many exceptions, some of them excellent; examples will be given in later chapters.

Beyond Parkinson's Law

Some years ago, Parkinson (1957) stated his famous law: Work expands to fill available time. In other words, if people have time on a job they will find work to fill the time. "Busy work" is a manifestation of this law. In an interesting experiment, Aronson and Gerard (1966) tested a variation on Parkinson's law: Individuals who are given excess time to complete a task on one occasion will use more time to complete a similar task on a subsequent occasion than individuals who have been given minimal time on the first task. This hypothesis has startling and disturbing implications—if confirmed. It is loosely derived from a learning theory (Guthrie, 1935) which says that a combination of stimuli accompanying a movement will tend, on the recurrence of the stimuli, to be accompanied by the movement. In the present case, if a subject spends too much time doing something on one occasion, he will tend to spend too much time on it on subsequent occasions.

Aronson and Gerard also gave a brief theoretical explanation (at the end of their report) derived from the theory of cognitive dissonance (Festinger, 1957). This theory says, in part, that if one does something that is incongruent with, say, perception of the self or the situation, then one will experience psychological discomfort, or "cognitive dissonance." In relation to Parkinson's statement, if a person spends more time than necessary on a task, this will create cognitive dissonance because the excessive time spent is incongruent with a realistic and accurate appraisal of the time necessary to do the task. To reduce the cognitive dissonance, the person may inflate the importance and complexity of the task: "After all, it's very important; it takes time." Consequently, he may take the same amount or even more time the next time he is confronted with the same or similar task.

The independent variables were time, incentive, and sex. We are concerned only with time; incentive, sex, and all interactions were not significant. Half the subjects were given 5 minutes to do a task; the other half were given 15 minutes. The task, which was extremely easy, required only 5 minutes. It consisted of choosing several arguments from a list of arguments and arranging them in a logical sequence. Later, the subjects were asked to prepare a 2-minute talk on athletics and to use as much time as they needed to prepare a convincing speech. The dependent variable was the time the subjects spent in preparing the speech (in seconds). Half the subjects were also given an incentive to finish sooner to counteract the "excess time effect." This variable was not significant, as indicated earlier.

Subjects in the excess-time (15 minutes) condition spent an average of 468 seconds on the second task, whereas the minimum-time (5 minutes) subjects spent an average of 321 seconds on the second task. This difference was statistically significant. The evidence, then, indicates that the subjects of the excess-time group did indeed take excessive time to finish the task.

The reader may wonder whether this result is generalizable; that is, does it apply to other people in actual work situations. It is often said that experiments like this are trivial because they have little or no applicability beyond the laboratory. It must be borne in mind, however, that the purpose of the experiment—and of most such experiments—was to test an implication of a theory. It did this successfully. It was not its purpose to do more than this. If the researchers wanted to know something of its applicability to other situations, they would have to do more research in other situations with representative samples of people. This frequently misunderstood point will be discussed again in the next chapter.

Race, Sex, and College Admissions

Much educational research lacks theoretical direction because it is applied research that is directed to solving particular problems or research that has not developed theoretical bases. The study we now consider (Walster, Cleary, & Clifford, 1971) is an excellent example of such applied research. It has several strengths, two of which are its clever manipulation of variables that are usually not manipulable and its generalizability. An interesting methodological feature was the unit of analysis of the study: instead of individuals it was colleges, and the colleges were a random sample of American colleges.[5]

The study was directed to finding an answer to a difficult, complex, and important social and educational problem: discrimination in college admissions. Walster and her colleagues asked: Do colleges discriminate against women applicants? Do they discriminate against (or for) black applicants? They randomly selected 240 colleges in the United States and sent prepared applications to each of these colleges. They used a $2 \times 2 \times 3$ factorial design. The independent variables were sex, race, and ability level. These are interesting and unusual because they are all experimental or manipulated variables. Ordinarily, these variables are nonexperimental, or attribute, variables—variables that cannot be manipulated. But Walster et al. manipulated them in a clever, imaginative, yet simple way.[6]

They prepared a master form for application to college, which attempted to provide answers to any questions a college might ask. These

[5] The reader should take the following proposition on faith: The use of random selection (of individuals or institutions) permits a researcher to assume that the probability of the sample being representative is substantial. Thus the probability that results obtained in such a sample are approximately applicable to the population from which the sample was drawn is high. This conclusion holds only for large samples. In simpler words, this means that large random samples enable researchers to generalize to the populations from which the samples were drawn. They can never be sure, however. They can assume only that their samples are representative because of their faith in the proposition just enunciated. For further details, see Kerlinger (1973, Ch. 7, especially pp. 118–122).

[6] A point not yet stressed should now be made. Good experiments require, besides knowledge and competence, ingenuity, imagination, and even creativity. The experiment of Walster and her colleagues is a good example. The ideas in it seem simple, once heard. But to my knowledge a clean, controlled experiment to test bias in admissions had not been done before.

applications were sent out to the 240 randomly selected schools. (They were randomly selected from a college guide.) Each application form came presumably from a legitimate applicant. One quarter of them indicated that the applicant was a white male, another quarter black male, another white female, and still another black female. In addition, three levels of applicant ability were included. In effect, then, there were three independent variables, race, sex, and ability, and there were twelve kinds of forms, corresponding to a $2 \times 2 \times 3$ factorial design. The 240 schools were randomly assigned to the 12 cells of the design. Thus there were 20 schools per cell. The main dependent variable was acceptance or rejection of the presumed applicant. A five-point scale, ranging from outright rejection (1) to acceptance with encouragement or financial aid offered (5). Certain other independent and dependent variables were included, too, but we are not concerned with them.

The researchers expected that males would be preferred to females and blacks to white. (At the time of the study colleges were seeking black students.) They were wrong. The factorial analysis of variance showed that the sex and the race main effects were not significant, nor was the difference between the means of whites and blacks (3.38 and 3.18). A much more interesting and unanticipated interaction was found, however. This is shown in Table 7.3, which shows the male and female means (mean scores on the acceptance variable, males and females) according to the three ability levels.

Study this table carefully: it is important methodologically and socially. The means of the three ability levels were significantly different. But this is a finding of no great importance, since it merely reflects the customary practice of rejecting applicants of lower ability. The difference between the male and female means of 3.41 and 3.15 was not significant. Evidently there was no *overall* discrimination on the basis of sex. The interaction of sex and ability in their joint effect on acceptance, however, was statistically significant. To interpret the interaction, we can omit the medium means (3.48 and 3.48), since they are equal. The high ability means are 3.75 and 4.05, not too different. At the high ability level there is no sex discrimination. Look, now, at the low ability means, 3.00 and 1.93. This relatively large difference is the major reason for the significant interaction. Evidently male applicants of low ability are accepted significantly more than female

TABLE 7.3   **Means of College Acceptance Variable, Sex and Ability Levels: Walster, Cleary, and Clifford Study**

		ABILITY			
		High	Medium	Low	
SEX	*Male*	3.75	3.48	3.00	3.41
	Female	4.05	3.48	1.93	3.15
		3.90	3.48	2.47	

applicants of low ability. Discrimination seems to be practiced at the low level of ability. The authors say that this finding agrees with the feminist observation that only exceptional women can ever transcend sexual stereotypes and be judged objectively. Women of more modest abilities are judged first as women—and thus as "inferior."

This is a particularly good example of the strength of factorial design and the usefulness of studying interaction. It would probably not have been possible to unearth the interesting and important finding of this study without the idea of the interaction of independent variables in their effect on a dependent variable.

Hostility Arousal, Displaced Aggression, and Anti-Semitism

Berkowitz (1959), in studying the relation between displacement of aggression and anti-Semitism, asked whether prejudiced persons are more likely than nonprejudiced persons to respond to frustration with displaced aggression. This is a most interesting interaction hypothesis based on two lines of psychological theory. One line can be called frustration-aggression theory, which is based on the general idea that frustration leads to aggression (Dollard et al., 1939). Another theoretical line, of psychoanalytic origin, says in effect that under certain circumstances people will displace their aggression. To displace aggression means to shift the aggression from whatever may have caused it to something else perhaps unrelated to the source of the aggression. We need not elaborate all the details of the theoretical reasoning. Suffice it to say that in many cases Jews will become targets of aggression, and there is no necessary relation between the source of the aggression and its target, Jews.

Berkowitz used this reasoning to try to explain aggression against Jews. The experiment he set up was ingenious and efficient. It was more than that: it was, and still is, a sophisticated wedding of theory and methodology and shows the good results of bringing the two together satisfactorily. (It does have a defect, however. See Footnote 7.) He split 48 female subjects into two groups on the basis of their scores on a measure of anti-Semitism. Each of these two groups was then split into two groups based on aggressive drive, but we drop this control variable from consideration for the sake of simplicity. The experimental manipulated variable was hostility arousal. In one experimental group the experimenter used sarcasm, deprecated the subjects' performances, and questioned the students' ability to do college work. The nonhostility students were treated in a neutral manner. Each subject was paired with a confederate of the experimenter with whom the subject was to solve a problem. The subjects were asked whether they liked their partners by means of two questions that could be scored 0 ("definitely yes") to 23 ("definitely no"). This measure of liking was the dependent variable. It was predicted that the more anti-Semitic subjects would exhibit more displaced aggression induced by the hostility

TABLE 7.4   Mean Liking-for-Partner Scores as Related to
Hostility and Anti-Semitism, Berkowitz (1959)
Study[a]

	HOSTILITY AROUSAL A_1	NO HOSTILITY AROUSAL A_2
HIGH ANTI-SEMITISM B_1	18.4	14.2
LOW ANTI-SEMITISM B_2	12.2	16.3

[a] The higher the score, the less the liking for partner. Main effects were not significant; the interaction was significant.

arousal than the less anti-Semitic subjects. This should be exhibited by less liking for the work partners by the high anti-Semitic subjects. This is, then, an interaction hypothesis: the hostility arousal should work differently at the different levels of anti-Semitism.

The mean liking-for-partner as a function of hostility arousal, A, and anti-Semitism, B, are given in Table 7.4. Neither of the main effects was in and of itself significant. Their interaction, however, *was* significant. When hostility was aroused, high anti-Semitic individuals responded with more displaced aggression (less liking for partner) than low anti-Semitic individuals. The interaction hypothesis was supported—a finding of both theoretical and practical significance.[7]

A CONCEPTUAL RETROSPECT

In the earlier chapters of this book, the purpose of science as theory and explanation was strongly emphasized. Explanation was described in part as specifying the relations among variables. We now have some conceptual and methodological tools to help us understand better how behavioral scientists try to explain phenomena. They separate variables into independent and dependent variables, using the former to explain the latter. The simplest possible explanation consists in relating one independent variable to one dependent variable. Examples of this were the Clark and Walberg and the Aronson and Mills studies. The reader will find many similar examples in the literature. The conceptual basis of the design and analysis of such research is a statement of the form if p, then q. No matter whether

[7] The questionable point of the study was pointed out to me by two of my students at the University of Amsterdam. They said that there should be a significant difference between A_1 and A_2 at B_1, but not at B_2. The reader can see, however, that the predicted difference of A_1 and A_2 does show up at B_1, but an unpredicted difference in the opposite direction also showed up at B_2. And there does not seem to be a theoretical reason why there should be such a difference at B_2. The reader can profit from reflection on this problem.

there are two experimental groups, as in the Clark and Walberg study, or more than two groups, as in the Aronson and Mills study, the conception of explanation is the same.

But explanations are often more complex, as in the Walster, Cleary, and Clifford study, the Berkowitz study, and the Aronson and Gerard study. More than one independent variable is used to explain a dependent variable. In the simplest case, the underlying conception is if p, then q, under condition r. This is the conceptual basis of many published studies. Many other studies, however, use a more complex conceptual basis: they assess the separate and combined effects of more than two independent variables on a dependent variable. The conceptual basis is if p, then q, under conditions r, s, and t. This example has four independent variables: p, r, s, and t. No matter how many variables are used and how they are symbolized, the basic approach is the same: the effect of one or more independent variables on a dependent variable is studied.

8

Experimental and nonexperimental research

Examples of actual research that we have summarized and discussed in earlier chapters have been mostly experimental: Clark and Walberg, Aronson and Mills, Walster, Cleary, and Clifford, and so on. Only the Miller and Swanson study described in Chapter 1 was nonexperimental. There is good reason for this preoccupation: experimental research can be called the ideal of science because answers to research questions obtained in experiments are on the whole clearer and less ambiguous than answers obtained in nonexperimental research. But there is a large body of important and significant research that is nonexperimental, or *ex post facto* research, as it has been called. It can even be argued that *ex post facto* research is more important than experimental research. The position taken in this book seems more reasonable: both kinds of research are important and necessary. Both have value. Both must be done.

In this chapter we examine the major characteristics of experimental and nonexperimental research and the major differences between them. The task is not an easy one because it will be necessary to explore in some depth the difference between the conclusions reached in experimental and in nonexperimental research. Fortunately, we have already discussed experimentation and can use what we have learned. We begin with reexamination of experimental research and use a series of experimental studies by Milgram to stimulate and illustrate the discussion.   **107**

MILGRAM'S EXPERIMENTS ON OBEDIENCE AND AUTHORITY

Milgram (1974), interested in the phenomena of obedience and authority, has shown that people of a wide range of backgrounds will do morally objectionable things to other people, if they are told to do so by a clearly designated and respected authority. I have chosen the Milgram research to illustrate the nature and power of experiments, not because of any particular excellence of design but because the results are startling, hard to believe, and go against accepted morality. If we are to believe Milgram's results, then, we must have considerable faith in the way they were obtained. This means, in turn, that we must study his methodology carefully and skeptically.

Milgram asked several related questions to which he wanted empirical answers: What factors influence the willing obedience of individuals to authority? How does authority affect obedience? If the individual giving orders to a person has authoritative status, does this compel greater obedience? Why do individuals comply with orders that compel "immoral" behavior, behavior that inflicts suffering on a helpless individual? When people comply with an order that violates common morality, how do they react psychologically, how do they justify their behavior? This is a formidable set of questions which we will be able to answer only partially.

The experimental procedure was as follows. Two people come to the psychology laboratory to work together in a study of memory and learning. One is to be a "teacher," the other a "learner." The real experimental subject is the teacher. He is told that the purpose of the experiment is to study the effects of punishment on learning. The learner—always the same person, an actor who has been instructed how to react—is seated in a chair, his arms strapped to prevent movement, and an electrode attached to his wrist. The experimenter tells him that he will learn a list of word pairs. If he makes an error he will be shocked. The teacher watches all this and is then taken into the main experimental room and instructed how to use an impressive-looking shock generator, which has an array of 30 switches labeled from 15 to 450 volts, also labeled verbally from "Slight Shock" to "Danger—Severe Shock."

The teacher is then told that he will "teach" the man in the other room by reading paired words to him—nice day; blue box; and so on. In tests of the learning, the teacher reads a stimulus word and then four possible responses, for instance: blue: sky ink box lamp (Milgram, 1974, p. 19). The learner communicates which of the four responses is correct by pressing one switch among four switches. If the response is correct, the teacher goes on to the next set. If the response is incorrect, he is to administer a shock to the learner. The teacher is also told to move one level higher on the shock generator whenever a wrong response is given. The subject is told, if he asks about the shocks, that they can be very painful, but that they cause no permanent tissue damage. (No actual shocks were ever given the learner.)

After the teaching and learning were underway and, during the experiment, the subject, perhaps disturbed by shocking another person, asked the experimenter whether he should continue the shocks. The experimenter prodded him with one of four commands: Please continue; The experiment requires that you continue; It is absolutely essential that you continue; You have no other choice, you *must* go on. These commands were given in sequence, and only if the subject refused to obey.

The learner-confederate of the experimenter always gave the same set of responses or reactions to the procedure. He indicated no discomfort until the 75-volt shock, at which time he gave a little grunt. The same was true for the 90- and 105-volt shocks, but at the 120-volt shock, the learner shouted that the shocks were painful. At 135 volts, the "victim" groaned painfully, and at 150 volts he shouted to be let out and that he refused to continue. He gave similar responses but with greater intensity to subsequent shocks, and at 180 volts he cried out that he could not stand the pain. At 270 volts he screamed in agony, and at 300 volts he refused to continue giving answers.

The subject (the teacher) at this point—and earlier points—sought guidance from the experimenter, who instructed him to treat absence of response as no response and to continue the experiment. After 330 volts the learner was no longer heard from.

The question is, How far would the subjects go—all the way to 450 volts? Or would they refuse at some point along the way? Would they be obedient or disobedient? This is the core of the experiment. Milgram varied the instructions for different groups of individuals. For example, he manipulated proximity of the learner to the teacher, predicting that the more remote from the teacher the learner was, the greater the shocks the teacher would give. He also used other control variations. One group of subjects, for example, went through the experiment with the experimenter (the authority) absent. With another group the experiment was done in an office building in a city distant from Yale University where most of the experiments were done. This was to control for the possible authority effect of a great and prestigious university. (See below.)

In effect, then, the experiments used several independent variables and one dependent variable, obedience, as measured by the shock level to which subjects went before either concluding the shock series or discontinuing participation in the experiments.

The results defy common sense and violate common morality.[1] In the first experiment, in which proximity was the independent variable, 26 of 40 subjects in the basic remote situation continued the shocks to the maximum of 450 volts! (Note that the switches from 375 volts to 450 volts were labeled "Danger—Severe Shock" and that the numerical voltages and the verbal designation were clearly indicated.) Five subjects gave 300 volts before quitting, and eight gave between 315 and 360 volts. Most of the

---

[1] We will not comment on the ethics of these controversial and frightening experiments, which have stimulated much controversy among social scientists. See Milgram's (1974, pp. 193–202) excellent summary of comments on the ethical issues raised by his research.

subjects, then, were completely obedient, and all of them gave at least what were supposed to be intense shocks! The closer they were to the victim, however, the less they obeyed. Nevertheless, substantial numbers still gave the full treatment to the victim.

It is tempting to pursue the psychological implications of this remarkable study. My main point in citing it at such length, however, is not psychological but methodological. I want the reader to know clearly that we are here dealing with highly controversial, debatable, and difficult matters and that belief in the results is difficult. I want to illustrate the point that an experiment, other things equal, compels more belief than an *ex post facto* study. If Milgram's results are empirically valid—and, despite certain methodological weaknesses, they appear to be—then we face a very disturbing fact about many people: they will cruelly hurt other people provided they are told to do so by recognized authority and despite their moral qualms. And they are not Hitlerian monsters; on the contrary, they are mostly decent and morally sound people who would not ordinarily dream of hurting other people. Can we believe the results, then? (The answer seems to be Yes.)

Most people, when asked what they or other people would do in such a situation, predict that they and others would not shock the victim, or would do so only to a low shock level. This is precisely Milgram's point and part of the central psychological meaning of his discovery: decent and kind people behave cruelly given the appropriate circumstances—and the main circumstance is authority. Again, can we believe him? Would I shock people if told to do so and despite the protest of the victim?

CONTROL

In general, results obtained from experimental research can be believed more than the results of other sources of knowledge. Put somewhat differently, given competence and the satisfaction of scientific criteria and standards, the results of experiments can be trusted more than the results of other kinds of research. This is the prime reason why experimental research is so important and why scientists, given a choice, will probably do experiments. The scientific experiment is one of the great inventions of all times. It is also the most trustworthy source of knowledge and of understanding natural phenomena, other things equal.

The reasons are not difficult to understand. The major and central one is expressed by the word "control." In a well-conducted experiment control is relatively great. But what does "control" mean in an experimental context? Basically it means the definition, delimitation, restriction, and isolation of the conditions of the research situation such that belief in the empirical validity of the results of the research is maximized. The possibilities of alternative explanations of the phenomena under study are minimized.

In Milgram's case, the basic statement tested was, If authority, then obedience. To be able to say that this statement is empirically valid means in part that other plausible and possible explanatory statements are not empirically valid. For example, is it possible that the prestigious atmosphere and surroundings of Yale University may have engendered the obedience? To answer this question, Milgram did the experiment in an unpretentious office building in another city. The results were virtually the same. Thus it was not prestigious surroundings that engendered the obedience.

A more subtle possible alternative explanation of the obedience of the subjects was contractual obligation. The subjects had contracted with the experimenter to give up some of their freedom to advance scientific knowledge. They also perceived that the victim had entered into a contract. Both teacher and learner, therefore, have to honor their contractual obligations. The subjects were therefore obedient. Milgram ruled this out by highlighting a release form which both teacher and learner signed. During the signing, the learner stressed that he had a heart condition and demanded that he be let out of the experiment when he said so. The experimenter grunted in apparent agreement. The "contract" was thus made preeminent. At 150 volts the learner protested, but the experimenter disregarded him and instructed the teacher to go on in the usual manner. The "contract" was thus not honored by the experimenter. Did it make a difference? If the contractual arrangement had force, then subjects should cease obeying. They did not; they continued obeying the experimenter. As the results showed and as Milgram says, "the social contract doctrine is a feeble determinant of behavior" (Milgram, 1974, p. 66).

But testing alternative explanations or hypotheses, a powerful and indispensable form of scientific control (Platt, 1964), is not exclusively an experimental prerogative. Such testing can be and is done in nonexperimental research. It is, however, more characteristic and more feasible in experimental than in nonexperimental research because experimenters have rather complete control over what they can do and how they do it.

Definition and Characteristics of Experiments

In an earlier chapter it was said that there were two essential characteristics of experiments: manipulation of independent variables and randomization. It was also pointed out that randomization is not absolutely essential in an experiment, though highly desirable. The real meaning of the essential quality of randomization in the definition is simply that only in experiments can randomization be used. As we will see later, random assignment is completely impossible in nonexperimental research.

An *experiment* is a research study in which one or more independent variables are manipulated and in which the influence of all or nearly all possible influential variables not pertinent to the problem of the investigation is kept to a minimum. In so-called laboratory experiments—as contrasted to field experiments—experimenters do this by isolating the research in a delimited physical situation and by manipulating and measuring variables under carefully specified and controlled conditions.

What all this boils down to, of course, is relatively greater assurance that the independent variables of the research study can, if effective, act upon the dependent variable without "contamination" by other influences or variables. This is what Milgram did. He carefully controlled the experimental laboratory situation so that he could have relatively greater assurance that the authority of the experimenter could, if effective, operate on the dependent variable, obedience, without contamination by other variables.

It should be obvious that experimental situations, especially in laboratories, are restricted and tight environments in which there is relatively high precision of manipulation and measurement. And the necessity or desirability of such tightly circumscribed situations in research comes from the greater confidence in the results they yield, the flexibility offered experimenters to test various aspects of research problems at will, and, closely related and highly important, the ability to test various aspects of theories at will. We have already discussed the confidence aspect of experiments. The flexibility aspect needs elaboration. So does the theory-testing aspect.

A highly important aspect of Milgram's obedience research, as brought out earlier, was the varying of experimental conditions in order to rule out alternative explanations of the obedience phenomenon. The hypothesis under test was, If authority, then obedience. If the empirical validity of this hypothesis is supported by the research, this is evidence for the empirical validity of Milgram's ideas about the relation between authority and obedience. But there are other plausible explanations. Only if these other explanations are shown not to be empirically valid can the researcher put strong faith in his original if-then statement.

This is essentially though not exactly what Milgram did, and it is a strong methodological feature of his research. He used the flexibility feature of experimental research to vary independent variables and to rule out other possible explanations or independent variables and thus to strengthen his basic statement or hypothesis. For example, if it is true that it is the experimenter's authority that compels obedience, then sources of possible influence other than the experimenter must be ruled out. Recall that one of these was the prestigious surroundings of Yale University. Milgram ruled this out by doing the research in another environment without status and prestige. Other plausible explanations were similarly tested, as we saw earlier. The point is that in most experimental situations such varied and fruitful testing is possible and desirable.

Part of Milgram's theory to explain his findings is as follows. Persons who enter an authority situation change internally, and this is shown by a change in attitude. The person who enters an authority situation suspends his own purposes for a time and acts as an executive agent of the wishes and commands of others (Milgram, 1974, pp. 132–134). Milgram calls the state of the person the *agentic state*, the condition a person is in when he perceives himself as an agent of another's wishes and commands. A key idea here is that when a person is in the agentic state his own values, attitudes, and motivations are suspended, or at least subordinated, and he can and will behave as he cannot and will not behave in his "own state." He sees himself as not responsible for his actions and can even perform acts of cruelty to others.

Supplied with a "good" theory, the researcher can deduce several or many consequences from the theory. If it is true that people in an agentic state lose their usual sense of responsibility, then an experiment can be set up to see if this is indeed so. One would somehow produce the agentic state in a group of individuals by experimental instructions, and then measure their sense of responsibility as compared to, say, the sense of responsibility of another group of individuals not in an agentic state.

Another experiment implied by the theory might be simply to compare the obedience of groups in different "intensities" of the agentic state. Still another experiment might be to vary the strength and legitimacy of the authority of the experimenter. Presumably the depth of the agentic state and the degree of obedience of subjects should be differently affected by different strengths and legitimacies of authority.

Call these experimental possibilities "flexibility." This characteristic of experiments, together with the ability to manipulate variables, to randomize subjects and conditions, and to achieve relatively tight and close control over the operation of variables add up to a most potent method of testing theory and hypotheses and advancing knowledge. This does *not* mean that all experiments add significantly to knowledge. Indeed, many are poorly conceived and poorly executed. There is no guarantee of validity or value, in other words, just because a research study is experimental. But the potential is there. Before studying *ex post facto* research, it will be well to look at both the strengths and weaknesses of experiments, but especially of laboratory experiments.[2]

Strengths and Weaknesses of Experimental Research

To outline the strengths of experimental research, we first recapitulate the points made above. The basic strength of experimental research lies in relatively high control of the experimental situation and consequently of possible independent variables that can affect the dependent variable. This means that relations can be studied in isolation from the cacophony of the outside world; the "pure" relations can be studied. A second strength is that variables can be manipulated alone and in concert with other variables. The reader may by now be convinced of the power of manipulation

---

[2] Much of the discussion will also apply to field experiments. For a more complete discussion, see Festinger and Katz (1953).

of variables. Third, experimental situations are flexible in the sense that many and varied aspects of theory can be tested almost at will. The only restriction is often the limits of ingenuity.

A fourth strength of experiments has not yet been mentioned: experiments can be "replicated" with or without variations. Some of Milgram's experiments in his series of experiments were replications. It has become almost a rule of behavioral research: Replicate all studies. And it is much easier to replicate experimental than nonexperimental research because so much of the research situation is under the control of the researcher. Unfortunately, too few studies are replicated.

"Replication" is a broader term than "repetition" or "duplication." It means repeating a research study, but usually with variations. In a strict sense, simple duplication is never possible because different subjects are used, a variable may be added or another deleted, the replication has to be done at another time when conditions may have changed, and the locale of the research may be, and often should be, changed. In any case, if obtained relations are the same or similar under replication, their empirical validity is strengthened. Milgram's replication of his basic experiment away from Yale University is an example of this strengthening of the empirical validity of research results.

Experiments do have weaknesses. One, the independent variables of laboratory experiments rarely have much strength compared to the strength of "natural" variables outside the laboratory. Milgram's experiment seems to be an exception. Most experimental studies, however, do not have the dramatic force of the authority-obedience studies. This is a disadvantage because it makes the effects of such variables hard to detect. Indeed, relations that actually exist may not be detected, perhaps misleading scientists about the true state of affairs in a defined field. When a researcher studies the effects of repetition on memory, it may be very hard to detect such effects, especially in the short term. One reason for laboratory precision and refined statistics is the need to detect the effects of weak independent variables.

Experimentation is often criticized on two related counts: artificiality and lack of generality. It is difficult to know whether the artificiality of experiments is actually a weakness. There is little doubt of artificiality. Indeed, since manipulated variables are contrived, they are almost by definition "artificial." On the other hand, it is often remarkable how realistic experiments can be made to be. Read Milgram's book and see if you can charge his experiments with being artificial! A more subtle point is that a certain amount of artificiality is a natural part of experimentation. Sophisticated experimenters know this, of course. They also believe that, because of the artificiality and weak effects, if a relation is detected in the laboratory, the probability is substantial that the relation will be stronger in more realistic situations, other things equal. Many researchers will not even care about artificiality. They will say that they are testing theory and have no interest in applications of their research. Their point is well taken. Too often so-called impractical theoretical research has yielded results with far-reaching practical consequences (see Comroe & Dripps, 1976; Deutsch, Platt, & Senghaas, 1971; Townes, 1968). We return to this problem at the end of the book.

In general, the results of laboratory experiments cannot be generalized beyond the laboratory. Because a certain result has been obtained in the laboratory, one cannot say that the same or similar result will hold outside the laboratory—though it well may. One must show by further research that the results apply in the field. This is *strictly speaking*. One is puzzled by Milgram's research and certain other powerful laboratory researches. Are Milgram's findings applicable to schools, corporations, churches, armies, and other groups and organizations? No one can really say until more research is done. My own opinion is that Milgram has made a strong case, but the research must be extended to field situations. (But how to do this?) It is possible that the relation between authority and obedience may break down when studied in certain types of realistic situations.

In thinking about the applicability of laboratory experimentation to real life, it must be borne in mind that the basic purpose of experimentation is *not* to find out what will happen or what will work in life situations. The basic purpose is to study relations and to test hypotheses derived from theory under carefully controlled and circumscribed conditions. To be sure, much research—a conspicuous example is medicine—is done in the laboratory mainly to determine what has happened or what will happen. For example, does such-and-such a method of therapy have efficacious results? Though highly useful, such experimentation, scientifically speaking, is peripheral to the conceptual basis of scientific experimentation. Whether or not this rather puristic interpretation is completely correct, however, is not important. What is important is that laboratory experimentation should not be expected to do what it is basically not designed to do: generalize to real-life situations.

Perhaps the reader will understand all this better if we briefly focus on another related criticism of experiments and experimentation in behavioral research. It is often said that laboratory experiments are trivial. There is little doubt that many experiments are trivial. It is important to know, however, what the critic is saying. He is saying that experiments are artificial, and he means by this that they are not life itself. They are thus trivial. The core of the criticism is that experiments lack generality. Their results do not apply to real people in real-life situations.

The argument is fundamentally irrelevant rather than wrong because experiments and their results are not meant to apply to real life, as indicated a moment ago. The experiment is a specialized invention whose purpose is almost wholly divorced from real life. Its purpose is specifically to be separated and shielded from outside "noise." Its scientific purpose is to study relations and to test propositions derived from theory in as uncontaminated an environment as it is possible to achieve. Its purpose is *not* to improve social and human conditions. Therefore a generalizability criticism is, strictly speaking, irrelevant. It is like criticizing something for not being what it can't be anyway.

NONEXPERIMENTAL RESEARCH

No one knows exactly what the proportions of experimental and nonexperimental research are in behavioral research. It can clearly be said, however, that much nonexperimental research is of high significance and importance, just as much experimental research is significant and important. Neither kind of research can or should enjoy any monopoly on validity and prestige. There is nothing inherently meritorious in doing either experimental research or nonexperimental research as such. One does research on problems of interest, and some problems can be experimental and others cannot.

Nonexperimental, or *ex post facto*, research is any research in which it is not possible to manipulate variables or to assign subjects or conditions at random. Inferences are made and conclusions drawn in nonexperimental research as in experimental research, and the basic logic of inquiry is fundamentally the same. But the conclusions are empirically not as strong in the former as in the latter. To explain this statement completely would be difficult and cumbersome. We content ourselves, therefore, with a less than complete explanation based on the idea of control discussed earlier.

The basis of the structure in which the scientist operates is relatively simple. He asks questions like: How is x related to y? Under what conditions does x affect y, x being an independent variable and y a dependent variable? Or, how do x_1, x_2, and x_3 affect y—or even y_1 and y_2? He then hypothesizes that x influences y in such-and-such a way, the hypothesis being derived, hopefully, from a theory. Most succinctly put, he sets up statements of the form "if p, then q" and tests the empirical validity of the statements in some manner.

There is no difference whatever between experimental research and nonexperimental research in this basic form of reasoning. The primary difference is in control of p, the independent variables. In experiments the p's can be manipulated at the will of the experimenter. Suppose, for instance, that I am interested in equitable relationships in general and specifically in how people deal psychologically with inequity.[3] I can set up different groups of individuals and have the groups experience different forms or amounts of inequity. That is, I manipulate equity or inequity. This is a form of control because the differences in equity among the

---

[3] This example comes from so-called equity theory and research (Berkowitz & Walster, 1976). Actually, Milgram's obedience studies can be conceptualized in the equity theory framework, though Milgram apparently did not do so.

groups come entirely from me. They did not happen "out there," so to speak. A good example with which we are already familiar is the Aronson and Mills experiment in which three groups of young women were subjected to different degrees of unpleasant initiation before presumably joining a group.

In *ex post facto* research manipulation of independent variables is not possible. This is the primary characteristic of nonexperimental research: independent variables come to the researcher, as it were, ready-made. They have already exercised their effects, if any. If I were studying how people deal psychologically with inequity and my research was nonexperimental, I would not be able to have different groups of individuals experience different degrees of inequity at will. I would probably have to try to find different groups of individuals who have already experienced inequity and then study how they deal with it psychologically. The difference between the experimental and nonexperimental approaches is great, then. Indeed, the difference is so great that we really have quite different approaches to research and research problems and different degrees of faith in the inferences we make from research data.

In experiments, since we have virtual control of the independent variables and the situation in which the independent variables operate, we can be more sure—never certain, of course—that contomitant observed variations in a dependent variable are due to the influence of the independent variables. In studies that are not experiments, our faith, other things equal, must be less, primarily because of lack of manipulative control of independent variables.[4] In much nonexperimental research we observe y, the dependent variable, and then "go back" to find the x or x's that presumably influenced y. Examples may make clear what is meant.

Cigarette-Smoking and Lung Cancer

Research on the presumed relation between cigarette-smoking and lung cancer has engendered much controversy. Many nonsmokers are completely convinced that cigarette-smoking causes lung cancer, and they cite research that seems to support their conviction. Many smokers are not convinced—perhaps because they don't want to be. What are the facts? There seems to be little doubt that, as it is said, there is a statistical relation between cigarette-smoking and lung cancer. Quite simply, much research has found that more smokers than nonsmokers become afflicted with lung

---

[4] Some researchers and writers seem to believe that the fundamental difference between experimental and nonexperimental research is that in the former causal inferences can be made, whereas they cannot be so made in the latter. This is oversimplified. Strictly speaking, neither kind of research can say that one thing causes another. The most one can say is that such-and-such a relation exists and it is of so-and-so nature. The question, however, is really academic, since there is no need for making causal statements in science. So-called conditional statements of the kind if p, then q, which lack causal implication, are sufficient.

cancer. So there is agreement on the findings. But can one agree with the conclusion, which is, remember, that cigarette-smoking causes lung cancer?

First, let us dispose of the word "cause." Scientists do not use the word, primarily because it is virtually impossible, strictly speaking, to say that one thing causes another—and make it stick. There is always a possibility that a presumed cause of something is not the real cause. Take a slightly ridiculous example. It would be easy to show that when it rains one can count more umbrellas than when it doesn't rain—except, perhaps, in London. Therefore the umbrellas cause the rain! The example is ridiculous only because it is so obvious and because we know the causes of rain. The smoking–cancer example is more subtle. Nevertheless, it has the same features as the umbrella–rain example. It differs in that we do not really know what causes lung cancer, and cigarette-smoking seems to be a plausible cause.

Suppose we could take a large group of people who were a random sample of, say, the people of a country or part of a country. We split the group into three subgroups at random. We instruct the members of one of the groups to smoke two packs of cigarettes a day, and we make sure somehow that they do. We require the members of the second group to smoke one pack of cigarettes a day. The members of the third group are not permitted to smoke at all. This "experiment" goes on for 10 years, at the end of which time we measure the dependent variable, presence of lung cancer or actual death from lung cancer. Disregarding two or three technical difficulties in the research design, we could have considerably more faith in the outcome than we can in the outcome of an *ex post facto* study. Such experiments are, of course, not possible for obvious reasons. Do we therefore abandon research on cigarette-smoking and lung cancer? By no means. But we are hemmed in by the main difficulty of nonexperimental research.

Is it possible that cigarette-smoking is not really a "cause" of lung cancer? Suppose there were a psychological syndrome, call it "discombulism," and individuals who are discombulists are also highly prone to lung cancer. Let us assume that discombulists, along with the characteristics they share—hyperactivity, nervousness, sleeplessness, mercurial moods, and slight paranoia—have a strong predisposition to lung cancer, *and* they smoke cigarettes heavily. In other words, discombulism is the basic cause of lung cancer, not smoking. Smoking is merely a concomitant characteristic. It just happens to be present in the discombulistic syndrome. Researchers, knowing nothing about discombulism, repeatedly note that lung cancer patients smoke heavily. The correlation between cigarette-smoking and lung cancer is, of course, high, and the researchers are deceived into believing that cigarette-smoking causes lung cancer.

Fanciful? A bit. But certainly not impossible. The point is that nonexperimental research is more vulnerable to erroneous conclusions than experimental research.

The Nature of Variables in Nonexperimental Research

In a perfect behavioral scientific world, researchers would always be able to draw random samples, manipulate independent variables, and assign subjects to groups at random. Alas, all three are often not possible, and in *ex post facto* research the last two are never possible. This does not mean that such research is not significant and important. Far from it.

One of the key differences between the two kinds of research is in the nature of the variables. Nonexperimental research deals with variables that are by their nature not manipulable: social class, sex, intelligence, prejudice, authoritarianism, anxiety, aptitude, achievement, values, and so on. If one is interested, for example, in authoritarianism and prejudice, or in intelligence, social class, and achievement, or in social class and values, then one must (usually) do nonexperimental research. And one is therefore faced with more difficult problems of inference than if one is interested in problems that include manipulated variables.

All variables that are characteristics of people—call them "status" variables—are not ordinarily manipulable. Take intelligence. You can't tell one group of individuals to "be intelligent" and another group "don't be intelligent"! People bring many status variables with them to research situations. And the differences among people on such variables are already relatively fixed.[5]

NONEXPERIMENTAL RESEARCH STUDIES

Of the many nonexperimental research studies published, we choose three as examples. They are highly significant, theoretically and practically. The first to be discussed has become famous and the source of much educational controversy.

Equality of Educational Opportunity

In the largest educational research study done in the United States, Coleman, Campbell, Hobson, McPartland, Mood, Weinfeld, and York (1966) attempted to answer a number of significant questions about educational inequality in America. Two of them were: What is the extent of inequality in American education? That is, are there differences in the educational opportunities and facilities available for majority and minority groups, and how extensive are such differences? (One of the answers was that the great majority of American children attend segregated schools, and

---

[5] It is worth noting that many variables—for example, anxiety, authoritarianism, group atmosphere, group cohesiveness, aggression—can be both manipulated and measured variables. This does not mean, however, that they are the same. Manipulated anxiety and measured anxiety are probably not the same variable, though there should, of course, be some substantial relation between them.

that black children are most segregated.) From the point of view of this book, a more interesting question was: What is the relation between student achievement and the kind and quality of schools they attend?

More than 600,000 pupils in the third, sixth, ninth, and twelfth grades in over 4,000 schools were studied. The basic method of observation was a questionnaire answered by superintendents, principals, teachers, and students. The enormous amount of data was analyzed with rather complex methods. There were over 100 variables grouped in major categories, such as home background variables, school variables, and teacher variables. The major analyses focused on the achievement of the children and rather boldly and certainly competently tried to discover major and minor influences on achievement.

The results were surprising. In general, home background variables were very important in accounting for the achievement of the children— more important, in fact, than any other set of variables except, perhaps, the children's attitudes (sense of control of the environment, for instance). School variables—differences among schools in facilities, curriculum, and staff—did not account for differences in achievement nearly as much as home background variables or attitude variables. This was the most controversial finding, one that has been debated and misunderstood. Many people have jumped to the incorrect conclusion that the Coleman report said that schools and their facilities, curricula, and staff were not important! This is an absurd conclusion that illustrates one of the difficulties of interpreting complex research results. A more nearly correct interpretation—and "correct" only in the context of the study—is that school variables did not add much to accounting for achievement *after* home background variables. To explain this statement adequately would take us too far afield technically and conceptually. We therefore relinquish it and other findings in order to highlight the nonexperimental nature of the study.

Insofar as possible, the Coleman study used modern research techniques competently and gave the people of the United States information about American education that will be discussed and debated for another decade. We must understand, however, that it is *ex post facto* research. Here the difficulties become dramatic because the conclusions of the research can well affect important policy decisions in education.

Consider the conclusion just mentioned: school variables contribute less to the prediction of achievement than home background variables. There is little doubt that this conclusion is empirically valid in the *Equality* research. But consider the possibility—a remote one, to be sure—that large experimental studies could be done in which school variables could be systematically manipulated and their effects on achievement assessed. The outcome might be very different because random assignment (of classes, say) to experimental conditions and manipulation of independent variables can yield less ambiguous results. We would know, in other words, that the influences of other independent variables were minimized. Coleman et al. analyzed the data in a way that approximated the findings of an experimental approach (through what is called multiple regression and related methods), but this is not at all the same thing. The influence of other possible independent variables is difficult to control, and only "statistical control" is possible in contrast to the powerful experimental controls of manipulation, randomization, and isolation.

Freedom and Equality Study

In an unusual series of studies on values, Rokeach (1968) combined *ex post facto* and experimental approaches. We address ourselves here to only a part of the *ex post facto* research, a part that is characteristic of much of this kind of research.

Rokeach had a number of groups and a national sample rank order two sets of what he called instrumental and terminal values—*a comfortable life, family security, equality, wisdom* (terminal); *ambitious, capable, independent, loving* (instrumental). Two of the terminal values, *freedom* and *equality*, had been found to be particularly important because they were apparently keys to fundamental differences in social and political value outlooks. One of Rokeach's sets of results is given in Table 8.1.

It seems clear that the four groups are quite different in their views on *freedom* and *equality* values. Policemen put a very high value on *freedom* and a very low value on *equality*, while unemployed blacks do almost the opposite (10 to *freedom* and 1 to *equality*)! Evidently the social values of policemen and blacks, at least in this sample, are dramatically different.

It is fairly typical of *ex post facto* research to study relations by determining if groups, selected on some basis relevant to the problem under study, possess different amounts of a dependent variable. (Recall the lung cancer research.) In the above example, Rokeach chose the four different groups, presumably, because he expected that their values would be different on his measurement instrument. Policemen and Calvinists, for example, are more conservative than the other two groups and are not known for their espousal of equality. Blacks, on the other hand, strongly espouse equality. Unemployed whites will probably not rank equality

TABLE 8.1   Composite Ranks of *Freedom* and *Equality* of Different Groups

	POLICEMEN (50)	UN-EMPLOYED WHITES (141)	UN-EMPLOYED NEGROES (28)	CALVINIST STUDENTS (75)
Freedom	1[a]	3	10	8
Equality	12	9	1	9

[a] 1 is the highest rank, 12 the lowest. The tabled entries are averages of the ranks assigned by each group. For example, the average rank assigned to *equality* by 141 unemployed whites was 9 compared to the average rank of 3 assigned to *freedom* [footnote added].

high. If the obtained values come out as expected, this is evidence both for whatever theory is explicit or implied *and* for the validity of the measurement instrument.

The Effects of Deprivation

In these last two examples we examine briefly both experimental and nonexperimental approaches to the same subject or relation: the effects of deprivation on later development. Such effects are important theoretically and highly important practically. They are theoretically important because to understand the effects of deprivation is to understand more about development and developmental processes and about learning in general. Consider the following questions: How does deprivation in early childhood affect later mental development and later learning? Are the effects of deprivation reversible? How can remedial programs counteract deprivation effects?

Many years ago Goldfarb (1943) studied the effects of institutional life on children. He was interested in the effect of institutional life, assumed to be a deprivation, on intellectual performance, among other things. He compared the intelligence of adolescent children who had spent their first three years in an institution with the intelligence of children who had not spent their first three years in an institution. He found that the institutional group's average intelligence was substantially lower than the average intelligence of the noninstitutional "control group." He also made a number of comparisons on other variables with similar results.

The weaknesses of the study are obvious and we need not spend much time on them. Our concern is only with its *ex post facto* nature and the consequent relative difficulties in interpreting its results. This study was chosen out of many similar studies because it was cited by Berelson and Steiner (1964) in their encyclopedic book on research on human behavior. Let us assume that the study was done impeccably and examine only its findings as *ex post facto* research.

Is it possible that children who have lived in institutions have lower average intelligence than children who have not lived in institutions because they are more likely to come from parents of lower intelligence? Take another possibility. It is well known that social class status is correlated with intelligence: children of lower-class status tend to have lower measured intelligence than children of middle-class status. Is it not likely that children who have lived in institutions later live in lower-class settings? If so, the observed difference in intelligence might have been due largely to lower-class background, which is less verbally and culturally oriented than middle-class background.[6]

[6] We must try to keep things balanced. Today, a study like Goldfarb's can be much better handled, principally by measuring other possibly influential variables and controlling them statistically. That is, their presumed influence is assessed and either deleted or "subtracted" from the results using well-known statistical methods.

Could this same research have been done experimentally? It is conceivable but hardly possible. A large sample of children can be taken at birth and half of them assigned at random to institutions! The other half will stay with their families. Careful controls will be used. After a period of years the average intelligence of the two groups will be compared. The impossibility of such an experimental procedure with children is apparent. We must, therefore, take things as they are and study them—in an *ex post facto* way. We now examine an experimental approach to the deprivation problem.

For a number of years researchers at the University of California at Berkeley have studied the later effects of deprivation on animals (Bennett, Diamond, Krech, & Rosenzweig, 1964). The unique feature of their researches has been the relatively direct physical examination and measurement of parts of the brain and chemical secretions in the brain. The research must be classed among the few most significant behavioral researches of our time. The sheer technical feat of measuring the presumed effects of deprivation on the physiology of the brain is staggering. The researchers did considerably more than this, however. Only one of their studies is summarized.

Bennett et al. (1964) hypothesized that differential experience very early in animals' lives will lead to quantitative changes in the brain. They used, in one study, three experimental groups of rats: Environmental Complexity and Training (ECT), Isolated Condition (IC), and Social Condition (SC). In ECT, 10 to 12 animals were housed at time of weaning in large cages with "interesting" equipment which they could use and play with. They were also allowed out of the cages each day to explore and play. In IC (isolated), animals were caged singly in a quiet room where they could not see or touch other animals. The control group rats (SC) were kept under the usual colony conditions, three to a cage and exposed to activity in the room, but with no special treatment. (A type of randomization was done in the analysis stage.) The initial study was replicated a number of times, but only the enriched environment (ECT) and the impoverished environment (IC) were used in the replications.

These conditions were maintained for 80 days. The animals were then killed for brain analysis. Samples of various parts of the brain were measured for thickness, weight, and chemical secretion. The anatomists who did the analyses did not know to which experimental groups the animals belonged.

The results were remarkable. There were significant differences in the weights of the cerebral cortex between the enriched and the impoverished environments. The mean weights in milligrams of the total cortex of the rats studied during the period 1960 to 1963 were 700 (ECT) and 669 (IC). The difference was statistically significant. Evidently the enriched experiences altered the weights of the rats' cortices! A "control analysis" of the rest of the brains of the animals showed no significant differences. It is the cerebral cortex that increased in weight relative to the rest of the brain.

The Berkeley researchers measured a certain enzyme in the brains of the animals and found differences between the experimental groups that supported the weight findings. They also measured the thicknesses of the cortices of the rats: the cortices of the enriched-experience rats were about 6 percent thicker than those of the isolated-condition rats.

The experimental evidence thus supported the enriched-environment hypothesis. Tests of alternative hypotheses—age of animals and isolation stress, for example—did not change the findings. There seems to be little doubt that enriched experience has fundamental physical effects on the brain—at least in rats under the Berkeley laboratory conditions. Are these results applicable to human experience and brains? No one knows.[7] For obvious reasons, similar experimental research cannot be done with human subjects. Future technical advances in brain research and technology may make it possible. But until such advances are made, the question cannot be unambiguously answered. Researchers using human beings as subjects and interested in real-life effects like the effects of ghetto environments must do mostly *ex post facto* research in which already developed ghetto and nonghetto individuals are compared on intelligence, aptitude, achievement, and other relevant variables—with the attendant *ex post facto* difficulties.

The above discussion may leave one a bit discouraged. The bases of human knowledge of human behavior, processes, and institutions seem frail. In one way, yes. In another way, no. There is really no need for despair. Quite the contrary. One of the conditions that increases hope is replication. If a study is replicated and the same or similar results are found, our trust and confidence in the results are increased. If the study is again replicated and the same results are obtained, our trust and confidence are greatly increased because the probability of obtaining the same results three times by chance is lower than the probability of obtaining the same results twice.

Another condition that strengthens research findings and our confidence in them is when experimental and nonexperimental results agree. Although it would be difficult to calculate probabilities, there is little doubt that convergence of research evidence—evidence yielded by different approaches and different studies—strengthens the empirical validity of research findings. The experimental example of the effects of deprived environments on the brains of rats and the nonexperimental example of the effects of ghetto environment on the mental development of ghetto children illustrate nicely what is meant. The two kinds of research are very different, perhaps not even directly comparable. But if the results of both seem to indicate that impoverished environments have effects sufficient to

---

[7] It is important to remember that these results say nothing about intelligence or other characteristics. They demonstrate only that enriched and deficient environments have physical effects on the brains of animals. Such findings, however, are fundamental and richly suggestive for research with human beings and for the whole problem of deprivation and its amelioration.

be reliably detected, then faith in the environmental deprivation hypothesis is strengthened.

We have spent much time and space trying to clarify the differences between experimental and *ex post facto* research. We found that the basic logic is the same: both kinds of research pursue the empirical validity of statements of the if *p*, then *q* kind. But we also found that they do it very differently because in *ex post facto* research it is not possible to manipulate independent variables nor to assign subjects and treatments to experimental groups at random. The difference is profound and significant. Other things equal and in general, the conclusions obtained in *ex post facto* research are not on as firm ground as conclusions obtained in experimental research because of the inevitable lesser control of the effects of independent variables and of the research situation. (The lack is sometimes compensated by greater realism and stronger effects, however.)

Many problems in the behavioral sciences are *ex post facto* problems and require *ex post facto* research simply because the independent variables are not manipulable. Researchers whose interest is mainly in the nature of intelligence or the structure of values and attitudes, for instance, must reconcile themselves to nonexperimental research. Does its nonexperimental nature make the research less significant, less scientific? In any case, both kinds of research must and will be done, and the student of science and behavioral research must understand the strengths and weaknesses of both.

ADDENDUM

The position taken in this book is that an experiment requires at least two experimental groups. These two groups may be designated as "experimental" and "control," or A_1 and A_2, or any other convenient way. The two groups are two aspects of some variable. If the variable, for example, is reinforcement, then the two groups might be "regular reinforcement" and "random reinforcement," or "massive reinforcement" and "regular reinforcement," as in the Clark and Walberg study. Naturally, an experiment can have more than two experimental groups. Recall that the Aronson and Mills experiment had three groups. And we learned in Chapter 7 that factorial experiments, in which more than one independent variable is used, are possible and desirable.

The basis of the requirement of at least two experimental groups is highly important. A "true" experiment must have at least one comparison (see Campbell & Stanley, 1963, p. 6). Indeed, in any study there must be at least one comparison. Say that an experimenter wants to enhance problem-solving ability by a special method. He uses the method with a group of students, perhaps his own class, and observes, after he has used the method, that the problem solving of the members of the group has improved. While this procedure is satisfactory for practical demonstrations, it is scientifically inadequate. The reason is the reason labored in this chapter: with only one group there is no assurance that something other than the method of the researcher was at work and helped to improve problem-solving ability.

For example, just teaching the students anything at all about problem solving may have a salutary effect. Or the method used by the researcher may simply have been a good vehicle for his personal style of teaching, and it was his personal style of teaching that helped the problem solving and not the method. Any method that the experimenter as teacher found congenial would work as well. Moreover, it is quite possible that the subjects' problem-solving ability improved as a result of their exposure to the problem. Or, over a period of time, the subjects might have improved with any method; their insight into the various aspects of problem solving may have matured.

It might well have been the method that helped to improve problem solving, but it can never unambiguously be said until at least one other group is used. Then the results obtained with the method should be compared with the results obtained without the method or with another method—with all other conditions the same.

In short, a research design having only one experimental group is always theoretically unsatisfactory. If I tell the researcher that it was not the method that improved the problem solving but rather his own personality and enthusiasm, for which the method acted as a vehicle, what can he say? Nothing! At least nothing convincing. If he had a second experimental group whose members had had all the same conditions as the first group except the method, and the results favored the first group, then the researcher is in a strong position to answer me. He can say, "No, it was not my personality and enthusiasm because I also taught the second group and I tried to teach in precisely the same way as I did with the first group. Therefore the difference in results between the groups must have been due to the method."

Although the argument still has weaknesses, it is much stronger than it was. Virtually all scientific conclusions, then, require comparisons. The function of the comparisons is to isolate the effect of the crucial independent variable, so to speak. This means, essentially, to show that some other influence did not produce the observed effect; only the hypothesized influence produced it.

Despite this obvious requirement to strengthen inference, there is a considerable body of research in which, in effect, only one group is used. In some research on reinforcement, for example, the effects of reinforcement are assessed by reinforcing one group of animals. The responses of the animals are observed to assess the effect of the reinforcement. In some research on memory, a stimulus like illumination may be varied, and the effects of the variations on the same subjects' retention of letters may be measured. It is not claimed here that such research is incorrect. One of the important methods of science, for example, is to ascertain functions (mathematical equations) that express the precise relations between stimuli and responses. And in reinforcement research on animals, it can hardly be disputed that it is the reinforcement—some sort of food, for instance—that produces the responses. There is little danger of confusion about the effective independent variable. Most other research in the behavioral sciences, however, is not so simple and easily controlled.

The Milgram studies described in this chapter come close to the edge of the definition of experiment. Note that all the experimental subjects in any one "experiment" received the same treatment: they were all given the same instructions to administer shocks. The satisfaction of the definition of an experiment, therefore, was not provided by the basic experimental situation but by the variations introduced: the experimenter present or not present; doing the experiment in a location other than Yale University; remoteness of the teacher to the learner.

The point of this addendum is that the basic definition and meaning of the word "experiment" are not the only definitions and meanings of the word in use. The position taken in this book, however, is that at least one comparison is necessary—that is, a minimum of two experimental groups—for an experiment to be a "true" experiment. This does not necessarily rule out the possible adequacy of more limited definitions in some situations. It simply sets what is believed to be an adequate standard for inferences to be made from experimental data.

$\mathbf{9}$

Observation and the measurement of variables

Scientists "observe" phenomena; they "make observations." What does it mean to say "make observations"? The expression is vague. Does it mean that the behavioral scientist looks at people and what they do, forms impressions of their behavior, and then concludes something about the behavior observed? Yes and no. When it is said that scientists make observations it means basically that they measure variables, or gather the information necessary to measure variables. There must, of course, be more to it—subjective impressions, hunches, insights—but basically the purposing of observing anything in science is to measure it. And it is measured so that it can be related to other variables.

An experimenter manipulates an independent variable, say reinforcement, by giving the members of three experimental groups three kinds of reinforcement in order "to observe" their different effects on memory. The observations in this case are of behavior that can be assumed to reflect memory. The purpose of the observations is to obtain measures of the dependent variable memory so that the experimenter can quantitatively assess the effects of the different reinforcements. The experimenter may "observe" that the memories of the three groups are different, a sort of subjective feeling or hunch. Such feelings and hunches are important in science but they are not enough. We have to know *how much* memory, how much of anything.

A researcher doing nonexperimental work is ordinarily faced with "observing" two or more variables: almost always at least one dependent variable and often one or more independent variables. Consider a problem of the presumed effects of role conflict on performance effectiveness of role-related activities. Getzels and Guba (1954), in a study of military officers and their role performance, predicted that the greater the conflict officers experienced, the less effective their role performance, in this case as teachers. They also predicted that career military officers would experience greater conflict when they had to be teachers for a period of time than would noncareer officers (because advancement of military officers depends more on command functions than on teaching functions). They would therefore be less effective as teachers than noncareer officers.

Getzels and Guba measured the conflict of the officers with a special scale constructed for the purpose. They also checked the validity of the scale by comparing the average scores of Air Force schools differing in degree of involvement with military matters. As predicted, the more military the school, the less the conflict, and vice versa. They also had to "observe" teaching performance and effectiveness. This was done by having teaching officers rate each other for effectiveness. In other words, Getzels and Guba "observed" conflict and teaching effectiveness. What they actually did, in other words, was to "measure" both variables. What does this mean?

MEASUREMENT

Measurement is the assignment of numerals to objects or events according to rules (Stevens, 1951). This is an excellent example of a powerful definition, in the sense that it is simple, general, and unambiguous. If you want to measure something, make up a set of rules that specifies how to assign numerals to objects. Like all general definitions, this one says nothing about the quality or virtue of any particular measurement procedure or instrument. A test or scale (see Chapter 2) can be good or bad. If it enables one to assign numerals to defined objects systematically, then it is measurement. This point is here stressed because the distinction between what measurement is and the quality of measurement instruments has been blurred in some discussions of psychological measurement. Because some measurement instruments have been questionable does not mean that all are, or that all psychological measurement is questionable.

To understand the definition of measurement recall the discussion of sets, variables, and relations in Chapters 2 and 4. A "relation" was defined as a set of ordered pairs, in which the symbols or numbers of one set were systematically paired with the symbols or numbers of another set. (See Figures 4.1, 4.2, 4.3, and 4.4.) The definition of measurement implies relations. That is, a measurement procedure is always a relation, with the objects (persons or groups, for instance) being measured coming first and the numerals used in the measurement coming second. To make all this concrete, let's revive an example used in Chapter 4 in which two variables, *discrimination* and *violence,* were related.

Measuring Discrimination

To study this relation, a researcher has to "observe" both discrimination and violence, the former being the independent variable and the latter the dependent variable. He is testing the hypothesis that those groups discriminated against in a society will exhibit violence. Moreover, the greater the discrimination, the greater the violence. To observe the two variables and to study the relation, he must measure the variables. This means that he must assign to different groups in a society different numbers, the different numbers reflecting different degrees of discrimination and violence.[1] How can he do this?

Take just one of the variables, discrimination. Suppose the researcher asks three sociologists who are specialists in prejudice and minorities to rate on a seven-point scale the general degree of discrimination suffered at the present time by seven groups. (He includes English as an anchor or comparison group, assuming that English people or people of English extraction have suffered the least discrimination.) The average ratings of the three experts of the seven groups are given in Figure 9.1 in a diagram such as was used earlier to exemplify relations.[2] The values of Figure 9.1 indicate that the judges believed that blacks suffered the most discrimination (6.1), American Indians the next most (5.7), down through the English who, as expected, were judged to suffer the least discrimination (1.3).

The figure represents a relation because there is a set of ordered pairs. It is also measurement since numbers (average ratings) have been assigned to objects (groups) according to rules. The rules included specification of the choice of expert judges or raters, the number scale used, 1 through 7, and the variable measured, discrimination. Is this "good" measurement? We do not yet know; it may or may not be.

In Chapter 4, rankings were used instead of ratings. While this changes the nature of the measurement procedure, particularly the numbers used to assign to the objects, it represents no change in the conception of measurement as numerals assigned to objects according to rules. It may be profitable to examine another example of measurement before continuing the discussion.

---

[1] The distinction between a numeral and a number is important. A *numeral* is a symbol of the form: 1, 2, 3, . . . , or I, II, III, . . . It has no quantitative meaning unless it is given such meaning; it is only a symbol that can be used to label objects. When a numeral is given quantitative meaning, as, for example, in the averages used in Figure 9.1, it becomes a number.

[2] This example is loosely modeled after a famous study of stereotypes by Katz and Braly (1935).

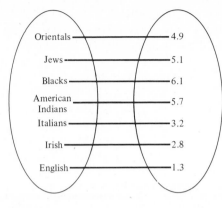

FIG. 9.1

Measuring Intelligence

There is hardly anything more controversial in contemporary behavioral research than the measurement of intelligence. Some have labeled it a great achievement, one of the greatest of our times. (I agree with this assessment.) Some critics, however, have damned it for not really measuring intelligence, sometimes claiming that intelligence itself cannot be measured, or for having evil and pernicious effects on children, especially minority group children. Although this is not the place to examine the whole controversy, perhaps it will be possible to clarify at least its measurement aspect.

"Intelligence" is, of course, a highly abstract concept or construct. Thus measurement of it is not easy. Before it can be measured, it will be necessary, first, to agree on some operational definition of intelligence. (It will be extremely difficult, perhaps impossible, however, to get even experts to agree on an operational definition.) Recall that an operational definition spells out the activity of the researcher in measuring a variable. Intelligence can clearly be a variable since a variable is a symbol to which numerals are assigned. (See Chapters 2 and 3, and note the similarity of the definitions of "variable" and "measurement.") "Intelligence" is the symbol.

One can think of different ways to measure intelligence. We can ask experts to observe a group of individuals and to assign ratings to the individuals corresponding to the perceived amounts of their intelligence. Or, more likely, we can use a well-accepted and well-tested test of intelligence, for example the famous Stanford-Binet test. Such a test and the instructions that go with it constitute an operational definition of intelligence. The numbers yielded by the test—called intelligence quotients, or IQ's, with some tests—will be assigned to the individuals and will presumably reflect the different magnitudes of their intelligence. Turn back to

Figure 4.2, in which five individuals, Marie, Jacob, and so on, were assigned numbers that were intelligence test scores: 131, 127, and so on. In Chapter 4, we were illustrating a relation. But the figure also represents measurement.

There is little doubt that some measures of intelligence are not adequate. There is also little doubt that even the best measures of intelligence are not valid in some situations. For example, if several members of a group of individuals whose intelligence is being measured happen to be ill during the test, doubt is cast on the results of the measurement. Or if a group of children has been raised in a remote place where there has been little cultural stimulation, the usual measures of intelligence will not be valid in the sense of measuring the children's "actual" intelligence. (It will, however, probably be valid as a measure of what is called their "functional intelligence," which means their ability to cope with middle-class American environment.) This does not mean, however, that measuring intelligence is not really measurement or that intelligence cannot be measured. Indeed, it is more or less agreed by many psychologists that intelligence can and has been measured with great success.

RELIABILITY

Study the numbers in Table 9.1 carefully. They are supposed to be the results of a judging or rating task given to four judges, who were told to rate each of five office managers on their competence in managing a set of assigned administrative tasks. The five managers were each observed by four judges. The judges used a seven-point rating scale, 6 meaning very high competence and 0 meaning very low competence. One of the first questions we ask of any measurement procedure is, How reliable is it?

Definition and Nature of Reliability

In common-sense terms, reliability means stability, predictability, dependability, consistency. The reliable person is one we can depend on; we can predict what he or she will do. An unreliable person is one whose behavior we cannot predict, a person on whom we cannot depend. His

TABLE 9.1   Data on Ratings by Four Judges of Five Persons' Competence, High Reliability

| | JUDGES | | | | | |
PERSONS	a	b	c	d	SUM	MEAN
1	6	6	5	4	21	5.25
2	4	6	4	3	17	4.25
3	4	4	5	2	15	3.75
4	3	1	3	1	8	2.00
5	1	2	2	0	5	1.25

behavior fluctuates a good deal, and it fluctuates rather unpredictably. We say that such a person is "not reliable." The predictable person, on the other hand, we say is "reliable."

Part of the essence of reliability is thus variability. In general, if someone's performance varies a great deal from time to time, we categorize it as unreliable. It is unpredictably variable, in other words. We don't know what to expect.

Another way to express reliability and unreliability is with the words "accuracy" or "precision." If someone has a gun, he wants it to be accurate; it must hit a target whenever it is shot—assuming, of course, a good shot is firing it. In this case, we can talk about the reliability of the gun and the reliability of the person firing it. We are interested mostly in the former.

A test is like a gun in its purpose. When we measure human attributes and abilities and achievements, we want to measure the "true" amounts of attributes that individuals possess. This is like hitting a target with a gun. With a test we want to hit the attribute. If a gun consistently hits a target—the shots cluster close together at or near the center of the target; they are not spread all over—we say it is reliable. Similarly with psychological and sociological measures. If they hit the target, they are reliable. But what does it mean for a test to "hit a target"?

In modern test theory it is assumed that each individual being measured on some variable has a "true score" on the variable. Since no one can ever know what any individual's true score is, the following reasoning is used. If a tester were able to measure the same person with the same test a very large number of times, and the average of all the scores on all the trials were calculated, this average would be an estimate of the true score. But an individual is usually tested only once. How can we know or even estimate what the true score is? We can't, but an estimate of the reliability of a test can be had through certain statistical procedures, which use the scores of a number of individuals to provide statistical estimates.

Reliable and Unreliable Measurement: Two Examples

Now, return to the data of Table 9.1. We want to know how reliable the judges' ratings of the office managers' competence are. They happen to be very high in this contrived example. Each of the four judges produced approximately the same rank order for the five managers. Remember that we want an estimate of the competence of each of the managers. We are not really interested in the judges. Their function is to increase the reliability of the overall ratings of the managers, as well as to rate them. If we add the ratings across each row, and then calculate the means of the ratings of each person (for example, for person 1: $(6 + 6 + 5 + 4)/4 = 21/4 = 5.25$), we have a set of average ratings for each person. We ask: How close are these averages to the "true scores" or "true ratings" of competence of each individual? It is possible only to get an approximate answer.

This approximate way to determine the reliability of the ratings is based on all the ratings and all the averages calculated from the four judges' ratings. If the individuals being rated differ in competence—if individuals do not differ in whatever is being measured, reliability cannot really be estimated—then the means in the column labeled "Mean" should differ. The more they differ, the greater the reliability. If the measurement procedure is a good one, then the same approximate rank order of average ratings should appear on subsequent measurements, assuming that the judges are expert and competent. Notice that the rank orders of the five individuals tend to be the same with each judge. For example, the scores of judges a and b of the five persons tend to go together: high ratings are given to individual 1 (6 and 6) and low ratings to individual 5 (1 and 2). The ratings of individuals 2, 3, and 4 are not inconsistent with these extreme ratings.

Similarly, if we examine the ratings of judges c and d, we find again general correspondence in the ratings. Such agreement will produce average ratings (column labeled "Mean") that clearly differ from each other, provided, of course, the individuals do actually differ from each other in competence. The greater these differences, the higher the reliability, other things equal.

No doubt the reader is still a little mystified. So let's make up a highly contrasting situation. Suppose the whole judging procedure was not at all reliable. Suppose the judges did not know how to rate competence and, moreover, they were careless. Such a situation would almost certainly produce a set of ratings of low reliability. An example is given in Table 9.2. The numbers (ratings) in the table are random numbers generated by a programmable calculator.

If we can know why this set of ratings is unreliable and why the set of Table 9.1 is reliable, we will be a long way along toward understanding reliability. First, study the individual columns. We know that the five individuals differ in competence—a safe assumption: most people differ in almost anything. The ratings should be different. If the judges are expert at judging competence, then their ratings should be more or less the same. That is, their ratings of the same individual should agree approximately. It is difficult or impossible to find much agreement in Table 9.2. It is as

TABLE 9.2   Data on Ratings by Four Judges of Five
Individuals' Competence, Low Reliability

| | JUDGES | | | | | |
PERSONS	a	b	c	d	SUM	MEAN
1	2	5	6	1	14	3.50
2	5	2	6	4	17	4.25
3	2	3	1	5	11	2.75
4	3	1	3	2	9	2.25
5	6	3	4	4	17	4.25

TABLE 9.3   Means of Persons Taken from Tables 9.1 and 9.2

PERSONS	HIGH RELIABILITY (TABLE 9.1)	PERSONS	LOW RELIABILITY[a] (TABLE 9.2)
1	5.25	2	4.25
2	4.25	5	4.25
3	3.75	1	3.50
4	2.00	3	2.75
5	1.25	4	2.25

[a] The means of Table 9.2 have been rearranged in rank order of size to emphasize the difference between the two sets of ratings.

though the judges made judgments of four unrelated characteristics. Or, closer to the truth, it is as though they made their judgments at random.

Now look at the ratings of Table 9.1. There is general agreement among the four sets of ratings, as pointed out earlier. If judge a gives person 1 a high rating, so do judges b, c, and d—and similarly for the four judges on lower ratings. There is, in other words, high agreement among the judges. To the extent that the ratings agree, to that extent the set of ratings is reliable.

Another and perhaps more subtle difference between the two tables is in the means of the persons. (The means of the items, while important in some situations, are not so important here. They do not in general affect reliability as much as the means of the persons.) The two sets of means have been reproduced in Table 9.3. The first difference to note is that the means of 9.1 are more variable than the means of 9.2. The ranges, which are crude indices of variability, are $5.25 - 1.25 = 4$, for 9.1, and $4.25 - 2.25 = 2$, for 9.2. Since the ratings of 9.2 were really random numbers, then the five means of 9.2 should be pretty much the same. (Why?) The range would, of course, reflect this lack of variability.

Turn back and examine Table 5.1, a set of 100 numbers arranged in groups of 10. Examine the means given in Tables 5.2 and 5.3, also calculated from random numbers. Skim through the discussions of the three tables. Note, in Table 5.1, that the 10 means are rather alike. The chance expectation is 4.56, the total mean. Since the 10 means are means of random numbers, they should be rather near this chance expectation. Random numbers are by definition not reliable. They are numbers without system or regularity, and reliability means, among other things, that the numbers are systematic; they exhibit regularity.

One definition of reliability is through the back door: Reliability is lack of "error" in a set of measures. The "error" here means, in effect, random or chance fluctuations. "Error" is the variability, the fluctuations, of the measures not due to whatever is being measured. To the extent that a set of measures has such variability, to that extent it is not reliable. (Such variability should not be confused with the variability of individuals discussed earlier, a variability that reflects differences among individuals. See below.) The random numbers, of course, reflect only such back-and-forth, up-and-down, nonsystematic variability.

The means of the five experts, "Experimental Group," Table 5.2, are much like the means of Table 9.3, "Low Reliability." They are not too different. They shouldn't be: they were calculated from random numbers. Similarly, the means of Table 5.3 are not too dissimilar. But the means of Table 9.3, "High Reliability," differ about as much as they can, if one realizes that means are always less variable than the numbers from which they are calculated. The greater range presumably more *accurately* reflects the individual differences in competence of the five persons whose competence is being measured. If the means resemble means calculated from random numbers, then, they will probably be like each other; they will not differ much. If we obtain numbers in a real measurement situation that resemble such random numbers, then their reliability will be low. They cannot accurately reflect whatever individual differences there are in the persons being measured.

A somewhat easier, though incomplete, way to think of reliability is as *stability*. Suppose the four judges rated the five managers for competence a second time, say two months later. Assuming that nothing has happened during the two months to change the managers' competence, the average ratings the managers receive should be approximately the same the second time as the first time. To the extent that they are the same, to that extent the scores are reliable. To the extent that the ratings from the two times differ, to that extent the scores are not reliable. If one calculated some sort of index that reflected the similarity of the two sets of scores, this index would be called a reliability coefficient. When such indices are calculated and reported in the literature, they are called repeat reliability coefficients.

One can also calculate reliability coefficients from the data of Tables 9.1 and 9.2. They are called internal consistency coefficients. The two coefficients for Tables 9.1 and 9.2 are .94 and .01. Reliability coefficients like these vary from 0 to 1.00, 0 indicating very low reliability ("no" reliability) and 1.00 indicating perfect reliability. The ratings of Table 9.1, then, are highly reliable, while those of Table 9.2 are not at all reliable.

The example used to illustrate reliability has used ratings because they are probably easier to understand than had we used a test and test items. The same reasoning, however, applies to tests. Just replace "judges" with "items." The persons being rated are the same; the only difference is that they are now "tested" instead of being "rated." That is, any test or scale consists of a certain number of items, and these items are each supposed to measure the same thing, just as the judges were supposed to rate or measure the same thing. For instance, suppose you are measuring authoritarianism. You might use the well-known F Scale. Here are two of the items (Adorno et al., 1950, pp. 255–257):

Obedience and respect for authority are the most important virtues children should learn.

Science has its place, but there are many important things that can never possibly be understood by the human mind.

Subjects respond to these items on a scale of agreement-disagreement. The more they agree, the more authoritarian they are presumed to be.

Many more than two items are used. (In general, the more items, the greater the reliability, provided the items all measure the same thing and measure it equally well.) If the two items just given measure the same thing, then they should yield approximately the same rank order of individuals. If they do, then the two-item scale is reliable. If they do not, it is not reliable. The same reasoning is extended to the many items of a test or scale. If we had 40 items on an intelligence test, then each of the items is a "judge": it will yield similar rank orders of intelligence among individuals.[3]

Why Is Reliability Important?

Before they are anything else, measures of variables must be reliable. We must know, for instance, that we are accurately measuring competence, because of what use is it to measure a variable if we do not come close to the "true" scores of the individuals (or objects) being measured? That is one of the main reasons for doing the measuring. We must be able to trust the scores. We must know, for instance, that if we measured the competence or creativity or dominance or intelligence of a group of individuals, we will get the same or similar scores on a subsequent measurement of the same individuals. This means, among other things, that we will get the same or similar rank orders of the scores.

Conceive of the relation between two variables, intelligence and competence. We want to know, say, what role intelligence plays in a certain kind of competence. If one or both of the measures of intelligence and competence are not reliable, then it is not possible to determine accurately how they are related—or "correlated," as it is said. The magnitude of the relation may be high, but if one or both of the measures are not reliable, the calculated relation will be low simply because of lack of reliability. If we accept the calculated magnitude of the relation at face value, we will be led seriously astray. Suppose the magnitude of the relation was really high, but the measure of competence was not reliable and we did not know it was not reliable. We might believe that the relation between intelligence and competence was low or even zero. We might then conclude that intelligence had little to do with the sort of competence we were trying to measure. Such a conclusion would, of course, be very much in error.

[3] Note, however, that individual items are much less reliable than whole tests. Nevertheless, items of relatively low reliability can, when used in sufficient numbers, produce a reliable test or scale. It is this useful feature or principle that makes reliable tests of human characteristics possible.

Similarly, in the practical use of measures of variables, reliability is an indispensable feature of measurement. Of what use is an intelligence test of children that is not reliable? Of what use is a measure of attitudes toward minority groups if it is not reliable? If tests and scales are not reliable, then the predictions we make with them—and they are predictive instruments as well as measures of variables—are useless, or worse than useless because they can lead us astray in our conclusions about the abilities and attributes of the individuals we are measuring, as well as about the relations among the abilities and attributes.

VALIDITY

Reliability is virtually a solved problem. The theory of the reliability of psychological and sociological measurement instruments is well developed and widely understood.[4] Principles of practice and how to put the principles into practice are also well understood. Psychologists and sociologists know how to construct measurement instruments of substantial reliability. They know, for example, that when a test or scale is too short it will probably be unreliable, that items must be written unambiguously (except for special purposes), and that there must be an adequate range of stimuli to capture the usually great range of human attributes. Many years ago, there was some excuse for a research study either to have one or more instruments of low reliability or not to say anything about reliability. Those days are gone, even though remnants of poor practice remain. There is no longer any excuse for low reliability. It is, in short, a largely solved theoretical and practical problem.

This is unfortunately not so with validity, which poses much deeper and more difficult problems than does reliability, partly because validity ideas are relatively new and partly because validity is a much more complex problem. Psychologists and sociologists were hardly aware of validity in earlier years. Fortunately, attention has lately been strongly focused on this most important aspect of measurement and behavioral science problems, and an excellent start toward understanding, if not practical mastery, has been made.

Definition and Nature of Validity

Validity is often defined by asking the question: Are you measuring what you think you are measuring? If so, your measure is valid; if not, it is not valid. The emphasis here is on *what* is being measured. Suppose a group of teachers of social studies writes a test to measure students' understanding of certain social concepts: justice, equality, and cooperation, for instance. The teachers want to know whether their students understand and can apply the ideas. But they write a test of only factual items about

[4] For excellent discussions see Guilford (1954) or Nunnally (1967).

contemporary institutions. The test is then not valid for the purpose they had in mind. It may be a good test of *factual knowledge,* but it does not measure *understanding* of social concepts. For a test to be valid, in the most elementary and perhaps fundamental meaning of the word, it must measure what the test-maker wants to measure and thinks he is measuring.

There is more than one kind of validity. Although we cannot go deeply into the different kinds and definitions of validity in this book, we must try to survey the major definitions because they will help us understand the general scientific approach to the observation of behavior and the measurement of variables. This understanding, in turn, will give us a better foundation for assessing some of the fundamental measurement controversies that plague both scientists and nonscientists.

Kinds of Validity

Sometimes researchers and practitioners use tests only to predict future performance. In fact, this is probably the most frequent use of tests. School authorities, for example, want to know the abilities and aptitudes of children in order to predict their later performance and achievement. The emphasis in such use of tests in schools and elsewhere is more on this prediction of present and future ability and performance than it is on measuring variables. While what the tests measure is of interest, of course, it is not of central interest. The main thing is that the test successfully measures what has been found to be essential to successful performance in school or on the job. It has even been said that if a test predicts to some criterion successfully, it doesn't matter what it measures! In any case, a test is conceived as valid if it predicts successfully to some criterion. Such validity used to be called *predictive validity;* more recently it has been named *criterion-related validity*.

Another form of validity is called *content validity,* which is directed at the substance, or the content, of what is being measured. If the teachers who wrote the test to measure understanding of social concepts were to ask colleagues whether, after study of the test, they thought that it really did measure understanding of social concepts, they would be asking a content validity question. Content validity is thus closely related to the question: Are you measuring what you think you are measuring?

A third kind of validity, called *construct validity,* is probably the most significant and important, at least from the point of view of this book. When researchers inquire into the construct validity of a measure, they are most interested in the psychological or other property or properties the instrument measures. They are interested in the variable under consideration, or perhaps more accurately, the construct or constructs underlying the variable. Criterion-related and content validities are comparatively easy to understand. Construct validity is not because it is embedded in much of the scientific framework of research and its methodology. As usual, an example may help clarify what is meant.

Measuring Dogmatism

The F Scale, mentioned earlier, purports to measure authoritarianism. It was constructed on the basis of rather complex social psychological and psychoanalytic theory. There has been much discussion of the validity of the scale, which is also discussion of the validity of the theory behind the scale. This discussion has really been of the construct validity of the scale.

Rokeach (1960), disputing to some extent the validity of the F Scale as a measure of authoritarianism, constructed his own scale, the D Scale, to measure dogmatism. He too used involved theoretical reasoning. One of his criticisms of the F Scale was that it measured only authoritarianism of the right, only fascistic tendencies. (The "F" of the F Scale stands for "Fascism.") Thus it is limited if indeed it omits measurement of authoritarianism of the left. Its validity as a general measure of authoritarianism is therefore questionable. With his D Scale Rokeach hoped to measure dogmatism, which includes authoritarianism of both the right and the left.

The D Scale consists of a number of items that Rokeach believed would measure closed-mindedness, a way of thinking associated with an ideology regardless of content. Central to his thinking is the idea that the ideological orientations of individuals are related to their personalities, behaviors, and thought processes. (This idea was also in the minds of the authors of the F Scale.) Two examples among the many that can be given are that dogmatism is related to intolerance and to opinionation. Rokeach did a series of investigations aimed at testing both his ideas and the validity of his scales.

For example, one of the ways often used to validate tests and scales is the *known-groups method*. In this method groups of people with "known" characteristics are administered an instrument and the differences between the groups predicted. We encountered this method in Chapter 8 when we examined Rokeach's study of the differences among policemen, unemployed whites, unemployed blacks, and Calvinist students in their responses to the social ideas of freedom and equality. Rokeach, as hinted above, believed that the core of dogmatism was closed-mindedness. Therefore, he had professors and graduate students select graduate students and friends whom they believed to be open-minded and closed-minded. The D Scale successfully differentiated the two groups. He also administered the scale to different religious groups; the results generally supported his reasoning. Still another test of the scale's validity was Rokeach's study of the relation between dogmatism and problem solving in situations different from any encountered in everyday life. Again, his ideas were supported.

In other words, Rokeach's efforts were directed both toward the theory behind the D Scale and the properties of the scale, a clear example of construct validation. "Construct validation" is perhaps a more accurate expression than "construct validity" to express what is involved. The researcher tries in varied ways to bring evidence to bear on the theory behind a measure as well as on the measure. It is a divergent and convergent process in which deductions from the theory are tested in different ways with the idea that the evidence from the different tests will all converge on the validity of the measure. Construct validation, then, is of the essence of science itself in its testing of deductions and implications derived from theory. It is a major achievement in measurement and in behavioral research, an achievement that is revolutionizing psychological and sociological measurement.[5]

MEASUREMENT IN PERSPECTIVE

Measurement can be the Achilles' heel of behavioral research. Too often investigations are carefully planned and executed with too little attention paid to the measurement of the variables of the research. Here is an interesting case history demonstrating a lack of adequate concern for reliability. A researcher planned an elaborate set of experiments to test a theory of attitudes. The chain of reasoning from the experimental implications of the theory seemed valid. If it is true, as the theory predicts, that if such-and-such is so, then so-and-so will happen. The experimental procedure was carefully planned and executed to test the deductions. Specific statistical predictions were made about differences between experimental groups. None of the predictions came out as predicted! Indeed, virtually no differences were statistically significant. The set of experiments was a complete failure. It was as though the numbers analyzed were random numbers. Why? Because the theory was faulty? Because the experiment was badly handled? Because the subjects were poorly chosen?

The real reason appeared to be the measurement of the dependent variable. The researcher had spent much of his professional life telling students that in order to measure a variable adequately, one has to use a number of items to measure the variable. To depend on one or two items, as many researchers do, is folly because it is well known and can be easily demonstrated that one or two items simply will not be reliable enough to justify their use. If an experiment is done and the dependent variable is measured with only one or two items, the probability is high that even if significant differences between groups exist, they will not be detected simply because the measure of the dependent variable is not reliable enough to pick up the differences! In this experiment, however, the researcher used only one item to measure the dependent variable! If there were actual differences between the experimental groups, as predicted, they did not have much chance of being detected.[6]

[5] The first real breakthrough probably came from an article by Cronbach and Meehl (1955) in which the basic ideas behind construct validity were elaborated. Construct validity has been officially recognized as a central kind of validity by the American Psychological Association in its manual on tests and testing (American Psychological Association, 1966).

[6] The researcher was the author of this book.

All fields of human effort have their shares of mythology and nonsense. Measurement is unfortunately particularly burdened with both. Negative attitudes toward psychological measurement are part of the cause. But ignorance and misunderstanding are probably a greater part. One of the core difficulties seems to be that the basic purpose of measurement in science is misunderstood. It is believed that psychologists, for example, measure people, and that you can't measure people. It is true that you can't measure people. But scientists do not really measure people, nor do they say they do (or they should not say they do). They measure variables, just as in experiments they do not manipulate people but variables. They *do* measure the behavior of people, the observable indicants of hypothetical constructs like intelligence and dogmatism. No one can measure intelligence directly. "Intelligence" is a construct used to epitomize an unbelievably complex set of behaviors that have the common characteristic of being "intelligent." To believe that psychologists measure people, then, is naive. To criticize measurement because it doesn't measure people is also naive.

Indeed, the whole measurement procedure, even of relatively "simple" variables, is highly indirect, complex, and often difficult. In view of these difficulties, the success of behavioral scientists in measuring behavioral variables is remarkable. And it *has* been a success, despite the critics who claim that it has been a failure. Here are some variables that have been successfully measured: intelligence, aptitudes (verbal, numerical, and so on), attitudes (toward a variety of objects), introversion, cohesiveness (of groups), needs, social class, authoritarianism, dogmatism. Many more can be named. This does not mean that the measurement of such variables has been perfect, or ever will be perfect. On the contrary, it has been ridden with difficulties, the greatest of which is, of course, validity. But scientists, especially psychologists, know the limitations and the difficulties and are usually quite cautious in their assessment and use of tests and scales and their results.[7]

Like anything else, tests and measures must be used with caution and discretion. When we talk about measurement in the behavioral sciences, we are at quite a different level than when we talk about measurement in the natural sciences. We must always be very careful to ascertain the reliability and validity of our measures. And we must realize that so-called errors of measurement play an unfortunately large part in our measures. In the natural sciences, there are far fewer problems of reliability; a high

---

[7] One of the interesting points about much criticism of measurement, especially psychological measurement, is that critics criticize in a way that seems to say that psychologists do not know the difficulties and weaknesses of psychological tests and scales. Critics say, for instance, that tests cannot measure human beings and their complexity, that "real intelligence" or "real creativity" cannot be measured, and that psychological measurement cannot in general be trusted. The statements imply that psychologists are not aware of the difficulties and that it is hopeless even to think of measuring people's behavior and characteristics. The facts are usually quite otherwise.

degree of precision and accuracy is usually attained with the help of powerful measurement instruments. Validity is more of a problem, but not nearly the problem it is with variables like intelligence, home background, school atmosphere, attitudes toward foreigners, creativity, and the like. Nevertheless, measurement is measurement in the natural sciences and in the behavioral sciences. The basic definition and general procedures are the same. It is no less legitimate and scientific to measure the attitudes and opinions of people, for example, than it is to measure the circumference of the earth or the force of earthquakes. If there are variables, they are potentially measurable, even though degrees of precision, accuracy, and validity vary widely.

10

Sociological inquiry, survey research, and frequency analysis

In our preoccupation with fundamental issues of behavioral research, we have neglected a number of topics that a complete study would have to include. Two or three of these topics—types of research and methods of observation, for example—will be discussed in the Appendix. We must consider now, however, a highly important form of behavioral inquiry and a common and important kind of analysis. For want of better rubrics, we call the form of inquiry "sociological inquiry" and the type of analysis "frequency analysis."

SOCIOLOGICAL INQUIRY

As used in this chapter, "sociological inquiry" is a broad term that means a set of related forms of nonexperimental inquiry directed toward the study of relations among "social variables." Sociological inquiry, as here used, is done mostly but not exclusively by sociologists and includes a range of variables characterized by their social orientation: social class status, political preference, religious preference, association membership, education, income, occupation, race, sex, and so on. These "social variables" are attributes of individuals (or groups) that have the common characteristic of membership in large and small social groups and thus of being shared by many or most individuals. For example, all of us have occupations, income, sex, religious preference, and the like, and they spring, at least in part, from our various group memberships. They are the basic stuff of much sociological inquiry.

I do not mean to imply that sociologists use only these variables and that psychologists or economists do not use them. Indeed, in recent years sociologists have been more and more using "psychological variables" and psychologists have been using "sociological variables"—and that is as it should be. I am using the terms "sociological inquiry" and "social variables" partly for convenience and partly because they reflect research reality. Another reason is that we have to direct ourselves to a large body of varied research studies that seem to have the common characteristics of using sociological variables, being nonexperimental, often being directed toward important social problems, and using a related set of analytic techniques. Many of these researches have been called "survey research" or "field studies."

To be more concrete, here are summaries of four sociological inquiries. That they may include "psychological variables" does not change their basically sociological nature.

Stouffer Study: Tolerance and Intolerance

In this large and important study Stouffer (1955) asked questions about, among other things, tolerance and so-called correlates of tolerance.[1] To obtain answers to the questions, Stouffer interviewed two random samples of the people of the United States. (Interviewing is a powerful form of obtaining information that is used a great deal in sociological inquiry.) One of the questions he asked was aimed at the relation between tolerance and community leadership. Put somewhat differently, the question was aimed at studying the difference in tolerance between leaders and ordinary citizens. The question asked was: "If a person wanted to make a speech in your community against churches and religions, should he be allowed to speak or not?" Part of the data obtained in one of the national samples is given in Table 10.1.

The answers to Stouffer's question seem clear, if we read the table correctly. There is a relation between position in the community and tolerance: community leaders seem to be considerably more tolerant than average citizens: 66 percent of the leaders said Yes, permit the speech, but only 37 percent of the average citizens said Yes. (Note that the Yes percentages, the No percentages, and the No Opinion percentages add, in each row, to 100 percent.)

---

[1] "Correlates" are variables that are related to other variables of interest, and that are usually used to "explain" a variable or variables of interest. For instance, researchers may be interested in voting behavior. To try to understand voting behavior, they study the religious preferences, political preferences, sex, and social-class status of, say, voters in an important election. In other words, they relate these sociological variables, or "correlates," to how people vote.

TABLE 10.1   Responses to Question on Tolerance of Religious
Nonconformity, Stouffer (1955) Study[a]

	RESPONSE		
	Yes	No Opinion	No
Community Leaders	66%	1%	33%
National Cross-Section	37%	3%	60%

[a] These data were obtained by the American Institute of Public Opinion. They are given in the form of percentages.

Miller and Swanson Revisited

In Chapter 1 a study of the relation between social class membership and type of upbringing of children was cited (Miller & Swanson, 1960). One of the specific relations studied was between social-class membership of parents and time of weaning of children. Miller and Swanson interviewed 103 middle-class and working-class mothers in Detroit. They asked the mothers, in one part of their study, when they had weaned their children. The responses of the mothers, already given in Table 1.1, are reproduced here in Table 10.2. In this table, both the frequencies of the responses and the percentages, calculated across the rows, are given.

The relation between the two variables is evident. In fact, the percentages are quite similar in their magnitudes to the Stouffer percentages.[2] Middle-class mothers of this sample weaned their children at an earlier age than working-class mothers. (See discussion in Chapter 1 for more details.)

TABLE 10.2   Social Class and Time of Weaning, Miller and
Swanson (1960) Study (Reproduction of Table 1.1)[a]

SOCIAL CLASS	WEANING		
	Early	Late	
Middle Class	33 (60%)	22 (40%)	55
Working Class	17 (35%)	31 (65%)	48
	50	53	103

[a] The main cell entries are frequencies; the entries in parentheses are percentages calculated across rows. See footnote a, Table 1.1.

---

[2] Percentages are often used in tables like these because they "transform" the frequencies of the two rows to a comparable scale based on 100. Since the sums of the row frequencies, 55 and 48, are unequal, it is more difficult to "see" the relation merely by studying the frequencies. When the frequencies are transformed to percentages, however, the relation becomes clearer. The more the sums of the row and column frequencies differ, the more useful the percentage transformation becomes. We will discuss some of these matters later. See Kerlinger (1973, Ch. 10) on the principles and practice of constructing and interpreting such tables and analyses.

People-Oriented Values and Occupational Choice

Some years ago teachers used to leave teaching, thus causing difficult staffing problems in many school districts. Why did they leave teaching? (The past tense is used because it is presumed, but, of course, may not be true, that teachers do not leave teaching as often as they used to because of the change in the need for teachers in the last half decade.) Rosenberg (1955) threw some indirect light on the problem when he asked students in 1950 and 1952 whether they would like to become teachers. He also determined whether they were "people-oriented" (want to work with people rather than with things; be helpful to others) or "non-people-oriented." One of the relations he reported is given in Table 10.3.

The percentages in the table seem to say that teachers who are not people-oriented tend to leave teaching. The numbers on which the table is based are comparatively small (a total of 108 teachers), and the study is much more limited than the Stouffer and the Miller and Swanson studies. Yet it shows the characteristics of sociological inquiry being illustrated: one variable, Remained Teachers or Left Teaching (Occupational Choice), is a sociological variable, which is studied in relation to a psychological variable, People-Oriented and Non-People-Oriented. The responses of the sample were analyzed in a table of percentages (calculated from frequencies).

TABLE 10.3   **People-Oriented Values and Change of Occupational Choice, 1952**

	REMAINED TEACHERS	LEFT TEACHING
People-Oriented	57%	43%
Non-People-Oriented	19%	81%

Enduring Effects of Education

The last study to be cited in this section cannot really be called survey research or a field study. It is, however, what is being called in this chapter sociological inquiry. It is also one of a new kind of study that is increasingly being done as archives of data are built from the results of many studies. Hyman, Wright, and Reed (1975) wished answers to the extremely important but seldom empirically asked question, How enduring are the effects of education?

One of the great difficulties in studying the long-range effects of education and social programs or changes is the difficulty researchers have in following people over time. Studies that follow people over time are called *longitudinal* studies. If we want to assess the long-range effects of schools and schooling, we should study the people when they are in school, have

TABLE 10.4 Educational Level and Mean Percentages of
Academic Knowledge of Four Age Cohorts in the
1960's, Hyman et al. (1975) Study[a]

| | EDUCATIONAL LEVEL | | |
Age	Elementary School	High School Graduate	College Graduate
25–36	36%	42%	71%
37–48	31	41	75
49–60	28	53	64
61–72	32	55	62

[a] Tabled entries are mean percentages, each calculated from three percentages associated with individual items of knowledge. The 36 percent in the upper left cell, for instance, means that an average of 36 percent of those with elementary school education *and* in the age category 25–36 succeeded in answering the knowledge questions.

just left school, and at later points in time. But this is one of the most difficult kinds of research to do for a number of practical and technical reasons that we cannot elaborate here. Suffice it to say that there is little longitudinal empirical evidence on the question of the enduring effects of education.

Hyman and his colleagues solved the problem of the difficulty of answering their question on the enduring effects of education by doing secondary analysis of data collected in a number of national surveys. In effect, they combined and compared the results of the various survey studies bearing on their question. That is, they extracted information on the educational status of thousands of Americans from 54 surveys, with a total of about 80,000 individuals. The surveys were done during the period 1949 to 1971. They were chosen to cluster around four points in time so that longitudinal studies could be approximated. The reader, whose critical acumen should have been sharpened by our earlier study, will find this study and its problems and results a fine exercise in critical interpretation.

In Table 10.4, some of Hyman et al.'s results are given in highly condensed and summarized form. These results are fairly typical of the many results presented in their book. The table primarily expresses the relation between amount of education as independent variable (*Educational Level*) and knowledge of three pieces of information: know number of terms a President can serve; know length of terms of Senators; know length of term of members of the House of Representatives.[3] Another "variable" in the table is age, which has the four categories indicated.

Hyman et al. wished to study the relation between amount of education and later knowledge of a wide variety of "knowledges." They were also centrally interested in the enduring effects of education: Does the influence of school persist through time? Do the "seeds of knowledge implanted long

[3] These three items and the tabled entries were chosen out of a large mass of similar tables almost arbitrarily. Most of the items used by the surveys, however, were similar in being applied functional knowledge.

ago . . . wither with time or endure throughout the vicissitudes of experience into old age" (Hyman et al., 1975, p. 29)? The ideal approach to such a problem is longitudinal: study the knowledge of children in school and follow them over time, measuring their knowledge at different points in time, also taking account of amount of education received. This approach is difficult if not impossible because of expense, loss of subjects, and other possible influences on knowledge and its acquisition that operate over time. Most studies of the effects of education are done at one point in time. The relation may, of course, be studied this way, but the results tell us nothing about the effects of education over time.

Hyman et al., in a fine attempt to "simulate" the longitudinal aspect, used the data of the national surveys and categorized the data obtained during different time periods with the "Age" category given in Table 10.4. That is, there are four age cohorts, as they are called: 25–36, 37–48, 49–60, and 61–72. The authors reasoned that the effects of education would be shown by increased knowledge with increased education and that the patterns of differences should be the same or similar in the different cohorts.

It is clear from Table 10.4 that the authors' main question is answered: from elementary school through college amount of knowledge increases, and it increases in a similar way in the four cohorts (different age levels). This finding is monotonously repeated in Hyman et al.'s tables. Rarely are such consistency of results seen and the power of "replication" demonstrated, if one can call the different age levels and the many tests of knowledge replications. The nagging questions always come back, however: Can we believe the results? Is it possible that these strong results are spurious in the sense that it is not education that produces greater knowledge the higher one goes in the educational system but some other variable or variables?

Consider intelligence. Is it possible that differing levels of intelligence of the sample respondents produced the observed differences in percentages at the three educational levels? It seems quite plausible to suppose that the more intelligent individuals go farther in the educational system than the less intelligent individuals. If, indeed, this is the case, then the results of Table 10.4 (and other similar results) lead to the wrong conclusion. It is not education but intelligence that is influential. Or perhaps more accurately, it is education *and* intelligence. Hyman et al. (1975, p. 294) used an apt phrase that expresses the frustrating difficulty facing interpreters of research results, especially nonexperimental research: "terrible indeterminancy." Naturally, there are other variables in this study that contribute to the terrible indeterminancy. We concentrate briefly only on intelligence.

Hyman et al. controlled competing variables and competing explanations competently. Indeed, I recommend their book to the reader as a model of careful reasoning, scientific objectivity, clear exposition, and the use of archival research materials to test important practical questions. It also uses liberally the kind of alternative hypothesis reasoning we have encountered in earlier chapters, but especially in Chapter 9 on experimental and nonexperimental research. Let us look briefly, however, at what may be the weakest part of Hyman et al.'s arguments, that on intelligence.

The authors say that the variable one wishes one could control is intelligence, measured during childhood before the test scores can be influenced by education. But such measures needed for direct control, they say, are beyond anyone's reach; survey subjects are already adult, too late to measure intelligence before education has had an influence. (Education, of course, has a strong influence on tested intelligence.) Conversely, measurement of children's intelligence comes too early to measure the enduring effects of education.

To bolster their contention that intelligence did not produce the effects they report, they used opposing arguments. First, social and biological characteristics have declined as criteria of educational selection. More and more children in recent years can and do gain entry into education. Intelligence should therefore play a larger role in determining achievement. Second, earlier more stringent standards of academic performance in the nation's schools have been relaxed. Thus, students of recent generations are allowed to pursue education and have gone higher in the educational system even though their intelligence is more limited. The first argument, then, says that intelligence plays more of a role, and the second argument says that it plays a lesser role. Hyman et al. point out that both arguments lead to the conclusion that the contribution of intelligence must have changed over time. Therefore, if it is found, as it was found in their analyses, that the effects of education do not vary across time periods and cohorts, intelligence is not the explanation. They also cite the results of other studies, which they say indicate that the general influence of intelligence on educational attainment is modest (a possibly doubtful conclusion).

My own conclusion is that Hyman et al.'s results are empirically valid because of the rather large effects—the differences in the percentages—and their remarkable consistency over time. But I am still nagged by the possibility that a substantial portion of the effects observed is due to intelligence. The most accurate conclusion is probably that both intelligence and education are substantial and interacting enduring influences on knowledge. I would have liked to see intelligence controlled. But that was not directly possible. Nevertheless, the researchers did about as well as they could under the circumstances.[4] One can say, in fact, that their "control analyses" (see, especially, Ch. 3) are excellent examples of control in the analysis of difficult and controversial materials and problems. The whole

[4] My doubt is increased, however, by what Hyman et al. (1975, p. 25) say about a brief intelligence test (vocabulary) that was administered on one of the surveys they used. The educated adults scored higher. In other words, there is a positive relation between intelligence and the educational effects. One often wishes in research, especially educational research, that all people had exactly the same intelligence!

study, in fact, is a fine example of careful and competent sociological inquiry.

SURVEY RESEARCH

In *survey research* large and small populations are studied by means of samples to discover the relative incidence, distribution, and interrelations of sociological and psychological variables. Survey research is part of social scientific research and has had strong influence on research in the behavioral sciences. It has been used mainly, but certainly not exclusively, to find out what exists and how it exists in the social environment of a group, a geographical or political area, or even a whole country. One of its chief virtues for practical people, especially administrators and government and business leaders and policy makers, is its surprising ability to provide accurate information on whole populations of people using relatively small samples. The technology of survey research—and related forms of inquiry—is highly developed. Modern society has a powerful tool for fact-gathering and for testing theory and hypotheses.

The Stouffer and the Miller and Swanson studies are both survey research. Stouffer studied his problem by using two large random samples (over 2,400 cases each) of the whole United States. Miller and Swanson interviewed a random sample of the Detroit population. Hyman et al. used results obtained in a number of sample surveys, as they are also called, to answer their questions. These studies used this large-scale form of research primarily to study relations. Their authors were not so much interested in survey research as a descriptive tool but as a relation-seeking and testing tool. This emphasis in survey research has increased in recent years. Much, perhaps most, survey research, however, has been what can be called descriptive.

Descriptive surveys seek to determine the incidence and distribution of the characteristics and opinions of populations of people by obtaining and studying the characteristics and opinions of relatively small and presumably representative samples of such people. They are used extensively by government, business, and organizations. The basic purpose of surveys used in this way is not scientific but rather action- and policy-oriented. Nevertheless, descriptive survey research has had very strong effects on behavioral research in general, mainly through its highly sophisticated and developed sampling and interview procedures. Earlier we discussed random sampling and its characteristics. For practical purposes, it is highly desirable that samples studied be representative. One wishes to say of a result obtained in a large-scale study that it is representative. If the sample is indeed representative, then the results obtained from it can be generalized to the whole population. If 80 percent of a sample responds favorably to a question about a possible government policy, for instance, one wants to believe that if all the people of a country, a state, a city, or an

TABLE 10.5 Comparisons of Sample with Census Data,
Stouffer (1955) Study

CHARACTERISTIC	SURVEY	CENSUS
Urban	66.0%	64.0%
Male	46.6	47.7
Negro	8.9	9.2
College	17.1	15.4
High School	45.4	43.5
Grade School (or none)	37.5	41.1

organization were asked the same question, close to 80 percent of them
would be favorable.

There are several ways to draw samples for survey purposes, but the
only one that gives reasonable and general assurance of being representative is some form of random sample. Surveys often use what is called a
stratified random probability sampling procedure, which has been shown
a number of times to have a high probability of being representative.
Table 10.5 contains some remarkable and reassuring evidence of the repre-
sentativeness of large random samples *of the whole United States.* The
method consists of checking the incidence of readily available sociological
characteristics of a sample with the same characteristics obtained in the
most recent census—or with some other reliable source of such data.

Comparison of the sample and census percentages in Table 10.5 shows
close agreement. The sample estimates, with the exception of grade school,
are all within 2 percent of the census estimates. Similar checking in other
surveys has shown sample estimates of the incidence of such characteristics in the population to come quite close to census estimates.[5] In Stouffer's
study the percentages obtained in response to different questions in two
independent random samples of the United States were compared. In
Table 10.1 we reported the responses of community leaders and nonleaders
to a question on tolerance of religious nonconformity. The percentages
reported in the table were those obtained in only one of Stouffer's samples.
The percentages obtained in the two samples, however, were all within 3
percent or less of each other. For the six percentages of Table 10.1, the
differences between them and those of the second sample were 2, 1, 3, 1, 1,
and 0 percentage points. This is a highly convincing demonstration of the
power of the random sample survey. It is all the more convincing when it is
realized that the sizes of survey samples are less than 3,000 individuals,
usually considerably less.

[5] The curious reader may ask: Can you trust the census "estimates"? After all, census
figures, even though presumably population values, have a number of sources of error
that reduce their ideal accuracy. There are some who even say that they trust the sample
estimates more than they do the census figures! In any case, census figures are usually
quite accurate. And, after all, something must be used against which to check sample
estimates!

Survey research and related forms of inquiry are important for both scientific relation purposes and practical action- and decision-oriented purposes, but particularly the latter. Examples of surveys for scientific purposes have already been given in this chapter. (The emphasis of this book on science and scientific behavioral research has dictated such examples.) We mention only one practical policy-oriented use of the survey.

Since 1946 the Survey Research Center of the University of Michigan has conducted surveys of consumer finance for the federal government. Their purposes have been varied, but one general purpose seems to be to supply the government and interested parties with accurate information on the actual and intended economic behavior of the American people so that the government can formulate economic policies to offset or prevent, for example, economic disturbances of a deleterious nature.[6] The annual surveys have evidently been highly effective and have provided accurate national information on income and its sources, savings, debts, consumer goods, consumer intentions, and so on.

Surveys of interest to behavioral researchers have focused on people, vital facts about people, and their beliefs, opinions, attitudes, values, motives, and behavior. While skilled interviewing and the use of carefully constructed interview schedules dominate survey research, other methods of observation are also used. In short, survey research is a form of sociological inquiry (with strong psychological overtones, of course) that is widely used, especially for practical and policy goals, and that has influenced behavioral research mostly by its interviewing and sampling procedures, as indicated earlier. Its results have usually been remarkably accurate and generalizable. One can usually trust such results, if they are obtained by random sampling done by the better survey organizations. We will now turn our attention to a common and important form of analysis that is used in survey research and in other sociological inquiry.

FREQUENCY ANALYSIS

A number of examples of frequency analysis were presented earlier without technical explanation. The reason the explanation was not given sooner is that the examples seemed so obvious that explanation was not necessary. Why not forego the explanation entirely? Because the prevalence of such analysis requires some understanding of the principles involved. Moreover, we need to balance our earlier preoccupation with analysis that uses statistics of central tendency and variability.

A *frequency* is simply a count of something. If one has a sample of 300 individuals and counts the men and women, these numbers are frequencies. More accurately, a frequency is the number of individuals in one of

---

[6] For a good brief account of these surveys and other applied studies, see Likert and Hayes (1957).

two or more categories or classes. If there were 152 women and 148 men in the sample, then 152 and 148 are frequencies, numbers that fall into the two categories, men and women.[7] In research, tabulations of a number of categories and the observed frequencies in them are called *frequency distributions*. It is such frequency distributions that are often published in popular publications. We are not much interested in them; they do not ordinarily express relations between variables.

Crossbreaks and Percentage Calculation

We *are* interested in setting up frequency distributions against each other. Such distributions are usually small, that is, with few categories. When we do so, they are called *crossbreaks* or, more technically, *cross partitions*. Table 10.2 contains a crossbreak. Note that the two variables, social class and weaning, are set against each other. That is, the cells of the table express the co-occurrence of the two variables. And the frequencies in the cells "express" the relation between the two variables. Talking directly, we find that 33 mothers who were middle class were also early weaners, 22 were late weaners, and so on. This is the simplest form of crossbreak, two cells by two cells, that expresses the simplest possible relation.

Tables 10.1 and 10.3 also contain two-by-two crossbreaks, but the frequencies have been converted to percentages to bring out the strength of the relations in the tables. The crossbreak of Table 10.4, also in percentage form, is really four crossbreaks. Each row is more a replication than it is a category of a variable—with half of one category, educational level, omitted. (The 36 percent in the first cell means that 36 percent of those who went to elementary school, of the age group 25–36, knew the knowledge items. This implies, of course, that 64 percent did not know them. Crossbreak tables are frequently truncated in this manner.)

The conversion of the frequencies in a table to percentages is done to facilitate "seeing the relation" and to assess its strength. The rule for conversion is: Calculate the percentages from the independent variable or variables to the dependent variable.[8] For example, in Table 10.2 the independent variable is social class and the dependent variable is weaning. Therefore, the percentages are calculated along the rows (33/55 = .60 = 60 percent, and so on). In Table 10.1, the independent variable is community leadership, or leaders and nonleaders, and the dependent variable is tolerance, or Yes and No responses to a question on religious nonconformity. Note how the strength of the relation comes out clearly in both tables. If the percentages were calculated the other way, down the columns, the

[7] Dictionaries give a different definition. They say that a frequency is the ratio of the number in a class or category to the total number being classified; in the above example, 152/300 and 148/300 would be frequencies. Actually, these are "relative frequencies." We use the simpler definition to avoid confusion.

[8] There is a statistical reason behind this rule. See Kerlinger (1973, pp. 162–166) for the technical explanation. A nontechnical explanation is given later.

direction of the relation would be incorrectly expressed and perhaps lead to the wrong conclusion. Such incorrectly calculated tables have been published. (It makes no difference if the percentages are calculated across the rows or down the columns provided the independent variable to the dependent variable calculation rule is followed.)

An Example of a Possible Incorrect Calculation of Percentages

Because it may help develop the reader's understanding of problems, relations, analysis, and inference, we now discuss a subtle and interesting problem in connection with what is probably an incorrect analysis from an important government report on civil disorders (*Report of the National Advisory Committee on Civil Disorders*, 1968). In 1967, President Lyndon Johnson appointed a commission to investigate and study the race riots that had occurred in American cities. His executive order had said: "The Commission shall investigate and make recommendations with respect to: (1) The origins of the recent major civil disorders in our cities, including the basic causes and factors leading to such disorders . . ." (*ibid.*, p. 534). From a survey done in Newark, the responses of rioters (*R*) and people not involved in riots (*NI*) to the question, "Sometimes I hate white people," were obtained. The table reported by the Commission is given in Table 10.6 (*ibid.*, p. 176).

The percentages in the table have been calculated from rioting, as a variable, to attitude toward whites, another variable (as indicated by agreement or disagreement with the statement). It can be shown, using probability theoretical reasoning, that percentages are really what are called conditional probabilities (Kerlinger, 1973, pp. 164–165) whose correct statement is derived from the original research problem. The original research problem in this case derives from the President's order. If the causes of the rioting is the problem, as indicated by the order, then the if p, then q statement is if p, then rioting, with rioting the dependent variable. The p stands for the causes being sought. But in Table 10.6 the way the percentages have been calculated makes rioting p and attitude q, which reverses the independent and dependent variables. The percentages in the table, in other words, imply the statement, if rioting, then attitude, or if rioter, then negative attitude toward whites.

TABLE 10.6   **Responses of Rioters (*R*) and People Not Involved (*NI*) to the Question, "Sometimes I hate white people," Civil Disorders Report**

	R (N = 105)	NI (N = 126)
Agree	72.4%	50.0%
Disagree	27.6%	50.0%
	100.0%	100.0%

The statement is not unreasonable, but it does not seem to be in conformity with the problem enunciated by President Johnson. It does seem to explain the attitudes, but not the rioting. What is wanted from the data is an answer to the question: What is the probability of rioting, given attitude? It can be shown that this probability is obtained by calculating the percentages (more accurately, the proportions) of the original frequencies across the rows. The original frequencies of the four cells of the table were obtained from the frequencies of R and NI (105 and 126) given by the Commission. The percentages were then calculated from attitude to rioting, or across the rows. These percentages are given in Table 10.7. (The values have been rounded.) They are equivalent to saying: If attitude, then rioting.

Taking these percentages as probabilities, one reads, for example: The probability of rioting, given agreement with the statement, "Sometimes I hate white people," is .55 (or 55 percent). It is obvious that these percentages or probabilities tell a different story from those of the Commission's report. In this table disagreement with the statement becomes important. Given disagreement with the statement, the probability is .68 that individuals will not be involved. Given agreement, the probability is .55 that individuals will riot. Most important, the percentages or probabilities of Table 10.7 are in consonance with the President's order; those of Table 10.6 appear not to be in consonance with the order.

This is a particularly difficult example because, in this case, reasonable arguments can be advanced for both methods of calculating the percentages. Since it was the Commission's assignment and purpose, however, to determine why the disorders occurred, the weight of argument seems to come down on the side of the Table 10.7 percentage calculation and against that of Table 10.6. The correct statement of the problem in if p, then q form is if attitude, then riot, and not if riot(er), then attitude.

The example has been developed at some length to give the reader a bit more than a glance at an interesting and important problem of analysis and interpretation. Insight into simple crossbreak analysis may also have been gained. The substantive problem is also both theoretically and practically important. The President's charge to the Commission is almost tantamount to setting a scientific problem: What caused the race riots? This is really a charge to psychologists and sociologists to build theory to explain racial violence, racial tension, and racial attitudes, as well as to determine the facts of discrimination and prejudice. I don't think I need to labor the practical importance of the problem.

TABLE 10.7   Responses of Rioters (R) and People Not Involved (NI), with Percentages Calculated across Rows

	R	NI	
Agree	55%	45%	100%
Disagree	32%	68%	100%

Other Forms of Crossbreak and Frequency Analysis

Crossbreaks come in many forms and shapes. To now we have examined mainly the simplest kind with only two variables, one independent and one dependent, and two cells for each variable. Other forms are, of course, possible: 2 × 4, 3 × 4, and so on. More than two variables is also possible. Beyond three variables, however—two independent variables and one dependent variable—frequency analysis and interpretation become difficult and troublesome. There are also other forms of tables. A frequent one omits part of the partitioning. That is, instead of "complete" tables that express all the aspects of the variables, one or more of the cells are omitted. Table 10.4 is an example. The reported percentages are only half the story. For example, in the 25–36 age level, 36 percent of those who had had elementary school education had the tested academic knowledge. How about the percentage of those who did not have the academic knowledge? It is implied. In this case it is, of course, 64 percent. If the reader understands the basic principles, most frequency and percentage tables are fairly easy to read and interpret.

SOCIOLOGICAL INQUIRY: A BRIEF PERSPECTIVE

It is easily possible to write a whole book on what has here been called sociological inquiry. Indeed, such books have been written. The approach adopted in this book, however, stresses experimental research and the measurement of continuous variables at the expense of sociological inquiry because such an approach is probably closer to the nature of science as in large part the study of relations experimentally and nonexperimentally. When possible and suitable, experimentation should be done in the laboratory and in the field for the reasons given earlier. When possible, variables should be measured using scales of values that can be assigned to the objects being measured. This does not mean that nonexperimental research is not necessary and important. Nor does it mean that measurement that permits only counting[9]—such as Stouffer's counting of Yes and No responses (Table 10.1) or Hyman et al.'s counting of numbers of individuals at different educational levels (Table 10.4)—is not necessary and important. On balance, both approaches are necessary and indispensable in behavioral research.

Sociological inquiry, then, is a large and highly significant part of contemporary behavioral research. It can even be said—and certainly would

[9] Some experts say that counting objects in categories is not really measurement. Other experts say that it *is* measurement (called *nominal* measurement). I take the latter position because of the definition of measurement as the assignment of numerals to objects according to rules. One assigns, in effect, 1's and 0's to individuals. The rule is: If an individual belongs in a category, assign a 1; if he does not belong in the category assign 0. An example is sex: assign 1 if male, 0 if female (or vice versa).

be said by some thinkers—that it is more important than experimental inquiry. Consider survey research and large-scale studies like the Coleman report, *Equality of Educational Opportunity.* Can one say or even imply that because there is less control and less certainty of inference that the research is not important? One of the purposes of this book is to help the reader to comprehend the broad canvas on which behavioral research is painted and the richness and variety of the colors that behavioral scientists use in the painting. Enormous scientific strides have been taken in this century, especially in the conceptualization of research problems and in methodology. And sociological inquiry has been and will continue to be an active, creative, and highly significant part of the general effort.

11

The multivariate approach
multiple regression and variance partitioning

The achievement of children in school has become the focus of intense research attention. Psychologists, sociologists, economists, and educators are doing studies and analyses aimed at understanding and predicting achievement. Achievement has, of course, always been more or less studied. The approach today, however, is what can be called multi-variable or multivariate. "Multivariate" means "many variables." It has become common knowledge among behavioral scientists that almost any phenomenon has many determinants and not just one or two. The school achievement of children is a prime example. So, if we want to understand and be able to predict achievement, we must somehow study the effects of many variables on achievement. Indeed, if we want to understand any complex psychological, sociological, or educational phenomenon, we must often approach the phenomenon in a multivariable manner.

A TECHNICAL DIVERGENCE: VARIANCE PARTITIONING

To be able to talk intelligently about the multivariate approach to behavioral phenomena and data, we need to understand a relatively simple but highly useful technical idea, the partitioning of variance. If we mea- **159** sure the verbal achievement of children with some sort of test, we will obtain scores on verbal achievement for each child. These scores will differ from each other; there will usually be wide individual differences. Some children will do very well, and we assume that they have achieved a good deal. Other children will not do well, and we assume that they have not achieved as much as we would like. The scores vary; in other words, they exhibit variability or, more technically, variance.

Variance means two things in research. First, it is used as a general term to express the variability of characteristics of individuals and objects, to express the differences in the characteristics. Researchers say, "The achievement variance in that school is greater than the achievement variance in this school." This means that the achievement differences among pupils in the first school are greater than the achievement differences in the second school. More specifically, the range of achievement scores in the first school is greater than the range of achievement scores in the second school. This meaning of variance is usually associated with individual differences among children in psychological characteristics. It can also be associated, however, with differences among objects and groups. It is said, for instance, that the average achievement scores of classes or schools differ. Here we are talking about the variances of classes and schools. The idea of individual differences, then, is general, provided we define "individual" broadly.

The second meaning or use of variance is more subtle and more technical, but highly useful, as we will see. Here researchers talk about the amount of variance in a dependent variable being "due to" or "accounted for" by an experimental manipulation or by other variables. For example, "The authority manipulation accounted for 20 percent of the variance of the obedience measures." Supposing that there were two experimental groups, the statement means that the mean difference between the two groups—or the variance between the groups—"accounted for" 20 percent of the total variance of the dependent variable obedience measures.

A more complex statement that reflects this second meaning and use of "variance" is: "Intelligence accounted for a major portion of the variance of achievement. The children's attitudes and their home backgrounds also accounted for substantial portions of the variance. School variables accounted for only a small portion of the variance." This statement specifies the influence on the variability of a dependent variable, achievement, of four independent variables: intelligence, attitudes, home background, and school variables.

The statement on the authority manipulation accounting for 20 percent of the variance of obedience is a univariate statement: only one independent variable, authority, is said to affect the dependent variable, obedience. The more complex statement specifies the influence on the variability of a dependent variable of four independent variables. It is a multivariate statement: more than one independent variable is said to influence a de-

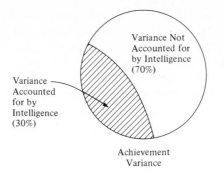

FIG. 11.1

pendent variable.[1] We have, of course, encountered such problems in earlier chapters. For example, factorial experimental designs were discussed in Chapter 7. Here and there in other chapters multivariate problems have been mentioned. Variation and variance have also been discussed. Now we must go farther and deeper.

Let's examine the school achievement of children from a variance point of view. We want to know the major influences on school achievement, and we have obtained in research with 300 school children, say, six measures of variables presumed to influence achievement. We need to study the rather complex relations between, on the one hand, verbal achievement as measured by a comprehensive test of verbal achievement, and, on the other hand, intelligence, motivation, attitude toward school, home background, social class, and sex. We assume that we have reliable and valid measures of all variables.

First, consider Figure 11.1, which is supposed to represent the effect of intelligence alone on achievement. The area of the whole circle represents the total variance of the test scores of 300 children in the ninth grade, say. We know that some portion of this total variance, which represents the individual differences of the children on the achievement test, is due to the differences in the children's intelligence. That is, some children achieve more and better because they have superior intelligence; some do not achieve as well as others because they have less intelligence. The portion of the variance "due to" intelligence is represented in the figure by the shaded area.[2] It occupies about one-third of the area of the circle. This is

---

[1] This statement is not quite accurate. "Multivariate," strictly speaking, refers to more than one independent variable and more than one dependent variable. In this book, we consider any situation in which there are two or more independent variables and one or more dependent variables as multivariate.

[2] Expressions that imply "cause" are hard to avoid. For example, expressions like "due to," "variance accounted for," "influences," and the like, have at least slight causal connotations. This is not intended, however. It is a byproduct of language, which is always rich in causal attributions. We will return to this difficulty later.

fairly realistic: intelligence often accounts for about this much variance of verbal achievement. If we let the entire area of the circle equal 100 percent, we can show approximately how much variance of achievement intelligence and the other variables "account for." In this case, intelligence accounts for about 30 percent.

We know, of course, that intelligence is not the only variable that is influential. The larger unshaded area expresses the variance not accounted for by intelligence (70 percent). If we knew more about achievement, we might be able to shade more of the circle. In fact, if we had complete knowledge—if we knew all the influences on achievement—we could shade all of it. We can probably never know all the influences. Indeed, we can rarely shade more than half the circle when talking about achievement. Anyway, take another variable, home background. In Figure 11.2 the variance of achievement accounted for by home background is shown. It is about 10 percent of the total variance, say.

Figures 11.1 and 11.2 express the separate effects of intelligence and of home background. If these two variables were completely independent, or unrelated to each other—if the magnitude of the relation between them was zero—then the variance situation would look like that in Figure 11.3. The total shaded area occupies 30% + 10% = 40% of the total area, and the two shaded areas do not overlap. If the condition of independence is met (the lack of overlap in the figure), then it can be said that 40 percent of the achievement variance is accounted for by intelligence and home background together.

In the best of all possible research worlds, independent variables would be independent of each other, or uncorrelated. (They are, of course, not called "independent" because they are independent of each other.) That is, the magnitude of their relations would be zero. It is hard to express these ideas clearly without technical details, especially technical details about the subject of "correlation" and the calculation of coefficients of correlation or relation. We therefore compromise and sidetrack the discussion a little to

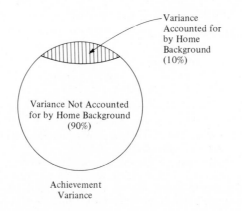

Variance Accounted for by Home Background (10%)

Variance Not Accounted for by Home Background (90%)

Achievement Variance

FIG. 11.2

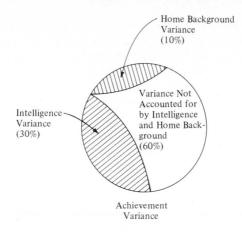

Home Background
Variance
(10%)

Variance Not
Accounted for
by Intelligence
and Home Back-
ground
(60%)

Intelligence
Variance
(30%)

Achievement
Variance

FIG. 11.3

discuss correlation and correlation coefficients in a nontechnical way. Our earlier discussions of correlation, while sufficient for the earlier discussions, are not sufficient to permit the more complex discussion now necessary.

Correlation, Correlation Coefficients, and Shared Variance

In Chapter 4 relations were discussed and illustrated. It was learned that a relation is a set of ordered pairs and that it is possible to calculate the direction and magnitude of relations. (It is suggested that the reader read again the section in Chapter 4 labeled "The Direction and Magnitude of Relations.") The varying together of two sets of measures produces correlation, positive or negative, with magnitudes varying from -1.00 through 0 to $+1.00$, $+1.00$ indicating a perfect positive correlation, -1.00 a perfect negative correlation, and 0 "no correlation" or lack of correlation. These three magnitudes of correlation were illustrated with simple numbers in Table 4.1. Magnitudes between these extreme values are much more likely to occur: .60, .42, $-.28$, and so on.

The reader must now again accept what follows on faith because statistical calculation and mathematical proof are not part of this book. He or she must also have a little patience. (It will probably be worth it.) The symbol r is used to mean correlation coefficient. $r = .70$, for example, means that the correlation between two variables is .70. If $r = 0$, there is no varying together or concomitant variation between two variables. One can say nothing about one variable from knowledge of the other variable. It can be said that the two variables are "independent." If the correlation between intelligence and achievement were zero, one can predict nothing about children's achievement from their intelligence test scores. If the correlation between two sets of random numbers is calculated, the correlation coefficient should be close to 0.

An important application of the idea of independence in this sense was introduced by a hint given in Chapter 7 where factorial designs of research were discussed. Manipulated independent variables in factorial designs are said to be independent, meaning that their correlation is zero—by definition, since subjects are assigned to the cells of such a design at random. This is a highly important technical property of experiments whose complete discussion we must also forego. Suffice it to say that it means that the effects of such independent variables can be assessed and interpreted independently of each other. This means we can talk about the effect of variable A without having to take into account variable B, and vice versa.

Correlation coefficients (those called product-moment correlations, which are most used) have a nice property that enhances their interpretation. If the correlation coefficient between two variables is squared, the squared coefficient indicates the variance the two variables share. In Chapter 4 such shared variance was called *covariance*. For example, if the correlation between intelligence and achievement is .60, then the shared variance is indicated by $(.60)^2 = .36$, which means that the two variables have 36 percent of their variance in common. In Figure 11.1 the variance of achievement accounted for by intelligence was given as 30 percent. This is really a squared correlation coefficient and can be interpreted as a percentage or proportion. (We can easily calculate the original coefficient by reversing the procedure: take the square root of the percentage [the proportion]: $\sqrt{.30} = .55$. The correlation coefficient between intelligence and achievement in this case is .55.)

Accounting for Variance When the Independent Variables Are Correlated

Again, if independent variables are not correlated ($r = 0$), analyzing and interpreting research with more than one independent variable is relatively easy. Under such "pure" and simple conditions, one can calculate the correlation coefficients between each of the independent variables and the dependent variable, add the separate r^2's, and then conclude how much of the total variance of achievement is accounted for by the independent variables. In Figure 11.3, for instance, one adds $.30 + .10 = .40$, or 40 percent of the variance is accounted for. Moreover, one can talk unequivocally about the separate contributions to the variance of achievement of the two independent variables: in this case of two independent variables, 30 percent and 10 percent.

The same reasoning and calculations can be applied to all six independent variables mentioned earlier—*provided the six variables are independent of each other*. A hypothetical situation showing the correlation coefficients between each of the six independent variables and achievement is depicted in Figure 11.4. Although the example is fictitious, the indicated percentages of variance are not unrealistic, though they are probably too

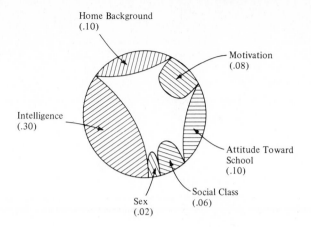

Home Background
(.10)

Motivation
(.08)

Intelligence
(.30)

Attitude Toward
School
(.10)

Sex
(.02)

Social Class
(.06)

FIG. 11.4

large compared to the proportions of variance obtained in actual research. The point is the addition of the variances under the condition of independence and the interpretation of the separate contributions to the achievement variance. The total variance accounted for is .30 + .10 + .08 + .10 + .06 + .02 = .66, or 66 percent of the variance of achievement is accounted for by the six variables.

The big difficulty in this not-best-of-all-possible-research worlds, however, is that independent variables like these are almost always correlated, often substantially so. (We give examples from actual research later.) For example, there is a positive correlation between intelligence and home background. Suppose it is $r = .30$, a not unrealistic figure. Then intelligence and home background share something in common ($r^2 = [.30]^2 = .09$), which of course means that they are not independent of each other. This means that the assumption of independence of the independent variables accepted earlier is false, which in turn means that the interpretations of the data made earlier are also false!

Look at Figure 11.5 in which the new correlation situation of the three variables is roughly depicted. The correlations between intelligence and achievement and between home background and achievement are still the same. But now the correlation between intelligence and home background is no longer zero, as in Figure 11.3, but rather .30. This is equivalent, in Figure 11.5, to $.30^2 = .09$, or 9 percent of the variances of intelligence and home background are shared. We can no longer talk about the effect of intelligence on achievement without to some extent taking account of home background. In other words, when there are correlations greater than zero (or less than zero) between independent variables, interpretation of research results are more complex and difficult.

To depict the situation of Figure 11.4 when the variables are correlated is difficult and clumsy. Not only does such a figure become confusing because of the overlaps of variances; the actual situations (the correlations

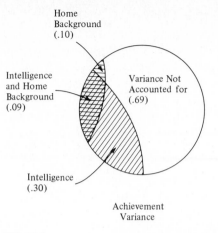

FIG. 11.5

among the variables and their covariances) can and do exceed the two dimensions of the paper surface. We abandon diagrams, at least temporarily, and change the subject though not the main theme.

MULTIPLE REGRESSION

Many experts might consider the subject of multiple regression—and factor analysis and other multivariate approaches and methods— inappropriate in a book like this. After all, the purpose of the book is to introduce the reader conceptually and nontechnically to scientific behavioral research. The answer is simple: It is not possible to understand modern behavioral research without understanding multivariate approaches and the ideas behind them. Moreover, a book on behavioral research that did not consider such enormously important approaches and analytic techniques as multiple regression and factor analysis would be immediately obsolete. These approaches are too important to neglect. They are too much a functional and active part of the contemporary and future scenes of behavioral research. In any case, we face the task of understanding these complex methodologies without much technical elaboration. Perhaps the best way to do the job is the way we have already used a great deal: through an actual research example followed by semitechnical explanations of the ideas behind the thinking and analysis.

Predicting High School Achievement: Holtzman and Brown Study

There have been many studies of success or lack of success in high school and college. They are usually what are called predictive studies: researchers predict high school or college achievement using a variety of independent variables as predictors. For example, intelligence and high school grade-point average (the average of all grades a student receives in high school) are good predictors in the sense that they account for substantial portions of the variance of success and lack of success in college. (Remember that variance of the dependent variable means differences among students, in this case, let us say, the differences that are reflected by grades in college.) In such research a common procedure is to administer two or more measures to students—or to use measures already administered by school systems—and to correlate these measures with a measure of presumed success in academic work. Through a statistical procedure, the joint or combined "effect" of the independent variables on the dependent variable is assessed. An attempt is also usually made to assess the contributions of each of the independent variables, as well as combinations of independent variables. The former is comparatively simple; the latter is more difficult and hazardous.

Prediction of success in school is often partially accomplished by using as a predictor some measure of scholastic aptitude, or general measure of ability to do school work. Holtzman and Brown (1968) used such a measure with 1,648 seventh-graders. Used alone the measure accounted for 37 percent of the variance of high school grades. The prediction, then, from the independent variable, scholastic aptitude, to the dependent variable, high school grades, was successful in the sense that a substantial portion of the variance of high school grades was shared with the predictor variable, scholastic aptitude. This is a common finding in educational research: general ability tests such as intelligence tests, general aptitude tests (especially verbal aptitude), and academic aptitude tests predict well to success in school.

The predictive approach is much more sophisticated than this, however. It has long been known that there is much more to scholastic achievement than intellectual ability, important as such ability is. For years, then, educational researchers have used other measures to enhance the prediction. Suppose we have two tests and we know that each of them predicts rather well to school success. Can we put them together in the manner of the example shown in Figure 11.3 and improve the prediction? If one test, a test of general ability, accounts for 30 percent of the variance of school success, and a second test accounts for 10 percent, can we add the two percentages to obtain the total amount of variance accounted for by both tests? If the two predictor tests are independent of each other—if r_{12} (the correlation coefficient between tests 1 and 2) is 0, in other words—the answer is Yes. But if the two tests are not independent of each other, then the two percentages cannot be added in a simple way. Such a situation was depicted in Figure 11.5 where the independent variables were positively correlated and thus shared variance with each other as well as with the dependent variable.

In the Holtzman and Brown study, the test of scholastic aptitude accounted for 37 percent of the variance of high school grades. Holtzman and

Brown also used a complex measure of study habits and attitudes, which alone accounted for 30 percent of the variance of high school grades. But scholastic aptitude and study habits and attitudes also shared variance, some portion of which was also shared with high school grades. There are two main problems: How much of the variance of high school grades do both variables account for? What does each variable contribute independently of the other variable? Because of the comparatively nontechnical nature of our discussion, we can answer only the first question—and that only roughly. The answer to the second question is quite complex. We will try, however, to give an approximate answer.

Shared Variance, the Multiple Regression Equation and Regression Weights

The shared variance situation of the Holtzman and Brown data is roughly depicted in Figure 11.6. Each circle in the figure stands for the variance of the labeled variable (spelled out). The lower left circle, for example, stands for the variance of scholastic aptitude. The dependent variable, the phenomenon to be explained (or predicted), is represented by the circle high school achievement. The other two circles represent the predictors. To the extent that the area of high school achievement is taken up by the other two circles, to that extent is prediction successful. The hatched overlapping area, labeled SA and HSA, represents the variance shared by the variables scholastic aptitude and high school achievement (grade-point averages). The hatched portion SHA and HSA represents the shared variance of study habits and attitudes and high school achievement. The doubly hatched area represents that part of the variance of high school achievement that is accounted for or predicted by the two independent variables "working together." It is that portion of the variance of high school achievement that scholastic aptitude and study habits share. For predictive purposes it is, so to speak, redundant. It also represents part of the total correlation between scholastic aptitude and study habits and at-

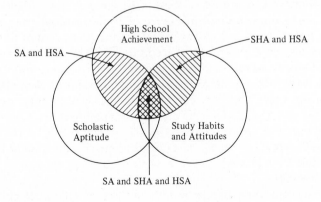

FIG. 11.6

titudes. (Note that there is also a small portion of the overlap between the two independent variables that is not part of the dependent variable; it is the small unhatched area below the doubly hatched area.)

Multiple regression analysis efficiently and expeditiously analyzes situations like this. First, a so-called regression equation is calculated. It can also be called a prediction equation. With two independent variables the equation looks like this:

$$Y' = a + b_1 X_1 + b_2 X_2$$

It will be worth the reader's time and trouble to understand this equation. It is both theoretically and practically important and useful. Y' stands for the dependent variable, or it can stand for the predicted score for any individual in the sample studied. a can be disregarded: it is a constant used to adjust the calculated values produced by substituting appropriate values in the equation. X_1 and X_2 stand for values or scores on the two independent variables. b_1 and b_2 are called regression coefficients. They express the relative weights of the two independent variables in the prediction. (But see below.)

The X's—X_1, X_2, . . . , X_k—are scores on variables 1, 2, . . . , k. That is, if we had two independent variables, as in the above equation, and 200 subjects, each of the subjects would have two scores, one on X_1 and one on X_2. A b coefficient expresses how much weight a particular independent variable has in the regression situation. "$b_1 X_1$" means that any score of any individual on independent variable 1 is weighted (multipled) by b_1. "$b_2 X_2$" and, if there were more independent variables, other b's and X's, have similar meanings. A low coefficient means that the variable to which the coefficient is attached is given less weight in the equation. A high coefficient, of course, has the opposite meaning.

Suppose a regression equation has been calculated from a set of data and is:

$$Y' = .10 + .68X_1 + .39X_2$$

The b weights of .68 and .39 indicate that X_1 scores will be weighted more than X_2 scores. Does this mean that X_1 is really more important than X_2 scores in the prediction? We cannot say clearly. The interpretation of regression weights is usually not simple and easy. Certainly if the above equation were used to predict the Y score of any individual from knowledge of his scores on variables 1 and 2, X_1 would get greater weight than X_2. This does not always mean, however, greater importance.

Take two cases, say individuals 7 and 41 in a sample of 50 individuals. Their X_1 and X_2 scores are (2,4) and (10,5), respectively. Then, substituting in the regression equation:

Individual 7: $.10 + (.68)(2) + (.39)(4) = 3.02$
Individual 41: $.10 + (.68)(10) + (.39)(5) = 8.85$

The predicted scores, or Y', given the two sets of X_1 and X_2 scores, are 3.02 and 8.85. Individual 41 gets a considerably higher score on Y' because his score on X_1 is high and X_1 is weighted more heavily (.68) than X_2 (.39). The opposite is true, though much less sharply, for individual 7: his higher score (4) is X_2, which is weighted less than X_1.

Regression equations such as the one above give the best possible prediction with given sets of data. No other equation or method (for example, one can simply add the X_1 and X_2 values to yield Y' scores) will give as good a prediction.

If random numbers instead of the actual test scores were used, then prediction would be futile because the correlations between X_1 and Y and X_2 and Y would be close to zero. To the extent that X_1 and X_2 are correlated with Y, to that extent the prediction is "good," other things equal. The "best" predictions are obtained when the independent variables, X_1, X_2, . . . , X_k, are highly or substantially correlated with Y, the dependent variable, and the correlations among the independent variables are low. The higher the correlations among the independent variables, the less successive variables contribute to the prediction, and the more difficult and ambiguous interpretation is.

What multiple regression analysis does essentially is to estimate the relative weights of the regression coefficients to be attached to the X's, taking account of the relations (correlations) between the X's and Y *and* among the X's. For example, in the regression equation given above, .68 indicates the relative influence of X_1 on Y, taking into account X_1's correlation with Y *and* the correlation between X_1 and X_2.

In the regression equation given above, b's were the regression coefficients. If the independent variables are measured with different scales of measurement—for instance, X_1 scores may have two and three digits and X_2 scores may have only one digit—there will be difficulties of interpretation because one b may be larger or smaller than another simply because of the measurement scale. Some researchers therefore prefer to use a form of standardized regression weight called beta weights, or β's. Such regression weights are usually routinely calculated by computer programs and have certain interpretative virtues. (They also have weaknesses.) Most important, they can be compared with each other.[3] If we calculate betas for the Holtzman and Brown study, we obtain the following equation:

$$y' = .40x_1 + .49x_2$$

Note that there is no constant term, a, and that y' and x_1 and x_2 are given in lower-case letters. The lower-case letters are used here, in place of other symbols commonly used, for simplicity. They mean, in effect, scores

---

[3] In the equation and example given earlier, we talked as though the b's were β's. This was permissible because X_1 and X_2 had the same scale of measurement. In many situations, however, this would be difficult or even impossible.

transformed so as to be comparable. Taken at face value, the two variables have similar regression coefficients; they have approximately equal weights in the equation. We would get about the same relative y' values simply adding the x_1 and x_2 measures because neither variable gets much more weight than the other.

Assessing Effects: The Coefficient of Multiple Correlation

Perhaps more comprehensible, interesting, and useful to us is the question: How good is the prediction? The reader of contemporary behavioral research studies will often encounter an important statistic, R, the coefficient of multiple correlation. Recall that an ordinary coefficient of correlation, r, expresses the magnitude of the relation or correlation between two variables, X and Y. It expresses how much Y varies with variation in X, the "going-togetherness" of the X and Y scores. It also expresses how well Y can be predicted from X. We also learned earlier in this chapter that if r is squared, r^2, this expresses the amount of variance shared by X and Y. The use and interpretation of R are similar. R, the multiple correlation coefficient, expresses the magnitude of the relation between, on the one hand, the best possible combination of all the independent variables and, on the other hand, the dependent variable. Suppose we calculate with the regression equation the predicted Y's, or Y', for all the members of a group whose scores on several tests are being analyzed with multiple regression. We already have their scores on the dependent variable, Y. Now, if we calculate the correlation, r, between the two sets of scores, predicted (Y') and observed (Y), we obtain the multiple correlation coefficient, R.

Earlier we examined the nature of r^2, the squared coefficient of correlation, and learned that it expressed the variance shared by X and Y. If we do the same with R and obtain R^2, we can interpret the more complex relation similarly. R^2 expresses the variance shared by Y and Y'. More useful to us, R^2 expresses the amount of variance of Y, the dependent variable, accounted for by the regression combination of all the X's, the independent variables. Figure 11.4 expressed a hypothetical and unrealistic situation of the amount of variance of achievement scores accounted for by six independent variables assuming that all the correlations among all the independent variables were zero. Figure 11.5 expressed the variance of achievement accounted for by two independent variables, but the two independent variables were themselves correlated. It is very difficult to draw such a figure with three or more independent variables, trying visually to depict all the r^2's. It is quite possible to do so, however, if we use the Y and Y' reasoning just discussed.

Multiple regression analysis always yields an R and an R^2. R^2 is an index of the maximum amount of variance of Y accounted for by all the X's, as said above. Suppose we have a dependent variable, reading achievement (Y), and two independent variables, verbal aptitude (X_1) and achievement motivation (X_2). (Achievement motivation is a measure of students' orien-

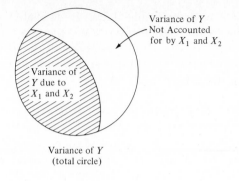

FIG. 11.7

tation toward achieving in school.) Further suppose the regression equation is that given above and that R^2 is .51. This R^2 is the percentage of the variance of reading achievement due to the best possible statistical combination of verbal aptitude and achievement motivation. The situation is depicted in Figure 11.7.

The total circle represents the variance of Y, reading achievement, the dependent variable. The hatched portion of the circle indicates, as usual, the variance of Y accounted for by a combination of X_1 and X_2, verbal aptitude and achievement motivation. The unhatched portion indicates the variance of Y not accounted for by X_1 and X_2. It is called the *residual variance*. In this case, it is $1.00 - R^2$, or $1.00 - .51 = .49$, or 49 percent of the variance of Y. (.51 is subtracted from 1.00 because 1.00 is the highest value R^2 can have.) Some of the residual variance is error variance, chance errors and errors of measurement. But future research using other independent variables may be able to reduce this residual variance. For example, if we added measures of arithmetic aptitude, social class, and home background to the regression analysis, the hatched area would undoubtedly grow larger and the unhatched area smaller. In other words, the prediction of reading achievement would be improved, and the amount of unknown variance would thus be decreased.

TWO RESEARCH STUDIES

Although multiple regression has been used a good deal in behavioral research, it can safely be said that its use has only begun. Certainly it has been used much less than analysis of variance, sometimes in cases where it should have been used instead of analysis of variance. In general, analysis of variance is appropriate for experimental data. Multiple regression, however, is appropriate for both experimental and nonexperimental data. It is admirably suited to the analysis of mixed data, data from research in which one or more variables have been manipulated and also in which there are one or more attribute variables. For this reason it has been called a general approach or method of data analysis (when there is one dependent variable).

We present summaries of two researches in which multiple regression was used as the principal analytic tool. As we will see, multiple regression was admirably suited to the problems of the studies. Indeed, one can hardly imagine any other approach. The two studies are quite different in their substance and purpose, but they share an important characteristic: they both used environmental or ecological variables to explain important phenomena. They also illustrate a number of points we have tried to make about the multivariate approach in general and about multiple regression in particular.

Marjoribanks: Environment, Ethnicity, and Mental Ability

Marjoribanks (1972), in a competent and imaginative study of influences on mental ability, used a method for measuring what he called environmental press, pressure or influence of the environment. There were eight "environmental forces": press for achievement, press for intellectuality, press for independence, and so on. Each environmental force was measured with several items called environmental characteristics. For example, press for achievement had the following items, among others: parental expectation for the education of the child, parent's own aspirations, and valuing educational accomplishments. The instrument was administered in interviews in children's homes. In short, the learning environment of the home was measured with the instrument under the assumption that the child's home environment was a potent influence on his mental ability and achievement.

Marjoribanks wished to study the influence of the environmental forces on mental development among five Canadian ethnic groups: Canadian Indians, French Canadians, Jews, southern Italians, white Anglo-Saxon Protestants. The dependent variable of the study was mental development; it was measured by four subtests of a well-known mental abilities test, the SRA Primary Abilities Test: Verbal, Number, Spatial, Reasoning. Thus there were actually four dependent variables, or four aspects of the basic dependent variable, mental ability. There were two independent variables: environmental force and ethnic group membership, or ethnicity. The basic question asked, then, was: How do environmental force and ethnicity affect mental development? Marjoribanks wanted to know how each independent variable separately affected mental development and how they affected mental development in concert.

The sample consisted of 37 families, 18 middle class and 19 lower class, from each ethnic group, or a total of 185 ethnic families. The five ethnic groups differed significantly on the profiles of the four mental abilities. The largest differences were on verbal ability, as might have been expected. We are more interested, however, in Marjoribanks' multiple regression analysis in which the additive (and subtractive) characteristics of R^2's were used. Let us examine the verbal ability and reasoning ability results.

The R that expressed the correlation between verbal ability, on the one hand, and the combination of environment and ethnicity, on the other hand, was .78. That is, the correlation between the predicted Y's, yielded by the regression equation that included the two independent variables environment and ethnicity, and the obtained Y's, the actual verbal ability scores, was .78. Squaring this R, Marjoribanks obtained $R^2 = .78^2 = .61$. This was interpreted as before: 61 percent of the variance of verbal ability was accounted for by environment and ethnicity in combination, a substantial portion of the variance. If the finding is taken at face value, we can say that environmental factors and ethnic group membership—the differences between the ethnic groups—have a rather strong influence on verbal ability. And this is certainly important and valuable information. It tells us little, however, about the separate "influences" of the two variables.

Marjoribanks then calculated separate regression analyses, one between verbal ability and environment and one between verbal ability and ethnicity. The R^2's were: .50 for verbal ability and environment and .45 for verbal ability and ethnicity. To obtain estimates of the separate influences of each of these variables, he subtracted their R^2's in turn from the R^2 obtained with both together. The latter was .61, recall. Therefore the separate effect of environment is estimated by subtracting the R^2 for ethnicity, or .45, from .61: $.61 - .45 = .16$. Thus 16 percent of the variance of verbal ability was accounted for by environment alone. The separate effect of ethnicity was similarly obtained: the R^2 for environment was subtracted from the R^2 for both environment and ethnicity: $.61 - .50 = .11$. Thus 11 percent of the variance of verbal ability was accounted for by ethnicity, or ethnic group membership.

This apparently complex procedure is really rather simple. One calculates the R^2 of the joint effect of the two variables. This yields the total variance of verbal ability due to both the variables working together, so to speak. Then one subtracts in turn the R^2's due to each variable. This yields estimates of the influence of each variable purged of the influence of the other variable. What about the variance of the joint effect of both variables that is still not accounted for? After all, the separate effects of environment and ethnicity only add to: $.16 + .11 = .27$. There is thus $.61 - .27 = .34$ left. This R^2 is that part of the total variance accounted for by both environment and ethnicity that is due to both variables evidently working together and that cannot be disentangled. In other words, the two variables have separate influences and a joint influence that cannot be dismembered.

As far as the best prediction of verbal ability is concerned, the above analysis doesn't matter. Marjoribanks could simply say that 61 percent of the variance of verbal ability is due to environment and ethnicity, and in future situations he can use both—and others, perhaps—to predict verbal ability. Scientific explanation, however, requires more than this. We want to know the relative influences of independent variables in their effects on a dependent variable. We want to explain in as much depth and detail as possible the phenomenon of interest, and not just predict it. Marjoribanks' analysis, then, was aimed at both prediction and explanation. Let me try to express these ideas in a somewhat different way.

Some of the results of Marjoribanks' multiple regression analysis are given in Table 11.1. Of the four dependent variables, only the verbal ability and reasoning ability analyses are included in the table. The total variances for both abilities together, Environment + Ethnicity, are .61 for verbal ability and .22 for reasoning ability. The .61 is the proportion (or percentage) of the verbal ability variance that environment *and* ethnicity account for. The comparable figure for reasoning ability is .22, much less. These can be considered to be "total" variances accounted for, and we wish to estimate the separate contributions of the two independent variables, environment and ethnicity. Environment accounts for .50 of the variance of verbal ability. Ethnicity accounts for .45 of the variance. The comparable figures for reasoning ability are .16 and .08. Henceforth we concentrate on verbal ability to reinforce the earlier discussion.

The proportions .50 for environment and .45 for ethnicity, however, are not "pure" estimates of the contributions to the variance of verbal ability of these variables because part of each proportion of variance is shared with the other independent variable. Therefore, that part due to the other variable must be subtracted from the joint contribution of both variables. These remainders are indicated by $A - B$ and $A - C$ in the table. $A - B = .11$, for instance, means: of the "total" contribution of both environment and ethnicity (A), .11, or 11 percent, remains after subtracting the effect of environment, or $.61 - .50 = .11$.

If we go back to using the circles of earlier figures, things may become clear. In Figure 11.8 we use the method of variance portrayal of Figure 11.6. The upper circle represents the variance of verbal ability, the two lower circles the variances of environment and ethnicity. The hatched area be-

TABLE 11.1 **Variances Accounted for by Environment and Ethnicity, Marjoribanks (1972) Study[a]**

DEPENDENT VARIABLE	INDEPENDENT VARIABLE	R^2	
Verbal Ability	Environment + Ethnicity (A)	.61	
	Environment (B)	.50	
	Ethnicity (C)	.45	
Effect of Ethnicity Alone = $A - B$ =			.11
Effect of Environment Alone = $A - C$ =			.16
Reasoning Ability	Environment + Ethnicity (A)	.22	
	Environment (B)	.16	
	Ethnicity (C)	.08	
Effect of Ethnicity Alone = $A - B$ =			.06
Effect of Environment Alone = $A - C$ =			.14

[a] This table was derived from Marjoribanks' Tables 5 and 6. It is in somewhat different form than his tables.

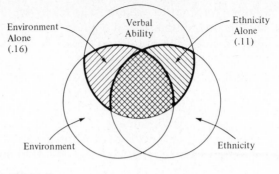

FIG. 11.8

tween verbal ability and environment represents the .50 of Table 11.1, and the hatched area between verbal ability and ethnicity represents the .45 of Table 11.1. The area outlined in heavy lines on the left represents the variance of verbal ability accounted for by environment alone (.16), while the similar area on the right represents the variance of verbal ability accounted for by ethnicity alone (.11). Note, too, that a substantial portion of the variance of verbal ability is accounted for by both variables in concert (the doubly hatched area). So the two influences to a substantial extent work together; they cannot be disentangled (.34: .50 − .16, or .45 − .11). There is also variance shared by environment and ethnicity that is not related to verbal ability (the unhatched area shared by them).

Taking the values in Table 11.1 at face value, we can reach two or three conclusions. Both environment and ethnicity seem to have considerable "influence" on verbal ability, especially when they "work together" (34 percent). Their contributions alone, while not large, are appreciable (11 percent and 16 percent). The "influence" of environment independent of ethnicity appears to be larger than the "influence" of ethnicity independent of environment (16 percent versus 11 percent). A similar analysis can be applied to reasoning ability. We note especially that environment and ethnicity evidently are not nearly as strongly related to reasoning ability as to verbal ability. It is not hard to understand this rather important finding. The reason is left for the reader to deduce.

We have discussed this example at length because of the importance and significance of the subject itself and because of the importance of the regression analysis. A method of analysis that can disentangle complex influences in this way is most valuable. Moreover, we have examined its use with only two independent variables. It is also applicable with more than two independent variables, though analysis and interpretation become much more complex, difficult, and sometimes even elusive. (Marjoribanks wisely chose to treat his eight environmental measures as one independent variable in his partitioning analysis—after first establishing that they were all substantially positively correlated, indicating that they were all more or less measuring the same thing.) The reader must also be cautioned. Like all methods of statistical analysis, this method yields only estimates of the values of the R^2's. Sometimes the R^2's can be biased and misleading. Competent researchers and analysts will not use the R^2's alone in their analyses and interpretations. They will also use regression coefficients, the original correlations from which the R^2's emerge, other statistics, and the results of other researchers.

Perhaps above all, researchers will be extremely cautious about making causal statements. Even though we used expressions like "accounted for" and "effects," causal implications, while perhaps inescapable because of language connotations, were not intended. In the Marjoribanks research, it is particularly important to keep one's bearings. When we talk about the influence of ethnicity on verbal ability, for example, we certainly intend the meaning that the ethnic group to which a child belongs influences his verbal ability—for obvious reasons. But the more accurate research statement is that there are differences in verbal ability between, say, Anglo-Saxon Canadians and French Canadians. But this is a functional difference in ability in the English language. We do not mean that being Anglo-Saxon, in and of itself, somehow "causes" better verbal ability in general than being French Canadian. The safest way to reason is probably the conditional statement usage emphasized throughout this book: If p, then q, with a relative absence of causal implication.

Cutright: Regression Analysis and High Correlations

The analysis and results of a study by Cutright (1963) may increase our understanding of a multivariate approach to scientific and practical problems. It may also alert us to a particular difficulty of interpretation that occurs fairly often in sociological inquiry. It will also illustrate interesting measurement of so-called ecological variables.

Cutright wished to study the political development of 77 nations. Rather than to use individuals or small groups as the unit of analysis, Cutright used whole countries. To do this, he constructed a complex measure of political development by giving varying numbers of points to countries for their relative development in the legislative and executive branches of government, for example, one point for each year a nation had a chief executive who had been elected by direct vote in a competitive election. The resulting measure was the dependent variable. The independent variables were also complex measures—of communication, urbanization, education, and agriculture.

The correlations between each of the individual variables and the dependent variable, political development, were high: from .69 to .81 (one was negative and also high). But the correlations among the independent variables were even higher: .74 to .88. This poses a problem in multiple regression analysis. Recall that the ideal prediction situation is high correlations between independent variables and the dependent variable, and low correlations among the independent variables. (Marjoribanks got around this problem by combining the independent variables into one independent variable after a separate analysis showed that the eight environmental variables were more or less measures of the same underlying variable, as indicated earlier.) When the correlations among the independent variables are substantial, technical problems arise which make interpretation of results difficult and ambiguous. Cutright was well aware of the problem and interpreted his results cautiously.

In any case, the multiple coefficient of correlation, R, was .82 and R^2 was .67. But the R^2 (really r^2) between political development and only one of his independent variables, communication, was .65! Thus, the additional independent variables added only .02 to the prediction of political development! Cutright was not content, however, merely with this high prediction. Using clever regression reasoning, he was able to interpret the political development of individual nations. His idea, basically, was to predict the *expected* development of each nation using the calculated regression equation. This is the same as calculating the predicted Y's, or Y'''s, discussed earlier, using the obtained information on the independent variables. That is, for each nation he substituted the values he obtained for each independent variable for that nation and then calculated Y', the expected value based on the equation.

For example, suppose he obtained for a particular country the following X scores: 7 for communication, 6 for urbanization, 6 for education, and 2 for agriculture. And suppose the regression equation calculated from all the data was:

$$Y' = 9. + .82X_1 + .74X_2 + .60X_3 - .65X_4$$

Then the predicted Y, or Y', would be:

$$Y' = 9. + (.82)(7) + (.74)(6) + (.60)(6) - (.65)(2) = 21.48$$

Further suppose that the obtained Y score, the score on political development, was 14.50. Cutright could then reason that the political development of the nation under analysis was lower than expectation. Given its communication, urbanization, education, and agriculture, it "should have" had a score on political development of about 21.48. Instead it was considerably lower, 14.50. In any case, Cutright's study is a good example of contemporary social scientific research into an interesting and important phenomenon, political development, in which multiple regression analysis was fruitfully used.

12

The multivariate approach
factor analysis

When I think of factor analysis, two words come to mind: "curiosity" and "parsimony." This seems a rather strange pair—but not in relation to factor analysis. Curiosity means wanting to know what is there, how it works, and why it is there and why it works. It also means the wish or the itch to penetrate things, to know what is behind them. Scientists are curious. They want to know what's there and why. They want to know what is behind things. And they want to do this in as parsimonious a fashion as possible. They do not want an elaborate explanation when it is not needed. The simplest possible explanation is the best explanation—though not always. This ideal we can call the principle of parsimony.

In order to explain things, we have to try to reduce the masses of information and phenomena that surround us to manageable form and size. In our efforts to explain phenomena, we try to reduce the large and often confusing domains of variables, for example, to smaller and more comprehensible domains. Suppose we are working in some area of interest and are confronted with a hundred variables that are perhaps related to the area of interest. A hundred variables is too much; we can't really grasp so many variables. Is it possible to reduce the number? We know from experience that many of the hundred variables are correlated with each other. Is it possible to discover which of the variables are correlated with each other and how much they are correlated? Is it possible through this information to somehow combine or cluster the variables that are correlated with each other to "create" new and fewer variables?

179

Suppose all this *is* possible. Will creating new and fewer variables satisfy my original curiosity about whatever it is I am curious about? Certainly the reduction of the number of variables seems parsimonious. If we have, say, twelve instead of a hundred variables, we have a more parsimonious situation. Or so we think and hope. Why do we insist on parsimony? Is it so important?

In general scientists believe that the most parsimonious, the simplest, explanation is the best explanation, other things equal. This is because if we let explanations and reasons multiply we end up with confusion, or with a situation so complex that we cannot really grasp it. But part of all this is faith. We have faith that somehow there is usually a simple explanation for most phenomena. That this is often not true does not change the faith. In any case, seeking simpler explanations and then testing their implications are strong scientific preoccupations.

One of the most powerful methods yet invented for reducing variable complexity to greater simplicity is factor analysis. *Factor analysis* is an analytic method for determining the number and nature of the variables that underlie larger numbers of variables or measures. It tells the researcher, in effect, what tests or measures belong together—which ones virtually measure the same thing, in other words, and how much they do so. The "underlying variables" in this definition are called "factors." Someone has called factor analysis the queen of analytic methods. Why? Let us take a famous example, intelligence and its nature, to try to understand this remarkable invention and the definition just given. Intelligence is a good example because of its intrinsic theoretical and practical interest and because a great deal is now known about it—though much of it still remains a mystery. Before starting this discussion, we digress to define certain terms and expressions that are commonly used in factor analysis and multivariate analysis.

A Definitional Digression

As just indicated, a *factor* is an underlying and unobserved variable that presumably "explains" observed tests, items, or measures. In the next section of this chapter an example of a factor analysis of intelligence tests is given. Three of the tests measure three aspects of verbal intelligence: Sentences, Vocabulary, and Completion. It has been found that these tests measure something in common. Study of the content of the tests seems to indicate that the underlying something being measured is verbal ability. "Verbal Ability," then, is a factor.

More precisely, a *factor* is a construct, a hypothetical entity, an unobserved variable that is assumed to underlie tests, scales, items, and, indeed, measures of any kind. There has been controversy over factors and factor analysis, a good deal of it stemming from the presumed "reality" of factors. Let us say here that the only "reality" factors have inheres in their accounting for the variance of observed variables, as revealed through the correlations among the variables.

A frequently occurring word in factor analysis and multivariate analysis generally is "matrix." Indeed, matrix algebra, algebra that uses matrices rather than individual symbols, is a key tool in the mathematics of multivariate analysis. A *matrix* is a rectangular array of numbers—though one can have a matrix of other symbols, too. Matrices can have virtually any dimensions: 2×2 (read "two by two"), 3×20, 15×15, and so on. The first number usually stands for the number of rows, and the second number for the number of columns. A 7×3 matrix, then, has seven rows and three columns. The matrix of Table 12.1 is an 8×3 matrix. The matrix of Table 12.2 is a 6×6 correlation matrix, often symbolized by R. Correlation matrices are symmetric because the lower half below the diagonal from upper left to lower right is a mirror image of the upper half. The type of matrix given in Table 12.1 is called a matrix of factor loadings or coefficients.

The expression "factor loading" occurs frequently. A matrix of factor loadings is one of the final products of factor analysis. A *factor loading* is a coefficient—a positive or negative decimal number usually less than 1—that expresses how much a test or observed variable is "loaded" or "saturated" on a factor. In Table 12.1, the columns are the factors, as we shall see, and the rows the tests or observed variables. The test Sentences, for example, is "loaded" .66 on Verbal (the first factor), whereas its loading on Number (the second factor) is only .01. Factor matrices are said to be unrotated or rotated. We need not define what these terms mean. Suffice it to say that final factor analytic solutions almost always require rotated matrices or solution. Factor loadings are further defined later.

For our purposes, a *factor structure* is a (usually) rotated factor matrix that shows the "structure," pattern, or configuration of the factors and the variables. ("Factor structure" also has a technical meaning that we do not need in our conceptual presentation.) In general, this means which tests or variables are loaded on which factors. Table 12.1 shows a "factor structure." So does Table 12.4. But a graph can also show a factor structure. In Figures 12.3 and 12.4 factor structures are shown.

The reader should not be too concerned if he or she does not now completely grasp the meanings of these terms. They should become clear as we work our way through the chapter. Now, to intelligence approached through factor analysis.

INTELLIGENCE AND ITS NATURE

We have always known that there are large differences in the way people handle problems. Some people grasp problems quickly, efficiently, and deeply. Others are not so quick and efficient. The range is enormous:

from those individuals capable of the highest degree of intellectual comprehension and mastery of abstract thought to those individuals almost completely incapable of any abstract thought. In an earlier chapter, we said that from a research point of view it would be much simpler if all people had the same intelligence, if there were no individual differences in mental ability. But the brute fact of large differences in intellectual ability is there, and it won't go away.

One of the most difficult and intriguing problems that has faced the modern psychologist is the nature of intelligence. What is intelligence? Is it a single unitary capacity that we all possess to a greater or lesser degree? Or is it not an "it" at all? Is it, rather, a set—perhaps a rather large set—of more or less related abilities? The experience of centuries has produced arguments for both views—and for others. Such arguments, however, are not scientifically satisfying. Is there systematic scientific evidence on the nature of intelligence?

Fortunately, there is a great deal of scientific evidence. Moreover, great strides have been made in its measurement. Paradoxically, however, psychologists are still far from knowing precisely what intelligence is. Indeed, they cannot even agree on a definition of intelligence. This is by no means unusual in science, however. Great strides can be made and knowledge advanced and ignorance decreased, even though a basic problem that started scientific investigation is still not solved.

A Research Example: Thurstone

In the earlier years of this century, there was much theory, speculation, and research on the nature of intelligence (Guilford, 1967). The nature of intelligence is highly significant, theoretically and practically. Scientific knowledge of the nature of intelligence can greatly advance psychological understanding of human (and animal) mental processes. And so it has. The practical effects, too, can be great. But our interest is in the principal method of analysis used to study intelligence: factor analysis. We try to understand factor analysis first by considering research into intelligence by one of the great psychologists of the century, Leon Thurstone.

Thurstone believed that intelligence was a set of separate but related fundamental abilities. After considerable work writing tests, giving the tests to many children, and analyzing the results, he concluded that there were a number of underlying entities behind many of the tests he had written and administered to children: Perception, Number, Word Fluency, Verbal, Space, Memory, Reasoning. In effect, he proposed a theory of the structure of intelligence, and the foundation of the theory was these entities, or "factors," as he and others called them.

To make clear what is meant, look at the tests named in Table 12.1. In one study, Thurstone and his wife (Thurstone & Thurstone, 1941) administered 60 tests of many kinds—vocabulary, addition, multiplication, mirror reading, letter groups, figure recognition, and so on—to 710 eighth-grade

TABLE 12.1   Selected Thurstone Tests and Rotated
Factor Matrix[a]

TESTS	VERBAL	NUMBER	PERCEPTION
Sentences	.66	.01	.00
Vocabulary	.66	.02	−.01
Completion	.67	.00	−.01
Addition	.01	.64	.01
Multiplication	−.03	.67	.01
Identification			
Numbers	.06	.40	.42
Faces	.04	.17	.45
Mirror Reading	−.02	.09	.36

[a] The entries in the table are called factor loadings. They can be interpreted like correlation coefficients.

pupils. In earlier research, Thurstone had found that appropriate analysis showed that certain sets of tests clustered together. They were positively correlated, in other words. To the extent that two tests correlate positively, to that extent (other things equal) they measure the same thing. Suppose we have three tests, and their intercorrelations are $r_{12} = .70$, $r_{13} = .64$, $r_{23} = .57$. The tests are vocabulary, reading and writing sentences, and completion of sentences (when presented with words omitted). What is the common element in these three tests? What makes them correlate so substantially? Thurstone concluded that it was basic ability associated with verbal learning and materials. He called it "Verbal," or "Verbal Ability."

Table 12.1 gives only a small part of the Thurstone and Thurstone results. I have selected for illustrative purposes only three of their seven factors (see below): *Verbal, Number,* and *Perception.* They are sufficient, however, for the present purpose. The names of eight of Thurstone and Thurstone's 60 tests are given on the left side of the table. The numbers in the body of the table are like correlation coefficients and are called "factor loadings." (See definition given earlier.) The larger a number that goes with a test—for example, the test Vocabulary has .66 under *Verbal,* .02 under *Number,* and −.01 under *Perception*—the more the test is associated with the factor. These loadings indicate that the test Vocabulary belongs to the factor *Verbal* and not to the factors *Number* or *Perception.*

Examine the loadings under *Verbal.* The three tests named above have the substantial loadings of .66, .66, and .67. The other five tests have loadings near zero (.01, −.03, and so on). A factor analyst would conclude that these tests share something in common—remember our earlier discussions of correlations, squared correlations, and shared variance. The three tests measure something in common. Had the loadings been 1.00, 1.00 and 1.00 (highly unlikely), the analyst could conclude that they are measuring the same thing perfectly. Had the loadings been .00, .00, and .00 (also unlikely), then he could conclude that they are not at all measuring the same thing.

Since the common element or elements of the three tests with the substantial loadings are all clearly associated with words, the analyst can conclude that the underlying common "factor" is verbal ability. Thus it is named "Verbal." Similar reasoning applies to the remaining five tests and two factors. The tests Addition, Multiplication, and Identification Numbers have substantial loadings of .64, .67, and .40 on the second factor. They share mental processes associated with numerical operations. The factor is thus called "Number."

Two of the tests, Faces and Mirror Reading, are loaded on the third factor, *Perception*, and on no other factor. The test Identification Numbers, however, is loaded on the third factor and also on the second factor. This means that it is a more complex test. One might say that it partakes of the essence of both *Perception* and *Number*. Such cases occur often in factor analytic investigations.

SOME ELEMENTS OF FACTOR ANALYSIS

If a test is given twice to the same sample of individuals, then the correlation between the two sets of scores should be 1.00. It is never 1.00, however, due to inevitable errors of measurement. But it should be high, if the test is reliable. If two tests measure the same thing, let's say verbal ability, then the correlation between them, after giving them to the same sample of individuals, should be high, or at least substantial. Even though all the items may be different—two different tests of vocabulary, for instance—they all more or less tap an aspect of verbal ability. Therefore individuals should respond to them similarly, and should be ranked by the two tests in much the same way.

On the other hand, the correlation between two tests that measure quite different things, say verbal ability and dogmatism, should be close to zero. There is no systematic relation between the two sets of scores yielded by the same sample of individuals. Of course, if there is some presently unknown relation between verbal ability and dogmatism—and there well may be—then there should be some correlation, positive or negative, greater than zero between the two tests. It may be that more verbal people are more dogmatic. At present, however, we know no reason for there to be a correlation between the two variables.

These two conditions of correlation are expressed in Figure 12.1. Each circle represents the variance of a test, as it did earlier. (It is suggested that the reader quickly review Chapters 4, 9, and, especially, 11. Understanding of factor analysis can be materially helped by understanding relations, correlations, measurement, and shared variance.) Consider the situation of the diagram, labeled (A). VA_1 stands for Verbal Ability 1, the first test of verbal ability; VA_2, of course, stands for the second test. The two circles, each standing for the variance of its test, overlap a great deal. The situation is comparable to that in Figure 11.6 of Chapter 11, except that that figure

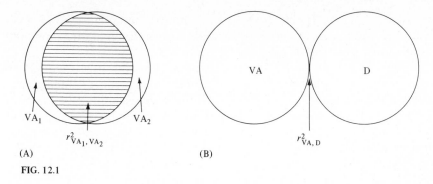

(A)   (B)

FIG. 12.1

was more complex. In the present case, the correlation is about .90 because most of the variances of the two tests are shared: some 80 percent ($r^2 = .90^2 = .81$). This means that the two tests are probably measuring the same thing, verbal ability.

The situation in Figure 12.1(B) is quite different. No variance is shared. The correlation between the two tests, verbal ability (VA) and dogmatism (D), is zero. They measure quite different things.

The two conditions depicted in Figure 12.1 show what factor analysts work with, shared variance, and the limits within which they work: between high or substantial correlation and zero correlation. They seek to discover the unities underlying tests and measures by studying and analyzing the correlations among tests, and, from the correlations, the shared variances. The method of factor analysis enables them to discover the shared variances of tests and measures and to determine the relations among the various shared variances. This is rather abstract talk. Let's be more concrete and specific.

A Fictitious, But Not Unrealistic, Example

Suppose, like Thurstone and many others, I am interested in "factors" of mental ability. I do not believe that mental ability is a unitary thing, a general intellectual power evident in all human thinking and doing. Rather, I suspect that there are a number of different facets or aspects of intelligence, and that individuals differ widely and variously on these facets. But I also know that there is a limit: there must be some relatively small number of the facets, and I want to know what they are. (A very big order, indeed!)

For the sake of simplicity, suppose that the psychological world of intelligence is two-dimensional, but no one knows it. Assume that a psychological scientist wants to understand the nature of human intelligence, that she is expert in psychological measurement, and that she believes the psychological "world" of intelligence has more than one dimension. Further assume that she is radical in her belief that almost all psychologists believe that intelligence is one-dimensional, and if it can be learned what the "nature" of this dimension is, then, assuming suitable expertise, psychologists can measure intelligence and can, in time, understand and know a great deal about intelligence.

Before continuing with the two-dimensional model, it is important to understand the implications of a one-dimensional world of intelligence. First, consider intelligence tests. Suppose there were six published tests of intelligence. If we gave a large group of people, say 300, all six tests and then calculated the correlations among all the tests, what would the correlations be like? They would be something like the correlations given in the correlation matrix of Table 12.2. All the correlations are positive and substantial. All six tests evidently measure the same thing, and, since the tests are intelligence tests, they must be measuring intelligence. Factor analysts would say that there is one factor to be derived from the correlation matrix of Table 12.2. In other words, we have done an inspectional armchair factor analysis and have concluded, because all the correlations among the tests were positive and substantial—and all of them more or less the same level of magnitude—that there is one factor in the data. And this conclusion fits the earlier notion that intelligence inhabits a one-dimensional psychological world.

But now take a two-dimensional psychological world. What would a correlation matrix obtained in such a world look like? Go back to our radical psychologist who believes that the psychological world of intelligence is two-dimensional. She believes that all the intelligence tests written hitherto are unsatisfactory because they inhabit the one-dimensional world. They might be satisfactory if intelligence were really only one-dimensional. Her strong hunch, however, is that it is not; it is two-dimensional! The "reality" of her intelligence world is quite different from the "reality" of the common belief of other psychologists. How can she demonstrate her belief and show the common belief to be wrong?

She believes that the underlying "entity" of the six tests of Table 12.2 to be verbal ability, since careful study of the tests shows that all six use predominantly verbal items. That is, they all demand verbal knowledge, verbal manipulation, and verbal reasoning. What would the matrix of correlations be like if half the tests demanded a different kind of knowl-

TABLE 12.2   Correlations among Six Tests in a
One-Dimensional Intelligence World

	TESTS					
	1	2	3	4	5	6
1	1.00	.62	.59	.81	.67	.50
2	.62	1.00	.47	.72	.52	.49
3	.59	.47	1.00	.69	.61	.53
4	.81	.72	.69	1.00	.47	.41
5	.67	.52	.61	.47	1.00	.52
6	.50	.49	.53	.41	.52	1.00

TABLE 12.3   Target Matrix and Obtained Correlation Matrix,
Six Tests of Intelligence[a]

	TARGET MATRIX[b]						OBTAINED MATRIX[c]					
	1	2	3	4	5	6	1	2	3	4	5	6
1	1.00	x	x	0	0	0	1.00	.71	.64	.15	.05	.02
2		1.00	x	0	0	0		1.00	.58	.06	.11	.01
3			1.00	0	0	0			1.00	.14	.05	.10
4				1.00	x	x				1.00	.59	.68
5					1.00	x					1.00	.64
6						1.00						1.00

[a] Tests 1, 2, and 3 are verbal tests; tests 4, 5, and 6 are mathematical tests.
[b] x: predicted substantial positive correlation; 0: predicted zero or near-zero correlation.
[c] Italicized correlations are those predicted in the target matrix.

edge, manipulation, and reasoning, say numerical or mathematical knowledge? The psychologist prepares three new tests, one to measure mathematical knowledge, another mathematical manipulation, and the third mathematical reasoning. She administers these tests and three of the verbal tests to a sample of persons and intercorrelates the six tests.

If the common belief that intelligence is one-dimensional is correct, then the correlation matrix the psychologist obtains should be very similar to that of Table 12.2; that is, all six tests should be positively and substantially correlated with each other. But if the psychologist's belief that intelligence is two-dimensional is correct, then what should the correlation matrix be like? In Table 12.3, on the left, a "target matrix" is given. It can also be called a "hypothesis matrix" because it expresses essentially what the psychologist has hypothesized. Tests 1, 2, and 3 are verbal tests; tests 4, 5, and 6 are the mathematical tests. The crosses represent hypothesized substantial correlations, and the zeros represent correlations of zero or close to zero.[1] On the right of Table 12.3 the matrix of correlations she actually obtained is given. The italicized correlations—.71, .64, .58, and so forth—are those predicted to be substantial by the target matrix. All other correlations should be close to zero.[2]

Evidently the psychologist's belief or hypothesis is correct. Tests 1, 2, and 3, the verbal tests, are positively and substantially correlated with each other: $r_{12} = .71$, $r_{13} = .64$, $r_{23} = .58$. Tests 4, 5, and 6, the mathematical tests, are likewise positively and substantially correlated with each other: $r_{45} = .59$, $r_{46} = .68$, and $r_{56} = .64$. And, very important, even crucial, the correlations between tests 1, 2, and 3, on the one hand, and tests 4, 5, and 6, on the other hand, are all low and near zero.

[1] Actually, with ability measures, one cannot expect zero correlations because most of them are positively correlated, at least to some extent. We use a model kind of exposition, however, to clarify the basic ideas behind factor analysis.
[2] Only the top halves of the matrices are given. This is possible because the matrices are symmetric, that is, their lower halves (below the diagonal running from upper left to lower right), if given, will be merely mirror images of the top halves of the matrices (above the diagonal).

The evidence of Table 12.3 is compelling. One is compelled along the way to belief in the empirical validity of the psychologist's theory. One study would never be enough; it is probably only suggestive. If more carefully controlled studies are done and the results are similar, then belief is compelled even further. If the psychologist's theory holds up under critical appraisal and deliberate efforts to show it not to be correct through rigorous research specifically designed to unseat it, then one may be compelled to accept the theory and its validity. The point pertinent to this chapter is that the attempts to bring empirical evidence to bear on the theory required factor analysis—or some comparable method—because the hypothesis being tested is structural, or can even be called spatial: instead of one dimension or factor of intelligence, there are two.

The example has aspects important enough to make us pause and dwell on them briefly. The most important has two facets. First, since we now know that intelligence has more than two dimensions or factors, neither theory is correct. The first theory says, in effect, that there is one dimension or factor of intelligence. The second theory says there are two. Second, although neither theory is correct, one is more "correct" than the other in the sense that it is nearer to the "truth," it is closer to empirical "reality." And this is the history of science: continual better approximations of the "truth," but never attaining complete "truth."

A Qualitative and Spatial Approach to Factor Analysis

The correlation matrices of Tables 12.2 and 12.3 provided the evidence for the conclusions reached in the above examples. All our reasoning was based on the correlations of those tables. And the examples were simple; they were deliberately concocted for the purpose in as simple a manner as possible. Correlation matrices are not usually so obliging, nor are theories and hypotheses so simple. For the most part, such matrices are much too complex to interpret directly. Their complexity and sheer size—a study of the correlations among 20 tests or variables, not too large a number in modern behavioral research, is the study of 190 correlations!—forbid direct interpretation. The correlations and the factors really say the same thing, of course, but the correlations cannot usually be grasped in their totality, while the factors often can. Factor analysis thus reduces the complexity of the original correlations of Table 12.2, for example, to the point where we can plot the tests as in Figures 12.2 and 12.3. The length of the line in Figure 12.2 has arbitrarily and conveniently been made equal to 1.00, so that each test has an index of its position on the line or dimension, the values of the index being all possible values between and including 0 and 1.00.[3]

---

[3] Strictly speaking, the possible values should include negative values. For simplicity we temporarily ignore negative values. They are not important in studying intelligence anyway, since almost all correlations between intelligence tests are positive.

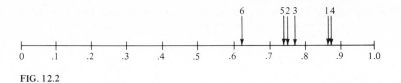

FIG. 12.2

To obtain the values plotted on the line, the correlations of Table 12.2 were factor analyzed. Through our earlier study of this correlation matrix, we learned that there was only one dimension or factor. One of the purposes of the factor analysis was to determine the values each test would have on the one dimension of Figure 12.2. The results of the factor analysis yielded the following values for the tests 1 through 6: .87, .75, .77, .87, .74, .62. (We need not concern ourselves with the actual calculations.) Their places on the line or dimension of Figure 12.2 are indicated by arrows with the numbers of the tests affixed. The six values are high and alike—in this artificial and unlikely example.

The six values are factor loadings, indices that report the degree of relation between each test and the presumed underlying dimension or factor. They are the correlations, in other words, between each test and the factor. The higher a factor loading, the more its test reflects or measures the factor, the more it "represents" the factor, so to speak. Loadings equal to or greater than .40 (sometimes .30; sometimes another criterion) are considered large enough to warrant interpretation. Obviously, all the loadings in this example are substantial. This was to be expected because the correlations among all the tests were substantial. Let us not take more time with this oversimplified example. Instead, we return to the more realistic two-dimensional example of Table 12.3.

We earlier decided, simply by inspecting the correlations of Table 12.3, that there were two dimensions or factors because tests 1, 2, and 3 were correlated with each other and not with tests 4, 5, and 6, and tests 4, 5, and 6 were correlated with each other and not with tests 1, 2, and 3. It is as though we had one set of tests to measure religious propensity and another set to measure musical aptitude. (We assume that the propensity and the aptitude are not related.) Let's probe more. Factor analysis is essentially a method for determining the number of factors there are in a set of data, for ascertaining which tests or variables belong to which factor or factors, and the extent the tests or variables "belong to," or are "saturated with" whatever the factor is. If we factor analyze the correlation matrix of Table 12.3, we will finally obtain a table like that given in Table 12.4.

The two factors reported in the table and labeled A and B are "factors" or "dimensions" in the sense that the three verbal tests are on one factor and the three mathematical tests are on the other factor. We knew this earlier, of course; the data of the original correlation matrix were so clear we could easily "see the factors": they were indicated by the pattern of the larger and smaller correlations. In most cases of actual research, with more

TABLE 12.4   Final Factor Analytic Solution of Data of Table 12.3

TESTS	A^a	B	TYPE OF TEST
1	.83	.07	Verbal
2	.79	.06	Verbal
3	.71	.11	Verbal
4	.07	.77	Mathematical
5	.02	.74	Mathematical
6	−.02	.81	Mathematical

[a] Loadings equal to or greater than .40 are considered significant. They are italicized.

variables that are correlated in complex ways, it is not possible to "see the factors" as it was in Table 12.3. In other words, the data of Table 12.4 demonstrate the obvious, what we already know. This is precisely why the example was manufactured: to demonstrate the obvious in an attempt to show what factor analysis is and what it does.

To repeat, if factor loadings are substantial or large, we assume that the tests or variables with which they are associated are "on" that factor. We say that a test is "loaded" on a factor. For example, tests 1, 2, and 3 are "loaded" on factor A, and tests 4, 5, and 6 are "loaded" on factor B. But the loadings of tests 1, 2, and 3 on factor B are low and insubstantial, and the loadings of tests 4, 5, and 6 on factor A are low and insubstantial. In factor analysis, both high and low loadings are important in interpretation. One may even say that the "ideal" factor analytic situation is one in which there are factor loadings that are high and low with no intermediate values.

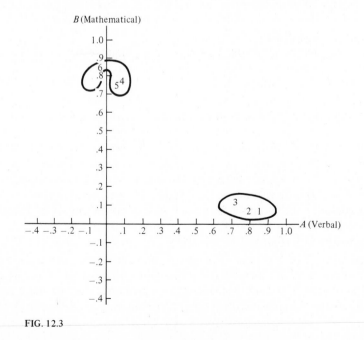

FIG. 12.3

Even though such situations seldom occur, it is good to remember them because they define clear-cut factors relatively unrelated to each other.

The interpretation of Table 12.4 is easy. Since tests 1, 2, and 3 are verbal tests and have high loadings on factor *A*, and since tests 4, 5, and 6 have low loadings on *A*, the factor is obviously a verbal factor. We call it, then, "Verbal." Similar analysis and reasoning apply to factor *B*. We call it "Mathematical." To clarify even more what Table 12.4 says, let's plot the factors. This has been done in Figure 12.3. Two axes, *A* and *B*, have been set up at right angles to each other. Recall that it is said that the axes are orthogonal to each other. The paired *A* and *B* values of Table 12.4 are then simply plotted. For example, .83 of test 1 on *A* and .07 of test 1 on *B* are realized by the point indicated by "1" on the graph of Figure 12.3. The remaining five pairs are similarly plotted.[4]

The clusters, 1, 2, and 3 and 4, 5, and 6, appear clearly. They are encircled on the graph. Tests 1, 2, and 3 are close together and near to and high on *A*; tests 4, 5, and 6 are close together and high on *B*. And, very important, the two clusters are far from each other. One is an *A* type and the other a *B* type. The two factors and the tests "defining" them are quite different kinds of entities. When I examine the three tests of *A* to find out its "nature," what it is, I see that all three tests are verbal. When I examine the *B* tests, on the other hand, I find that they share mathematical understanding, processes, and operations.

This example is oversimplified, of course. Most domains in the behavioral sciences have more than two factors. We would hardly study only six tests. And actual correlations and correlation matrices are rarely as obliging as this one with the beautiful orthogonal structure of Figure 12.3. Usually, then, the picture is not as clear; it is more muddied. In fact, the example is unrealistic because verbal tests and mathematical tests are always positively correlated. Indeed, all ability tests are positively corre-

[4] The justification for setting up the two axes against which to plot factor loadings as has been done in Figure 12.3 rests in the mathematical procedure that extracts or calculates the factors or factor loadings. The nature of the method is such that each factor extracted is independent of all the other factors extracted. This means that the factors extracted are all at right angles to each other. (Substantively, this in turn means that the factors are independent or different entities.) Thus, if we wish to plot the factor loadings, we do so using axes that are at right angles, or "orthogonal," to each other.

It should be emphasized that the factors and factor loadings of Table 12.4 and plotted in Figure 12.3 are "rotated." The method of factor extraction yields "unrotated" factors and loadings, and the magnitudes of the latter are usually not readily interpretable. What rotation does, in effect, is to put as many of the loadings as possible close to the axes, which represent the factors. Note in Figure 12.3 that the plotted points are all near the *A* or the *B* axes. In the original unrotated solution these points were rather far from the axes. Why should the points be near the two axes? The closer the points are to an axis, the greater the magnitude of the loadings on that axis; and, since the second axis is orthogonal (right angled) to the first axis, the lower the loadings will be on the second axis. Note that tests 1, 2, and 3 are close to and thus high on *A* and, at the same time, low on *B*, and, similarly, tests 4, 5, and 6 are near to and thus high on *B* and low on *A*. In short, the rotated factors and loadings give a more parsimonious and thus interpretable factor solution than the unrotated factors and loadings.

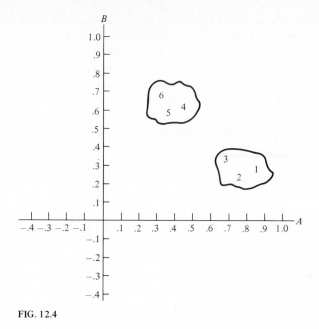

FIG. 12.4

lated, and such positive correlations make the results of factor analyses less clear and less easy to interpret. If, for example, tests 1, 2, and 3 of Table 12.3 were positively and substantially correlated with tests 4, 5, and 6, then the graph of Figure 12.3 would look something like the graph of Figure 12.4. Notice that the two clusters are closer together than they were. They are also some distance from the axes. The higher the correlations between the two kinds of tests, the closer together the clusters will be.

The above reasoning with only two dimensions generalizes readily to more than two, or k, dimensions. It is easy for most people to visualize two dimensions. Many can also easily handle three dimensions. But almost no one can visualize four or more dimensions. Yet factor analysts habitually extract four and more factors from correlation matrices and report the results of such factor analyses. It is easily possible to have 10 factors in a study, with all 10 factors being orthogonal to each other, that is, virtually independent of each other, at least in a technical sense. Because it is completely impossible to visualize 10 orthogonal dimensions does not all detract from our understanding of the factors and their meaning and interpretation!

RESEARCH EXAMPLES OF FACTOR ANALYSIS

The discussion has to now be separated from research reality, except for the earlier brief reference to Thurstone and his studies of intelligence. Indeed, our whole discussion has been much too narrow because it has been focused exclusively on intelligence and the factor analysis of intelligence test results. But factor analysis has been used with a wide variety of measures: aptitudes, attitudes and values, personality traits, environmental variables, cultural patterns, traits of honesty, even boxes and coffee cups! We now summarize and discuss three actual factor analytic research studies, preceded by a discussion of large-scale attempts by Guilford and his colleagues to test an ambitious theory of the structure of intelligence. The three studies have been chosen for their variety and possible intrinsic interest.

Guilford's Structure of Intellect Studies

As indicated earlier, there are several theories of the structure of intelligence—"structure" means, loosely, factors and their relations. At one extreme is the theory that claims intelligence to be one broad dimension, called general intelligence. Virtually no psychologists accept so simple a theory, though many of them accept the idea of a broad general intelligence factor plus other factors. In an earlier chapter, we saw that Cattell (1963) developed a theory in which two general "intelligences" are proposed: crystallized intelligence and fluid intelligence.

Perhaps the most radical of theories of intelligence, and certainly a controversial and heuristically fruitful theory, is the structure of intellect (SI) model proposed by Guilford (1956, 1967). Guilford says, in effect, that there are many factors of intelligence, and he specifies what their nature has to be. The theory is really an organization of factors into a complex categorial system consisting of three broad kinds of mental categories: operation, product, and content. Guilford has put these three organizing or structural principles into a large cube consisting of many cubes formed by the intersections of the subclasses of the three general structural principles.

This abstract description perhaps does not help us too well to understand Guilford's basic idea. Take the simplified cube of Figure 12.5, which is supposed to represent a highly simplified structural theory of intelligence like Guilford's. (There is no "reality" to this figure. It is only an intellectual convenience.) The figure is the simplest possible cube consisting of $2 \times 2 \times 2 = 8$ cubes. Each dimension of the cube has been dichotomized and labeled A B, I II, and 1 2. Let A and B represent verbal and numerical, I and II perceptual and memory, and 1 and 2 relations and implications. These three kinds of intellectual ability are called, respectively, *content, operation,* and *product.*

One can use the cube of Figure 12.5—Guilford's cube is much more complex, of course—as a model of the structure of intellect or intelligence. Each cube of the model spells out a factor. For example, AI1 would be a factor with content A, operation I, and product 1. Since there are eight cubes, there are eight factors. In other words, the cube is a theoretical model that can be used to write tests. For example, three tests for each cube

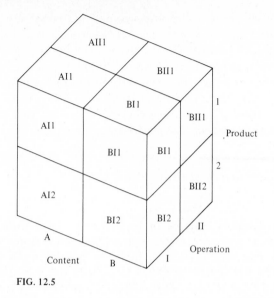

FIG. 12.5

cell can be written, a total of 24 tests. These tests can be given to a large number of children and can be intercorrelated and factor analyzed.

The empirical validity of the model rests in the results of the factor analysis. Are there, indeed, eight factors, and does their nature correspond to the nature "predicted" by the model? Moreover, and very important, as yet undiscovered factors may be predicted from the model. Suppose, for instance, that the model has a cube that describes a kind of operation or mental ability not yet encountered. Why not write three or four tests to measure the nature of the predicted factor, administer them with other tests to a suitable sample, factor analyze the results, and then see if the new tests appear together on a new factor? This is what Guilford and his colleagues have done, often with valuable results. One of these valuable findings, or perhaps confirmations, is the set of factors believed to be, and to some extent found to be, associated with creativity. It has been found, for example, that an important difference between thinking abilities is convergent thinking and divergent thinking, and that the latter is associated with creativity. (Convergent thinking is the usual kind of deductive analytic reasoning. Divergent thinking is associated with elaboration, originality, flexibility, creativity, and varied and fluent responses.)

As indicated earlier, factor analysis has been used with aptitudes, attitudes, personality traits, and even environmental variables. Moreover, it is not necessary that the correlations that are factor analyzed be calculated only from tests. Factor analysis has in recent years been more and more used with items, to determine the factors in a single test or scale. It has also been used to factor analyze the correlations between persons. We give examples of both possibilities later.

In other words, the method is more than a method; it is also an approach in the sense that it searches out and identifies underlying relations among variables. In this context, tests are variables, items are variables, and even persons are variables. The examples to be summarized each represent different aspects of the factor analytic approach to problems and data. In the first example, the researchers pursued the search for the factors behind attitudes toward blacks. In the second example, persons were treated as variables and factor analyzed. And in the third and last study to be summarized, the factors underlying social attitudes were studied mainly to test a structural theory of attitudes.

Racial Attitudes: Woodmansee and Cook Study

Most people probably conceive racial prejudice as a one-dimensional phenomenon. Individuals who differ in the degree of their attitudes toward blacks, for instance, do so on a single continuum of like-dislike. This is an oversimplified view. Actually, attitudes toward blacks, or toward any ethnic group, are complex. There are different facets of liking and disliking blacks, Jews, Russians, Americans, or any group. The scientific study of attitudes, therefore, demands the use of some approach or method that will help behavioral scientists to determine what these facets are. The study we now consider is an excellent example of the approach.

Woodmansee and Cook (1967), in a set of studies on prejudice against blacks, showed unmistakeably that such attitudes are multidimensional. Indeed, any simple-minded conception of ethnic attitudes as one-dimensional has little support from factor analytic attitude research. In their studies, Woodmansee and Cook's two main purposes were to determine the components (factors) of racial attitudes, in particular attitudes toward blacks, and to construct a reliable and valid scale, or more accurately, to construct sets of scales, to measure such attitudes.

In their first study they administered an existing attitude scale of 120 items to 593 white American college students from the Northeast, Midwest, and border South. In the second study they revised the attitude scale on the basis of the results of the first study and administered the scale to 609 similar college students. The third study concentrated on improving the scale even more, on obtaining evidence of the reliability and validity of the final version of the scale, and to continue the investigation of the factors underlying attitudes toward blacks.

We concentrate on Woodmansee and Cook's factor analytic results. They found 11 factors. The multidimensional picture they offer is interesting and important both scientifically and practically. Bear in mind when reading what follows that each factor can be a different way of perceiving blacks, of reacting to them, of having beliefs about them. But before going further, we must take a rather simple-minded look at what factors really are. There has been too much mystery about factors and factor analysis.

Some of what was said earlier will necessarily be repeated, but such repetition may help us understand factors.

An Explanatory Digression: What Are Factors?

What is a factor in the most mundane sense? A factor can be viewed as reflecting a particular rank ordering of the items of a scale or test that a sufficient number of people of a sample responding to the scale more or less agree to (or otherwise commonly respond to). Or it can be viewed as a subset of items of a test or scale to which a sufficient number of people in a sample respond similarly. Here is a simple example. Suppose that six persons are asked to rate four social attitude items on a six-point scale. They express their approval (or disapproval) of the social ideas implied by the items with the ratings 1 through 6, 1 indicating very little agreement or approval and 6 indicating strong agreement or approval. The items are single words and short phrases that have been found to measure social attitudes reliably and validly. They are *equality of women, birth control, private property, business*. We wish to discover the factors underlying the four-item attitude scale. (Bear in mind that many more items and persons would, of course, be used.)

The six persons responded to the scale as just indicated, yielding the ratings, or scores, given in Table 12.5. Person 3, for example, disapproved, or at least did not approve *equality of women* and *birth control*. He gave each of them the relatively low rating of 2. On the other hand, he rather strongly approved *private property* and *business;* he gave them ratings of 5 and 6, respectively. Contrast person 3 with person 6, who exhibited the opposite pattern: approval of *equality of women* and *birth control* and relative disapproval of *private property* and *business*. These are probably the clearest examples in the table. The other sample members had less clear and more mixed responses.

TABLE 12.5 **Responses of Six Persons to Four Social Attitude Items**[a]

	ITEMS			
Persons	1 Equality of Women	2 Birth Control	3 Private Property	4 Business
1	1	2	4	2
2	1	3	2	2
3	2	2	5	6
4	5	6	5	5
5	6	5	3	4
6	6	6	2	1

[a] The numbers in the table are the ratings of the six persons of the four referents on a scale from 1 to 6, 1 indicating very little approval and 6 indicating strong approval.

TABLE 12.6   Matrix of Correlations among Four Social
Attitude Items

	EQUALITY OF WOMEN	BIRTH CONTROL	PRIVATE PROPERTY	BUSINESS
EQUALITY OF WOMEN	1.00	.91	−.15	.04
BIRTH CONTROL	.91	1.00	−.23	−.11
PRIVATE PROPERTY	−.15	−.23	1.00	.81
BUSINESS	.04	−.11	.81	1.00

Notice, now, that the values of the columns of ratings under *equality of women* and *birth control* "go together": when there is a high value in the first column, there is usually a high value in the second column, and similarly for the low values. The columns of ratings under *private property* and *business* also tend to go together, though not quite as clearly as the ratings in the first two columns. This means, then, that *equality of women* and *birth control* are positively and substantially correlated. The correlations are .91 and .81. The correlations between the ratings of columns 1 and 3 and 1 and 4, and between 2 and 3 and 2 and 4 seem to be low; it is difficult, even impossible, to discern regular patterns of "going together."

The correlations between the referent pairs were calculated; they are given in Table 12.6. The correlations form a very clear pattern similar to the pattern of Table 12.3 where the correlations among six tests of intelligence were displayed. *Equality of women* and *birth control* are highly correlated, as our earlier inspection led us to believe. *Private property* and *business*, too, are highly correlated. Evidently we have two different kinds of referents: the sample of persons responded to them quite differently. Yet the correlations between 1 and 3 and 2 and 3 and between 2 and 3 and 2 and 4 are all low, most of them low and negative.

Taken at face value, the correlation matrix of Table 12.6 means that there are two separate and distinct factors, call them *A* and *B*. On *A* there are two items, *equality of women* and *birth control*, and on *B* there are two items, *private property* and *business*. There appears to be little relation between the two factors, judging from the low, near zero, correlations between the referents of *A* and the referents of *B* (−.15, .04, −.23, and −.11). It is said that the factors are uncorrelated, independent, or orthogonal. They are two separate and distinct entities, as it were. If we did a factor analysis of the correlation matrix of Table 12.6, we would obtain the same sort of factor structure that we saw in Table 12.4 and in Figure 12.3.

Factors are no more than this. They are defined by the correlations between tests or scales. If scores of individuals on items or tests "go together" to the extent that there are substantial correlations among them, then a factor is defined. The nature of factors is decided by researchers from study of the tests, scales, or items with high loadings on the factors. The final result of a factor analysis of the correlations of Table 12.6, the rotated factor matrix, is given in Table 12.7. From this table a researcher must try to deduce what the nature of the two factors is. In this case even though the evidence is slim—only four items, two loaded substantially on each of the two factors—it is not difficult to deduce that factor *A* is a liberal factor, since its two high loadings are associated with two items, *equality of women* and *birth control,* which express ideas ordinarily espoused by liberals. With considerably more evidence, then, we might call the factor "liberalism." The items with substantial loadings on factor *B, private property* and *business,* express ideas usually espoused by conservatives. We might, therefore, call the factor "conservatism."

This highly oversimplified example should not mislead us into believing that factors are "realities" and that it is always easy to interpret factor analytic results and to name factors. On the contrary, it is often very difficult. The only scientific "reality" that factors have comes from the correlations among the tests or variables being analyzed. The factor loadings obtained are in effect reductions of much more complex data to manageable size so that the researcher can better interpret the results.

Interpretation can always be wrong, however. First, a substantial factor loading can occur by chance. Thus the analyst may try to interpret what is an uninterpretable result. Second, a researcher can simply be mistaken when he deduces the "nature" of a factor. It may be that in a particular factor analysis, items or tests other than those used may be more fundamental than the ones actually used. In such a case the items used may be only a superficial aspect of the factor. It is quite possible, for instance, that the items *private property* and *business* may be only superficial aspects of a factor more fundamental than conservatism, the adopted name of the factor. Third, the results of factor analysis can be flawed by technical difficulties and shortcomings. Factor analysis *is* complex and has complex technical problems. For instance, it is often difficult to know how many factors there are in a set of data. If the "wrong" number of factors are extracted, the data can be misleading. While computers and computer programs have made it possible to do factor analysis rather easily, they give no really satisfactory answer to the number-of-factors problem.

TABLE 12.7   **Rotated Factor Matrix: Result of Factor Analysis of Correlation Matrix of Table 12.6**

	FACTORS	
ITEMS	A	B
Equality of women	.94	.13
Birth control	.94	.00
Private property	−.25	.83
Business	−.10	.87

In any case, we should now be in a better position to read and understand Woodmansee and Cook's study and the other studies summarized below. So let's return to Woodmansee and Cook.

Return to Woodmansee and Cook

Recall that Woodmansee and Cook found 11 factors or dimensions of attitudes toward blacks. Our purpose is to understand factor analysis and factors and not the complex substance of the Woodmansee and Cook results. Therefore, we take only four of their factors to try to see what the factors may mean and to understand the importance of factor analysis in behavioral research. Suppose a social psychologist is doing research on changing attitudes toward blacks and sets up a well-conceived experiment to do so. Suppose that he holds the notion that attitudes toward blacks is a relatively simple variable consisting of stereotypical ideas about blacks, and he wants to change these ideas to more accurate perceptions. His dependent variable, which reflects what he wants to change, is then stereotypes of blacks. Suppose, further, that his research is unsuccessful, that is, his independent variables have no effect on the dependent variables.

If a number of social psychologists do similar experiments with the same results, they may conclude that attitudes toward blacks cannot be changed. This statement, of course, may not be true. A more accurate statement is: Stereotypes of blacks have not been changed, and it may be difficult or even impossible to change them. The point is that the researcher drew a conclusion about attitudes toward blacks on the basis of evidence obtained on stereotypes of blacks. Stereotypes are only one part of attitudes, one dimension or factor (and even this statement may not be true because stereotypes themselves may have more than one factor). Thus it is possible that reports that this independent variable has had no effect on that variable may be weak because "that variable" may in fact not be "that variable" but only one aspect of it.

Woodmansee and Cook's factor A, "Integration-Segregation Policy," as the name indicates, centered around the subjects' positions on the propriety of racial segregation and integration. Factor B's items expressed "Acceptance in Close Personal Relations": How much would subjects accept blacks in relatively close interpersonal situations? Factor C, "Negro Inferiority," has been traditionally associated with attitudes toward blacks in the sense that such attitudes have focused on the perception of blacks as inferior to whites. (Another factor, "Derogatory Beliefs," was rather closely related to Factor C.) Factor D, "Negro Superiority," is a bit surprising. Its items attributed characteristics to blacks that made them superior to whites, for example, "I think that the Negroes have a kind of quiet courage which few whites have."

With the remaining factors we need not be concerned. The point is that the factor analyses of the intercorrelations of the large numbers of items that Woodmansee and Cook used showed that attitudes toward blacks is a complex domain of eleven facets or factors that reflect various aspects of attitudes toward blacks: integration and segregation, personal relations, black inferiority, black superiority, and others. If, for example, one wanted to change attitudes toward blacks then one has to decide what aspects of such attitudes are to be changed. Certainly attitudes toward blacks are far from being a simple unidimensional variable. Their study and understanding obviously require a multidimensional approach.

Perceptions of Teacher Behavior: Correlations among Individuals

It was said earlier that the responses of persons to an instrument can be intercorrelated and factor analyzed. This approach to behavioral research is called Q methodology (Stephenson, 1953). It is an interesting and potentially powerful approach, particularly in psychology. Its basic tool is the Q sort, a deck of from 40 to about 100 cards on which items are typed or otherwise depicted. (Drawings and abstract figures, for example, have been used.) Individuals are instructed to sort the cards into six to ten or even more piles according to various criteria: like-dislike, approval-disapproval, like me-not like me, and so on. Different values are assigned to each pile—usually 0 through 7, 8, 9, or 10—and these numbers are used to intercorrelate the sets of responses of different individuals with each other.

In other words, Q methodology's central focus is on the correlations among individuals. If, for example, two individuals sort a Q sort whose items are attitude items, say attitudes toward blacks, and if the correlation between their two sorts is high, then their attitudes toward blacks are similar. Further, if a sufficient number of individuals respond to the same Q sort, the responses to the Q sort can be intercorrelated and factor analyzed. The resulting factors are called *persons factors*. We examine rather briefly a study that has used this interesting approach.

Sontag (1968), in order to study the relation between teachers' attitudes toward education, his independent variable, and their perceptions of teacher behaviors, his dependent variable, constructed a Q sort for describing teacher behaviors. Some of the items are given below. Sontag believed that the judgments by teachers of the desirability of teaching behaviors are influenced by their basic attitudes toward education. For instance, a teacher whose attitudes are "progressive" would consider a certain set of teaching behaviors desirable, whereas a "traditional" teacher would consider another set of behaviors desirable.

Sontag indeed found that progressive and traditional teachers, as measured by another instrument designed to measure such attitudes, differed in their perceptions of desirable teaching behaviors. Our interest, however, is only in the factors he obtained with the teacher behavior Q sort. It is possible to determine the items of a Q sort to which the persons of a

TABLE 12.8   Selected Items from High School Teaching
             Behavior Factor Arrays, Sontag Q Study

"General Subject-Matter Presentation"
  Presents well-planned lessons.
  In his presentations, shows competent knowledge of subject matter.
  Takes advantage of student interest in planning lessons.
"Concern for Students"
  Keeps his promises to students.
  Teaches students to be sensitive to the needs of others.
  Shows interest in the viewpoints of pupils.
"Structure and Subject Matter"
  Conveys his enjoyment of subject matter to pupils.
  Demands attention from students during lessons.
  In his presentations, shows competent knowledge of subject matter.
"Norms and Rules"
  Stresses respect for fellow students as much as for teacher.
  Encourages pupils to be constructively critical in their approach to subject matter.
  Teaches respect for all ethnic groups.

---

persons factor—the persons who correlate highly with each other—have common or similar reactions. Sontag found four such factors at both the elementary and the high school levels. Selected items from the factor arrays associated with the teaching of secondary school teachers, together with the names Sontag gave them, are given in Table 12.8.

The reader can perhaps get a feeling for the nature of these factors by reading the items a few times. "Concern for Students" is obviously pupil-centered: for the teachers who find these behaviors desirable, the pupils' needs and views seem paramount. "Structure and Subject Matter," on the other hand, is centered in the things taught: for the teachers who find them desirable, knowledge, competence, discipline, and the planning and structure of teaching seem important. The factor analysis of persons' perceptions of teaching behaviors in Sontag's study has yielded valuable insights into different perceptions of teaching.

Testing a Theory of Social Attitudes

Decades ago there was a good deal of research into the general attitudes or ideologies of conservatism and liberalism. Do such sets of attitudes really "exist"? Is it possible to categorize people, scales, and items as "conservative" and "liberal"? Some psychologists seem to believe that social attitudes are far too complex to permit them to be so categorized. Moreover, there are too many exceptions. For example, there are many people who espouse mixtures of what can be called conservative and liberal viewpoints. In addition, some social scientists believe that many people hold virtually "no" attitudes, since they know little about economic, political, and educational issues.

My research (Kerlinger, 1972b; Kerlinger, Middendorp, & Amón, 1976) seems to indicate that conservatism and liberalism do indeed "exist" in the sense that conservative and liberal items and persons factors have been repeatedly found in different parts of the United States and in two European countries. The picture is roughly as follows. Liberals believe that social welfare programs should be strong, that blacks and women should have complete equality, that incomes should be taxed progressively, that business must be regulated, and that women should be allowed abortion if they wish it. Conservatives, on the other hand, stress the importance of religion and church, express faith in capitalism, private property, and business, espouse discipline and duty, and believe that social relations must be anchored in authority. There are many exceptions but these two pictures in general conform to research "reality." They are much more complicated than this, of course, but the general descriptions are accurate.

From the point of view of the present research summary, however, there is another popular belief—to which many social scientists also subscribe—that has important theoretical and practical implications. This is that liberalism and conservatism form a single dimension of social attitudes, with extreme liberals, even radicals, at one end and extreme conservatives, even reactionaries, at the other end. Similarly, social concepts and issues are also on this single dimension. To be sure, there are social scientists who believe that social attitudes are more complex than this, that there are several factors of liberalism-conservatism. Nevertheless, the several factors are still conceived as containing both liberal and conservative issues and beliefs. In other words, conservatism and liberalism are thought to lie on a single dimension, or single dimensions, that have both conservative and liberal issues (or people) on the same dimensions. In this view, conservatism and liberalism and conservatives and liberals are conceived as opposed: what one espouses the other opposes. This is what is called a bipolar conception. A bipolar dimension is one that has two ends, one positive and the other negative.

Years ago I questioned these ideas because the results of my research seemed to contradict them, or at least to cast serious doubt on them. After working with the ideas and doing more research, I published what I called a criterial referents theory of attitudes (Kerlinger, 1967). The theory can be called a structural theory because it outlined the general factor structure and some of the characteristics of social attitudes. It contradicted the validity of the bipolar conception of social attitudes, and said that conservatism and liberalism were separate and distinct "ideologies," or large sets of beliefs, not necessarily opposed to each other. (Radicalism of the right or the left was excluded from consideration, although it was said that attitudes may indeed be bipolar in the framework of radicalism.) This means that there are sets of individuals who have predominantly conservative or predominantly liberal attitudes toward social issues, but that conservative individuals are not necessarily opposed to liberal issues, and liberal individuals are not necessarily opposed to conservative issues. In short, the common bipolarity belief is denied, and a distinct and separate life for each of conservatism and liberalism is affirmed.

There is considerably more to the theory than this, of course, but this is sufficient to illustrate the use of factor analysis, in this case to test a structural theory of attitudes. The theory has been tested in the United States a number of times using attitude scales that consist of sentence items—for example, "A first consideration in any society is the protection of property rights" (conservative) and "There must be more effective birth control if the world is to solve its social and political problems" (liberal)—and referent items (single words and short phrases expressing social ideas)—for example, "private property," "competition" (conservative) and "equality," "socialized medicine" (liberal). The scales have been administered to large groups of individuals in different parts of the country and the correlations among the items factor analyzed.

The results of the factor analyses have been highly similar in almost all samples. Six or more factors have been obtained, and in most cases liberal items have appeared together on factors and conservative items have appeared together on other factors. The two kinds of items have rarely appeared together on the same factors. Since the factors are relatively independent of each other, it seems that liberalism and conservatism, as defined by the items, are separate and distinct entities. Moreover, a so-called higher-order factor analysis, a factor analysis of the correlations among the factors themselves, showed that the factors with liberal items were correlated positively, and similarly the factors with conservative items. There has been little evidence in these studies of bipolarity, that is, liberal items appearing with negative loadings on conservative factors, and conservative items appearing with negative loadings on liberal factors. Q studies have also supported the results just summarized. The structural theory, then, seems to be supported by the evidence of these studies.

To give the reader a feeling for the kind of results obtained in the studies, the factor arrays of one of the most recent of the studies (Kerlinger, 1972b) are given in Table 12.9. The major purpose of the study was to test the criterial referents theory described above by using referents themselves as items. Another purpose was to learn more about the nature of social attitudes by determining through factor analysis the factors underlying social attitudes. The data of Table 12.9 serve this purpose.

A seven-point social attitudes scale of 50 items of single words and short phrases (see Table 12.9), all presumably related to social attitudes, was administered to samples of graduate students of education in New York, North Carolina, and Texas. Although the data from each of these states were analyzed separately, the North Carolina and Texas samples were combined to create a large sample ($N = 530$) and thus, presumably, more reliable factor analytic results. (Factor analysis requires large samples mainly because of errors of measurement and many variables being analyzed.) The New York sample results were used to compare to the North Carolina-Texas combined sample results. We are concerned only with

TABLE 12.9   Social Attitude Factors, Referent Items, and Factor
Loadings, North Carolina and Texas Combined
Sample, $N = 530$[a]

CONSERVATIVE FACTORS		
Religiosity	Educational Traditionalism	Economic Conservatism
religion (.78)	subject matter (.59)	free enterprise (.62)
church (.73)	education as intellectual	real estate (.53)
faith in God (.72)	training (.52)	private property (.43)
Christian (.69)	school discipline (.44)	capitalism (.37)
religious education (.57)	homogeneous grouping	national sovereignty (.30)
teaching of spiritual values	(.30)	(scientific knowledge (.30))
(.53)		
moral standards in		
education (.36)		
patriotism (.33)		

LIBERAL FACTORS		
Civil Rights	Child-Centered Education	Social Liberalism
Negroes (.60)	children's interests (.56)	Social Security (.53)
civil rights (.57)	child-centered curriculum	Supreme Court (.50)
racial integration (.57)	(.54)	federal aid to education
Jews (.46)	pupil personality (.54)	(.49)
desegregation (.43)	self-expression of children	socialized medicine (.47)
(racial purity (−.37))	(.47)	United Nations (.43)
	pupil interaction (.44)	
	child freedom (.37)	

[a] The loadings are given in parentheses. Loadings .30 or greater were considered significant. The two parenthesized referents are one *L* item loaded on a *C* factor and one *C* item loaded on an *L* factor.

the combined sample. The data were factor analyzed and six factors extracted from the intercorrelations of the 50 referent items. The results of the
factor analysis are given in Table 12.9.

Three of the six factors had items that had been previously determined
to be conservative, and three factors had items previously determined to
be liberal. This determination of liberal and conservative is, of course,
important. Judgments were made on the basis of the literature on conservatism and liberalism (Hartz, 1955; Kirk, 1960; Rossiter, 1962), previous
research, anthologies of attitude measures (Robinson, Rusk, & Head, 1968;
Robinson & Shaver, 1969; Shaw & Wright, 1967), and experience and
knowledge. It is not hard to see that *free enterprise, religion,* and *subject
matter* are conservative referents and that *civil rights, equality,* and *socialized
medicine* are liberal referents. In any case, most of the designations of the
referents as conservative or liberal turned out to be empirically "correct" in
the sense that they grouped themselves together on predominantly conservative or predominantly liberal factors as predicted by the theory.

Table 12.9 is worth studying. First note that, with only one exception, *racial purity* on the factor "Civil Rights," there are no negative loadings in the table. Second, all items on any single factor array are either conservative or liberal, but not both. For example, all the items on the factor "Social Liberalism" are liberal items, while all the items on the factor "Economic Conservatism" are conservative—with one possible exception, *scientific knowledge*.

Third, and most important from the viewpoint of this chapter, note the common theme or character of each factor. Do you agree with the name it has been given? Can you think of a better name? Note, for example, that one item, *national security*, does not quite fit with the factor name, "Economic Conservatism." Is "Economic Conservatism," then, not correct? (One does not always get "perfect" factors, of course.) And *scientific knowledge* seems not to fit. The main thing to note, however, is that most of the items, sometimes all, share some central idea, some core of attitude meaning that makes it possible to identify the factor. Moreover, since the first three factors share the general characteristic of having conservative items, one can speculate that there is a "general" factor of conservatism. Similarly, perhaps the last three factors, whose items are all liberal, define a general factor of liberalism. The evidence of this study and other studies, even in Spain and the Netherlands where similar studies have been done (Kerlinger, Middendorp, & Amón, 1976), indicates that this is so.

FACTOR ANALYSIS: AN APPRECIATION

The scientist pursues explanations of phenomena. As has been pointed out several times in this book, the only way to explain anything is to say what is related to it. Before the relations among variables can be studied, we must know what the variables are; we must know something of the phenomena we want to study. This seems so obvious as not to require mentioning. But it is not obvious; indeed, it turns out to be maddeningly elusive and difficult. Psychological scientists want to explain intelligence, as well as to use intelligence as a variable to help explain other psychological phenomena. To explain intelligence, however, they must have some idea what they mean by intelligence. This means knowing something of the categories, the kinds, of intelligence that make up what is known as "intelligent behavior" ("intelligent behavior" must itself be constitutively and operationally defined).

These problems form a set of the most difficult problems of understanding behavioral sciences. (I find it very difficult even to express the problem so that I can understand it before trying to explain it.) As usual, take an example or two. We saw earlier in this chapter that Guilford has created a highly complex classification of kinds of intelligence. His classification system—formally a taxonomy—forms in effect a theory of intelligence, or at least the elements and underpinnings of a theory of intelligence. He used three types of categories—operation, content, and product—each with subcategories. The combinations of these categories and sub-categories "predict" aspects of intelligent behavior. Guilford and his colleagues write items and tests that seem to flow from these "definitions," administer them to appropriate samples of persons, and then use factor analysis to test the adequacy of the theoretical conception. Do the factors that Guilford predicted turn up as he has said they should? Do the items and tests appear on the factors Guilford has predicted?

Understanding phenomena depends in part on taxonomy. *Taxonomy* is the discipline of classification. All sciences have some sort of taxonomy or classification system. To classify things means to put them into categories. But what categories? Where do the categories come from? One of the main jobs of a science is to invent adequate taxonomies of the phenomena or variables of the science—and then to test the empirical validity of the taxonomic systems. Factor analysis is probably the most important method available to accomplish this testing and also to explore the variable world of the science to discover, or rather, get hints for taxonomic systems. This is what Thurstone and Guilford did in their pursuit of intelligence phenomena and what I did in trying to understand social attitudes. Without factor analysis, of course, these theoretical and empirical attempts to understand complex psychological phenomena would be impossible, or at least extremely difficult.

Factor analysis is, then, a basic tool of behavioral science. Earlier conceived as only an exploratory tool, a method for "finding" or "discovering" factors, which it is, of course, we now know it to be much more. We now conceive it and use it to test the empirical validity of primarily structural or taxonomic theories. As such, it is fundamental and indispensable. It is a highly important approach and analytic tool for understanding the basic stuff of a science: its phenomena and variables.

The multivariate approach
canonical correlation, discriminant analysis, and covariance structure analysis

Most of the discussion of research in this book has been dominated by the idea of one dependent variable. Think back to the discussion
of experiments, and note that a single dependent variable, a single effect,
has been considered to be influenced by one or more independent variables. It can be said that most research in the behavioral sciences has had
only one dependent variable, or at least one dependent variable at a time.
Even the method of multiple regression, with its many independent variables, has only one dependent variable. (Factor analysis is different: we do
not usually think of independent and dependent variables in factor analytic studies, even though we *can* do so if we wish.) Are we limited, then,
to only one dependent variable? No, not at all.

There is no good reason why we should not extend our thinking to
more than one independent variable and more than one dependent variable. There are often compelling practical reasons for limiting the numbers
of variables in research, but, conceptually at least, we need not so limit
ourselves. Indeed, we can think of all research, no matter how many variables of any kind, as being special cases of the one general case of k
independent variables and m dependent variables, k and m being any
numbers. Multivariate research, then, is research in which there is more
than one independent variable, or more than one dependent variable, or
both. The term commonly used is "multivariate analysis," which is a family of forms of analysis that are similar to multiple regression analysis, **207**

except that there is more than one dependent variable. In this book we consider multiple regression, too, as part of the multivariate analysis family, even though there is only one dependent variable.

Multivariate methods are indeed complex and often difficult to understand, partly because of the forbidding arrays of mathematical and statistical symbols the potential student needs to know. Ideally, one should know differential calculus to understand multiple regression and other multivariate methods. But one can attain satisfactory understanding without the calculus. One can even understand multivariate methods without knowing matrix symbols and algebra. But one cannot understand contemporary behavioral research without a fairly good understanding of multivariate approaches and methods. The reasons will become apparent as we get into the subject.

SOME MULTIVARIATE EXPERIMENTAL EXAMPLES

In Chapter 7 we discussed an interesting experiment by Berkowitz (1959), in which an answer to the following question was sought: Do anti-Semites displace aggression toward Jews when their hostility is aroused? We extend Berkowitz's univariate experiment (one dependent variable) in a multivariate way. Suppose that hostility arousal has been shown to produce displaced aggression toward Jews among anti-Semites. With an extension of the theoretical reasoning, we may ask whether hostility arousal also produces *direct* or overt aggression against Jews. There are now two dependent variables, displaced aggression and overt aggression, and two independent variables, hostility arousal and anti-Semitism. This would be a multivariate experiment with two independent variables and two dependent variables.

It is quite possible, of course, to test the effect of hostility arousal on the two dependent variables separately. Such a procedure would be like those described earlier. Instead of one experiment, there would be two. In one of them the effect of hostility arousal and anti-Semitism on displaced aggression would be assessed. In the other, the effect of hostility arousal on overt aggression would be assessed. Why not just do two experiments? Why bother with a considerably more complicated multivariate experiment? We now attempt to answer these questions, though it must be confessed that only partial answers can be given.

Consider educational experimentation to study the effects of different methods of teaching on achievement. Go back to the Clark and Walberg study, for instance, in which the effect of massive and regular reinforcement on reading achievement was studied. Recall that massive reinforcement had a considerably greater effect on reading achievement than regular reinforcement. What would be the effect of massive reinforcement on arithmetic achievement? The same? Perhaps different? Here again, two experiments can be done, each with a different dependent variable. It is possible, however, that a better answer to the research question on the effect of reinforcement on achievement can be obtained by including both dependent variables in one experiment. Why? What might the benefit be? One answer is that the reinforcement methods may affect the two kinds of achievement differently, and the differences may not emerge in two experiments, whereas they may merge in one experiment that includes both dependent variables.

There are many practical situations in which individuals have to be "assigned" to different groups on the basis of their possession of different traits, abilities, experience, and so on. For example, in schools children are "assigned" to passed and failed groups on the basis of their effort and achievement. Prospective employees of a company are assigned to a hired group or a not-hired group on the basis of ability and experience. Psychiatrists assign mentally ill people to categories such as neurotic, schizophrenic, and manic-depressive on the basis of tests and observations. In such cases, researchers consider the group membership to be the dependent variable and the various tests and other devices as independent variables. While there is only one dependent variable, as in multiple regression analysis, methods of analysis in such situations are considered and called multivariate analysis.

One last more complex example before going into more detail. Roe and Siegelman (1964) believed that early experiences in life led to later differences in orientation to people. Their interest in orientation stemmed from their assumption that orientation toward people influenced interests in different occupations. An individual strongly oriented toward people would be more likely to become a teacher or a counselor, for example. To test the hypothesis, they administered two sets of instruments to a number of college seniors. The first set measured variables associated with home environment: early experience of social activities, closeness to mother and father, interest and energy that father (or mother) devoted to activities other than family or work. The variables of the second set reflected orientation toward people, for example, curiosity about people, desire for close personal relations, and warmth and sociableness. Their hypothesis was that extensive and satisfying personal relationships early in life produce adults who are primarily person-oriented, while inadequate and unsatisfying relationships produce adults who are primarily oriented to nonpersonal aspects of the environment.

This research is multivariate because there were several independent variables and several dependent variables. The problem is how to study the relation between them. The most obvious thing to do is simply to correlate each of the independent variables with each of the dependent variables and then study the many correlations. If early experiences of social activities correlates highly with, say, a measure of orientation toward people—that is, the more the early experience of social activities, the greater the orientation toward people—then the researchers can probably conclude that early experience influences later orientation. One can also calculate all the correlations among all the variables and factor analyze the correlations. This may be a good way to attack the problem because the results of the factor analysis should show the relations between the early experiences and the orientations.

Another way to approach the analytic problem, a way that is more appropriate because its results will bear directly on the original hypothesis, is to calculate a composite of the independent variables and another composite of the dependent variables and then to correlate the composites. This is the method Roe and Siegelman used.[1] The composites, calculated in a way to maximize the correlation between the two sets of variables, eight measures in each set, was .47. This canonical correlation, as it is called, was statistically significant, indicating a moderate relation between early experience and orientation toward people.

The method also enables the researcher, in addition to obtaining the overall correlation between the two sets of variables, to obtain estimates of the relative influences of the separate variables on the composites. In the present case the most influential independent variable was a variable called "Early experience of social activities," and the most important dependent variable was called "Orientation toward people," calculated from selected pertinent scale and inventory items. Roe and Siegelman's hypothesis was supported, since the canonical correlation coefficient was statistically significant. Moreover, information was obtained on which variables contributed most to the correlation between the two sets of variables.

The method just described is called *canonical correlation analysis*. It is the most general of the multivariate methods in the sense that other multivariate methods can be considered special cases of canonical correlation.[2] It is also powerful and elegant, even though the interpretation of its results can be difficult, even ambiguous. (Why this is so cannot be explained here because the explanation requires technical equipment beyond the scope of the book. In general, the more complex an analysis, the more difficult the interpretation.) To give the reader somewhat more feeling for and understanding of the method, we invent a fictitious example and clothe it with variables related to foreign language learning. It must be emphasized, however, that the example is wholly fictitious. Indeed, I know of no actual research that even resembles the problem and its variables.

Canonical Correlation Analysis: A Fictitious Example

Recall the earlier discussion on multiple regression: there were k independent variables and always one dependent variable. Suppose that in a

---

[1] The analysis reported here was actually done by Cooley and Lohnes (1962, pp. 40–44).

[2] This statement is a little clumsy. A more satisfactory statement is that almost all multivariate analytic methods are special cases of the so-called linear model—and canonical correlation analysis is one of the most general of linear model methods. This means, in effect, that it analyzes virtually any kinds of data with k independent variables and m dependent variables, extracts factors from the data, assesses the relations within and between the independent and dependent variables, and especially the maximum possible correlation between composites of the independent and dependent variables.

study of foreign language learning a psychologist-linguist is interested in the abilities that contribute to speaking a foreign language. He believes that three important variables are influential in foreign language learning: memory, vocabulary, and cognition of relations. (Just take these variables at face value, except the last, which we can here take to be ability to grasp connections between items of information.) He administers tests of the three variables to 200 individuals who have been studying Italian for one year. In addition, he has spoken language fluency scores for each individual, obtained by Italian-speaking experts from observation and testing under controlled conditions. Spoken language fluency, then, is the dependent variable.

The researcher analyzed the scores on the three tests and the spoken language fluency observations with multiple regression analysis. The scores of eight of the subjects are given in Table 13.1. (Assume that the calculations reported here have been done with all 200 subjects. We use eight scores for convenience.) The scores on the three tests, the independent variables, are reported under X_1, X_2, and X_3. The language fluency or speaking scores are reported in the column labeled Y_1. The multiple regression analysis yielded a multiple correlation coefficient, R, between a regression composite of the three independent variables and the dependent variable of .37. The researcher was disappointed: he had expected that more than $.37^2 = .14$ (R^2), or 14 percent of the variance of Y would be accounted for by the three independent variables.

He then had a hunch. Perhaps the three independent variables were more related to the learning of *reading* a foreign language. Fortunately, he had Italian reading scores obtained from a test that had been given to the same language students. These scores are reported in the column labeled Y_2 in Table 13.1. A multiple regression analysis of this variable and the

TABLE 13.1   Fictitious Scores of Three Independent Variable Measures of Language-Related Abilities and Two Dependent Measures of Language Proficiency (Italian)

	INDEPENDENT VARIABLES			DEPENDENT VARIABLES			
Per-sons	Mem-ory X_1	Vocab-ulary X_2	Rela-tions X_3	$\overline{X}$	Speak-ing Y_1	Read-ing Y_2	$\overline{Y}$
1	12	9	9	10.00	11	10	10.50
2	10	8	11	9.67	9	8	8.50
3	14	11	11	12.00	9	9	9.00
4	21	10	8	13.00	7	7	7.00
5	24	19	20	21.00	12	14	13.00
6	18	16	21	18.33	14	12	13.00
7	15	17	14	15.33	7	15	11.00
8	20	14	10	14.67	18	16	17.00

same independent variables yielded an R of .89 and an R^2 of .80. Therefore, 80 percent of the variance of Y_2, reading of Italian, was accounted for by the combination of memory, vocabulary, and cognition of relations scores. The researcher was pleased. Although the three independent variables were related to Y_1, speaking Italian, the relation was comparatively weak (though many researchers would in this case be pleased by an R^2 of .14). The three independent variables were much more strongly related, on the other hand, to reading Italian.

The reader will realize that such a finding would be an important one—if it held up on replication. It is important theoretically because increased understanding of learning a foreign language has been gained. It makes a difference, for example, whether learning a language means learning to speak or learning to read. The magnitude of the R^2 of the reading scores was gratifying to the researcher: a substantial advance was perhaps made in explaining reading of a foreign language. After all, to account for 80 percent of the variance is no mean achievement.[3] Perhaps further searching and work may raise the R^2 with the speaking scores.

Instead of two separate analyses, is it possible to use one analysis that includes the three independent variables *and* the two dependent variables? Is it possible to study the relations between the two *sets* of variables, in other words? The ingredients of such an analysis are given in Table 13.1. The X_1, X_2, and X_3 scores have been averaged in each row, yielding the means of 10.00, 9.67, 12.00, and so on, in the column headed $\overline{X}$. The Y_1 and Y_2 scores have been similarly averaged, yielding means of 10.50, 8.50, 9.00, and so on, in the column headed $\overline{Y}$. We have, then, an X component and a Y component that are, in this case, the means of the X scores of each individual and the means of the Y scores of each individual. The correlation between the X component, $\overline{X}$, and the Y component, $\overline{Y}$, is .54. If we square this r, we obtain .29. If we accept the $\overline{X}$'s as "representative" of the three X variables and the $\overline{Y}$'s as representative of the two Y variables, then the correlation between the three X variables, on the one hand, and the three Y variables, on the other hand, is .54, and 29 percent of the variance of Y is shared with X.

The procedure just described would *not* ordinarily be used in actual research. We have used it to illustrate an idea, the idea of determining the correlation between *sets* of scores rather than single scores, in this case the correlation between the X set and the Y set. In most cases of actual research with sets of X and Y variables, we would use canonical correlation analysis, which calculates, among other things, the maximum correlation possible between sets of X and Y variables. Correlating the means of the X and Y scores does not correctly estimate the "true" relation between the two sets of scores. It does not estimate the maximum correlation possible given the two sets of scores and all the relations between them. Therefore, in this case it gives much too low an estimate.

---

[3] It must be emphasized that such a high R^2 is unlikely. It was contrived in this example for dramatic effect.

Hark back to our discussion of multiple regression analysis. Recall that a multiple correlation coefficient expresses the correlation between a "best" combination of independent variables, or X's, and a dependent variable, Y. Canonical correlation extends the idea to more than one Y variable. Although the calculations are complex, the basic ideas are simple. The coefficient of correlation between the means of the X variables and the means of the Y variables of Table 13.1 was .54. Had we calculated the correlation between the X and Y variables using canonical correlation analysis, it would have yielded a so-called canonical correlation coefficient, which would be the maximum correlation possible between the X and Y sets of scores, given those scores and the relations between the X variables, between the Y variables, and between the X and Y sets of variables. The canonical correlation between the X and Y sets of scores, then, will be larger than the correlation obtained by our simplified procedure using means of the X and Y scores. (The canonical correlation is actually .99, very high indeed. But such a high canonical correlation rarely occurs with behavioral data. In this case it is due to the synthetic nature of the scores and the high correlation of .80 between X_2 and Y_2.)

In addition, canonical correlation analysis yields assessments of the relative contributions of the separate independent and dependent variables to the canonical correlation. For example, in the language-learning example, weights similar to the factor loadings discussed in Chapter 12 could have been calculated, and these weights would tell the researcher which independent variable or variables had relatively greater influence on which dependent variable or variables. The results of a canonical correlation analysis of the data of Table 13.1, for example, showed that X_2, Vocabulary, and Y_2, Reading Italian, were much more important than the other variables in determining the canonical correlation. In other words, the analysis, if successful, determines the magnitude of the overall relation between the two sets of variables, or measures, and also indicates which variables, both independent and dependent, contribute most to the relation between the sets. Although there is much more to canonical analysis, including limitations of the method and certain difficulties of interpreting canonical data, we forego further discussion. Our purpose of suggesting the basic ideas has been served.

DISCRIMINANT ANALYSIS

Think of a multiple regression analysis in which the dependent variable expresses group membership. For example, sex, social class, religious preference, political preference, and the like, are variables that express group membership. Any individual can be assigned to one group on the basis of possession of the characteristics "suitable" to that group. We can usually see whether an individual is male or female, but if in doubt we can ask him or her. The identification in effect assigns the individual to one of two groups, male or female.

The same reasoning applies to political preference, except that the identification and assignment to groups are more complex. Political preference, for instance, is usually simple in the United States: most voters are either Republican or Democrat. In Western Europe where political parties proliferate—in the Netherlands, for example, there are more than 30 political parties—identification and assignment to membership groups are more complex and difficult. In the Soviet Union, on the other hand, where there is only one political party, no question of assignment to membership groups exists; indeed, there can be no variable political preference.

In many research situations, then, researchers assign people to groups on the basis of their membership in the groups. This sounds almost silly: How can a researcher assign people to groups that they are already in? One point is that he may not know to which groups they belong, and if one of his variables is one that in effect expresses group membership, then he must somehow determine the group membership. This is usually not difficult, fortunately. He can do so by checking records or simply by asking people well-directed questions.

Suppose, however, that a group membership variable is one that is to be predicted. Now we have to extend our thinking. In some situations people are not yet "in a group" but will be "assigned" to it by the researcher on the basis of information obtained from variables other than the group membership variables. Let's see what this means, because much behavioral research has this essential character of "predicting" group membership.

A famous example was given earlier: predicting lung cancer from cigarette-smoking. The researcher in effect assigns people to a lung cancer group or a no lung cancer group on the basis of knowledge of cigarette-smoking. The greater the relation between cigarette-smoking and lung cancer, the more successful the prediction. Educational researchers assign children to an adequate achievement group or an inadequate achievement group on the basis of aptitude test scores, grades, attitude measures, social-class measures, sex measures, and other variables and measures. Professors similarly assign college students to grade groups—A, B, C, D, and F, for example—on the basis of test performance, term paper quality, special assignments, and even personal judgments.

The reader will no doubt recall from an earlier discussion that this is called nominal measurement. If a person has such-and-such a characteristic, assign him to Group A_1; if, on the other hand, he has this-and-that characteristic, assign him to Group A_2; and so on for other characteristics and groups. A key point is that the individuals are assigned to groups not to which they may really belong but to which they "should belong" on the basis of evidence on the individuals that is independent of the group membership. That is, group membership is "predicted" based on evidence obtained independently and apart from group membership, but that is known or believed to predict that group membership successfully.

The above rather long aside was necessary in order to understand the method of discriminant analysis and research that involves, in effect, predicting group membership. *Discriminant analysis* is a highly useful form of multivariate analysis whose main task is to predict group membership. Research of this kind is done somewhat as follows. A researcher wishes to understand, for instance, the problem of language acquisition. Some people can learn to speak and understand a foreign language with comparative ease; other people have great difficulty. Why? Suppose the researcher first identifies two groups of individuals. She calls one group "good learners" because they seem to have learned Italian well and with relative ease and the other group "poor learners" because, after a year of study, they speak and understand Italian poorly or only with difficulty. In an effort to understand the differences between the two groups, the researcher administers three tests to them, the same three tests that were used earlier: memory, vocabulary, and cognition of relations. She reasons that if the canonical correlation coefficient was so high in the earlier study, then perhaps the three variables used as independent variables earlier, if used jointly, may be capable of substantially accurate prediction of success or lack of success in learning a foreign language.

The idea is highly similar to earlier ideas discussed in Chapter 11: several tests or measures were used to "predict" performance on some dependent variable. For example, Holtzman and Brown (1968) used measures of scholastic aptitude and study habits and attitudes to predict high school grades. Instead of high school grade-point averages, a continuous variable, they could have used a measure of success in high school. Such a measure might be obtained by asking teachers to categorize each student as "successful" or "not successful." Or the criterion of finishing high school or not finishing high school might be used to indicate "successful" and "not successful." In other words, group membership, a two-valued or dichotomous variable, is used. Quantification is simple: assign a 1 to "successful" and a 0 to "not successful." If a multiple regression analysis is now done, with scholastic aptitude and study habits and attitudes measures as independent variables and the dichotomous variable, "success," as the dependent variable, we have in effect a discriminant analysis.

Language Learning Revisited

Return to the language-learning problem. Suppose that instead of two dependent variables, as in Table 13.1, we had one dichotomous dependent variable. Such a situation is given in Table 13.2. Conceive of a problem similar to that of Table 13.1 and its discussion. Suppose the problem is explaining or predicting success in learning a foreign language, this time Dutch. Eight individuals who have studied Dutch for one year have been judged by three expert judges to be "successful" or "unsuccessful" in speaking Dutch. Four of them were characterized by the judges as "unsuccessful"; they are Persons 1 through 4 in Table 13.2, and have been assigned 0's to indicate lack of success (Y column of the table). The other four

TABLE 13.2 Fictitious Scores from Three Independent Variable Measures of Language-Related Abilities and a Dichotomous Measure of Success in Language Learning (Dutch)

| | INDEPENDENT VARIABLE | | | DEPENDENT VARIABLE | |
| | X_1 | X_2 | X_3 | | Y |
PERSONS	Memory	Vocab-ulary	Relations	Category	Success, Language
1	12	9	9	not success	0
2	10	8	11	not success	0
3	14	11	11	not success	0
4	21	10	8	not success	0
5	24	19	20	success	1
6	18	16	21	success	1
7	15	17	14	success	1
8	20	14	10	success	1

persons, Persons 5 through 8, were characterized as "successful." They have been assigned 1's in the table. In other words, the "data" of Table 13.2 consist of the scores on the three independent variables of memory, vocabulary, and relations, and scores of 1 and 0 on the dependent variable, language success, 1 indicating "successful" and 0 "unsuccessful."

Assigning 1's and 0's like this seems to puzzle some people. It is a natural, simple, and effective way to quantify a variable that expresses group membership. Actually, it was introduced earlier when variables like sex, social class, alive-dead, and political preference were discussed. Such variables are usually quantified by counting and the results put into crossbreak tables, which have frequencies in the cells. But they can be quantified with 1's and 0's and their correlations with other variables easily calculated. The correlations between the success variable of Table 13.2, for example, and the independent variables of the table are, in order, .56, .92, and .70, indicating that language success is substantially correlated with the memory, vocabulary, and relations variables, but especially highly correlated with vocabulary. *How* the 1's and 0's were assigned is harder to explain. In this case, the assignment was deliberately done to enhance the correlations. In actual research, however, other and better methods are used.

If a multiple regression analysis is done with the data of Table 13.2 and it was successful—with the data of Table 13.2 it *was* successful: $R^2 = .85$— then the obtained regression equation can be used with future students. Say that a new set of students is about to begin the study of Dutch. We can administer the three tests to them, and, using the regression equation obtained in the earlier analysis, calculate a predicted score for each of them. These scores can then be used to indicate probable "success" or "lack of success" in learning Dutch.

The regression equation calculated with the data of Table 13.2 is:

$$Y' = -.99 + .01X_1 + .14X_2 - .01X_3$$

Suppose one individual's scores are $X_1 = 12$, $X_2 = 9$, and $X_3 = 9$ (scores taken from person 1 in Table 13.2). Then, substituting these scores in the above equation, $Y' = .06$. Suppose another individual's scores are $X_1 = 24$, $X_2 = 19$, and $X_3 = 20$ (scores of Person 5 in Table 13.2). Substituting in the equation yields $Y' = 1.23$. We can then predict that the first student will not succeed and the second student will succeed. We are, in effect, predicting group membership, or predicting either 1 or 0. The first student's predicted score of .06 is close to 0; therefore he probably will not succeed. The second student's score of 1.23 is close to 1; he will therefore probably succeed.

The procedure is, of course, fallible, as all procedures are. Our predictions are probabilistic: we say only, on the basis of the three scores, that a student will probably succeed or not succeed. Given a "good" regression or prediction equation, we will, other things equal, be correct a large proportion of the times we use the equation. But we will also sometimes be incorrect. Readers dissatisfied with such lack of perfect prediction can console themselves with the thought that without the knowledge yielded by the tests any predictions made—perhaps based on intuition, experience, or other more or less subjective criteria—will probably not be as good.

In any case, discriminant analysis is a powerful tool with both practical and theoretical problems. The practical use was illustrated with the example just given. The theoretical use is suggested by the regression equation. The equation itself yields clues to the relative importance of the three independent variables in their presumed influence on language learning—if, indeed, the learning of Dutch can be considered representative of language learning, and if the sample whose data determined the equation and other regression statistics is like other samples of language students.[4]

Human or Chimpanzee? A Research Example of Discriminant Analysis

In a study of fossils (Howells, 1972) anthropologists had to know whether a particular bone—from the lower end of the upper arm—had belonged to a human being or to a chimpanzee. This is a difficult problem because there are resemblances and overlaps of the two kinds of bones,

[4] A good case can be made against Dutch as representative of other languages. It seems to be more difficult to learn to speak and read than other Western languages. Whether this is true, however, is really not known. If it is true, then generalization is weakened. If Dutch is harder than other languages, then it is possible that quite different regression equations might be obtained with other languages and thus quite different predictions.

especially in the body region of this particular bone. The anthropologists knew, however, that seven bone measures could be used to distinguish human and chimpanzee bones. The problem is still difficult, because each of these measures for both humans and chimpanzees has considerable variability, and thus overlap between human and ape measures. To see some of the problem, look at Figure 13.1 in which two overlapping distributions are drawn. (These are so-called normal distributions. This means roughly that most of the scores, the middle range, will occur in the middle of the distribution, and fewer and fewer of the scores occur at the low and high ends.)

Distribution A has a mean of 57, and distribution B has a mean of 70. Suppose the scale of measurement, indicated by the baseline of the figure, represents a certain bone measure that has reliably distinguished human and chimpanzee bones. Distribution A represents human measures and distribution B ape measures. The mean of A is 57 and the mean of B is 70; the difference of 13 has been found to be statistically significant. Suppose we have five measures, a, b, c, d, and e. Measures a and b, because they are extreme, can rather clearly be categorized as human and chimpanzee, respectively. They fall in places of no overlap on the scale (the baseline). But measures c and d, although each near the two means, fall in the area of overlap (indicated by the horizontal hatching). To which group do they belong? c is probably human and d is probably ape. But you can't be too sure because they are both in the area of the overlap of the two distributions. And with e, a measure that falls near the middle of both distributions, you must be in even greater doubt.

This illustrates the problem with only one measure. If, however, we have several measures, all of which have been found to differentiate human and ape fossils in this same statistical way, perhaps we can be more confident of the categorization of bones whose identity is not known. In his analysis Howells (and a colleague, Patterson) used seven such

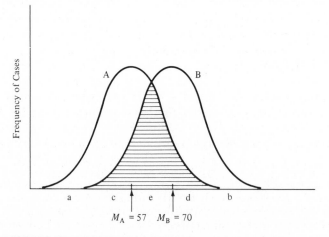

FIG. 13.1

measures—we need not name them; they are technical and are not pertinent to our immediate interest—and discriminant analysis to identify the unknown bone. Suffice it to say that the seven measures had been found to differentiate human and ape bones. The seven measurements were made on 40 human bones and 40 chimpanzee bones in two museums. The particular bone under investigation was compared to the means of the seven measures of the 40 human bones and also to the means of the seven measures of the 40 chimpanzee bones. Unfortunately, this procedure did not lead to clear identification because of overlap in the measures.

In the discriminant function technique it is possible to extract from the data a weighted combination of measures that will maximally distinguish groups. (A "weighted combination" means that the variables in a combination are given different greater or lesser quantitative emphasis by assigning different "weights," like .94, .72, .05, −.40, 1.00, and so on, to them.) Howells wanted to differentiate the two groups of bones as much as possible using the seven measures. How best to combine the measures to achieve this purpose? Discriminant analysis, in effect, discovers this maximally distinguishing combination, as indicated earlier. The combination, really a profile of the seven measures, was then applied to the fossil under investigation. The point is not so much to solve this particular problem as it is to understand how this fascinating multivariate method works. We therefore diverge briefly and geometrically to illustrate how discriminant analysis works. In so doing we borrow and adapt a nice demonstration given by Tatsuoka (1970, pp. 5–7) in his lucid manual on discriminant analysis. This demonstration, in addition to elucidating discriminant analysis, also throws more light on multivariate analysis in general, in part because it approaches the problem of conceptualizing spaces of k (more than two) dimensions.

An Illustrative Geometric Divergence

Suppose we have six bones, three human and three anthropoid. Suppose, further, that we have only two measures, X_1 and X_2, instead of seven, and that these measures, in pairs for each of the six bones, are (1,5), (1,3), (3,5), (3,2), (4,5), and (5,4). The first set of three pairs of measures comes from human bones and the second set of three pairs comes from chimpanzee bones. We have found a new bone and want to determine to which of the two groups it belongs. The two measures, X_1 and X_2, of this bone are (3,3).

The six pairs of X_1 and X_2 measures are plotted in Figure 13.2. The three human bones are indicated with crosses and the three anthropoid bones with circles. The unknown bone is plotted with a cross inside a circle. From this plot, as it is, it is virtually impossible to tell to which group it belongs: it falls near the middle of both sets of measures. (I did this deliberately, as the reader may suspect.) A case can be made for assigning it to either group.

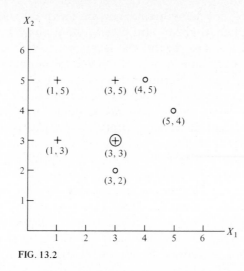

FIG. 13.2

Take an idea presented earlier, that of a linear combination of X_1 and X_2, each so weighted that a single Y score can be calculated from each pair of X scores. Let the weights be .83 and −.37. (These values were estimated by assigning Y scores of 0 to the first three pairs and Y scores of 1 to the second three pairs, and then doing a regular regression analysis. The values are regression weights.) Then, a Y line is drawn as a projection of all six plotted points in such a way as to maximize (roughly) the difference between the two groups. This has been done in Figure 13.3, where per-

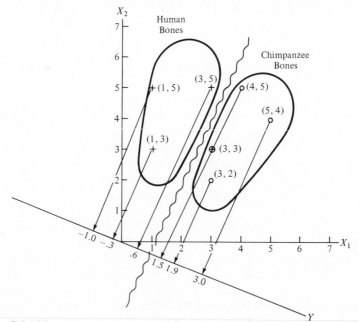

FIG. 13.3

pendiculars have been dropped to the Y line from each of the plotted pairs of scores. The points on the Y line reflecting each of the plotted points are -1.0, $-.3$, $.6$, 1.5, 1.9, and 3.0.[5]

The mean of these six Y values is $.95$. Note that this splits the two groups of points cleanly apart. In Figure 13.3 the two groups of plotted points are separately encircled, and a wavy line drawn between them accentuates the separation. We now have two sets of points corresponding to the two groups of bones and the measurements associated with them. The "system" can be used for the identification and categorization of bones found in the future. The rules are: Take measurements X_1 and X_2 of the bone; plot these values in a graph like that of Figure 13.3; drop a perpendicular to the Y line and read off the value; if the value is greater than $.95$, assign to chimpanzee, otherwise assign to human.

This example, then, illustrates roughly how discriminant analysis works. In the example with seven measurements of bones, instead of only X_1 and X_2 being used, X_1, X_2, X_3, X_4, X_5, X_6, and X_7 are used. Intuitive understanding, which we have used in the above example, deserts us. The basic ideas, however, are the same, or at least similar. The seven bone measures or variables are used in a multiple regression way to predict to group membership. The original groups of 40 human bones and 40 chimpanzee bones are used like subjects in a psychological or educational experiment to do the regression analysis. The dependent variable is group membership. The quantitative rule is simple: If a chimpanzee bone, assign a 1; if a human bone, assign a 0. The discriminant method then in effect does what is depicted in Figure 13.3: it "projects" a linear combination of the seven variables or measures on to a Y line to produce the maximum possible separation of the two groups. Of course, it doesn't actually do this. The analysis of the data produces a set of weights that are used in a discriminant (regression) equation. The seven measures from new subjects—in this case subjects are bones—are plugged into the equation to obtain discriminant scores, which are then used to categorize the subjects or bones.

Suppose the discriminant equation for the above two-measure example was:

$$Y = .80X_1 - .40X_2$$

and $X_1 = 2$ and $X_2 = 5$. Then

$$Y = (.80)(2) - (.40)(5) = -.40$$

This is well below the "separation score" of $.95$ given earlier (the mean of the six measures on the Y line of Figure 13.3); so the fossil is a human bone.

---

[5] The reader interested in knowing more about how to do this and in the reasoning involved should consult Tatsuoka's manual (Tatsuoka, 1970, pp. 5ff.).

Note, too, that the same outcome could have been obtained by plotting (2,5) in Figure 13.3 and then dropping a perpendicular to the Y line.

Return to Howells

In Howells' research the human mean on a Y line was 61.42 and the chimpanzee mean was 99.71. These are the means of the "discriminant scores" calculated for the 40 human bones and the 40 chimpanzee bones. The seven measures of the unknown bone produced a discriminant score of 59.40. This is, of course, close to the human means of 61.42, and the bone is categorized as human. The probability is high that the bone belonged to a human being and not to a chimpanzee.[6]

Discriminant analysis and other forms of multivariate analysis are, of course, much more complex than this. Nevertheless, the basic ideas are relatively simple—once they are understood. The main point of the examples is that many problems in the behavioral sciences are too complex to be adequately solved by simpler methods. A multivariate approach is required. One should naturally never use a complex method when a simple method will do. The question is: Will a simple method do? The answer to this question inheres in the problem and in the judgment of the researcher.

Discriminant analysis in a more general sense is a method for assigning individuals to groups on the basis of information on the individuals on two or more variables. So far we have used only dichotomous dependent variables and have said that this is nothing more than multiple regression with a dichotomous dependent variable, usually quantified as $\{1,0\}$. Discriminant analysis, however, is by no means limited to such dichotomous variables. For instance, Cooley and Lohnes (1962) used the method to discriminate three groups using value and personality measures as predictors (independent variables). The three career groups were a research group, students who enter graduate work to do basic research; an applied-science group, those who continue in science and engineering, but who do not plan to do research; and a nonscience group, those who leave the field to enter fields that have direct involvement with people. Students from six eastern colleges were given the personality and values measures, and three years later their membership in the three groups, as described above, was determined. Cooley and Lohnes successfully differentiated the members of the groups and were able to describe some of the group differences.

Discriminant analysis has been used mostly for applied research purposes. Its use is generally as follows. On the basis of theory, previous knowledge, or hunch, appropriate measures of ability, personality, and other variables are administered to members of known groups. Discriminant analysis is done and discriminant equations (like the regression equa-

---

[6] At the end of his paper Howells says that his colleague, Patterson, returned to the area where the fossil was found and turned up other evidence that supported the discriminant conclusion.

tions described earlier) are calculated. The equations are then used to predict the (later) group membership of individuals whose group memberships are not known, just as we did in the bones example. A psychologist, for instance, might use a set of tests with selected samples of delinquent and nondelinquent boys and calculate a discriminant equation to "predict" delinquency, or membership in the delinquent and nondelinquent groups. He calculates the equation, in other words, with individuals of known group membership, delinquent and nondelinquent. He can then use the equation to predict the later group membership, later delinquency and nondelinquency, of other individuals. He simply administers the same measures to other individuals and, on the basis of the scores they obtain, calculates their future group membership, their future delinquency or nondelinquency. This must, of course, be done with great care and suitable reservations. After all, the application of an equation obtained from one group may not be applicable to another group for a variety of reasons. Nevertheless, discriminant analysis is a useful and powerful prediction device in applied research.

Suppose, however, a basic researcher is more interested in describing the differences among groups and in understanding *why* groups are different. Discriminant analysis can be used to help in such description and understanding. Indeed, it was so used by Cooley and Lohnes in the research just summarized. This is a more scientific use of the method than simply to predict group membership, because Cooley and Lohnes were seeking to understand why career choices are made, to know something of their personality and value determinants, and not just to predict to such choices. This difference between basic and applied research objectives is important and is nicely illustrated by basic and applied use of discriminant analysis.

This point is so important that it should be discussed further. Let us return to the example of learning Dutch, illustrated by the data of Table 13.2. Educators interested in the teaching of foreign languages would ordinarily use a method like discriminant analysis predictively. That is, they want to know how well they can predict success in the learning of Dutch. They usually want to know which students will succeed and which will probably have more difficulty. They can thus perhaps better provide for individual differences in their teaching. Researchers more oriented toward basic research, on the other hand, will more likely want to know why and how some individuals are more successful than others. To them, prediction is more a by-product of the method. They are more likely to be interested in language learning as a natural phenomenon to be probed and understood.

This sketch of the two general research orientations is a little overdrawn, of course. The teacher of Dutch will no doubt also be interested in why and how some individuals are more successful than others. And the basic researcher will want to be able to predict to successful and unsuccessful learning. Nevertheless, the distinction remains and is often important. The point being illustrated is that discriminant analysis—and, to be sure, other multivariate approaches and methods—can be nicely used for both purposes. We return to the basic-applied distinction in Chapter 16.

ANALYSIS OF COVARIANCE STRUCTURES

Multivariate approaches and methods have freed researchers from the restrictions of studying the influence of only one or two variables on a dependent variable. In experimental research two, three, and even more variables can be simultaneously manipulated (though there are practical limitations). Multivariate analysis, however, has perhaps its most important and useful applications in nonexperimental research, where identifying and controlling various sources of variance are major problems. In the study of school achievement or the study of determinants of intelligence, for instance, it is almost absurd to think of one or two variables as determinants. Both school achievement and intelligence, like other psychological and sociological phenomena, are complex. They are therefore complexly determined. This complexity requires multivariate conceptions. Indeed, psychological, sociological, anthropological, and political science research has been and is being transformed. In 1930, for instance, an applied study like *Equality of Educational Opportunity* (Coleman et al., 1966), discussed earlier in Chapter 8, in which the effects of more than a hundred independent variables on achievement were studied, could hardly have been conceived let alone actually done. Likewise, Guilford's (1967) and Cattell's (1963) theoretical studies of intelligence would probably not even have been conceptualized. It is quite possible, in fact, that behavioral research is being revolutionized, certainly radically changed, due to the impact of multivariate conceptions and the modern computer.

To illustrate the radical development, even conversion, of behavioral research due to multivariate thinking, I want to describe and illustrate what is probably the most complex and powerful synthesis of multivariate methods to achieve theoretical and applied scientific purposes. It is called analysis of covariance structures, and is part of the system of Karl Jöreskog (1974, 1976), who has brought the work of a number of analysts together into a brilliant and productive synthesis.[7] The analysis of covariance struc-

---

[7] My discussion will sound as though Jöreskog has been solely responsible for the development of analysis of covariance structures. But such a way of talking is only for convenience. Actually, there have been several individuals important in the development of the methodology, whose contributions Jöreskog acknowledges (for example, Bock & Bargmann, 1966; Wiley, Schmidt, & Bramble, 1973). Nevertheless, Jöreskog has integrated various approaches and methods of analysis into one (or two) general systems in which mathematics, statistics, and computer technology have been integrated. In fact, Jöreskog's two main systems have been loosely named by the names of the computer programs used to implement the system: ACOVS and LISREL. The first of the two references given above (1974) uses the simpler of the two approaches, ACOVS. The second reference (1976) uses LISREL, which is more general and more complex. It is also more powerful. In the above description, I limit myself to a simplified view of the core of research and theory in the system.

tures means, essentially, the analysis of the varying together of variables that are in a structure, an edifice, dictated by theory. The system does several kinds of multivariate analysis but in such a way that one need not ask what form of analysis is being done. This is because the analytic possibilities are part of the larger system. In other words, Jöreskog has created an abstract mathematical and statistical formulation that can be expressed in algebraic equations, and this formulation encompasses a number of multivariate methods.

Computer programs have been integrated into the system (see footnote 7) in such a way that a research conception is "realized" by use of the computer program. This rather abstract description of Jöreskog's system is unsatisfactory for adequate understanding. To get the feel of it better, let's take two examples. The first is factor analytic because it is the easiest and clearest way to show the idea of the system. It should be emphasized, however, that the system's actual use usually involves more complex and involved problems. Indeed, one of its chief strengths is its ability to handle successfully sets of variables related in complex ways. The second example is path analytic. We will explain later what path analysis is.

A Theoretical Example Revisited

In Chapter 12 the elements of a structural theory of social attitudes were presented. The theory "says" that two general dimensions or factors underlie social attitudes, "conservatism" and "liberalism," and that these two general dimensions are relatively independent of each other (Kerlinger, 1967). The last phrase means that the correlation between the two factors is close to zero. This implies that conservatives espouse conservative principles and are not necessarily opposed to liberal principles. Conversely, liberals espouse liberal principles and are not necessarily opposed to conservative principles.

The usual conception of social attitudes is quite different. Whereas the "theory" just mentioned, and given in more detail in Chapter 12, says that conservatism and liberalism are separate and distinct entities, generally accepted and popular notions say that attitudes are bipolar. A bipolar, or two-ended, conception of social attitudes implies that conservative principles and people are at one end of a continuum of social attitudes and liberal principles and people at the other end of the continuum. This means, in effect, not only that conservatives espouse conservative principles, but that they also oppose liberal principles—and similarly for liberals and liberal principles.

Rational arguments can be and have been advanced for both conceptions. But what does empirical evidence say? The empirical evidence, obtained in a number of mostly factor analytic studies (for example, Kerlinger, 1972; Kerlinger, Middendorp, & Amón, 1976) seems to support the relative independence of conservatism and liberalism. But the matter is not yet settled. How can the two conceptions, or theories, be tested with the Jöreskog system?

TABLE 13.3   Responses of Six Persons to Four Social Attitude
Items (Reproduced from Table 12.5)[a]

	ITEMS			
	1	*2*	*3*	*4*
	Equality of	Birth	Private	
PERSONS	Women	Control	Property	Business
1	1	2	4	2
2	1	3	2	2
3	2	2	5	6
4	5	6	5	5
5	6	5	3	4
6	6	6	2	1

[a] The numbers in the table are the ratings of the six persons of the four referents on a scale from 1 to 6, 1 indicating very little approval and 6 indicating strong approval.

Let us use the attitude item example of Chapter 12. Suppose we administer four attitude items, two known to be liberal—*equality of women* and *birth control*—and two known to be conservative—*private property* and *business*—to six persons. (Again, many more items of "known" and "unknown" attitude affiliation would be administered to many more persons.) The results are those given in Table 12.5 and are reproduced for convenient reference in Table 13.3. The correlations among the items were reported in Table 12.6 and are reproduced here in Table 13.4. The results of factor analyzing this correlation matrix, originally given in Table 12.7, is reported again in Table 13.5. These results seem to support the independence and duality conception because the two liberal items are loaded on one factor (italicized loadings) and the two conservative items on another factor (also italicized). Negative loadings are low and inconsequential. If a bipolar conception were correct, then we should obtain one factor with the two liberal items having substantial positive loadings and the two conservative items having substantial negative loadings.

Using Jöreskog's approach, one first sets up the theoretical situation with diagrams. The diagrams in Figure 13.4 express the two alternatives. On the left (A) of the figure is the two-factor hypothesis. The numbers 1, 2, 3, and 4 represent the four attitude items, 1 and 2 being *equality of women* and *birth control*, the liberal items, and 3 and 4 *private property* and *business*, the conservative items. The circles represent the presumed factors, *L*

TABLE 13.4   Correlations among Four Social Attitude Items of
Six Persons (Reproduced from Table 12.6)

	EQUALITY OF WOMEN	*BIRTH CONTROL*	*PRIVATE PROPERTY*	*BUSINESS*
Equality of women	*1.00*	*.91*	−.15	.04
Birth control	*.91*	*1.00*	−.23	−.11
Private property	−.15	−.23	*1.00*	*.81*
Business	.04	−.11	*.81*	*1.00*

TABLE 13.5   Rotated Factor Matrix: Result of Factor Analysis of Correlation Matrix of Table 13.4 (Reproduced from Table 12.7)

	FACTORS	
ITEMS	A	B
Equality of women	.94	.13
Birth control	.94	.00
Private property	−.25	.83
Business	−.10	.87

and C, or liberalism and conservatism. The arrows represent influence or determination in the directions from L to 1 and 2 and from C to 3 and 4. That is, factor L "determines" or underlies items 1 and 2, and factor C "determines" or underlies items 3 and 4.

The diagram on the right (B) expresses the bipolar hypothesis. One factor, labeled appropriately LC, or L versus C, in Figure 13.4 (B), determines all four items, but it determines items 1 and 2 positively and 3 and 4 negatively. Therefore plus and minus signs have been attached to the arrows. (Note that the figure is oversimplified. For example, since there are always errors of measurement in measuring variables, such errors should be included in the figure—and estimated by the system.)

The next step is to express the situations diagrammed in Figure 13.4 in algebraic equations and then fit them into the general equations of Jöreskog's system. We omit this step and, instead, set up so-called hypothesis, or "target," matrices. A target matrix is usually a matrix of 1's and 0's, 1 indicating where substantial factor loadings (or other statistics) are expected and 0 where close-to-zero loadings are expected. (In the present example we will also use −1's.) Call the two-factor hypothesis or theory A and the one-factor hypothesis or theory B. If the intercorrelations of the four items—see Table 13.4—are factor analyzed, what sort of factor matrices do we expect for A and for B? What sort of matrices do the two theories "predict"? The two target matrices that express the alternative situations are given in Table 13.6.

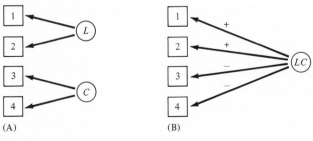

(A)   (B)

(See text for explanation of symbols.)

FIG. 13.4

TABLE 13.6   Target of Hypothesis Matrices Expressing
Alternative Factor Structure Hypotheses of
Correlation Matrix of Table 13.4[a]

DUALITY HYPOTHESIS		BIPOLARITY HYPOTHESIS	
I	II	I	II
1	0	1	0
1	0	1	0
0	1	−1	0
0	1	−1	0

[a] Entries in the table have the following meanings: 1: significant positive factor loading; −1: significant negative factor loading; 0: factor loading close to zero.

The next step in the procedure is to factor analyze the correlation matrix of Table 13.4. When this is done the results are compared to the target matrices using a quantitative procedure whose ultimate outcome indicates the degree of agreement between the factor matrix obtained from the data—it is given in Table 13.5—and each of the two target matrices of Table 13.6. This is *not* the actual procedure. It is suggested only to indicate the idea. The actual procedure is more powerful; it will be outlined below. In any case, the two coefficients of agreement—these are coefficients that are often used to compare factor matrices—calculated between, on the one hand, all eight factor loadings of Table 13.5 and all the 1 and 0 values of the two-factor target matrix of Table 13.6, and between the Table 13.5 loadings and the 1, −1, and 0 values of the bipolar target matrix, are .99 for the two-factor hypothesis and .61 for the bipolar hypothesis. Evidently the two-factor target matrix agrees much more with the research data than does the bipolar target matrix.

The above method is insufficient and is not the one actually formulated by Jöreskog. What is needed is a method that will take us back to the original correlations among the four items. The method just outlined puts all its faith in comparing the hypothesis matrix to the matrix obtained from the data. It is desirable to go back further and somehow generate a matrix like the correlation matrix. And this correlation matrix should be "produced" from the hypothesis factor matrix and the obtained factor matrix. In other words, we want to manipulate the obtained factor loadings and the values of the hypothesis matrix in a way that will produce a correlation matrix. If the hypothesis is correct, then this "produced" matrix will be very much like the correlation matrix obtained from the data. If, on the other hand, the hypothesis is not correct—if, for instance, there are really four factors or perhaps three rather than two factors, or the factor loadings obtained from the data do not fall into the structure or pattern specified by the 1's and 0's of the hypothesis matrix—then the "produced" correlation matrix will not be in agreement with the correlation matrix obtained from the observed data.

One of the central and basic ideas of the Jöreskog system is the comparison of covariance matrices. A correlation matrix is one kind of covariance matrix. So, for our purpose, we can say that one of the central ideas of the system is to compare correlation matrices, one yielded by the correlations among the obtained variables and another produced from a mathematical manipulation of the hypothesis matrix, as shown above, and the results as constrained by the demands of the hypothesis or hypotheses.

To give some flavor of what is meant, consider the two matrices, I and II, in Table 13.7. Matrix I is the same matrix of observed correlations among the four social attitude items already reported in Table 13.4. Matrix II is a set of "constrained" correlations produced by a well-known method from the factor loadings of Table 13.5. The operation was simple: the matrix was multiplied by itself. (The details need not concern us. The interested reader can consult a text on matrix algebra, or a matrix algebra section of a statistics text, for example, Cooley and Lohnes, 1971, pp. 15–20; Sullins, 1973; Tatsuoka, 1971, Ch. 2.) When we do this we obtain matrix II of Table 13.7.

We want to express and test the quantitative implications of the duality hypothesis and those of the bipolarity hypothesis. The two hypotheses were simply expressed in the target matrices of Table 13.6. We want somehow to operate on the obtained factors of Table 13.5 to transform the factor loadings into a set that expresses the duality hypothesis and into another set that expresses the bipolarity hypothesis. What the operation amounts to is to use the theoretical models expressed in Table 13.6 and to make the data of Table 13.5, the obtained factor loadings, look as much as possible like the models expressed in Table 13.6. When this was done, the two factor matrices of Table 13.8 were obtained.

TABLE 13.7   Obtained Correlations, Constrained Correlations, and Residual Matrix: Duality Hypothesis

	I: OBTAINED CORRELATIONS					*II: CONSTRAINED CORRELATIONS*			
	1	*2*	*3*	*4*		*1*	*2*	*3*	*4*
1	1.00	.91	−.15	.04	*1*	.90	.88	−.13	.02
2	.91	1.00	−.23	−.11	*2*	.88	.88	−.24	−.09
3	−.15	−.23	1.00	.81	*3*	−.13	−.24	.75	.75
4	.04	−.11	.81	1.00	*4*	.02	−.09	.75	.77

	RESIDUAL MATRIX			
	1	*2*	*3*	*4*
1	.10	.03	−.02	.02
2	.03	.12	.01	−.02
3	−.02	.01	.25	.06
4	.02	−.02	.06	.23

TABLE 13.8 Factor Loading Matrices That Express the Duality and Bipolarity Hypotheses

| | DUALITY HYPOTHESIS | | | BIPOLARITY HYPOTHESIS | |
	I	II		I	II
1	.94	.13	1	.81	.00
2	.94	.00	2	.94	.00
3	−.25	.83	3	−1.08	.00
4	−.10	.87	4	− .97	.00

The matrix on the left of Table 13.8 is exactly the same as that of Table 13.5. So the obtained factor matrix of Table 13.5 already expressed the duality hypothesis. The matrix on the right of Table 13.8 expresses how the factor matrix would look, given the same data and the empirical validity of the bipolarity hypothesis. In other words, the matrix labeled Duality Hypothesis, if obtained from the original correlations, would support the duality hypothesis, and the matrix labeled Bipolarity Hypothesis, if obtained from the original correlations, would support the bipolarity hypothesis.

Suppose now, in turn, that each of the factor matrices of Table 13.8 had actually been obtained from the data. From each of them we want to generate a correlation matrix, and then we want to compare this correlation matrix to the original correlation matrix.

We have already "produced" a correlation matrix from the factor matrix of Table 13.5 and the hypothesis or target matrix of Table 13.6 (on the left). It was given in Table 13.7 under the heading Constrained Correlations. If we subtract the values in this matrix from the values in the matrix labeled

TABLE 13.9 Obtained Correlations, Constrained Correlations, and Residual Matrix: Bipolarity Hypothesis

| | I: OBTAINED CORRELATIONS | | | | | II: CONSTRAINED CORRELATIONS | | | |
	1	2	3	4		1	2	3	4
1	1.00	.91	−.15	.04	1	.66	.76	− .87	−.79
2	.91	1.00	−.23	−.11	2	.76	.88	−1.02	−.91
3	−.15	−.23	1.00	.81	3	−.87	−1.02	1.17	1.05
4	.04	−.11	.81	1.00	4	−.79	− .91	1.05	.94

| | RESIDUAL MATRIX | | | |
	1	2	3	4
1	.34	.15	.72	.83
2	.15	.12	.79	.80
3	.72	.79	−.17	−.24
4	.83	.80	−.24	.06

Obtained Correlations, we obtain what is known as a residual matrix. This matrix of residuals expresses the "difference" between the two matrices and thus their agreement: the smaller the residuals, the greater the agreement of the two matrices. The average value of the residuals, omitting the diagonal values from the calculation, is .03.

Using the same procedure to test the bipolarity hypothesis, we obtain the correlation matrix labeled Constrained Correlations of Table 13.9. Subtracting the values of this matrix from the values of the actual obtained correlations, again given on the left of the table, we obtain a residual matrix, given at the bottom of the table. It is obvious that the "agreement" between matrices I and II is poor: the values of the residuals are large. Indeed, their average is .59. Evidently the results obtained from the duality hypothesis agree with the obtained data much better than do the results obtained from the bipolarity hypothesis.

In a word, one can use covariance structure analysis to test which theoretical model among two or more such models best fits the observed data. This is scientifically powerful business. Recall from earlier discussions that one of the most significant and characteristic approaches or methods of science is to set up and test alternative hypotheses. The scientist does not trust the evidence, for example, that p_1 leads to q. He insists on testing plausible alternative explanations, p_2, p_3, and so on. The elimination of such alternative hypotheses by research strengthens the hypothesis p_1. The main strength of the Jöreskog system is its flexible ability to test complex hypotheses and to compare results obtained from alternative models.

An Added Note: Latent Variables

A highly important and invaluable characteristic of covariance structure analysis must be mentioned, if only briefly. This is the conception and use of so-called latent variables in the system. A *latent variable* is an unobserved variable that is used or hypothesized to "explain" or influence observed variables or other latent variables. An example was given in Figure 13.4 where liberalism (L) and conservatism (C) were underlying unobserved variables assumed to "explain" the four items (or variables) of the example. To make the point a bit clearer and to approach closer to the Jöreskog system, regard Figure 13.5 in which the situation on the left of Figure 13.4 is depicted more along Jöreskog lines.

L (liberalism) and C (conservatism) are latent or unobserved variables that are presumed to underlie the four observed variables (items), L underlying variables 1 and 2, and C underlying variables 3 and 4. Observed variables are given in boxes and latent variables in circles. The one-headed arrows indicate direction of influence—for example, L influences 1 and 2. The double-headed arrows indicate correlation—for instance, r_{12} is the correlation between variables 1 and 2. The e's indicate the measurement errors in the observed variables. Given the data—in this case the correla-

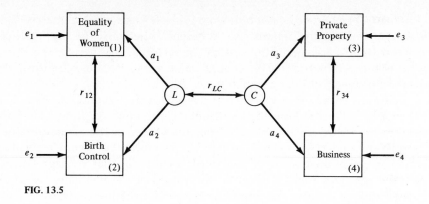

FIG. 13.5

tions among the four items—the system estimates the influence of L on variables 1 and 2 and the influence of C on 3 and 4. These influences are symbolized by a_1 and a_2 (for L) and a_3 and a_4 (for C), the values of which are estimated by the system. The system also estimates the correlation between L and C and the error variances e_1, e_2, e_3, and e_4. Analysis then proceeds along the lines outlined above.

The point of Figure 13.5 is to show that the method, unlike most other multivariate analysis methods, estimates the effects of latent variables on observed variables and even the relations among latent variables. This is, of course, the stuff of theory building and testing. It is also much like factor analysis. Recall Cattell's fluid and crystallized intelligence, second-order factors that can also be conceived as latent variables. The difference is that in covariance structure analysis the idea is generalized and applied to all kinds of theoretic and analytic situations. Moreover, factor analysis is a special case of the general system. Thus theories can be formulated, tested, and compared for their congruence with observed data.

A Path Analysis Example

To show the versatility and flexibility of covariance structure analysis, we now examine a different sort of research problem. Studies of achievement in college have sometimes used measures of intelligence and social class to predict such achievement. Suppose that an educational researcher believes that these two variables are insufficient and that a measure of motivation is also needed. He selects a measure of need for achievement, commonly written n Achievement, or simply n Ach (McClelland, Atkinson, Clark, & Lowell, 1953). He believes, in other words, that not only will the addition of n Ach to intelligence and social class improve the prediction of success in college but it will also supply a theoretically more satisfying explanation of such success. His proposed "explanation" is diagrammed in Figure 13.6.[8]

---

[8] This example is taken from Kerlinger and Pedhazur (1973, pp. 323–324).

Analysis of Covariance Structures   **233**

The arrows in the diagram indicate direction of influence: the influence flowing in the direction of the arrow heads. (Ignore for the moment the numbers attached to the arrows.) For example, SES (socioeconomic status) influences Ach (Achievement) directly. It also influences Ach indirectly through n Ach, which latter influence is direct. (A direct influence is represented by a single arrow from one variable to another. An indirect influence is shown by an arrow coming from a variable that itself is the "recipient" of another arrow. For example, as indicated above, SES influences n Ach directly and Ach indirectly, through n Ach.) The arrows are usually called "paths." Thus the term "path analysis." The path diagram, then, expresses the researcher's "small theory." SES and Intelligence (Intell.) both affect n Ach directly, for example; the higher the intelligence, the higher n Ach, and the "higher" the social class, the higher the achievement. They also both affect Achievement directly: if middle class, then higher Achievement, and if higher intelligence, then higher achievement. n Ach is also considered to affect Achievement directly, as indicated by the arrow between n Ach and Ach. But it is also presumed that, in addition to their direct effects on Achievement, SES and Intelligence exercise indirect effects on Achievement by their direct effect on n Ach. (Although SES and Intelligence are themselves correlated—this is indicated by the double-headed curved arrow between them—they are not considered to affect each other.)

Path analysts call the above formulation a causal model: by using it some notion of causes and effects may be determined. (We withhold comment here on the thorny problem of cause and effect.) Then, from the correlations among the variables of the model, they calculate path coefficients. A path coefficient is simply a regression weight yielded by the usual regression analysis. For instance, the regression of n Ach on SES and Intelligence (that is, SES and Intelligence are the independent variables and n Ach the dependent variable) yields regression coefficients (beta coefficients) of .40 for the path from SES to n Ach and .04 for the path from Intelligence to n Ach. These values indicate that SES has a substantial effect on n Ach, but that Intelligence has little effect.

Then the regression of Achievement on SES, Intelligence, and n Ach (that is, Achievement, the dependent variable, is predicted by the other three variables) is done. The analysis provides coefficients, as follows: from SES to Achievement, .01; from Intelligence to Achievement, .50; from

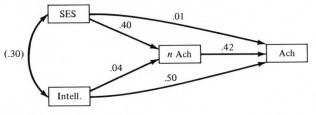

FIG. 13.6

n Ach to Achievement, .42. These path coefficients have been attached to their paths in Figure 13.6. Of course, the usual regression analysis in this situation would have yielded the latter coefficients. The difference between an ordinary regression analysis and the path analysis, however, is that the paths from SES and Intelligence to *n* Ach have been added because the researcher believes, on the basis of theoretical reasoning, that both direct *and* indirect influences are at work. In other words, not only do the three variables directly affect Achievement; SES and Intelligence affect Achievement indirectly through *n* Ach. (Note the similarity in reasoning to the interaction phenomenon studied earlier.) This is a richer, more sophisticated, and probably more accurate analysis of the influences on Achievement than we obtain with an ordinary regression analysis, in this case mainly because we have "explained" *n* Ach on the way to "explaining" Achievement.

When we inspect the path diagram of Figure 13.6, we see that two of the paths have near-zero path coefficients: from SES to Ach, .01, and from Intelligence to *n* Ach, .04. Since one of the goals of science is not only explanation but parsimonious explanation, we ask: If we delete these two paths and recalculate the path coefficients in the resulting more parsimonious model, will a test with the original data, as done with the factor analytic model above, show good agreement between the correlations among the four variables produced by the new model and the original correlations? That is, it is possible to calculate a set of correlations among the four variables from the path coefficients. This matrix of correlations is then compared to the matrix of original correlations. Then, a residual matrix—the result of subtracting one of these matrices from the other—is calculated, as before. If its values are quite small, we can conclude that the theoretical model as embodied in the path diagram is satisfactory.

The new model is given in the path diagram of Figure 13.7. The difference between this model and the model of Figure 13.6 is that the two paths mentioned above have been deleted. Here, Intelligence affects Achievement directly and does not affect *n* Ach. SES affects Achievement only through *n* Ach. That is, SES affects *n* Ach, which in turn affects Achievement. Obviously the model is considerably simpler and more parsimonious. The question again is: Is it consistent with the original data, the original correlations?

Table 13.10 gives the analysis to answer the question. The original

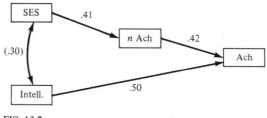

FIG. 13.7

TABLE 13.10   Original Correlations, A, Constrained
Correlations, B, and Residual Matrix, Four
Variables, Second Model

	A: ORIGINAL CORRELATIONS					B: CONSTRAINED CORRELATIONS			
	1	2	3	4		1	2	3	4
1	1.00	.30	.41	.33	1	1.00	.30	.41	.32
2	.30	1.00	.16	.57	2	.30	1.00	.12	.56
3	.41	.16	1.00	.50	3	.41	.12	1.00	.48
4	.33	.57	.50	1.00	4	.32	.56	.48	1.00

RESIDUAL MATRIX

	1	2	3	4
1	.00	.00	.00	.01
2	.00	.00	.04	.01
3	.00	.04	.00	.02
4	.01	.01	.02	.00

correlations are given on the left of the table, A, and the constrained correlations, the correlations calculated from the path coefficients of Figure 13.7, are given on the right, B. Subtracting matrix B from matrix A yields the residual matrix, given at the bottom of the table. It is obvious that the correlations produced from the path coefficients are highly similar to the original correlations: none of the residuals is greater than .04. We conclude, therefore, that the path model of Figure 13.7 is consistent with the data.[9] Evidently the "explanation" behind the model of Figure 13.7 is satisfactory. And, since it is a simpler "explanation" than the model of Figure 13.6, we accept it as a "better" explanation because it is more parsimonious *and* it yields correlations that agree with the original correlations.

An important point must be made. Because a theoretical model is consistent with obtained data does not mean that the theory behind the model is necessarily "correct." Indeed, more than one model may be consistent with obtained data. So, in this case, although the model of Figure 13.7 is consistent with the obtained correlations, the model itself may or may not be the "correct" theoretical explanation. The method being expounded can be said, therefore, to be negative in its virtue. If a model is not consistent with the data, it is unlikely to be "correct." But if it is consistent with the data, it may or may not be "correct." Its "correctness," in other words, has

[9] A caution is in order. Had we done the same analysis with the path model of Figure 13.6, the residual matrix would have been all zeroes. Thus the model of Figure 13.6 is also consistent with the data. But this does not mean that the model of Figure 13.6 is better than or even just as good as the model of Figure 13.7. The perfect reproduction of the correlations is almost an artifact. When all possible paths of a path diagram are used, and all possible path coefficients calculated, no matter what the model or the diagram, the original correlation matrix is perfectly reproduced.

to be judged on more than statistical grounds. This is one of the difficulties of all scientific (and other) theories and explanations. They can be shown to be probably incorrect in the sense that they are not consistent with empirical evidence, but they can never be shown to be absolutely correct. An explanation can be shown to be probably "better" than other alternative explanations, but the scientist can never be sure that it is the last word. If the reader will think back to the cigarette-smoking and lung cancer discussion in Chapter 8, he will perhaps understand better what was said then about explanations and alternative explanations.

In the above discussion nothing was said about covariance structure analysis. Indeed, it was a more or less conventional description of path analysis. It omitted covariance structure analysis so that the reader could get an overview of the path analytic approach in the usual multiple regression framework. We now try to show, though briefly and incompletely, how path analysis is a special case of covariance structure analysis and how the research analytic problem can be approached in the covariance structure framework.

In covariance structure analysis the problems depicted in Figures 13.6 and 13.7 can be solved with precisely the same results. More can be done, however. First, the measurement error variances associated with the fallible measures of the variables can be estimated. Such estimation will then change the solution, including the path coefficients. Path analysis usually assumes no errors and is thus vulnerable to criticism. Second, latent variables can be postulated and their influence estimated. For example, in the model of Figure 13.6 a latent variable might be thought to influence both n Achievement and Achievement.

Third, covariance structure analysis permits tests of the statistical significance of the agreement between theoretical models and observed data. Moreover, alternative theoretical models can be tested for their comparative congruence with observed data. For example, the congruence between the original correlations and the constrained correlations of Table 13.10 can be statistically tested. If the differences between the two matrices, shown in the residual matrix of Table 13.10, are relatively large, indicating lack of agreement between theory and data, the statistical test will indicate this. If the statistical test shows nonsignificance, then the agreement or congruence is acceptable.

Finally, the estimation of the magnitudes of the values of the coefficients of a model—in path analysis the path coefficients, for example—is done simultaneously. In the path analysis examples given above the path coefficients were estimated successively. For instance, in the problem of Figure 13.6 the coefficients leading from SES and Intelligence to n Achievement were first calculated and then the coefficients from SES, Intelligence, and n Achievement to Achievement were calculated. In covariance structure analysis, however, they are all estimated at the same time, so to speak, including the estimation of the influences of the latent variables, if any, and the errors. That is, *all* the information is taken into account in a truly multivariate fashion. It should be obvious that path analysis is a special case of covariance structure analysis.

As usual, we must end this discussion on a cautionary note. As powerful as it is, covariance structure analysis is not the perfect answer to theoretic and analytic problems. It cannot—or should not—be used for ordinary analyses. It is a waste of time and effort to use it, for example, for an ordinary exploratory factor analysis. It should be used only when testing relatively complex theoretical models or complex alternative hypotheses. A second limitation is that the assumptions behind its use are rather severe, making it at least theoretically inapplicable in some research situations (for example, with dichotomous variables). This limitation of the system may in time be overcome. There are one or two other limitations, but they can be ignored here. In sum, covariance structure analysis is a rich, potent, and powerful strategy and method of attack on research problems provided they are guided by theory and are of such nature that the assumptions of the method can be reasonably satisfied. One can even say that the method is a major breakthrough in conceptualization and methodology heralding a new direction and sophistication in behavioral research.

CONCLUSION

We have come almost full circle. We started the book with ideas of theory and explanation, and we have continually harped on theory and explanation throughout the book. Now we have reached the contemporary methodological ultimate in the abstract conceptualizing and testing of theory in a multivariate framework. With multivariate analysis, behavioral research methodology reaches a degree of complexity undreamed of in earlier years.

The most important strength of multivariate analysis is that scientists can get closer to the complex reality of human behavior by using multivariate methods. Another strength is that the conduct of nonexperimental research and the analysis of nonexperimental research data can be greatly fortified with multivariate approaches and analyses. Perhaps the most significant word is "control." With appropriate multivariate techniques identification and control of variance can be achieved. Thus research data can be more confidently interpreted. The path of inference from initial theory to final confirmation and interpretation has been made clearer, even though it has also been made much more complex.

The power and desirability of the multivariate approach should not deceive us, however, into believing that its development solves most of our scientific problems, or that there are no weaknesses, or that simpler univariate approaches are dead or dying. Not so. Behavioral research will always need simpler approaches, especially in experiments and certain applied research situations. After all, one can even say that the correlation coefficient, which expresses the magnitude and direction of the relation between two variables, is the heart of multivariate analysis. Note that in a sense a complex tool like canonical correlation results finally in a correlation coefficient. More germane to the point is that much research will require no more than a simple comparison of means using analysis of variance or other method, or a comparison of frequencies and percentages as in crossbreak tables, or the simplest of research designs, say one experimental group and one control group. No, the multivariate approach will not so much displace simpler methods as it will enrich behavioral research by making it possible to approach closer to the complex demands of behavioral theory. A theory is a set of constructs or variables systematically related to each other in specified ways. By definition, a theory has several variables in a unified structure. To test a theory adequately, then, multivariate methods are often needed. The purpose of this chapter has been to supply some of the flavor, if not much of the substance, of this necessity.

14

The computer

What is it about computers that mystifies and disturbs many people? Are computers beneficial aids or awesome monsters of frightening potential? Are they good for us or bad for us? Computers are not just machines; they are also social and psychological phenomena with important implications for science and research. In this chapter we try to understand some small part of what computers are, how they work, and what they mean for the scientist. We will also try to dispel some of the mythology about them.

One cannot understand modern behavioral research without understanding the computer, one of the strongest contemporary influences on research. It is not only that more and larger problems can be tackled than could be tackled before the 1950s, the first years of the modern high-speed electronic digital computer. The very nature of the problems we study is different; even our approach to problems is different.

For example, the multivariate analytic techniques studied in the last few chapters are today readily available to researchers because there are computers, computer centers, and multivariate computer programs available. Knowing this the researcher is free to conceive a large variety of research problems that, say, in the 1950s he would not even consider simply because there was no feasible way to do the lengthy and involved calculations needed. Sheer quantity of calculations, in other words, has drastically affected the nature and substance of theory and problems.   **239**

The computer has become so intimately and closely entwined with the thinking of researchers that it is difficult to conceive of a time when computers were not around. I clearly remember the time myself, but I now wonder how I could have existed professionally without them. And so it is with most research-minded psychologists, sociologists, economists, and educators. We cannot imagine what it is like not to have computers available.

Take one or two examples. Factor analysis is now almost routinely used to help determine what tests and scales measure. One can construct an aptitude test, as Thurstone did many years ago, and include what one believes to be three or four kinds of measures of aptitudes: verbal, numerical, and spatial, for instance. Does the test really measure the specified aptitudes, however? One important way to answer this question is to administer the test to large numbers of children or adults and then to factor analyze the correlations among the *items* of the test. Recall that factor analysis, among other things, is a method of analysis that enables a researcher to determine how tests or measures cluster together. It also determines how test or scale items cluster together. If certain items presumably measure verbal aptitude, and certain other items measure numerical aptitude, then they should each on analysis cluster together. The correlations between the verbal items should be positive and substantial, and the correlations between the numerical items should also be substantial, while the correlations between the two kinds of items, between the presumed verbal and numerical items, should be lower (because they are measuring different things). Factor analysis, as we saw earlier, does such analyses quite successfully—with the help of the computer. (See Chapter 12, especially the attitude scale example and Tables 12.5, 12.6, and 12.7.)

Before computers were generally available it was known—though not well known—that factor analysis of items was needed for satisfactory validity and other studies in measurement. Yet such studies were rare, almost nonexistent.[1] The sheer bulk of calculations effectively removed such ideas even from consideration, though some researchers wistfully thought about this approach. Thus an effective way of studying the validity of measures, of learning to some extent what tests and items really measure,

[1] In 1958 Kaya and I (Kerlinger & Kaya, 1959) wanted a factor analysis of the correlations among the items of a 20-item attitude scale in order to validate certain ideas we had about the attitude domain and the items. We calculated the 190 correlation coefficients ourselves on a mechanical desk calculator. Needless to say, this took many hours. The thought of doing the factor analysis, however, appalled us, though both of us had done factor analysis "by hand." We took the correlation matrix to the late Irving Lorge, who had the distinction of having one of the first and rather primitive computers in his office complex. Lorge did the factor analysis, without rotations, for us at the cost of about $600. The job took hours, if I remember correctly. Then Kaya and I did the rotations by hand—at the cost of about 10 to 20 hours. One can see why researchers hesitated before planning item factor analysis. Today a complete analysis of similar item data, from all item statistics to the final factor axes rotations, takes less than 20 seconds on the computer I now use!

was virtually unavailable before the modern high-speed computer became available. Today such analyses are routine.

In Chapter 11 we learned that multiple regression is a powerful way to study the single and joint effects of a number of independent variables on a dependent variable. To do multiple regression requires, in effect, the solution of a number of simultaneous equations. One common way to do this requires the calculation of the inverse of the matrix of correlations among the independent variables. To do this "by hand" with two independent variables is easy. To do it with three independent variables is harder but quite possible. To do it with four or more variables is much harder, time consuming, frustrating, and error prone. A computer does it very quickly, in a matter of seconds. Even a small programmable hand calculator can handle three independent variables in about two minutes. The point is that the calculations of a powerful method like multiple regression are now readily available to researchers who no longer have to face the time-consuming and error-prone desk calculations of the past.

One more example, this time a highly complex one, is covariance structure analysis, described in Chapter 13. Covariance structure analysis is virtually impossible to do with a desk calculator. Parts of the computations are so complex that they can be done only by a computer, and this in a matter of seconds. So we can say that this flexible, powerful, and fruitful method of approaching theory and theory testing has become possible only with the advent of high-speed computers. Indeed, the method would never have been conceived in the first place if its authors had not worked always with the availability of the computer in mind. And the same is true of almost all multivariate analysis with more than, say, six or seven variables. The influence of computers on research in the behavioral sciences, then, has been very great. And we have talked only of the effects of calculations. Computers have had great effects, of course, in noncomputational areas. In this chapter, we pretty much confine ourselves to the effects of computer calculations with numbers.

CHARACTERISTICS OF COMPUTERS AND COMPUTING

The basic function of machines has changed fundamentally. A machine is a mechanical or electrical device or system for accomplishing some useful work through routine operations. It is a template, so to speak, with which one produces something regularly and repeatedly. A sewing machine makes stitches regularly, repeatedly, and with variations. A typewriter produces series of letters. A piano produces series and clusters of tones. An automobile engine, through repeated explosions and intricate interaction of its parts, delivers power to wheels. Machines operate stereotypically. They do—or are supposed to do—what their users tell them to do, and no more. The basic function of most machines is to deliver power so that a certain relatively fixed job can be done: the up and down movement of the sewing machine needle, the mechanism of a piano that transforms the energy of fingers to the felt hammers that strike the strings, the working of the automobile engine to turn the wheels of a car.

Weizenbaum (1976), in his penetrating book on the computer, points out that the coming of electrical machines, especially the computer, has changed the fundamental purpose of machines from the transmission of power to the transformation of information. The observation is profound and its meaning important. The purpose of the computer is not to produce power so that some sort of work can be done. It transforms information from certain forms to certain other forms, and it does this at high speed and with great reliability. A pertinent example is the transformation of raw data in the form of numbers into other numbers called statistics, like adding long strings of numbers and then calculating a mean, multiplying many pairs of numbers, adding them, and then calculating covariances, or scanning verbal texts, counting key words, categorizing such words, and then counting the numbers of such words in each category.

A computer, then, is an electrical machine of great complexity whose basic function is to transform information at great speed and with high reliability. It is an elaborate complex of hardware whose major characteristics are ability to do many repetitive operations at tremendous speed and with a high degree of accuracy, flexibility, and what I like to call "ductility." The speed of modern computers is almost beyond belief. The modern large computer can do 200,000 operations or more per second! I gave one example earlier. Let me now be more specific with a more complex example. In an attitude study done in the Netherlands, a sample of 685 persons responded to a 72-item attitude scale (Kerlinger, Middendorp, & Amón, 1976). Means, standard deviations, the intercorrelations of the 72 items were calculated by a large computer. Then the correlation matrix was factor analyzed and the obtained factors rotated successively, starting with two factors, then three factors, and so on through twelve factors. The computer took about one minute and 40 seconds to do the work. To get some idea of the magnitude of the job, realize that there were 72 sums, 72 sums of squares, 72 means, 72 standard deviations, 2,556 cross-products, and thousands, even millions, of other calculations connected with the factor analysis!

The computer also operates with great reliability. It does all these complex operations with finite but high accuracy. The hardware—as computer people call the physical parts of computers—performs admirably; you can depend on most results you get from a computer, provided you have done your work properly and provided the program you use is adequate. Unfortunately, a good deal that comes out of computers is inaccurate, even meaningless. But this is not the fault of the computer; it is the fault of the people who use the computer. Most such questionable output is probably due to ignorance. We will return to this point later. The point is that modern computers are highly reliable and accurate machines that can be depended upon for most analyses in behavioral research.

Computers are not infallible, however. You cannot depend on them completely because they *do* have limitations. If prolonged calculations with very large or very small numbers are done, the results of the calculations can exceed the computer's capacity. Suppose I have a small computer with room for results no greater than the number 1,000,000, or seven places. But I have the following calculations to do:

$$467^2 \times 54^3 + 117/.005.$$

The result is, of course, greater than 1,000,000, and my computer cannot handle it. But the capacities of modern computers are greater than 1,000,000, and they can accommodate most computing needs of the behavioral sciences.

Occasionally, however, inaccuracies occur, even with well-written programs. ("Program" will be defined later.) For example, much multivariate analysis depends on a mathematical operation known as matrix inversion (mentioned earlier). The inverse of a matrix is like a reciprocal or a divisor or denominator in arithmetic. Although in algebra you can easily divide b by a, or b/a, to produce, say, c, or $c = b/a$, it is not possible in a strict sense to divide one matrix of numbers into another matrix of numbers. Instead, an inverse matrix is calculated, and the first matrix is multiplied by the inverse matrix. Calculating inverses of matrices requires many multiplications. If the numbers are large, then the computer capacity may be exceeded. If, as is often likely in multivariate analysis, the numbers are small—correlation coefficients are small, and two or three multiplied together produce even smaller numbers because they are fractions[2]—then the many multiplications may produce very small numbers that lead to inaccuracies and misleading results.

The computer's reliability is related to its "ductility." "Ductility" means "tractability." A tractable person does what others want him to do. A computer does what people tell it to do. In so doing it is stupid: it does exactly what it is told to do; it never shows any intelligence or common sense. The computer programmer doesn't exist who, at some time or other, hasn't said: "You dummy! That's not what I wanted." So it can be said that computers are stupid as well as tractable. This is an excellent characteristic because it means great reliability and dependability. It also puts large demands on people who use and program computers. They must spell out *everything* the computer must do to reach any goal. And this is, of course, not easy to do. In short, a programmer can omit nothing: computers must have complete and detailed instructions. A computer faithfully makes the mistakes it is told to make! It does no more and no less than its instructions dictate.

---

[2] For example, suppose we multiply .30, .40, and .05: $.30 \times .40 \times .05 = .006$.

Another characteristic of computers and computing is not really a characteristic of the machine. It inheres in the people working with the machine. Computers seem to have endless fascination for many people. This is especially true if one has successfully programmed a computer to do a useful job. The fun involved is like the fun a pianist has learning and playing a challenging piece of music or a chess player playing an equal opponent. It is as though one is driven to conquer not just the analysis one needs but also the computer—and oneself. The intense preoccupation and concentration involved seem to coalesce into a highly satisfying psychological experience. In short, computer programmers often get hooked, addicted to the computer.

This characteristic leads to productive results. Problems get solved that would not get solved without such investments of preoccupation, concentration, energy, and time. But the results can also be unfortunate. It is possible to become so absorbed in the machine, programming, and computations that what they are for is forgotten. Weizenbaum (1976, Ch. 4) has vividly described computer "hackers," individuals who virtually live with and for the computer. They don't program so much as they "hack." While technically brilliant—their knowledge of computers and programming is often profound—they don't really care what they program for. Weizenbaum says that theirs is a neurotic preoccupation not so much to solve or help solve substantive problems as it is to master the machine, to achieve power.

Weizenbaum's extreme case has been given to highlight the extreme fascination of this highly complex and powerful modern tool. While Weizenbaum's "hacker" is a neurotic manifestation of the fascination, there can be little doubt that many people, perhaps most of those who liberally interact with computers, get hooked. There is nothing wrong with strong interest; it often leads to creative achievement. But there is an additional dimension to the computer: it is basically a tool for helping to solve problems. If this is forgotten in preoccupation with the machine itself, then the enterprise becomes a game. Most games are harmless, and their avid pursuit does not hurt anyone. The avid pursuit of the computer without concern for the scientific and technical ends it is used for, however, can lead to meaningless triviality, or, far worse, to erosion of scientific values.

HOW COMPUTERS AND COMPUTER PROGRAMS WORK

The core of understanding the computer in its relation to research is to understand how it is made to do its work. In this book we do not really care *how* computers work internally, but we do care how we can make them perform. How, for instance, do you have a computer calculate the mean of a series of numbers? Perhaps the best way to understand computers and computer usage is to learn a little of computer programs and programming.

A computer program is a set of instructions in some special computer language that tells the computer precisely what to do to accomplish the purpose of the program. A factor analysis program, for example, is an elaborate set of instructions to a computer to read data from cards or tape, to calculate means and standard deviations of all the variables read in, to calculate the intercorrelations of all or some of the variables, to do the calculations necessary to obtain factors and rotate them, and finally to print out the results in appropriately labeled form. Such a program will be complex and long. The specific instructions will fill a number of pages. A program I use for factor analysis occupies 12 tightly packed large-size computer output pages. Another more complex factor analysis program occupies 26 pages. (Many programs, of course, are relatively short.)

A Simple Example of Programming

Programs are written in special computer languages. We use Fortran (FORmula TRANslation) here because it is probably the most-used computer language, at least in the behavioral sciences. There are, however, a number of other languages: Algol, Cobol, Pascal, and so on. Since our concern is only basic programming ideas, we need not dwell on the languages and their differences. We shall, however, also briefly discuss and illustrate the language used to program another remarkable development, a programmable pocket calculator. Such "smaller" languages have the virtues of relative simplicity and considerable flexibility and capability. Moreover, programmable calculators are now becoming readily available and will soon be more widely used and quite inexpensive. Indeed, within five years they will probably fill a number of the needs of behavioral scientists for lesser calculations.

Fortran is an intermediary language—as are Algol, Pascal, and other similar languages—that enables the researcher to communicate with the computer. It uses certain basic English statements or commands like: READ, WRITE, GO TO, CONTINUE, DO, and IF. These commands can be taken literally: *read* such-and-such data; *write* (or print) the results, *go to* another part of the program, *if* a computed quantity is positive (say), *go to* this part of the program, but *if* it is negative or zero, *go to* that part of the program. The power and flexibility of computer languages cannot be exaggerated. There is almost no logical or numerical operation that cannot be accomplished with them.

Suppose we wish to add two numbers, 6 and 4, and put the results into a storage place labeled SUM. A Fortran instruction to do this is:

$$SUM = 6 + 4$$

But this is too limited because we will certainly want to use the addition operation again. So we write:

$$SUM = A + B$$

Now, any two numbers can be read by the computer's "reader" and can be stored in the "places" called A and B. Then A and B can be used later in any arithmetic operations as well as in addition. The other arithmetic operations are handled similarly. For example, multiplication and division are accomplished as follows:

$$RESULT1 = A * B \quad \text{(multiplication)}$$
$$RESULT2 = A/B \quad \text{(division)}$$

("*" is the Fortran version of "×," multiply. "/" is the Fortran version of "÷," divide.) Operations are easily combined, like the following combination of the four basic arithmetic operations:

$$RESULT3 = ((RESULT1 + RESULT2)*A)/(A - B)$$

(If A = 6 and B = 4, then RESULT3 = 76.50.)

This very low level use of Fortran, while not particularly interesting or powerful, illustrates three important points about Fortran and programming. First, Fortran equations are not like ordinary algebraic equations. They always mean that the statement on the right is put into the "place" labeled on the left. Only one term can be on the left, any number of terms and expressions on the right. The statement SUM = A + B, above, means: Into the place called SUM, put the sum of A and B. Second, the result of an operation can be labeled almost anything subject to two or three simple rules (for example, the name can have one to seven letters or numbers or both: C, SUM, RESULT2, and so on).

Third, modern computers have a great deal of storage, and the storage places are accessed simply through their names or labels. In the above example, each of the values, A, B, SUM, RESULT1, RESULT2, and RESULT3, are stored in different and readily accessible places that in effect are labeled as indicated. The storing and storage places of the above example can be conceived like this (though this is not how it is really done):

6.	4.	10.	24.	1.50	76.50
A	B	SUM	RESULT1	RESULT2	RESULT3

Now, the programmer can do what he wishes with these values, or any other values he may have calculated, simply by writing new Fortran statements.

The real power of the computer, however, lies in its flexible ability to do repetitive operations over and over at great speed. Suppose we wish to add a series of numbers and then calculate their mean. There are several ways to do this in Fortran. We illustrate only two of them. They permit us to make two or three points. Here is one routine for adding numbers:

```
        DO 110     I = 1,N
   110  SUMX = SUMX + X(I)
```

These crisp statements can be translated as follows. DO whatever is indicated in the statement 110, using the values 1 through N $(1, 2, 3, . . ., N)$, N being the total number of values of X. Suppose that 100 different X values had been read into the machine's memory earlier $(N = 100)$. They would then be in 100 storage places. The Fortran statement instructs the machine to take these values of X from each memory in turn and add them to another place called SUMX. This is a characteristic way to cumulate values in Fortran. In effect, the machine repeatedly does the stated operation until it has used the Nth X value ("100" having been earlier read into a storage place labeled N). Then it stops for further instructions.

The above procedure, however, uses storage that need not be used. A programming precept is always to use as little storage as possible. A Fortran routine that is more economical would have the machine read one X value at a time from a card and then immediately do the required addition. There would then be no need to store the X's, unless, of course, one had to use them later. The Fortran to accomplish this and also to calculate the mean can be:

```
    10   (Read in N.)
         SUMX = 0.0               (Initialize SUMX.)
    30   I = I + 1                (Set I to 1.)
    40   (Read in X(I).)
   100   SUMX = SUMX + X(I)       (Adds X_i to SUMX.)
   105   IF (I.LT.N)   GO TO 30   (Conditional statement:
                                     see text.)

         AN = N                   (Puts N into AN.)
   107   AVER = SUMX/AN           (Calculates mean.)
   110   (Print SUMX and AVER.)
         END
```

In this routine the computer first reads in N, or 100, which the user has punched on a card. Statement 10, which has been omitted to avoid complexity, accomplishes this. Then SUMX, the name of what will ultimately become the sum of the X's, is set to zero. This is called *initialization* and is like clearing a calculator before beginning a calculation. Statement 30,

I = I + 1, is a standard form of cumulating a sum. A 1 is added to I and is put into the place called I. (I will be used as a subscript of X later.) Statement 40, the details of which are again omitted, reads in the first X, or X(1). At statement 100, X(I), which is of course X(1), is added to SUMX and put into the place SUMX. Statement 105 is the most interesting. Translated, it says: "If I is less than (LT) N, go to statement 30." Since I = 1 and is thus less than N, or 100, the computer goes back to statement 30. This completes one swing through the loop.

The computer is now back to statement 30, which adds 1 to I again. At 40, X(2) is read in, and at 100 is added to SUMX. If X(1) = 15 and X(2) = 17, then SUMX is now 32. The test at statement 105 is again made, and because I, or 2, is less than 100, the computer again loops back to 30. I is again incremented, the next X(I) is added to SUMX, the test at 105 is again made, and the computer again loops back to 30. The procedure continues until the 100th X, or I = 100. After X(100) is added to SUMX, the IF test at statement 105 is again made, but this time, since I = 100 and therefore not less than N, the computer will not loop back to 30. Instead it continues after 105.

The continuation of the program simply calculates the mean, called AVER, after converting N to AN, which is done to change the integer N to a decimal number so that the arithmetic of SUMX/AN can be performed. (In Fortran, variable names that begin with I, J, K, L, M, and N are integer variables; all others are decimal variables. The reader need not worry over this distinction.) AVER, the mean, is then calculated in statement 107, and SUMX and AVER are printed by statement 110 (not given). The program and calculations then end with the instruction END.

This is sufficient to give the reader some flavor of a computer language like Fortran and how the computer "works." The procedure may look cumbersome at first, but it works—and works very well. The above program would take only a second or two on a large computer. Moreover, we could easily have added the squares of all the X's, calculated the sums of squares, and then the standard deviations, had we wished to do so, with very little increase in computer time. Reading in data and printing results take more time than actual calculations, which are done so fast that if you pressed a button to start them they would be done before you released the button!

It would be almost silly to use a large computer for such simple computations. If one had, instead of one X, 30 X's, or variables, and wished to calculate all the means, standard deviations, and correlations among the X's, it would not be silly. And this is easily, accurately, and quickly done with a Fortran (or other) program. Of course, the program will be more complex. And if one wishes to do other analyses, like factor analysis or multiple regression analysis, then the program becomes much longer and more complex. (We have only shown a small fraction of Fortran's possibilities.) Nevertheless, the basic procedures are similar.

PROGRAMMABLE CALCULATOR-COMPUTERS

For its potential importance and intrinsic interest, we now look briefly at the language used with the Hewlett-Packard small programmable calculator, the HP-67.[3] (The same language, with slight alterations, is used with the larger HP-97.) The HP-67, like its TI cousins, has the capability of recording programs written for it on small pieces of plastic. When a program is needed, the plastic is inserted into the machine and the programmed calculator is ready to function. The flexibility and power of such machines—and in two or three years they will probably be even more flexible and powerful—are remarkable. They are not, of course, in the same universe of discourse as the large computers, but they are not toys. They are full-fledged calculator-computers capable of many important analytic jobs. In any case, we now illustrate some of the programming language and logic of the HP-67. Let's do the same job we did with Fortran, adding numbers and calculating a mean.

The complete program—the above Fortran program was not complete—is as follows:

(Enter X_i;	LBL A	Part A labeled.
Press A)	STO + 1	Accumulates X's in storage 1.
	1 ⎫	An increment of 1 is added
	STO + 2 ⎭	to storage 2.
	RCL 2	Recalls the incremented number in 2, the case number.
	RTN	Part A ended.
(Press B)	LBL B	Part B labeled.
	RCL 1	Recalls 1, the sum of the X's.
	RCL 2	Recalls N from 2.
	÷	Divides, $\Sigma X_i / N = $ Mean.
	STO 3	Stores mean in 3.
	RTN	Part B ended.

Explanatory notes have been given on the right of each program line. In "HP," each part of a program, or a whole program, has to be labeled, A, B, and so on: LBL A, LBL B. Our program has two subprograms, A and B. A's purpose is to add the X's and determine the number of cases, N. B's

---

[3] There are at the present writing several programmable calculators commercially available. The Hewlett-Packard (HP) and Texas Instruments (TI) machines are probably the most important because of their relatively large capacities—for such small machines—their sophistication, and their usefulness. And their prices keep getting lower, perhaps the only products that get cheaper during inflation. I have chosen to illustrate the HP language rather than the TI language because the former is more compact and sophisticated. Both kinds of machines, however, are very good.

purpose is to calculate the mean. Both are easily done with only six statements. In A, STO +1 is equivalent to the Fortran statement: SUM = SUM + X(I). It takes a number keyed in by the user and adds it to the contents of storage 1. If X had been needed for a later operation, it could have been stored for that purpose. This could have been done by inserting the statement STO 3 (or STO 4 or STO 5) immediately after LBL A and before STO +1.

The two statements, 1 and STO +2, are a "counter." They increment the cases in storage 2. Whatever number is written before STO +2 will be added to the contents of the storage place 2. When all X's have been entered, storage 2 will contain N, the number of cases, the statement RCL 2 means "Recall 2," or "Recall whatever is in storage 2." This is convenient because it shows the user what the case number is. The instruction RCL 2, in other words, brings whatever is in 2 to the display. The final statement of LBL A is RTN, or "Return." It stops the program running, and the computer returns to the beginning of LBL A.

In using the large computer, one records (punches) the X's on cards or tape and the computer reads the cards or tape. On the small programmable calculators, one keys in the X's (though there is a way for the calculator to read data from plastic cards). With our little program, one keys in the first X, or X_1, and then presses A. The calculator takes the value keyed in and adds it to the contents of storage 1. If, for example, you key in 15, 15 will be in storage 1. A 1 is then added to storage 2, or $0 + 1 = 1$. This 1 is recalled from storage 2 and displayed. The calculator then returns to LBL A ready for the new X entry. Let's say that X_2 is 21. It is added to the contents of storage 1, or $15 + 21 = 36$, and 36 is in storage 1. Again 1 is added to storage 2, or $1 + 1 = 2$.

When you have entered all the X's, say 40 of them, you press key B which activates LBL B. B recalls the contents of storage 1, recalls the contents of storage 2, and divides the latter into the former, or $\Sigma X_i / N$, the mean, of course, which appears in the display. It is also stored in storage 3 by the instruction STO 3 for possible future use. If the program is needed for future similar calculations, it can be recorded on a small plastic card (mentioned earlier), stored away, and used another time simply by entering the card in the machine. The program, as written, is then ready to operate on new data, just as a Fortran program is recorded on cards or tape and ready for future use.[4]

---

[4] The reader may wonder how the computer "understands" the instructions it gets in Fortran or other language and how it executes the commands. It would take almost a book by a computer expert to explain fully. This much can be said here, however. On any large computer there is a "translation" program, or set of programs, called the "compiler." The compiler examines the Fortran for "validity" (no mistakes in writing, punctuation, and so on), and then translates it into "machine language," the actual absolute machine instructions in whatever system has been built into the machine. For more details on compilers and related matters, the interested reader can consult the very good books on computers and their use in the behavioral sciences by Brier and Robinson (1974) and Green (1963).

OTHER COMPUTER OPERATIONS AND USES

We have talked only of rather straightforward numerical calculation uses of the computer: calculating means, standard deviations, correlations, and so on, and larger operations like multiple regression and factor analysis. The computer, however, has many other uses: the analysis of verbal materials, the simulation of theoretical models, planning and regulating traffic, and so on. Discussion of such uses is beyond the scope of this book. There is a class of usage, however, that it will be profitable to discuss because it will help us understand better the nature of the computer and its use in behavioral research. This is the solution of calculation problems that are difficult or impossible to do without a computer. For example, tables of random numbers are published in statistics books and are used constantly by researchers. (Recall our earlier discussion of randomness and randomization in Chapters 5 and 6.) Such numbers are difficult or even impossible to generate adequately "by hand" or with small calculators, but it is relatively easy to generate a large number of random numbers on a large computer. (Even the HP-67 and the TI programmable calculators can generate "good" random numbers.)

In an earlier discussion of testing statistical significance, the actual tests of significance used by researchers were neglected because the purpose of the book is not to teach statistics and analysis but rather the ideas behind statistics and analysis as vital parts of research. After a researcher has done an experiment, say like the Clark and Walberg or the Aronson and Mills experiments, he must test his statistical result for "significance" to see if the result departs sufficiently from chance expectation to warrant belief that it is in fact a "statistically significant" result. One such test is the so-called t test. A statistic, t, is calculated from experimental results from, for example, the difference between two means, as in Clark and Walberg. The calculated statistic is then checked against a table of such t's. If the calculated t is equal to or larger than the appropriate t-table entry—there are many t's in the table corresponding to the numbers of cases in the experimental groups—the result is considered to be statistically significant. (For further discussion of such statistical tests, see the Appendix at the end of the book.)

Statistics books always contain t tables—and other tables used with statistical tests. Strictly speaking, however, the computer has made such tables partly obsolete. The computer can calculate the specific t needed quite accurately. All that is needed is what is called a subroutine to do the necessary approximation.[5] The tabled values for different t's are distribu-

---

[5] A *subroutine* is a program within a *main program*. Subroutines have their own names, usually have special purposes, and are often used over and over again. One of their purposes is to save programming. Instead of cumulating the number of cases in the main program of the above example, for instance, we could have written the procedure in a subroutine and then "called" the subroutine at the appropriate places.

tion values. They are values that are expected by chance for various N's. Suppose a researcher obtains a difference between two means and he calculates t, which, say, is 3.714. Looking up the appropriate table entry at the .05 level of significance, he finds the tabled t to be 2.010. His t is 3.714, larger than the tabled entry. Since the tabled entry of 2.010 is the value expected by chance—the value expected if there was only a chance difference between the two means—he can conclude that the two means are significantly different.

The calculation of distribution values, as for the t distribution, is difficult because such calculation involves tedious calculus. The computer calculates the distribution values by using repetitive approximation procedures. (A simple form of such a procedure will be illustrated below.) Within a few years computer programs involving statistical distributions will probably have such approximation procedures built into most statistical programs. When a t, for example, has been calculated, the computer will then also calculate, through an approximation procedure, the probability that the calculated t (calculated from the data) would occur by chance. For example, the approximation of probability that $t = 3.714$ has occurred by chance is only about .0003, or 3 chances in 10,000. I had an HP-67 do the long repetitive calculations—many loops to effect the approximation—using a program supplied by the company. The calculator took about 30 seconds to do the job. A large computer would do the same job in much less time, a small fraction of a second. In short, while tables of distribution values will perhaps not become obsolete, they will not be as necessary and useful as they now are.

An Approximation Example: Square Root

Most of us learned how to calculate the square roots of numbers using a tiresome method that is quite impractical for more than a few square roots. Fifteen to 20 years ago slide rules gave fairly accurate approximations to square roots. Slide rules have virtually disappeared. Indeed, they will be collectors' items in two or three decades. Who needs a slide rule when a 15-dollar pocket calculator will do all a slide rule can do—and more accurately? Another method is to look up the square roots in tables. This method, too, is dead or dying. Still another method involves the old desk calculator: guessing at the root, squaring the guess, and gradually getting closer to the final root by guesses and approximations. Hardly an efficient method! It is similar, however, to the iterative approximation method on computers. The big difference is in speed, accuracy, and the avoidance of frustration and guessing. While like the enormous difference between a Vermeer and a Warhol, it will be profitable for us to examine the calculation of square root by an approximation method on the computer. The method to be described also has the distinction of having had no less a genius than Isaac Newton work on it.

An *algorithm* is a set of rules that tells us what to do to accomplish a given object or purpose. Many algebraic formulas are algorithms. If I tell you precisely how to solve a certain class of problems, I am giving you an algorithm. When you want the square root, or the logarithm, or the reciprocal of a number, you simply press the appropriate key of a calculator. But how does the calculator produce or calculate the number? Does it have a table built into it? Hardly. It has built into it a very efficient algorithm that works very, very fast.

Here is the mathematical expression for an algorithm to obtain the square root of any positive number:

$$r_{i+1} = 1/2 \left(r_i + \frac{x}{r_i} \right)$$

where $x =$ number whose square root is wanted, $r_i =$ the ith root, and $r_{i+1} =$ the root approximated after the ith root. I wrote a program for the HP-67 to do the iterations (repetitions with changes) or loops implied by this equation. In its essence it is like the algorithms used in large computers, except that the latter are usually more complicated, more sophisticated, and work much faster. The program works as follows. The number whose square root is wanted is entered into the calculator. The calculator divides this number by 2. This is inefficient, but it always works. The calculator then uses the above algorithm successively and repeatedly until the square root is obtained. The process will usually converge rapidly to the correct solution.

To see how it works, enter 15 into the machine. The successive iterations—I made the calculator stop after each loop to be able to see the result of each iteration and thus each approximation before final solutions—were:

$$4.75000 \quad 1/2 \left[\left(7.5 + \frac{15}{7.5} \right) \right]$$

$$3.95395 \quad 1/2 \left[\left(4.75 + \frac{15}{4.75} \right) \right]$$

$$3.87381 \quad 1/2 \left[\left(3.95395 + \frac{15}{3.95395} \right) \right]$$

$$3.87298 \quad 1/2 \left[\left(3.87381 + \frac{15}{3.87381} \right) \right]$$

and $3.87298^2 = 15$. Calculate $\sqrt{2}$. The algorithm and the iterations yielded:

1.50000
1.41667
1.41422

To show that it works with a large and more complex number, calculate $\sqrt{1587.8714}$. The iterations were longer:

       397.96785
       200.97890
       104.43979
        59.82175
        43.18256
        39.97684
        39.94831
        39.84810

and $39.84810^2 = 1587.8714$. Notice how the successive numbers converge on the final correct number. Does the procedure work with numbers less than 1? Try $\sqrt{.75}$. The iterations yielded:

        1.18750
         .90954
         .86707
         .86603
and $.86603^2 = .75$.

The first and last tasks each took about 7 seconds, $\sqrt{2}$ about 5 seconds. $\sqrt{1587.8714}$ took a long 14 seconds. It is possible to reduce the iterations and thus the times appreciably, but we are interested only in illustrating computer algorithms and how they work. So, although these are slow calculations by large computer standards, they show the idea of computer iterative procedures.[6]

Similarly, analysts write algorithmic procedures for other quantities for which there are no exact procedures. Highly sophisticated algorithms—or "little" programs—are incorporated into the computer's memory and are always ready for easy use. When you enter a number whose square root you want into a small calculator and then press the square root key, the square root of the number appears "instantaneously." It only appears to be instantaneous, however. All such calculations take some time. Computer analysts have been so skilful in writing and improving algorithms, and the technology of the computer and calculator hardware has advanced so greatly, that very high speeds have been attained. The skeptical reader

[6] The curious reader may wonder how the machine "knows" when to stop iterating. How does it know when it has the correct square root? This is a common problem in computer programming. The machine is instructed to stop looping or iterating when a certain criterion is reached. The criterion is given earlier, and a test is made after each iteration to see if the criterion has been reached. In the present case, the criterion is .00001. The square of r (the approximation to the root), or r^2, is calculated, and r^2 is subtracted from x, the number whose square root is wanted. When $r^2 - x$ is less than or equal to .00001, the test is satisfied and the computer no longer loops. If greater accuracy is wanted, then the criterion is made smaller, for example, .0000001 or .00000001.

can see a little of this for himself by first obtaining the square root of a number on a good pocket calculator. The square root of the number will appear to be instantaneous. Now obtain the logarithm of the same number. Note that there is a perceptible delay, not much of a delay but a slight one, nonetheless. This is because the programmed algorithm—and perhaps the hardware—for the logarithm does not work as fast as that for the square root.

LARGER ISSUES

Much has been written and published about computers and their presumed effects on people and society. Some of it, as usual with any complex issue, is sense, some of it nonsense. There is no doubt of the wide and deep effects of computers. The question is: On the whole are the effects good or bad? The question can probably not be answered unambiguously. The computer is an inevitable result of advancing technology and the computing needs of scientists, engineers, administrators, and others. Our concern is only with its effects on behavioral research. Most of these effects are clearly good.

First and most obvious, many calculations in behavioral research analysis are laborious, fatiguing, and error prone. Calculating square roots and sums of squares are obvious and frequently occurring examples. Even with the old mechanical calculators, still used in the 1950s or even later, it was never an easy job to do the basic calculations for standard deviations and correlations. On modern computers it is easy, convenient, fast, and accurate. Factor analysis is an excellent example. Before 1960, roughly, researchers took many hours and days to extract factors from a correlation matrix. For a 20 by 20 matrix of correlations—190 correlation coefficients—and, say, four factors, something like two or more days were needed. Let an error occur—an error that was discovered!—and the time might be doubled. Earlier we gave an example of the approximate time a large computer took to do a complete factor analysis of 72 variables: about 100 seconds. The earlier grinding labor is thus mostly gone.

Second, the computer has freed researchers to think about and work at ideas and tasks more challenging and important than calculations. Research has not become easier to do, however. If anything, it is more difficult. Twenty to 30 years ago, a good part of many researchers' work was analysis and sheer brute calculation. This no longer need be so; the computer does the brute work. With this relief from calculation, however, has come a rise in scientific expectation. Researchers are expected to develop theory, always a difficult job, to use appropriate research design, and to improve the measures of the variables they use. Years ago, for instance, there was almost cavalier disregard of the demands of validity of measures used; even reliability demands were neglected. Today such disregard is much less likely. While these improvements are not entirely the result of the availability of computers, there is little doubt that computers have helped to make conditions possible for improvement. In short, the computer has freed researchers for better things.

The third beneficial influence of the computer is more subtle. The mere presence of a computing center which most researchers must eventually use affects the lives and thinking of all near it. It is a physical manifestation of mathematics, science, research, and technology. Its status as the manifestation of one of the highest technological and intellectual achievements is a constant reminder of the values that influence our thinking and work. The great investment by universities—and other social agencies and institutions—in computers and computer personnel pervades researchers' lives. And one of the major values is objective problem solution and communication. The computer is, then, a powerful symbol of intellectuality, especially of scientific intellectuality. As such, it supports and reinforces intellectual and scientific norms and criteria. It is no wonder that writers, painters, historians, and philosophers worry about it. They are afraid that its potent influence may unbalance the university and even the society. And they may be right.

The fourth influence has been referred to earlier in this chapter. Research problems that could not readily be approached are now within reach. We have mentioned factor analysis and other forms of multivariate analysis earlier. Take a quite different kind of example not discussed heretofore: content analysis. Political scientists, historians, psychologists, and sociologists, among other scholars, have always analyzed documentary materials in order to establish facts and trends and to study relations. Such documentary study has been extremely laborious. Historians might have to spend months or years in libraries to study and document a subject being pursued. Indeed, the image of the scholar has always been of a person who more or less grubs, burrows, digs, and patiently records the results of his digging. Much of the scholar's work was of this kind. While wearisome, it could not be avoided.

Because of the computer and the development of content analysis within the behavioral sciences, the scholar's approach, outlook, and work are changing drastically—or perhaps I should say, *will* change drastically because many scholars are still not affected. There will never be any real substitute for the human judgments the scholar must continually make. And there will probably always be a certain amount of drudgery. But the computer can remove much of the drudgery. With a skillfully drawn-up list of key concepts, subjects, and names, a computer search of the literature—after the literature itself has been put into computer memory banks—is now feasible. The drudgery of literature search will be greatly lightened. After the scholar selects the sources he wishes from the lists the computer yields to his search request, the computer can even reproduce the source or send out instructions to do so.

Let us take a more interesting example. *Content analysis* is a method of studying and analyzing communications—documents of all kinds, including existing documents and documents deliberately produced for research purposes, books, letters, and so on—in systematic, objective, and quantitative ways to measure variables or to accomplish other research purposes. Suppose we wish to study the value systems of different groups or countries, and that certain value words have been found in earlier research to differentiate social groups, words like *equality, discipline, achievement, religion, freedom*.

A "dictionary" of such words can be put into the memory of a computer. Random samples of key publications—editorials, political speeches, and magazine articles, for instance—in different countries can be analyzed. Whole selections are punched on to cards and read into the computer. The computer scans the cards, notes the value words that have been put into its "dictionary," and then analyzes the "data" by counting, categorizing, and calculating appropriate statistics. The great labor of actually studying and analyzing the texts is saved, and researchers can concentrate on what is important: the theory behind the work, the "dictionary" and its contents, the selection of materials for analysis, and other essential substantive and methodological matters.

Another benefit of computers is that workers from different fields are thrown into contact not only with computer specialists but also with workers from other fields. It occasionally happens that a researcher, faced with an analytic or computer problem not known in his field, will find from someone in another field that the problem has already been solved. This is especially true of contact with mathematicians. Most behavioral researchers are not noted for strength in mathematics, and they will sometimes learn that an analytic problem that has eluded them has already been worked out by mathematicians or mathematical statisticians.

The last benefit to be mentioned springs from the international character of computers and computer science. Computer languages, although written in English, or what can be called a form of English, are truly international. Programs are written all over the world in Fortran, Algol, and other computer languages. Computer installations share programs internationally. Certain well-known and well-used package programs are available in universities in New York, Berkeley, and Amsterdam, to pick only three widely dispersed installations. It is also a common occurrence for computer users and specialists from different countries to meet at computer centers and sometimes to share their knowledge and know-how. The word "computer" and certain other computer-related words have become part of natural languages. Like music and mathematics, computer talk is a sort of international language.

The effect of this international exchange and influence is to help break down national and social barriers. Of course, science and technology have always had this international character and have sometimes helped to break down barriers. The computer's influence may be greater, however, because of the need of institutions to have computer centers and computer skills physically present in or near the institutions. The benefits to behavioral science come mainly from increased sharing of methodology—the analysis of covariance structures discussed in Chapter 13 is an excellent example—and broadened knowledge of theory and research.

The drawbacks of computers have been generously discussed by many observers. They are complex and much less obvious than the advantages in the sense that their negative or even baneful character and influence are more debatable. As we examine two or three of them we will see why.

The first and most obvious drawback of the computer is possible violation of confidentiality. One of the important values or rules governing behavioral science research is that all information about individuals and groups is confidential. The privacy and rights of individuals must be carefully safeguarded. Data gathered on individuals must not be identifiable. But if individuals' names are entered in computer memories together with their data, it becomes quite easy for unscrupulous individuals and organizations to obtain individual information and to violate individual and group privacy and rights. Unfortunately, this has been done and has been blamed on the computer. The problem will have to be solved if this important value is to be preserved.

A second deleterious influence springs from the problems raised by the question, Can computers think? At first blush, most sensible people will quickly respond, No, of course computers can't think—at least not as human beings "think." The trouble is that the question and its answer are very complex. To be sure, computers can do only what they are instructed to do. But sometimes no one knows for sure what they have really been instructed to do. Moreover, their tireless and relentless pursuit of logical possibilities can yield surprising results. That is, the results of a certain line of thinking cannot be known because the possibilities are so many. We would take weeks, even years, to explore even some of the possibilities. But a program can be written and the computer instructed to explore the possibilities and to print the results. In other words, where a person can carry a procedure forward for only a limited time and with limited possibilities, a computer can follow it for minutes, hours, even days (at great cost, however) and explore many more, even all, the possibilities. Is this "thinking"? If not precisely thinking, it is much like it.

Computer ability to do repetitive and varied operations at high speed, then, enables its users to follow the consequences of complex ideas and models. This great power has an aura of magic which makes many people suspicious, even afraid, of computers. In addition, the computer can simulate human thinking processes with great success. A famous example is a computer program that can prove logic theorems. These proofs are often very difficult even for logicians. Does the computer think when solving these problems? A more famous and better-known example is the computer's remarkable ability to play chess. Computers can beat most chess players (but not the best ones). Do they "think" when they do this?

The subject is highly controversial and debatable. Some say that the "thinking" of a computer is indistinguishable from that of people. Others say that there is a profound difference. There is probably no satisfactory resolution of the difficulty, meaning that it is not possible to answer the question, Can computers think? (The question has even been called meaningless.) Perhaps the best answer was Turing's (1956), who years ago, said that the test of the question is to give a problem requiring thinking to a computer and to a human expert. If an expert observer can discern no reliable difference in the produced solutions, then the computer can "think." There is little doubt that much of what computers do appears to be a form of thinking. And there is also no doubt that computers can successfully and repeatedly simulate known characteristics of human thought. We leave this perplexing problem and turn to easier matters—with considerable relief, it must be confessed.[7]

The next drawback of the computer has its roots in the relative ease of computer use, the wide and easy availability of what are called "package" programs, and the power and speed of modern machines. These characteristics and conditions make it possible for individuals with insufficient knowledge of the methods they use to produce analyses that can be and often are nonsense. Such users depend too much on the computer doing their work and thinking. The misuse of factor analysis package programs is a frequent and troublesome example. Objective methods for factor analysis suitable for computer use have been worked out and are widely available. The trouble is that a completely objective method does not always yield a satisfactory solution to a factor analytic problem. Human judgment has to enter the business in two or three crucial places.

For example, an important part of factor analysis is the number of factors to rotate after factor extraction. (See Chapter 12, footnote 4, for a brief explanation of rotated factors.) There is no completely satisfactory answer to the question: How many factors should be rotated? There are objective answers and methods, but they can give misleading if not downwright wrong answers. The only fairly satisfactory way at present involves objective methods *and* researcher judgment. The drawback, then, is the tendency for researchers to become too dependent on the computer, and, in so doing, to lose real understanding of the data and methodology they work with, and to relinquish control over their research and its results.

More insidious and harmful is the strong tendency of computer users all

---

[7] The reader can get a fair idea of the problems involved by reading Lindsay and Norman's (1977, pp. 593–599) analysis of a particular problem called day arithmetic (Monday + Wednesday = ?) along computing and thinking lines. Much of Lindsay and Norman's book, incidentally, is strongly influenced by computers and computer technology. A lucid description of computer problem solving and "thinking" is given by Green (1963, pp. 219ff.). Turing's (1956) brilliant essay will repay curious reading, too. To say the least, his essay will hardly leave even the most skeptical reader unmoved.

over the world to depend on so-called package programs for the solutions of their analytic problems. A "package program" is a generalized program that can handle all problems of a certain kind. It is written to be "general" across a class of analytic problems; your problem, my problem, and others' problems can be done with it. For example, there are package programs to do factor analysis and to do multiple regression analysis, and some of them are very good indeed. Others have questionable features. Many or most users of such programs know little or nothing of the computer and what it can and cannot do; and, worse, they know little about the methods packaged in the programs. They put total dependence on computer programs. The awful results show themselves again and again. It has occurred to few people, even researchers, that such overdependence is dangerous, even pernicious. It not only leads to incorrect and misleading results; it also cripples the abilities of many potentially able people. And it lowers the general quality of research in the behavioral sciences.

The final drawback to be discussed is the most elusive, complex, and hard to describe. The power, universal applicability, and tremendous speed of the computer help to generate awe and fear in many people. (Naturally, when automation makes jobs obsolete, dislike and hate follow.) The computer becomes viewed as a mysterious power whose ultimate effect will be to destroy humanity. The computer's work and the people who use it are perceived as dangerous threats to the integrity and existential uniqueness of whole men and women. In short, the computer, often together with science, is perceived as an enemy of humanity.

Fact and fiction are laced together here. The fact is that such attitudes are very real and influential (see Lee, 1970, for a nationwide study of such attitudes). The fiction is that the computer, essentially a machine though a potent machine, is anthropomorphized; it is given a "reality" and "power" it does not possess. Computers do not dehumanize people; people dehumanize themselves. Computers are human products and a part of the social structure; they should be controlled by men and women and by the social structure. If dehumanization is a threat, then look deeper than the computer.

As usual, the answer, if there is an answer, is not to blame science, technology, methods, and computers for human ills. Although there is no doubt that man's powerful human products help shape human beings, there is also no doubt that the ills of society are cured only by men and women working deliberately to effect cures.

This somewhat moralistic homily leads us to our last chapters. In them we discuss some of the important controversial issues associated with science and research. We will find that the computer is only a small part of a much larger and more difficult complex of problems.

15

Misconceptions and controversies
methodological issues

Our study of science and behavioral research has taken us a long way. In order to understand the how and why of scientific research, however, we had to talk methodologically much of the time. To round out our study and understanding, we now turn to more tenuous problems loosely related to lack of understanding of science and research. We end the book by returning to these and other problems for two reasons. First, they are highly interesting and important in their own right and should be known and understood. And second, misconceptions connected with them seriously impede understanding.

We must try to understand why science and empirical research have in recent years been under attack. Why do some people, for example, say that science is a destructive force? Why do they say that it is inhuman, abstract, cold, and remote and that it divorces us from human reality and leads to negation and despair? Why do they insist that the basic purpose of research must be to improve the lot of mankind? Why is there little understanding of what science is for and what it is not for?

The task of these last chapters, then, is to open up and study a number of controversial and difficult issues to give greater breadth and depth to the reader's understanding of science and research. In this chapter we explore what can loosely be called methodological controversial issues: objectivity, quantification, values, and science and the individual. In the last chapter the discussion is directed to the relation between research and practice. In **261** it we will talk about basic and applied research and about ideas that research must pay off. Finally, we will attempt to explain how research *does* influence practice—what it can and cannot do, and how it does it.

OBJECTIVITY

One of the most serious attacks on science stems from attacks on objectivity. Objectivity was earlier defined as agreement among expert judges on what is observed. This means that science seeks to remove scientific procedures from human concerns. All forms of knowing are biased by values, attitudes, and other predilections. It is not possible ever to be completely objective. In other words, objectivity is always a matter of degree. But science holds up the ideal and criterion of objectivity as indispensable. Without objectivity there can be no science.

As pointed out in Chapter 1, the criterion of objectivity enables scientists to get outside themselves. They set up procedures "out there," apart from themselves. The idea is to protect the procedures from predilections and biases. This is the essence and core of scientific empirical methods. One test of objectivity is whether, from a description of a research study, another competent investigator can replicate the research. If so, and the results are the same or similar, this is partial support for the "validity" of the research. Objectivity is one of the main reasons why scientific explanations supported by objective empirical evidence are considered more trustworthy than other methods of obtaining knowledge.

Criticisms of objectivity range from the naive to the highly sophisticated. The core of most criticism, however, seems to take two forms. The first has already been mentioned and was discussed in Chapter 1. Objectivity, it is said, leads to remoteness, coldness, inhumanity. To set up procedures divorced from people is to impoverish humanity. The remoteness and coldness of science destroy human values and dehumanize man. Thus science is fundamentally harmful. Moreover, the knowledge gained from such an inhuman and inhumane system cannot be trusted because it lacks real and deep wisdom, which comes only from intuitive apprehension of spiritual and human truths. Science is reductive: it reduces the essential whole of human beings and the world to desiccated fragments of knowledge, which are in essence distortions of reality. Psychologists, in objective attempts to study human intelligence and personality, miss the very essence of intelligence and personality, indivisible wholes not capable of being reduced to concepts and numbers. Objectivity, rather than being a neutral tool of the scientist, is in fact a dangerous enemy of man and of truth—so it is said.

The second argument is more sophisticated and more influential, especially in Europe where it is part of Marxist attacks on objectivity. It is said—with considerable truth, by the way—that no one can really be objective. When scientists set up objectivity as an ideal, they are deceiving themselves and others. All of us, scientists included, are ruled by our values and motives. We cannot be objective. Marxists and similar ideologists go further. They say, for example, that the values of the society influence the hypotheses and research of bourgeois scientists, and if these values are corrupt, as they are in capitalistic society, then the research and its results are inevitably corrupt. Objectivity, then, is a bourgeois myth; it is a tool of oppression.

It is even said that it is more important to know the history of a hypothesis than it is to test it. This means that the history or origin of hypotheses in Western capitalistic science is what is important. *Who* formulates hypotheses is the key question. Do they come from establishment-supported scientists? If so, they are biased and suspect. This kind of reasoning and the less ideological reasoning of sociologist and psychologist critics of behavioral research come together in their attack on objectivity.

A related argument was answered in Chapter 1. We limit the answer here to brief remarks centered mainly on the confusion of two definitions of objectivity. The scientific definition of objectivity was given above and elaborated in Chapter 1: agreement among expert judges, "judges" being defined as people or machines. The essence of this definition is procedural, methodological: it provides a general methodological rule. The rule says, in essence: All procedures must be public; they must be replicable; they must be apart from the investigator. And that is all it means.

The critics of objectivity, however, base their arguments on a definition that is focused on the investigator. They, or at least their arguments, assume that objectivity means a characteristic or trait of scientists. They are saying, in effect, that scientists claim objectivity for themselves, that they as a class of individuals are more objective than nonscientists. I am exaggerating to some extent, and I am aware that some critics of objectivity are more sophisticated than my encapsulation of their arguments indicates. Nevertheless, the confusion caused by the explicit or implicit definition of objectivity as a trait of scientists hampers communication and weakens understanding of objectivity as a scientific procedure.

Scientists make no claims to personal objectivity (there are, of course, exceptions). They insist, rather, on objectivity as a methodological procedure that can and must be set apart from scientists and their predilections. The procedures must be, in short, public. The arguments against objectivity outlined above miss this point. The first argument, that objectivity is remote, cold, and inhuman, is quite correct. That is what it is supposed to be. It is precisely this divorcing of scientific research from human predilections, together with the insistence on objective empirical testing of hypotheses—which, once enunciated publicly, are themselves outside human beings—that has so remarkably advanced our knowledge. That objectivity leads to destruction of important human values is part of a larger mythology. To be sure, the practice of science tends to challenge established values because of its basic nature of critical inquiry. But that it destroys human values or man himself is absurd. If values or men are to be destroyed, men will do it. Procedures can dehumanize us only if they are permitted to do so.

The second argument, too, has little weight, except for people who want to believe it. We are all, of course, influenced by our predilections. That we can or cannot be personally objective is debatable. But that is not the point. The point, as already pointed out, is that the procedures of science are objective—and not scientists. Scientists, like all men and women, are opinionated, dogmatic, ideological—influenced by the forces that influence all of us. That is the very reason for insisting on procedural objectivity: to get the whole business outside of ourselves, subject to critical public scrutiny.

Scientifically speaking, there are no absolute truths. We cannot "know" anything absolutely. There are only relative degrees of reliable and valid knowledge. Objective procedures increase the probability of obtaining more reliable and valid knowledge from research. In and of itself objectivity has little value. To be objective does not mean to be scientific. To remove objectivity from science, however, destroys the core of the scientific enterprise.

QUANTITATIVE METHODS

A second source of misunderstanding of science, especially of its methodology, is the high prominence of mathematics, especially statistics, in scientific analysis. Criticism of quantification in the natural sciences seems hardly to exist. It seems obvious and natural to measure chemical reactions, molecular movements, physical dimensions of bodies and materials. It does not seem to strain people to see the necessity for a high degree of quantification in physics, for example, where the relations between physical forces, among other things, are studied. So there is little controversy. In psychology, sociology, education, and other behavioral fields, however, controversy thrives.

How is it possible to measure intelligence? It can't be seen; no one can get inside heads (except surgeons and physiologists) to "see," let alone measure intelligence. Even granting that people differ in intelligence—though some even doubt this!—how is it possible to assign numbers to people suggesting that there are precise quantities of intelligence? Similarly, isn't it ridiculous to suggest that human characteristics and the characteristics of groups and organizations can be measured? Even assuming that some measurement can be successful, must we not then conclude that whatever has been successfully measured is too trivial to be of much importance? For example, assuming that some aspect of intelligence can be measured, do the measures reflect anything of the whole richness, complexity, and multifaceted nature of human intelligence? Or must we conclude that those aspects measured are relatively unimportant, quite fragmentary, and, in short, trivial? Certainly whatever numbers are yielded by such procedures are far removed from the reality, the rich wholeness, of human abilities. And then to use these numbers in statistical calculations stretches credulity far too far.

Carry the critics' arguments a bit further. What is the meaning of an average intelligence test score of a group of individuals? In the first place, how can you add such questionable numbers and then divide another number into them? How can you correlate two sets of numbers whose individual components are supposed to reflect human characteristics when, in fact, the numbers in both sets are far from the "reality" of the individual whose characteristics are supposed to be measured? What real meaning can be put in a coefficient of correlation between, say, a measure of self-concept and a measure of occupational status? There are other arguments against quantification, but these are sufficient to illustrate what is meant.

It is harder to answer such arguments than it is to argue them. Part of the answer was given in Chapter 9 where we studied the measurement of variables. There is no doubt that certain arithmetic operations with numbers on behavioral science variables are questionable. When, for example, one adds a set of intelligence test scores and calculates the mean of the set, one is assuming that the intervals between fixed points, like 80, 90, 100, 110, and 120, are equal, and that *numerically* equal distances, like 80 to 100 and 100 to 120, stand for *empirically* equal distances. Intelligence test measures—and many other measures used in psychological and educational research—may not satisfy the assumption. For instance, the difference between the intelligence quotients 150 and 140 may really be psychologically larger than the difference between the quotients 110 and 100. That is, the psychological distance between 140 and 150—the "real" difference between these two measured intelligence levels—may be considerably greater than the psychological distance between 100 and 110. The former numbers may represent a very much greater difference in intelligence, in other words, than the latter, even though the numerical differences are both 10.

There are several answers to the criticism of quantification in the behavioral sciences, the most important of which is empirical and pragmatic. The use of quantification works! Even though assumptions underlying the use of the numbers and their manipulation may be violated, quantification works very well indeed. When the intelligence of children is measured with a reliable and reasonably valid test, one can correlate the numbers obtained with other numbers obtained from another test given to the same children, say a test of verbal achievement, and obtain a rather good approximation of the magnitude of the relation. The evidence for the "truth" of this statement is that—in general and, of course, with the usual exceptions—those children who get high scores on the intelligence test also get high scores on the verbal achievement test, as well as on tests of other kinds of achievement; and the children who get low scores on intelligence tend also to get low scores on achievement. (See the discussion of validity in Chapter 9.)

While a scientist does not arbitrarily disregard important assumptions in the assignment of numbers to objects being measured, he knows that he often cannot satisfy all of them. Besides, he also knows from experience and evidence that with knowledge, care, and skill in devising and using his measures he can get reasonable approximations of his variables and the relations between them in the sense that his results, properly tested and checked, agree with "reality," as in the above example of intelligence and verbal achievement. Achieving this much he can use the "strong" methods of mathematics and statistics to aid him in making inferences about what is "out there."

There is a closely related empirical-experiential answer to the charges against quantification. Statistical tests of significance have certain assumptions behind them. For example, a t test, which we have discussed before, among other things assesses the statistical significance of the difference between two means. One of the assumptions behind the test (Edwards, 1967, pp. 214–215; Hays, 1973, pp. 409–410) is that the scores of the two populations from which the two groups are samples are normally distributed.[1] The theory behind the t test of the difference between two means requires this assumption. If it is violated, the results of a t test may not be valid. Similarly, it is assumed that the variances (variabilities) of the two populations are equal. Again, if this assumption is violated, if the two variances are not equal (statistically), then the results of the t test may not be valid.

Empirical tests (for example, Boneau, 1960) and experience have shown that the assumption of normality can be violated without great damage to the results of the t test. Researchers can use the test without worrying too much about the assumption, especially if their samples are large (Hays, 1973, p. 410). The assumption of equal variances is more important. But, in general, it too can be violated, if not with impunity. It has been shown, in other words, that the t test and similar tests are "robust." They are so strong that they work quite well even when the assumptions behind them are violated. No one in his right mind, of course, advocates disregard of the assumptions. But it is now known that they are not as important as they were once thought to be.

There are, of course, other arguments that support quantification in the behavioral sciences. But they would take us too far afield. We rest the case, therefore, with the pragmatic argument that the use of quantification has been highly successful, and, with increasing sophistication and computer help, will become even more successful. Indeed, the use of quantification in behavioral science, so essential in all science, has been one of the noteworthy achievements of the twentieth century. The argument that the

---

[1] Recall that a "normal distribution" means that the scores, if appropriately plotted on a graph, will form the lovely bell-shaped curve found so often in statistics texts and displayed earlier in this book. The "meaning" of a normal distribution is that most subjects have scores in the middle of the distribution, some few have low and very low scores, and some few have high and very high scores.

measurement of psychological and sociological attributes is questionable, for example, the measurement of intelligence or attitudes, is simply contradicted by the evidence. Intelligence, attitudes, and many other psychological and sociological variables—social class, achievement and need for achievement, aptitudes, and so on—have been successfully, if not perfectly, measured.

VALUES AND SCIENCE

Another somewhat murky area of concern is values and their relation to science, a subject touched upon in Chapter 3. *Values* are organizations of beliefs about principles, behavioral norms and standards, and end-states of life that express culturally weighted preferences and judge the "goodness" or "badness" of preferences, norms, and end-states of life. They also express moral judgments of norms and behavior (see Rokeach, 1973). A significant characteristic of value statements, pointed out in Chapter 3, is that they cannot be empirically tested. Therefore they are not amenable to scientific research. Statements like "It is wrong to practice discrimination on the basis of race, religion, sex, or national origin," "Private property is sacred," and "Religion is the opiate of the masses" are value propositions. There is no way to test them empirically. They are beyond the means and capabilities of science. Scientists therefore exclude such propositions from their work.

This does not mean that scientists as individuals, or even in groups, have no values. Such a statement is nonsensical. Nor does it mean that scientific research is value-free. The choices of research topics and even research methodology are influenced by the values the scientist holds. Values can also influence interpretation of research results. The knowledgeable psychologist or sociologist knows this, however, and uses safeguards to minimize this influence.

Because scientists eschew value propositions as nontestable does not mean that values themselves cannot be studied scientifically. Indeed, they have been so studied, but, strangely enough, not nearly as much as their importance warrants. Such scientific study of values is approached as objectively as possible; the scientist studying values has to be particularly careful that his own values do not bias the collection and analysis of data and the interpretation of results. Possible examples of value research are the influence of conservative and liberal values on voting behavior; the effect of religious values on issues like divorce and abortion; the relations between parents' and children's values; the connection between values put on concepts like *freedom* and *equality,* on the one hand, and values put on concepts like *private property* and *capitalism,* on the other hand.

In other words, it is perfectly possible to study values as a natural phenomenon. One can explore the factor structure of the values people say they espouse to learn the relations between general sets of values and how expressed values may cluster. One can study the various effects of stated values on different kinds of social behavior, or the relations between political values and religious values, or the ways in which values are learned by children. But one cannot empirically test value propositions themselves, propositions containing the words "good," "bad," "must," "should," "ought," and so on. There is simply no way to do so. Such propositions and words imply and reflect human judgment. There is nothing to test, no relation between variables that can be manipulated or measured.

SCIENTIFIC RESEARCH AND THE INDIVIDUAL

A source of considerable dissatisfaction with science and scientific research, especially scientific psychology and psychological research, centers in the presumed lack of concern of science for the individual. This problem was mentioned earlier in the book. Fortunately, it is easily settled—rationally. Unfortunately, it is psychologically not easy to settle. The concern springs from what people see as the abstractness, coldness, and remoteness of science—and a lack of concern for the human individual. Scientists are themselves seen as cold and remote. It is felt that science is therefore a dehumanizing influence, and that scientists are people to be feared and contained. We have here, then, rather strong feelings of antipathy to science, scientists, and scientific research on the basis of presumed remoteness from human concerns.

To argue that such feelings are based on misconceptions of science and scientists does not make the feelings go away. We must nevertheless try to explain and justify the correctly perceived remoteness and coldness of science. This explanation centers around the perceived abstractness of science and its lack of concern for the individual.

As was said earlier in the book, there is justification for perceiving science as cold and remote. Science is necessarily abstract. To be abstract means to be removed, separated, apart from specific things. A mathematical equation is highly abstract. All nouns are abstract: they are not the things they represent or name. Instead, they "stand for" the things, they represent them, they name them. Consider the words "book," "man," "map," "science," "research." The first three words stand for specific "objects" or delineable entities; they are abstract. The last two words also stand for "things," but they are more abstract than the first three words because they represent much more. They represent complex ideas and activities. The last three or four sentences have been deliberately made more abstract than they might have been. "The first three words," for example, was used instead of the specific words "book," "man," and "map."

One of the most important and indispensable characteristics of science is its abstractness. Indeed, scientists try to be as abstract as possible because abstractness means greater generality and power. The ultimate aim is to express theoretical and discovered relations and perhaps laws in mathematical symbols and expressions.[2] Suppose a scientist, in trying to explain memory, finds out that it is affected by intelligence, organization (of the information to be remembered), and mental imagery. He can and will, of course, describe the discovered relation in words. But it is more succinct, accurate, and fruitful if he expresses the relation with, say, a regression equation, which says rather clearly what the nature of the relation is.

Many more examples could be given of the necessity and power of abstraction. But this still does not get to the root of why the scientist, as scientist, has no concern for the individual case. In writing the regression equation, as in the above case, he has lost the individual persons who were his subjects. His regression equation is an average expression, an abstraction from the original data. Of course, he can use the regression equation to predict any subject's score on the dependent variable. But this, too, is an abstraction, an expression that says, in effect, "Here is the prediction for subject X_{14}, but it is only a prediction on the average." We have here a dilemma and a clue to the "group" nature of science, as it were. To understand this, let us look at a highly useful way of regarding disciplines and propositions.

The Nomothetic-Idiographic Distinction

There are two broad kinds of knowledge disciplines, nomothetic and idiographic. Physics is said to be nomothetic and history to be idiographic, for example. *Nomothetic* means law-making. A discipline can be characterized as nomothetic if its basic purpose is to set up general laws. Physics is a clear-cut example because its major purpose is to discover natural laws, or statements of relations among physical phenomena. The so-called law of gravity is a well-known example. Psychology and sociology are nomothetic, or law-making, disciplines. The behavioral sciences are generally considered to be nomothetic, though there is dispute on this point.

Idiographic means to describe things individually. Disciplines that are idiographic are not basically law-seeking; they are, rather, descriptive. History, for example, is idiographic: the historian tries to give accurate descriptions of singular events and their relations: a history of the Civil War, the causes of the Russian revolution, the origin and foundation of public schools in America. Relations and presumed causes and effects are studied, but the interest focuses on individual people, nations, organizations, and events. History is therefore not a science. This certainly does not mean that it is in any way inferior or superior to science. It is simply different—and idiographic.

[2] A "law" in science is a statement of relations that has a theoretical basis and considerable empirical support. A theory, of course, may or may not have empirical support. If a theory has been repeatedly supported by evidence, then it may be called a "law." There are no hard and fast rules, however, to tell when a supported theory becomes a law.

Within psychology and education there is often conflict between nomothetists and idiographers, as I will call them. Clinical psychologists are mostly idiographers. They are primarily concerned with individuals and their problems. Patients must be treated. People must be served. On the other hand, the nomothetic student of personality is not and cannot be concerned with the individual. He seeks laws to explain behavior. He wants to know the roots of neurosis, for instance. He is interested in the patient only as an example of the expression of a theory of personality. The patient's neurosis must be explained lawfully, nomothetically. The picture I am drawing is a bit extreme; there are psychological scientists who combine both nomothetic and idiographic approaches. I suspect, however, that it is not easy for them to do so. Many years ago Carl Rogers eloquently expressed his own conflict in trying to be both nomothetist and idiographer (Rogers, 1955).

Scientists, then, are not and cannot be concerned with the individual case.[3] They seek laws, systematic relations, explanations of phenomena. And their results are always statistical. They must learn to live and work with uncertainty. The laws they seek are statements of the kind if p, then q, but such statements are always understood to be if p, then probably q statements. Any predictions they make to individual cases are not "individual" in the idiographic clinical sense, but rather a sort of abstract "individual" of a statistical equation.

It seems to be hard for clinicians, teachers, and other people whose work is primarily with individuals to understand nomothetic science and the nomothetic scientist. Their main interest in science, if any, is in how it can help them cure or teach individuals. It is not so much in abstract laws that may or may not apply to particular individuals, or that applies to them only on the average.

Prediction

To understand the distinction a bit better we now look at two main empirical ways to study individuals: prediction and profile. (We omit all more or less subjective ways of studying individuals, like intuitive psychological speculation and astrology.) With prediction we forecast an individual's performance on some dependent variable on the basis of one or more scores on certain independent variables. Or, closely related, we predict the

[3] There is an apparent exception to this statement. Scientists often predict to individual cases, especially in psychology and education. For example, on the basis of three or four or more tests *and* a regression equation, occupational status of individuals can be predicted. Another example was given in Chapter 13 when we discussed discriminant analysis: the group membership of a single bone was predicted. I don't think, however, that these are really exceptions. The predictions are in all such cases statistical predictions. One calculates the probable score of Y, some measure to be predicted, on the basis of scores obtained from many subjects. The scientist is basically interested in the relations and not in the individuals, bones or people, of his samples. (See the discussion of prediction, below.)

individual's category or group membership on the basis of his performance or his measurements on one or more tests or measures. Common
examples are the prediction of school or college achievement on the basis
of measures of intelligence, social class, motivation, and previous
achievement, and the prediction of occupational success from measures of
education, social class, parents' education, and parents' occupation.

Perhaps the most frequently used method for making predictions is
multiple regression analysis. (This is only if there is one dependent variable being predicted, of course.) The researcher administers the measures
of the independent variables to a number of persons and ascertains or
measures the dependent variable. ("Ascertains" is used here because
when group membership—"success" or "no success" in finishing college,
for instance—is the dependent variable, all one has to do is determine to
what group or category the individual belongs.) He then does a multiple
regression analysis and uses the regression equation for prediction, as
outlined in Chapter 11.

As an example, take a very difficult phenomenon, creativity. The concept is difficult because it is hard to know what creativity is; it is hard to
define it, especially operationally. Let us assume, however, that a psychologist has two reasonably good measures that predict creativity in children,
the global concept of creativity itself being judged by experts. Call the two
measures X_1 and X_2 and creativity Y. At this point it is suggested that the
reader go back to Chapter 11 and review the section on the Holtzman and
Brown study and the section immediately following its description. There
we learned what a regression equation is, what it is used for, and how
individual predictions can be made using the regression equation.

An abstract regression equation with two independent variables is:

$$Y' = a + b_1 X_1 + b_2 X_2$$

Y' is the predicted score. a, the so-called intercept, we again ignore; it is
not important for our purpose. X_1 and X_2 are the independent variables,
and b_1 and b_2 are the regression weights for X_1 and X_2. They are part of the
fruits of the regression analysis. As their name indicates, they "weight" or
assign differential "importance" to the independent variable measures.

Assume that the psychologist has administered X_1 and X_2 and his
creativity measure, Y, to a large number of children, has done a regression
analysis, and has obtained the following regression equation—which is
the same one used to illustrate regression and prediction in Chapter 11:

$$Y' = .10 + .68X_1 + .39X_2$$

b_1 and b_2 are .68 and .39, respectively. They indicate that in any individual
prediction X_1 is "weighted" more heavily than X_2. X_1, in other words, has
been found to contribute more to the prediction of Y than X_2. Assume,
further, that two individuals, numbers 7 and 41 in a sample of 50 individ-

uals, have obtained X_1 and X_2 scores of (2,4) and (10,5), also as in Chapter 11. Then the predictions of the two Y or creativity scores are:

Individual 7: $.10 + (.68)(2) + (.39)(4) = 3.02$

Individual 41: $.10 + (.68)(10) + (.39)(5) = 8.85$

On the basis of these predictions, the psychologist can say that individual 41 is or will be more creative than individual 7 (naturally on whatever aspects of creativity that X_1 and X_2 measure).

This is the essence of prediction.[4] The psychologist has predicted the creativity scores of two individuals. He can use the equation to predict the creativity or Y' scores of any similar individuals. But note carefully that these predictions are really "group" predictions, in the sense that the weights have been obtained from the X_1, X_2, and Y scores of a group of individuals. They are, so to speak, averages, statistical abstractions derived from the original group data. The predictions are thus statistical in nature. They have greater or lesser probabilities attached to them. They are, therefore and strictly speaking, not individual predictions but, rather, predictions to classes of individuals who have obtained the given X_1 and X_2 scores. As such, they can be and often are very useful, but they are not "individual" in the existentially unique sense of the word. In other words, the existential individual, the core of individuality, forever escapes the scientist. He is chained to group data, statistical prediction, and probabilistic estimates.

It has been said that the above is true in the behavioral sciences; it is a function of the inexactness of these sciences. In the so-called hard and exact sciences, however, laws are known with virtual certainty, and predictions to individual cases can be confidentally made. Not quite so. There are, of course, differences between "hard" and "soft" sciences, but they are not differences in general ideas, conception, approach, and general methodology. They are differences in degree of precision of experimentation and measurement. But all scientific knowledge is knowledge of empirical relations, whose "existence" always has an attached probability tag. In the natural sciences the probabilities are higher, often much higher, than in the social sciences. Nevertheless, generalizations and predictions in all the sciences are group predictions and are probabilistic. The physicist can no more predict the movement of an atom with certainty than can the psychologist predict a child's creativity score with certainty.

Profiles

A second and highly useful way to study the individual is through profiles and profile analysis. Actually, profile analysis is closely related to

---

[4] The reader interested in statistical prediction will find Rozeboom's (1966) book enlightening, often amusing, sometimes difficult, even profound.

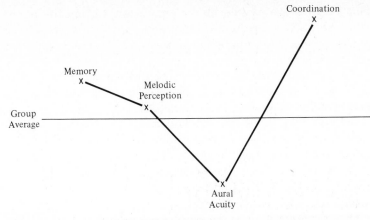

FIG. 15.1

prediction. It is more complex, to be sure, and perhaps more interesting, especially to the idiographically oriented person. A *profile* is a set of scores from a set of tests or measures. Profiles can be of individuals or of groups. Individual profiles consist of two, three, or more scores of some kind for a single individual. Group profiles are some kind of average scores obtained from a group of scores. A common group profile would be a set of means of some group on two, three, or more measures.

Profiles are often used by practitioners for diagnostic purposes. For instance, teachers study their pupils' achievement scores in different areas to diagnose strengths and weaknesses. Test batteries provide teachers, administrators, and counselors with profile information on both individuals and classes, even on whole schools. Clinicians often use profiles of personality tests to help them diagnose patient difficulties. Profiles are thus useful tools for working with individuals. They are, like multiple regression methods, also multivariate tools that, theoretically at least, are closer to the complexity of human attributes and behavior than single tests or measures.

Despite their seeming individual character and idiographic appeal, profiles, like the prediction equations discussed earlier, are group products. A profile derives its meaning only from the attachment of its constituent scores to group data. This is illustrated in Figure 15.1. The profile consists of the graphed scores of four measures of musical talent—another difficult concept, by the way—memory, melodic perception, aural acuity, and coordination.[5] Figure 15.1, let us say, portrays the (limited) musical talent profile of one individual. From it one can roughly assess the individual's musical ability. We assume that the four attributes given are important for any individual who aspires to musical achievement. The

---

[5] These measures have been chosen only to illustrate the points being made; they do not come from actual research. The technical details of how to set up profiles like this are here ignored since they do not bear directly on the problem.

individual's scores are plotted above and below the means of the four measures. (We further assume that the raw scores of the tests have been suitably transformed to comparable measures. Otherwise the profile would not make much sense.[6])

In the present case we can see that the individual has above average memory, melodic perception, and coordination. But his aural acuity is considerably below average. Since aural acuity is crucial (say) in most musical activity, the prognosis for his musical success is not good. Nevertheless, he might make a good drummer! But not a tympanist, since tympanists have to tune their drums, even during performance!

Again note that profiles, like regression equations, are tied to group measures. The means, calculated from a group's scores, are the comparative anchors that make interpretation possible. In short, the psychologist, teacher, and counselor who use profiles or the predicted scores of multiple regression are using an idiographic approach; they are describing individuals. But they must do this always on a basis of group measures and statistics.[7]

The nomothetic-idiographic distinction is important because it clarifies part of the fundamental nature of science and scientific research and because it highlights the limitations of both approaches. The good novelist is an idiographer. He describes and probes individuals and their loves, fears, motivations, and behavior. The great novelist does all this and more: he also somehow manages to project his characters on to the mankind backdrop. A Chaim Potok not only vividly creates a Hassidim character in Brooklyn faced with the conflict of rupture with Hassidism. He also makes the reader feel the pain of all such creedal rupture. In so doing he slips over to some extent to nomothesis. The great scientist can never slip over from a nomothetic approach to an idiographic approach. The rules of the game do not permit it. He must stick to them and leave idiography to the Potoks because the very definition of science as law-making, with its restriction to generality, does not permit dealing with the individual.

---

[6] A common way to do this, but not the only way, is to convert all scores of the individual to standard scores. A standard score is the difference between a raw score, X, and the group mean on that test, M, suitably adjusted for (divided by) the variability of the group.

[7] The related problem of a "statistics of the individual" is a difficult one. In theory, one can conceive of using statistics on the data of one individual. For example, Q methodology (Stephenson, 1953) is such an approach. Measurement instruments, usually card sorts, are constructed with one, two, or three variables embodied in the instrument's items. A single individual responds to the instrument, and, under certain circumstances, the results can be analyzed with analysis of variance. This can be called a statistics of the individual. Equally interesting, the responses of one individual can be correlated with those of another individual—and so on. The approach and methodology and its strengths and weaknesses are too complex to discuss here. Suffice it to say, however, that the group nature of the data does not change.

A Troublesome Paradox

We can conclude this troublesome chapter with a troublesome paradox. It is a paradox of science, but especially behavioral science, that centers in what can be called the "unit of speech." The unit of speech in science is always the set, the group. But behavioral scientists, and particularly psychologists, often talk as though the unit of speech were the individual. Psychological theories, for example, are sometimes enunciated as though they were explanations of what goes on inside a single individual. The social psychological scientist, for instance, may talk about the effect of perceived similarity of attitude toward social issues on liking for another person. In explaining the rationale of such a relation, the scientist may talk about the individual and the structure and content of his attitudes toward social issues. Or a cognitive theorist may talk about the structure of memory and its effects on certain behaviors. They mean, of course, the attitudes and memories of single individuals.

To be quite clear about this difficult problem, take a sociological example and contrast it with the above examples. Sociologists (for example, Duncan, Featherman, & Duncan, 1972) have tried to explain occupational status using the independent variables father's occupational status, father's education, and subject's education, among other variables. It is apparent that these variables are not as "individual" as memory and attitude. They are not as much "inside the individual," "inside the head." Occupational status and education are abstractions, of course. But they are less abstract than memory and attitude in the sense that it is easier to find the referents, the more or less specific and operational things, that "mean" education and occupational status. One readily ascertainable index of occupational status, for instance, is income. Operational indices of memory and attitudes, however, are more difficult to find. These variables are sunk in the brain of the individual, so to speak. The sociologist is less inclined to talk as though he were dealing with the single individual and his occupational status. The psychologist, by the very nature of his variables, can more easily slip into the individual level of discourse, more easily use the individual unit of speech. There is less danger, then, for the sociologist to talk at the individual level because his variables are "less individual," less tied to people—though the flavor of "individual talk" is sometimes present even in sociological discussions.

Take the discussion a bit further. When the psychologist discusses problems he often speaks of the psychological characteristics of single individuals. For example, in the conclusion of the report of a stimulating research study on the influence of traits as prototypes on memory (Cantor & Mischel, 1977, p. 47), the following sentence appears: "Storing material in terms of its relation to a consistent conceptual schema is likely to provide *one* (my italics) with a more stable, less redundant memory structure . . ." Here is a passage from another fine study (Markus, 1977, p. 63): "Self-schemata are cognitive generalizations about the self, derived from past experience, that organize and guide the processing of the self-related information contained in an *individual*'s (my italics) social experience." In these studies the authors could only work with groups of individuals and establish the relations they were studying by using groups of individuals. Both authors, however, slip from the group to the individual unit of speech. They more or less have to because their theories "explain" what is presumably inside the head of the individual. In the second study, since the hypothesized relations were supported by the empirical *group* evidence, the author assumes, perforce, that self-schemata existed in the brains of her individual subjects.[8] The paradox, then, is that scientists, especially psychological scientists, must hypothesize and test relations at the group or set level when they in fact often want to talk on the individual level—and may do so.

ADDENDUM

The discussion in this chapter of the "group" or collective nature of science and the necessary lack of scientific concern for the individual may, in the eyes of some people, not be completely accurate. In general the argument is valid, but certain ways of working may appear to be exceptions to the rule that the scientific unit of speech is always the group and not the individual. It can be argued, for instance, that so-called case studies of single individuals are legitimate tools of scientific investigation. Adhering to the position taken in this chapter and elsewhere in the book, we see that this can be so, strictly speaking, only if case studies are used to obtain measures of variables.

But case studies are not usually used for this purpose. They can be, of course. One can use what is called content analysis (mentioned in an earlier chapter) to obtain measures of variables. Their usual purpose, however, is diagnostic or clinical. One seeks to understand an individual in more depth than is usually possible for some sort of practical purpose. One looks for insights into an individual's characteristics or attributes, in other words. The clinical psychologist, for example, studies a detailed description of a patient for clues or symptoms of an ailment. The scientific psychologist, on the other hand, may select a few of many cases—the higher and lower scores on a dependent variable, say—to help understand the

---

[8] Negative criticism of the two reports cited is not intended. I am only trying to show how difficult it is in psychology to escape the individual level of discourse and the individual and his idiosyncratic motives, perceptions, attitudes, and so on. To make my point, I have deliberately selected what I believe to be good examples of psychological research. Other examples in which the individual orientation is more pronounced could easily have been cited. Indeed, it is virtually impossible to escape individual-level talk in psychological research writing.

relations under study. This is, of course, not the basic scientific approach to data.

Another seeming exception to the collective rule is more difficult and controversial. This is the approach in which a researcher—perhaps the most famous case is B. F. Skinner, the behavioristic psychologist—studies a phenomenon with one animal or one person. Say the problem is the effect of reinforcement (reward) on learning. The researcher can reinforce one or more times a certain response or class of responses of a single pigeon, as Skinner has done. He finds that learning improves with reinforcement. There is a relation here: we have a set of ordered pairs consisting of time points, or reinforcement at time points, being one set and responses the other set. Can this be considered a genuine exception to the collective rule?

The aim of nomothetic science is to establish laws, systematic explanations or relations that apply generally. The researcher in this case wants to be able to say that reinforcement produces certain responses, and from this he wants to be able to say that reinforcement produces learning. If every individual—rat, pigeon, person—were like every other individual, then studying a single individual might yield generalized results applicable to all individuals of a certain kind. The trouble is, as usual, the great differences among individuals. Even isopods, tiny marine crustaceans, show individual differences (Morrow & Smithson, 1969)! Therefore one has to have severe reservations about the conclusions reached from research using one individual. The principles of sampling and generalizing from samples apply to all situations, even though the demands may be somewhat less in research with animals and in the laboratory. The above example, then, is not really an exception to the collective requirement.

Stephenson (1953), whose ideas we mentioned earlier, has strongly claimed that a psychological theory can be tested with a single individual by using what he has called Q methodology. A single subject is asked to sort a deck of cards or items according to some criterion, say degrees of approval or degrees of importance in whatever area the cards represent. The cards are put into designated piles with varying numbers of cards in each pile. The six or more piles represent a rank order, and values are assigned to the cards in the piles, different values for each pile, and the same value within any pile.

The method is highly effective. And one can achieve a sort of "statistics of the individual." This is done by building categories into a Q sort and its items. For example, in measuring social attitudes, one might have half the items conservative and half liberal. Then, after a person has sorted the cards according to his beliefs and appropriate numbers have been assigned to the cards of each pile, a suitable statistical test of the significance of the difference between the mean of the conservative items and the mean of the liberal items is made. Obviously, two, even three, categories can be built into the items. The category "abstract-specific" can be used, for instance. Then factorial analysis of variance, as described in an earlier chapter, can be applied to the sort of one individual (the details are not pertinent here).

The method is really a sophisticated way of rank ordering a set of items. To rank order 60 or 80 items is difficult and tedious. Putting the cards in piles is much easier and still effective. In addition to statistical analysis of an individual's Q values, one can correlate one individual's values with those of another individual. In fact, the correlations among the Q sorts of a number of individuals can be intercorrelated and factor analyzed, often with valuable results.

Stephenson claims that a theory built into the Q items can be tested using the Q sort of one individual whose characteristics are known. A conservative who has sorted the social attitudes Q sort described above should have a mean of the conservative items greater than the mean of the liberal items. While this description is oversimplified, it is sufficient for the present purpose.

The idea is interesting and important. (It is strange that it has not been used more than it has.) Unfortunately, it is subject to the same assessment as the previous example of studying reinforcement with one animal. In brief, the relations of a theory cannot be established with the data of a single individual. One requires more generality than the data a single individual can provide. Indeed, one of the weaknesses of Q methodology is that the nature of the method—requiring almost personalized administration of Q sorts and thus large investments of time with each individual, for example—virtually precludes having large groups of subjects.

I believe that the nomothetic-idiographic distinction and the claim in this chapter that science is not and cannot be concerned with the individual is in general valid. Nevertheless, I want to leave the door of the reader's mind a little open. It is possible that legitimate exceptions—for example, in physiological psychology—may be developed in the future. Although I cannot myself see how science can be other than nomothetic, it may in the future be shown that science can work with the single individual. In any case, understanding of modern behavioral science can be considerably aided by knowing the nomothetic-idiographic distinction and the individual-group paradox of the psychologist.[9]

[9] The reader interested in pursuing the subject further should consult Nagel's (1961, pp. 547ff.) penetrating analysis. Nagel might even find some of the discussion of this chapter questionable. He says, for example, that it would be an error to say that singular statements play no role in science. He points out that general statements can be asserted only by using singular statements (p. 548). He means, I think, that empirical evidence has to be tied to specific instances. Nevertheless, he also says that by and large statements in the natural and social sciences "contain few if any references to specific objects . . . ," whereas statements in history "are almost without exception singular in form . . ." (p. 548).

A philosopher colleague (J. van Heerden) has pointed out to me that to say that singular statements are not used in science is too strong. In addition, one can say that the individual plays a role in science as a member of a class. On the other hand, science does not and cannot deal with uniqueness and the unique individual.

16

Misconceptions and controversies
research and practice[1]

How does research influence practice? What is research for? Why do scientists do research? Is the purpose of research to improve the lot of mankind? Is the goal of science to help men and women live better? Or is the purpose of science simply understanding of natural phenomena? These difficult questions and more like them need to have reasonable answers if we are to round out our understanding of behavioral research.

The problems and arguments of this chapter are not easy to understand. There is no great conceptual difficulty as there has been in some of the more technical chapters of this book. The difficulty is the sort of incomprehension and psychological resistance that arises when well-accepted and traditional beliefs are challenged, as they must now be challenged. When we say, as we will say, that the purpose of science is not to enhance the welfare of mankind, we may ignite a flame of incredulity, even resentment, in the minds of some readers. Of what use is science if it is not to improve human and social conditions? Shouldn't research yield practical dividends on the investment in it? Can you put an important activity like scientific research in a category separate from most other human activities?

To answer these questions we set the central question of the chapter: What is the relation between research and practice? Does scientific re-

[1] Part of the content and argument of this chapter has been borrowed from, or at least influenced by, an address given at the annual meeting of the American Educational Research Association in New York, April 6, 1977 (Kerlinger, 1977).

search get translated into practice? If so, how? Should scientists be required to show how their research will somehow benefit people and society before support is given for research? In attempting answers to these questions, we will, as in Chapter 15, return to themes introduced in Chapter 1. In other words, we begin and end the book with these major problems. We will briefly repeat the purpose of science and scientific research, define and discuss basic and applied research, outline an important misconception of the purpose of research, payoff, and, finally, discuss the complex relations between research and practice.

THE PURPOSE OF SCIENTIFIC RESEARCH REVISITED

The basic purpose of scientific research is theory. We have said this before and must repeat it here because of its importance. The statement at first seems enigmatic and puzzling mainly because we are so used to thinking that research must have practical goals. Once its meaning is grasped, however, the enigma disappears. It simply means that the purpose of scientific research is to understand and explain natural phenomena. As Braithwaite (1953, p. 2) puts it: "The fundamental concept for science is thus that of scientific law, and the fundamental aim of science is the establishment of such laws." A theory presents a systematic view of phenomena by specifying relations among variables, with the purpose of explaining and predicting the phenomena. Theory is held in high esteem by scientists—and rightly so. The esteem springs from the basic purpose of science, and theory is the vehicle for expressing the purpose. Science, then, has no other purpose than theory, or understanding and explanation.

Many people think that the purpose of scientific research is to solve human and technical problems and to improve practice. The goal of research in biology and chemistry, for instance, is thought to be the ultimate production of improved agriculture, superior medical practice, or other outcomes beneficial to society. Similarly, it is thought that research in sociology and psychology should be aimed at solving, among other things, problems of prejudice and discrimination, repairing learning deficiencies, improving learning and teaching, creating tests useful for education and industry, and helping people to be psychologically balanced and constructive.

It is quite true that much research is more or less aimed at such goals. We will discuss it later. In general, however, such practical and worthy goals are not the purposes of scientific research. The purpose is theory, and it has no other purpose. Since this point was elaborated in Chapter 1, we need not argue it further. Its acceptance, however, is the foundation of the argument of this chapter. Therefore, two examples of scientific psychological research, one actual and one invented, are given to illustrate what is meant.

Two Examples of Scientific Psychological Research

Earlier we presented the gist of Cattell's (1963) important research study on the nature of human intelligence. Recall that he claimed that there are two broad kinds of intelligence, called crystallized and fluid intelligence. Crystallized intelligence is the usual kind of intelligence tested by most intelligence tests. For instance, verbal ability is an important part of measured intelligence and is part of crystallized intelligence. Many psychologists believe, with considerable justification, that there is a general intelligence, or "*g*," that runs through intelligence tests; it is a general ability that is the prime source of human intelligence. Cattell would say that "*g*" is crystallized intelligence. In addition, however, he says that there is another important general form of intelligence quite different from crystallized intelligence, though obviously related to it. This he calls fluid intelligence.

Fluid intelligence is a sort of second "*g*." It shows itself in human performance characterized by adaptation to new situations. It is the "fluid" application of general ability, so to speak. Such ability is more characteristic of creative behavior than is crystallized intelligence. In short, Cattell says that there are two forms of general intelligence and not just one. In the study cited above he tested his hypothesis by administering tests that he believed to measure crystallized intelligence—verbal, numerical, and reasoning tests, for example—and also tests thought to measure fluid intelligence—more unusual perceptual tests that presumably require more openness of thought, greater flexibility, and so on.

Cattell administered tests of both kinds, together with personality measures, to eighth-grade children and factor analyzed the results. These results supported his hypothesis: the two kinds of tests appeared together on two different factors. Certain other predictions were also supported.

This research is scientific research. It seeks to explain important aspects of human intelligence by specifying the definitions and relations of a theory. It says nothing whatever about improving intelligence; it only "explains" it.

As a second example, suppose that a theory of learning has been found to be empirically valid and rather successfully explains the learning of concepts. The research that tested the theory was scientific research because it explains some aspect or aspects of human learning. It may or may not have implications for teaching concepts to children. Whether it does or does not has nothing to do with its status as scientific research. Further suppose that a teaching expert devises a method of teaching concepts based on the theory and research. He is an engineer, a technician. Although based on scientific research, what he does is not itself scientific research. He may, of course, test the efficacy of his method using techniques devised by scientists. His research is applied research which is in this case inspired by the original research. Actual teaching using the method is partly engineering, partly art. It is not science.

Science and Engineering

Much of the misunderstanding in many people's minds about research and its presumed ameliorative purpose has probably arisen from confusing science with engineering and technology. We diverge briefly, therefore, to explain the difference.

Engineering is a set of applied disciplines that depend mostly on science but that are not themselves science. It is the job of the engineer to devise technical solutions to practical problems. In so doing, he uses technology, which likewise often arises from science but is not itself science. Technology comprises technical methods and materials devised to achieve practical objectives. The teaching expert mentioned above devised a method to teach concepts. Computer experts devise machines and machine languages, as brought out in Chapter 14, to achieve solutions to analytic problems. The teaching expert and the computer expert are highly important members of the intellectual community. But they are not scientists; they are basically engineers, though, admittedly, it is sometimes hard to draw a clear line between engineering and science. The essential clue to understanding the difference is the basic purpose of each. The purpose of engineering and technology is to solve relatively specific practical problems. The purpose of science is to understand natural phenomena. It is right and proper to expect and ask for solutions to practical problems from engineers. It is not right and proper to expect and ask for solutions to practical problems from scientists, as we shall see.

BASIC AND APPLIED RESEARCH

Again, ask the question: What is research for? We have said in this book that the purpose of science is theory, or systematic explanation of natural phenomena. Let us assume that this statement is correct. If so, then the work of scientists should be centered on the study of the relations among phenomena. In the behavioral sciences this would mean research into such phenomena as learning, memory, perception, motivation, attribution, occupation, religious preference, organizations, personality, social class, social movements, ideology, attitudes, values, and so on. Such research is called basic research.

Basic research has had many definitions, most of them unsatisfactory in one way or another. It has even authoritatively been said that an adequate or operational definition of basic research is not possible (Kidd, 1959). Nevertheless, scientists and thinkers and writers on science know, if often vaguely, what the term means, especially in contrast to applied research. In any case, *basic research* is research done to test theory, to study relations among phenomena in order to understand the phenomena, with little or no thought of applications of the results of the research to practical problems. Despite the possible inadequacies of this definition, it is adequate to help us talk about basic research. It says what has been said throughout this book: that scientific research is disciplined inquiry into the relations among natural phenomena, and adds that it is not done to achieve practical goals.

Applied research is research directed toward the solution of specified practical problems in delineated areas and from which amelioration or improvement of some process or activity, or achievement of practical goals, is expected. So-called programmatic and directed research are applied research. Such research is directed toward particular goals that promise solutions of usually pressing problems. It is the kind of research often cited by newspapers when research is discussed, because it is easy to understand the rationale and motivation of applied researchers and their sources of finance. Examples should as usual help us grasp the important differences between basic and applied research.

The study of Aronson and Mills (1959) cited earlier is a good example of basic research in psychology. The researchers were interested in the influence of deprivation and difficulty of entrance into groups on the value group members put on group membership. They also were seeking further light on social psychological theory to help explain certain phenomena connected with membership in groups. Milgram's (1974) studies of obedience to authority, also cited earlier, are also good examples of basic research. Recall that subjects were asked to administer what were believed to be painful shocks to another person in an alleged learning experiment. The question was: How far would the experimental subjects go? How much pain would they inflict on someone at the behest of a "scientific investigator"? The relation studied was between the variables authority and obedience.

Neither of these researches seems to have been done with any idea in the minds of the researchers of practical consequences. They were pursuing explicit or implied explanations of natural phenomena: of the presumed higher value put on group membership when one has experienced deprivation or difficulty in attaining the group membership, and obedience to authority.

Memory and Flatworms

To further our understanding of basic research, let us look at a highly unusual and, in the minds of many people, thoroughly impractical study of memory done many years ago using flatworms as subjects. (Indeed, I have chosen this study because it would seem to be far from any practical application—and also because of its importance in the study and understanding of memory.)

Memory has always captured the concentrated attention of psychologists, not only because it is a brain function that is highly interesting, complex, and elusive but also because it is a key to understanding other psychological processes and functions. Without going too much into theories of learning, memory, and brain function,[2] we can say that scientific attention has been directed to learning the brain locations of speech, hearing, verbal learning and ability, musical learning, and so on. It has been discovered that if a part of the brain is damaged, in some cases another part of the brain can take over the function or functions of the damaged part. Since it is very difficult or impossible to do controlled experiments on human brains, animals and animal brains are often used. While the gap between human and animal brains is great, it is sometimes feasible to test hypotheses and explore brain functions and relations among these functions with animals. Even though the difference may be great, the similarity may be sufficient to warrant studying relations among functions.

McConnell, Jacobson, and Kimble (1959), in a classic study of learning in flatworms, or planaria, exploited the regeneration characteristic of these little animals to demonstrate that learning, as well as physical characteristics, is regenerated. If a planarium is cut in two, a "new" animal is regenerated. That is, both parts of the "cut" animals will be complete organisms! The researchers first "taught" an experimental group of five planaria to react physically to a light by pairing the appearance of the light with electric shock. Shock causes the planarium to contract longitudinally. "Learning" took place when the planaria's bodies contracted when only the light and not the shock was presented. A control group of five animals was not given this training.

After the training the experimenters cut the animals of both experimental and control groups in two. Would the tail sections of the experimental group animals that had originally not had brains—the head sections, of course, had the original brains, which were assumed to have "learned" the conditioned response to the light—show evidence of having "learned" the response to the light? After about four weeks, sufficient time for regeneration, the animals of the experimental and control groups were tested for the conditioned response. Both head and tail sections of both groups were tested. The situation is depicted in Figure 16.1. The figure is self-explanatory.

Did the experimental group tail sections of the regenerated worms exhibit the conditioned response to the light? Since the experimental group

---

[2] Good, clearly written accounts of these phenomena, as well as of other psychological phenomena, can be found in Hilgard, Atkinson; and Atkinson's (1975) *Introduction to Psychology*. The very beginning of this book (p. 4) is a good example of part of the main argument of this chapter. The authors give ten psychological research problems as examples of the work of psychologists. Of the ten, eight are applied research problems, one is a basic research problem, and one is a methodological problem. Nevertheless, much, perhaps most, of the text of the book is preoccupied with basic research.

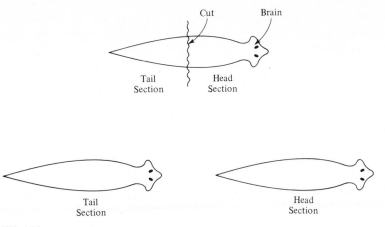

FIG. 16.1

head sections had the original brains that had learned the response, it was assumed that they would retain the learning. Since the control group worms had had no training, it was expected that both head and tail sections, after regeneration, would show no learning. The measure of the dependent variable was number of trials necessary to reach a criterion of 23 conditioned responses in 25 consecutive trials.

The results showed that the experimental group subjects' tails, as well as the heads, possessed the learning! The mean number of trials of the original training was 134. The mean of the head sections, after cutting and regeneration, was 40, and the mean of the tail sections was 43.2. The differences between the mean of the original training and both retest means after regeneration were statistically significant. The mean of the head sections of the control group animals was 248.6, and the mean of the tail sections was 207.8. These means did not differ significantly from each other. But both head and tail sections differed significantly from the experimental group postregeneration means.

These results are remarkable. Indeed, the experiment and its conception have a sort of strange beauty. Did the learning somehow get to the regenerated tails of the experimental group planarians? Our concern, however, is not with the results and the fascination of the research but with basic research. Of course, the researchers were probably interested in human learning, but it seems clear that they had little or no thought of practical application. Nevertheless, if such startling results are borne out in further research, theory and research on memory with both animals and human beings could be strongly affected. The next question, of course, is why and how the regenerated experimental group tail sections had "learned."

Examples of applied research are not hard to find. The Clark and Walberg study, cited so often in this book, is an applied study, though it certainly has aspects of basic research. It was aimed at obtaining a partial answer to a rather difficult question: How best to teach underachieving minority-group children to read? Much research in education is applied in nature: its object is to help improve educational practice. For example, most studies of methods of teaching, programmed instruction, exceptional children, and the like, are applied research. Because of its focus on specific practical problems and its lack of focus on basic understanding of phenomena, applied research is narrower in scope and more limited in potential impact. Applied studies in education are done not so much to enhance knowledge and broaden and deepen understanding of educational processes as they are to help children learn better. In other words, they are essentially pragmatic; they seek to find out what works, or to ascertain relations not for the sake of the relations and possible theory but for planning and decisions for educational action.

Two Important Applied Research Studies

One of the most important applied research studies of the century, cited earlier in this book, is the large-scale investigation of equality and inequality in American education done at the behest of the Congress, *Equality of Educational Opportunity* (Coleman et al., 1966). Its great influence shows clearly that applied research does not lack importance and significance. In seeking answers to the equality questions asked by the Congress, Coleman and his colleagues studied the effects of a large number of variables on educational achievement. The results of the study, as well as its methodology, are still having an impact today. Similar studies have been done in other countries under the general title International Studies of Educational Achievement (for example, Husén, 1967; Thorndike, 1973), and their importance and influence are also large.

Another applied research study of large practical importance to the welfare of the United States is a set of survey research studies done by the Survey Research Center of the University of Michigan to determine the attitudes of white people toward black people (Campbell, 1971). Actually, the attitudes of black people toward white people were also studied in the complete set of studies, but Campbell's book was limited to attitudes of white people toward black people. Surveys are usually applied research: they are done for specific practical purposes: ordinarily to obtain information on which to base decisions or actions. The study under consideration is no exception. Part of it was commissioned by the National Advisory Commission on Civil Disorders (see *Report of the National Advisory Commission on Civil Disorders*, 1968) to get information on race riots and related matters. Presumably the information obtained would help the Commission and other bodies better deal with racial problems. In the whole set of studies over 9,000 Americans were sampled and interviewed in 1964, 1968, and 1970.

The findings of the studies are surprising and important. But first, Campbell warns us in the very beginning of the book (p. 1) that there is no simple way to describe white attitudes toward black people. Nevertheless, he reaches three or four important conclusions. One, although there is no doubt of the widespread racistic attitudes of white Americans, the white population in the cities is not universally racist. Moreover, there has been a massive shift toward more favorable racial attitudes. While far from egalitarian, white Americans are much more egalitarian than they were. And only a small portion of the population expressed overtly hostile attitudes toward blacks.

Two, resistance to change in race relations is widespread, though by no means universal. Some forms of change, for instance acceptance of blacks in work situations, are accepted. Other more private kinds of change are resisted. Three, the idea of racial superiority does not characterize white attitudes. This conventional sign of racial doctrine seems to have changed for the better.

Four, those Americans who went to college after World War II are clearly more positive in their attitudes toward blacks than are those who did not go to college or who went to college before the war. This was the strongest relation of the study. In other words, there has been an important change in the intellectual climate of U.S. campuses: black people are accepted by younger white college graduates. Perhaps recent higher education has had a significant and beneficial impact. There are a number of other findings, of course, but these are the principal ones. Accepting the findings as valid indicators of American white attitudes toward blacks—and the results of the research of first-rate research organizations like the Survey Research Center are generally accepted by social scientists because of the excellent conceptual and technical quality of their work—we get a good idea of how important applied research can be.

There can be little doubt, then, that applied research often has large practical human and social importance. It would be hard to overestimate the importance of the two studies just outlined. Such studies, and others like them, however, lead many people to believe that applied research is more important and significant than basic research. The importance and significance of basic research are easy to overlook because basic research is usually not directed toward issues of obvious and compelling human importance. It is much easier to grasp, for instance, the social relevance of the above two studies than it is to grasp the importance of attribution theory studies or of studies of human memory.

Applied research is indispensable and often highly significant in two or three ways. First, it can, as intended, provide information that will help lead to problem solution. Second, it can sometimes suggest new or different lines of basic research. For instance, an unexpected relation between two variables may be discovered in a survey of opinions. This relation may suggest the alteration of a theory being tested in basic research. The needs of applied research can also stimulate basic methodological research. The need for more appropriate forms of analysis in studying such phenomena as school achievement, occupational status, later-life success, and similar variables apparently helped to reinforce the development of multivariate analysis, especially multiple regression analysis and path analysis. Third, and perhaps even more important, applied research sometimes has a heuristic quality. It can lead to theory development and basic research. It is often rich in potential hypotheses that cry out for testing and theoretical underpinning.

PAYOFF

The people of modern industrial nations are strongly pragmatic. They like and admire what works, especially what works quickly and efficiently. This attitude, probably strongest in the United States, is a healthy one in the sense that things get done. If there is a problem to be solved, bring in experts for advice, explore past solutions of similar problems, but above all do something. If the something works, fine. If it doesn't work, try something else. But find something that works.

There is a kind of slapdash style about many American solutions to problems, but there is little doubt that solutions are tried, which is probably better than ignoring problems, or analyzing them to death, or hoping that they will go away. Unfortunately, a strong pragmatic outlook and attitude is both a friend and an enemy of science. It is a friend as long as people, particularly people with power, perceive science as helpful in problem solution. If, on the other hand, they perceive science as ineffective in solving problems or as remote from practical concerns, then the pragmatic attitude becomes an enemy of science and basic research. This seems to be what is happening in Western countries today.

In keeping with this pragmatic attitude, most people assume that research can and should solve practical problems and improve human and social conditions. The assumption is false. Research does not lead directly to improvement in practice or in human and social conditions. The solution of a research problem is on a different level of discourse than the solution of an action problem. The outcome of research is usually the establishment of a relation of some kind between two or more phenomena. This is even true of applied research problems. Take a relatively simple applied outcome like that of the Clark and Walberg experiment. Recall that massive reinforcement had a fairly substantial effect on the reading achievement of black children who were seriously behind in reading.

Can these results be applied directly to educational practice? On the surface, it would seem so. If a research study shows that massive reinforcement helps underachieving children read better, then encourage teachers teaching such children to use massive reinforcement. Unfortunately, things are not so simple. Does massive reinforcement work with children of other ages? What difference does massive reinforcement make when used by different kinds of teachers? More subtle, is it possible that the prolonged use of massive reinforcement might have a deleterious effect on some or even all children? Might it, for example, have the effect of ultimately crippling children's internal motivation and initiative?

So even a seemingly obvious and simple outcome of research that is more applied than basic turns out to have no certain implications for practice. If we take the results of many basic research studies that seem to have implications for educational practice, we find an even greater gap. In most such studies the gulf between study findings and practice is wide and deep.

Studying relations and taking action are on two different levels of discourse which one cannot easily bridge.[3] Scientific research never has the purpose of solving human and social problems, making decisions, and taking action. The researcher is preoccupied with, and should be preoccupied with, variables and their relations. He should never be required to think about or to spell out the implications of what he is doing or has done. To require this is to require a leap from an abstract relational level of discourse to a much more concrete and specific level. This cannot be done directly; it is not possible to do a research study and then have practitioners immediately use the results.

The expectation that research should lead rather quickly to change in practice springs in good part, as mentioned earlier, from the pragmatic and practical orientation of people. They conceive the purpose of research as human, environmental, and technical improvement. Research, in this view, must pay off; there must be a return on the investment in research. Practical answers and problem solutions are demanded of science and scientists.

A strong pragmatic attitude, then, virtually forces focus upon outcomes and getting things done. What is good is what works! Why it works is less important; most important is that it works. This is, in science, a defeating attitude, because as Thomson (1960) has pointed out, "The best way to make advances in technology . . . turns out to be to understand the principle" (p. 997). He has also pointed out that this idea is a recent discovery and has only recently become true.

Practitioners often have little patience with what they conceive to be "impractical," "ivory tower" research. They want research to be put to practical work. One of the unfortunate manifestations of this general orien-

---

[3] It is important to know what is meant by "level of discourse." Whenever we talk about something we talk about it in a context or frame of reference. Call this frame of reference U, meaning "universe." A particular U is a level of discourse; it must include all the objects under discussion. If we shift from one level of discourse to another, say from U_1 to U_2, the new level of discourse will not contain all the objects. In fact, it may not have any of them. When discussing segregation and its implications, we should not shift to religious problems—"It is God's will that there are races; they were obviously meant to be kept apart." These are two levels or universes of discourse: segregation and religion. Shifting levels of discourse, without suitable transition, is a conscious and unconscious way of distorting communication. In the problem discussed above, the level of discourse of action problems is entirely different from the scientific research level of discourse. See Kerlinger (1973, pp. 57–58) for further discussion.

tation to research is an urgent desire and demand for research to pay off, to yield quick returns. To talk about research for the sake of understanding seems to many of us foolish, even pathetic. There must be payoff! This is a futile expectation. Scientific research does not pay off in any simple way because it is not and cannot be aimed at practical problems (Brain, 1965; Brooks, 1971; Dubos, 1961; Townes, 1968; Waterman, 1966).

How about applied research? Is the same argument pertinent? After all, applied research is by definition directed toward application. Shouldn't we therefore demand payoff from applied research? The answer seems to be a highly qualified Yes. One can *expect* payoff, but it is unrealistic to demand it. An example was given earlier. The direct application of the results of the Clark and Walberg massive reinforcement study findings, obtained from applied research of commendable quality, was shown to be questionable. A possible payoff of this study is its suggestion that massive reinforcement *might* help certain kinds of children.

The very comprehensive *Equality of Educational Opportunity* study was applied research, as indicated earlier. What payoff did it have? Strangely enough, its findings offer little to the practitioner. It documented inequality of resources and achievement. It offered no solutions, however. It also showed that a considerably greater portion of the variance of achievement was presumably due to home background and the characteristics the child brings to school than it was to differences between schools (or school resources). What does this mean for educational practice? Don't bother to spend money on schools? If only a relatively small portion of the achievement variance is due to schools, then why make great efforts to have excellent schools? Indeed, direct extrapolation from research studies can sometimes lead to absurd conclusions! Curiously, the real payoff of the *Equality* study was to emphasize that educational situations and achievement are very complex and require much more complex research than has usually been done. It also pointed out ways to study such situations. In short, it really pointed to a great need to *understand* educational phenomena.

Applied research can, of course, be used to help solve problems, but this problem solving does not ordinarily lead to understanding the complex phenomena of behavioral research. Like the *Equality* study, it frequently highlights research, theory, and methodological problems, but it is doubtful that direct applications are possible with the phenomena of interest in behavioral research. Its results, however, can *suggest* things to do. But as usual practitioners must do the things. The research results only provide possible support for the decisions.

Reading is a good example. Answers to reading problems lie not in many researches aimed at telling teachers how to teach reading. They lie in research aimed at understanding the many aspects of human learning and teaching connected with reading. Such understanding is arrived at, if it is ever arrived at, by invoking psychological and other theories related to reading and doing research over long periods directed at understanding reading-related phenomena. Research on reading itself is almost invariably unproductive. We must study reading in the context of perception, motivation, attitudes, values, intelligence, and so on. In other words, the goal should not be the improvement of reading! It should be understanding of the relations among the many complex phenomena related to reading. To improve something as complex as reading requires understanding of reading and many related phenomena, a very difficult task indeed. And there is, of course, no guarantee of improvement in children's reading, even if basic research on phenomena related to reading is done.

The demand for payoff of research, then, is an impossible demand. It is based on misunderstanding of what scientific research is and is not. Its persistence testifies to its strength. Its influence, unfortunately, can be particularly disturbing to individuals who seek to understand science and scientific research, because it implants erroneous notions of the purpose of research and what research can accomplish.[4]

Because of the importance of the issue, one would think that researchers would have studied the relative effects of basic and applied research on practice. But the problem appears not to have been studied empirically. So, from an empirical viewpoint we know little about the relative effects of, say, basic and applied research on practice. Most discussions and assertions are more or less informed opinion and speculation. Recently, however, an important empirical study in medicine was published (Comroe & Dripps, 1976). This study has the virtues of timeliness, importance, and competence. Most important, it brings good empirical evidence to bear on the difficult problem of the relation of research to practice. We turn to it now.

THE COMROE AND DRIPPS STUDY

Of all the research done that might have influenced modern medical practice, Comroe and Dripps (1976) wished to know what kind of research had the most influence. Their primary question was whether basic research or applied research had the greater impact on medical practice.

They asked 40 physicians to list the advances in medical practice that they considered the most important for their patients. They sent the selected advances to a large number of specialists and asked the specialists to vote on the list. The votes decided 10 advances in medicine in the last 30

---

[4] Another view that hampers understanding of science and behavioral research is that such research must be relevant. Like the payoff view, this view is hard to deal with because it is so plausible. It seems so obvious that behavioral research should be directed to significant human and social problems. The view of this book, however, is that relevance is a criterion completely external to research—indeed, it is essentially a political criterion—and that insistence on its use will seriously weaken research in the social sciences by politicizing it and by distracting researchers from the core scientific activity: basic research. (See Kerlinger, 1977, for further discussion of relevance and its effects.)

years. The authors, with 140 consultants, then identified the essential bodies of knowledge that had to be developed so that the advances could be made.

From some 2,500 research reports that were especially important to the development of one or more of the essential bodies of knowledge identified, they and their consultants selected more than 500 essential or key articles for careful study. A "key" article was one that had an important effect on subsequent research and development, reported new data or new ways of regarding old data, a new concept or hypothesis, and so on. In other words, it was a key article if it led to one of the 10 clinical advances.

Comroe and Dripps classified the articles as: (1) basic research unrelated to the solution of a clinical problem; (2) basic research related to the clinical problem; (3) studies not preoccupied with basic mechanisms; (4) reviews; (5) developmental work or engineering to create, improve, or perfect apparatus or a technique for research; (6) the same as (5) but for use with patients.

The results were clear: basic research was responsible for almost three times as many key articles as other types of research and almost twice as many articles as nonbasic research development taken together! (The figures were basic: 61.7%; not basic: 21.2%; development: 15.3%; review: 1.8%.) This remarkable research into research corrects distorted ideas of the contributions of basic and applied research to practice and strongly affirms what many scientists have been saying for the last 30 or more years: basic research done not for payoff ultimately is likely to have greater effect than so-called programmatic or targeted research. Even if one can quarrel with this statement, it is at least evident that faith in the plausibility of the payoff argument must be shaken.

THE INFLUENCE OF RESEARCH ON PRACTICE

How does research influence practice? No one really knows for sure. There is much opinion, of course, but little systematically obtained evidence. The Comroe and Dripps study is a rare and important bird. But it is limited. Would similar findings emerge in psychology, sociology, and education? It would be much more difficult to do similar studies in these fields because it would be difficult to get agreement on what are advances and what are key articles (for example). Although hard evidence is lacking, there does seem to be a consensus among many scientists of the great importance of both basic and applied research and the necessity of nourishing both. This consensus is healthy, I think; it is the position taken in this book. The following remarks on how research affects practice are based in part on the Comroe and Dripps study, on a study by Deutsch, Platt, and Senghaas (1971) about advances made in the social sciences, and on the published writings and reports of scientists and philosophers during the last 10 to 15 years. (Some of these have already been cited in this chapter.)

Possible Effects of Series of Studies

The effects of research are indirect and are felt only over appreciable periods of time. Deeper understanding of underlying phenomena is slow, even reluctant, because it has to combat or displace fixed sets of beliefs. Larger trends in theoretical thinking and series of research studies geared to answering general theoretical psychological and sociological questions have the greatest probability of having an impact. But the impact is in general not specific. A single piece of research or even a set of researches, for example, never tells practitioners what to do. Instead, it influences, if it influences anything, ways of thinking, perceiving, and reacting. This is particularly so with basic research. Applied research studies, virtually by definition, have less chance of having long-range and deep impact because they are aimed at specific and relatively narrow goals. Theoretically oriented studies aimed at understanding phenomena are general, abstract, and applicable in principle to many different problems and situations—if, indeed, they are applicable at all.

Take Cattell's theory of fluid and crystallized intelligence mentioned earlier. If further research supports Cattell's notions, it is possible that psychological and educational thinking might ultimately be changed. If it becomes accepted that there are two kinds of general intelligence, crystallized and fluid, might this not ultimately influence teaching? Much of contemporary teaching has been influenced by the notion that there is one general form of intelligence that runs through most ability tests and much human performance (the famous "g"). Providing for individual differences in teaching means in large part providing varied instruction for different levels of one general intelligence. But Cattell says there are two forms of general intelligence! It should be obvious, if this is true and if it becomes generally known and accepted, that providing for individual differences becomes more complex.

Attribution theory is another interesting example. In the last decade, a rather large literature has grown in social psychology on the phenomenon of attribution.[5] Attribution is the process people use to understand and explain the causes of behavior—especially the behavior of other people. If we see someone solve problems quickly and efficiently, we may attribute it to the person's ability. Or we may attribute it to the easiness of the problems. On the other hand, if we see someone else who has great difficulty with the problems we may attribute lack of success to laziness, lack of

---

[5] For example, Harvey, Ickes, and Kidd (1976), Jones, Kanouse, Kelley, Nisbett, Valins, and Weiner (1971) and Shaver (1975). Most of the references are heavy going, unfortunately. Perhaps the best introduction is Shaver (1975). A very brief but clear exposition can be found in Chapter 18 of the general psychology text by Hilgard, Atkinson, and Atkinson (1975). (The chapter was actually written by Daryl J. Bem.)

concentration, or even race or sex! What causes these and other attributions? How are they related to the characteristics of the individuals making them? Obviously, attribution is a highly general phenomenon. It is also heuristic: it stimulates a great deal of theory and research. Let's look at two studies briefly.

Harvey and Kelley (1974) asked the general question: What conditions affect an individual's sense of his own competence in making judgments? In one experiment they had subjects make comparisons of the relative sizes of figures, but the figures were presented to them in different ways. Pairs of figures of different sizes were presented 20 times, and the subjects were asked which was the larger of the two. The experimental manipulation was stability of presentation. The first 10 of the 20 presentations of one condition, for example, were unstable; that is, the figures were presented in random ways: sometimes the larger figure on the right, sometimes on the left. The second 10 presentations were all stable: the larger figure was always either on the left or the right. This was the unstable-stable condition. The other three conditions were stable-stable, stable-unstable, unstable-unstable.

In a second experiment stability and instability (with, this time, three conditions) were similarly manipulated. The modality, however, was hearing. The subjects were required to make judgments of the relative locations of sounds. Harvey and Kelley found, among other things, that stability and instability of presentation affected judgments of self-competence. The sequence unstable-stable led to the highest judgments of self-competence, while the other sequences in general led to lower judgments.

In another study stimulated by attribution theory Jones and his colleagues (Jones, Rock, Shaver, Goethals, & Ward, 1968) were interested in the effects of initial success and failure on observers' judgments. They had their subjects tackle a series of problems presented in such a way that observers saw some subjects first succeed and then fail, and other subjects first fail and then succeed. The observers judged those who first succeeded more able than those who first failed, despite later performance. That is, the observers attributed differing degrees of ability to the subjects depending on whether the subjects first succeeded or first failed.

Series of studies such as these should increase our understanding of attribution. This understanding should in turn increase our understanding of self-perception, social perception, and judgment. Many interpersonal and judgmental problems in practical situations, as in business and education, may be affected by this increased understanding. We may, for example, gain increased insight into teacher judgments of pupils and the school conditions and the teacher traits and behaviors that affect such judgments. Bonuses may be picked up on the way. The serendipity of theoretical and research exploration is often surprising and rewarding. Is it possible, for example, that the Harvey and Kelley study is an opening wedge into a highly important but little explored aspect of motivation: sense of competence?

None of these three studies by itself means much for practice—though all three are suggestive. A body of such studies, on the other hand, may help to change the thinking of psychologists, sociologists, and educators about important areas of human behaviors, in this case intelligence and making judgments and other attributions. Such gained insights can have an impact on practice—though there is never any guarantee that there will be significant and beneficial impact.

Another example of long-range research that is already changing education in Europe and America is the series of developmental-epistemological studies of Piaget and his colleagues. For many years Piaget has been carefully observing children of all ages, interviewing and talking to them, and devising "problems" for them to solve. He is evidently interested in trying to answer the ancient epistemological and psychological question: How do we know? He thinks that the question can be answered, in part at least, by understanding the development of the thinking processes of the child.[6] One of Piaget's general findings—congruent with what John Dewey had said many years earlier—is that the child has an intellectual life of his own, a way of regarding reality quite different from an adult's. In his thinking, in other words, the child is not just a small adult. Understanding by psychologists and educators of the child's conception of reality is likely to affect adult interaction with children profoundly, especially in education. Series of studies like these, then, will probably have an impact on practice.

The Influence of Methodology

A good deal of this book has been preoccupied with methodology, a general term meaning different ways of doing things for different purposes. Methodology includes ways of stating problems and hypotheses, methods of observation and data collection (not emphasized in this book; see Appendix), the measurement of variables, and techniques of data analysis. Methodology also includes aspects of philosophy of science and a general critical approach to research. Despite its great importance, we rarely think of methodology's possible influence on practice. This is strange because methodology has already had a profound influence on behavioral scientific knowledge.

If we can say that research has influence on practice, then it follows that anything that influences research strongly may ultimately influence practice. Methodology influences research strongly. Such influence, of course, will be quite indirect. After all, the influence of research itself is indirect. The influence of methodology is even more indirect. Take a rather obvious example. Before the 1930s, experiments were mostly two-variable affairs.

[6] The interested reader can try one or two of Piaget's many books, but better advice—unfortunately, Piaget's writing is not a model of clarity—is to try one of several explanations in book form. One of the oldest but still perhaps the best is the book by Flavell (1963).

One independent variable was manipulated, and its presumed effect on a dependent variable was observed. After the invention of analysis of variance, however, more realistic and more theoretically interesting experiments could be done using two or more independent variables. Some of them have been described in earlier chapters. The effect of advances in methodology is to help produce research whose results are more generalizable and to enlarge both experimental and nonexperimental research approaches and problems.

But is it possible that methodology can have deeper effects? Let us speculate, for example, about the possible effects of multiple regression on thinking habits some 10 to 20 years hence. The essence of multiple regression is the simultaneous effects of many variables on a dependent variable. Most people think usually of the effect of one variable on another variable. Is it possible that after repeated exposure to and use of multiple regression—and there is no doubt that the next decade or two will see much such exposure and use—we can no longer think of single influences? Is it possible that multiple influences will become part of our habitual ways of thinking? It seems so to me.

The Influence of Theory

The most important source of influence on practice is theory. I am thinking of theory at two levels. One is the larger kind of theory associated with psychological and sociological schools of thought. Psychology, for instance, has been influenced by gestalt (holistic), behavioristic, psychoanalytic, and cognitive theories. Each of these, and sometimes conjunctions of them, have their traditions in research. Social psychology in its early years was influenced by gestalt theory, by behavioristic theory, and by psychoanalytic theory. Experimental psychology has been influenced by behavioristic theory and by cognitive theory. Such theories probably influence practice, because they influence decisions on what research problems are important—attribution research arose mainly from gestalt (or field) theory and cognitive theory—and because ideas stimulated by the theory get into textbooks and sometimes even become part of dogma. Thus, quite indirectly practice may ultimately be affected. The widespread use of group dynamics by teachers and social workers in the 1950s and 1960s was a result in part of field theory, an offshoot of gestalt theory, which stimulated both research on group processes and the introduction and use of group techniques in practical situations.

The other kind of theoretical influence is the more specific theory, such as attribution theory, reinforcement theory, and theories of intelligence. Theories of intelligence can change educational and social welfare thinking and practice. Environmental and hereditarian theories of intelligence, for instance, can lead to quite different educational and social welfare practices. The influence of reinforcement theory has already been felt because of its strong emphasis on positive reinforcement. Parents and teachers are more likely to use reward than punishment, because their education and training cannot have helped but be influenced by reinforcement theory and research. They "know," often without explicit and specific knowledge, that the effect of reward is somehow better than the effect of punishment. (If the reader is inclined to take this for granted, realize that in the nineteenth century punishment was a more prevalent mode of dealing with children, at least in schools.)

Prejudice and Authoritarianism: A Mixed Example

Science and scientific behavioral theories and research change our ways of thinking about ourselves, others, and children, and about society, social problems, and possible solutions to social problems. As said earlier, however, such change is indirect and relatively slow. Moreover, it is very difficult, perhaps often impossible, to tell just how theory and research have affected, for example, approaches to and attempted solutions of social problems. Has it been research that has affected the thinking of many individuals on prejudice, for instance, or has it been a general change in social conditions that affected the thinking? Or was it both? I believe it was both—plus other factors. If research does have an effect, how does it have the effect? A major part of the difficulty in answering such questions is not just their complexity. It is also because the research that may have an effect was not usually done specifically to have the effect. It was done, to repeat perhaps tediously, to increase understanding of phenomena that happen to be related to the social problems.

Consider a social problem of enormous magnitude: equality of the black American. I label the problem this way because the related problems of race relations, prejudice, discrimination, and segregation can be subsumed under equality, since if black Americans had complete equality with white Americans then most of the other problems would in time probably disappear. There can be little doubt that considerable, even great, progress has been made in improving the condition of the American black. It is unnecessary to catalogue the laws passed and the changing statistics of jobs, residence, and acceptance. Few Americans will deny that black men, women, and children should have equal rights and equal opportunity under the law. (See the earlier discussion of Campbell's research.) Another sign of important social change is the disuse of derogatory and stereotyped language. In the early 1900s, derogatory words and expressions were commonly used to describe blacks—and one hardly thought it was wrong to do so. While such language is still used today, its use has greatly diminished. These are big changes. What has research had to do with these and other salutary changes in thinking and practice? No one knows for sure. There are no Comroe and Dripps studies. So what follows is necessarily speculation, though, it is hoped, informed speculation.

Sociological and psychological thinking and writing on race and prejudice made headway early in the century. Actual research in the sense of controlled inquiry really began to thrive in the third, fourth, and fifth decades of the century. Classic investigations into one of the foundations of prejudice, stereotypes, had significant impact on psychologists and sociologists (for example, Katz & Braly, 1935).[7] Many other studies on stereotypes and other aspects of prejudice were done, and the subject has been analyzed theoretically (for example, Krech & Crutchfield, 1948). Behavioral scientists have wanted to understand the phenomenon, as well as to contribute to its solution.

I have deliberately chosen a phenomenon whose investigation has had mixed motives. Because it has repeatedly been said that the purpose of science is theory, or understanding, this does not mean that theorists and researchers have only a pure desire for knowledge. Indeed, many researchers working in the general area of prejudice seemed to have had strong social motives based on egalitarian ideology. Nevertheless, progress in understanding prejudice—and today prejudice is rather well understood, though, as usual, much is not understood—has come from scientific research into the phenomenon and related phenomena. We turn now to a highly interesting, important, and influential set of investigations whose initial aim was to study and understand prejudice, but whose execution went considerably beyond prejudice. Although we examined aspects of these investigations earlier, their importance and their singular appropriateness for the problem of research and practice warrants repetition.

The influence of a remarkable book published in 1950, *The Authoritarian Personality* (Adorno et al., 1950), is still felt today. The ambitious aim of the research it reported was to study, understand, and explain prejudice. The researchers were men and women who were also dedicated to the amelioration of prejudice in modern society. Indeed, it is doubtful that the study would have been done had the researchers not had this motivation. On the very first page of the book, Horkheimer and Flowerman, the directors of the Department of Scientific Research of the American Jewish Committee, which sponsored the study, ask a number of disturbing questions stimulated by the persecution and extermination of millions of human beings by other human beings:

> How could it be . . . that in a culture of law, order, and reason, there could have survived the irrational remnants of ancient racial and religious hatreds? How . . . explain the willingness of great masses of people to tolerate the mass extermination of fellow citizens? What tissues in the life of our modern society remain cancerous, and despite our assumed enlightenment show the incongruous atavism of ancient peoples? (p. v)

These are profound questions. That they should have been asked as questions to be answered by empirical inquiry, in part at least, is one of

---

[7] A book by Simpson and Yinger (1965) discusses stereotypes and other aspects of prejudice. The literature is very large, and Simpson and Yinger ably summarize a good deal of it.

the most remarkable aspects of this research. Horkheimer and Flowerman say:

> But an aroused conscience is not enough if it does not stimulate a systematic search for an answer. Mankind has paid too dearly for its naive faith in the automatic effect of the mere passage of time; incantations have really never dispelled storms, disasters, pestilence, disease, or other evils . . . (p. v)

We are now not so concerned with the substance, methodology, and findings of the study as we are with its mixed motivation and how it may have affected practice. The researchers, deeply concerned over prejudice and its vicious accompaniments, wanted to contribute to the quest for practical answers for eradicating prejudice. After all, the study was initiated and financed by the American Jewish Committee, one of whose main tasks it was to combat anti-Semitism. They knew, however, that they had to understand it to combat it. "Our aim is not merely to describe prejudice but to explain it in order to help in its eradication" (p. vii).

Through a combination of research approaches, the researchers came to several important conclusions. One of these was that prejudice is a broad general phenomenon that is part of the personalities of individuals. This personality they called the "authoritarian personality" because they found, among other things, that the "authoritarian personality" possessed a syndrome of characteristics that predisposed the individuals who possessed it to be hostile toward groups other than their own.

A second conclusion was that prejudice tends to be generalized. The person who is prejudiced against one group is likely to be prejudiced against other groups. This conclusion, like the other conclusions of Adorno and his colleagues, has been supported in other research. The individual who doesn't like Jews is likely not to like blacks, foreigners, and so on. Notice that this explains much human social behavior, but especially that involving intergroup contact. It also means that, to understand anti-Semitism, one must also understand prejudice against other minority groups.

A third conclusion—the last one we will consider—is related to the first summarized above: political, religious, and other social attitudes are related to authoritarianism. That is, the authoritarian personality not only tends to be prejudiced against other groups than his own; he also has identifiable and predictable attitudes toward social issues. The general term that embraces these attitudes is "conservatism," but the authors carefully point out that they mean "pseudoconservatism," by which they seem to mean reactionary conservatism. There is no doubt, however, of the positive correlation between measured authoritarianism and measured conservatism.[8]

[8] An unfortunate outcome of this and other similar research is a tendency for some liberals to consider conservative ideology as somehow immature and evil. Such a view can be as dogmatic and prejudiced as the views of authoritarians toward Jews and blacks. Rokeach (1960) has correctly pointed out that dogmatism and authoritarianism can be of the left as well as of the right.

Prejudice is obviously highly complex, and understanding it not easy. Adorno et al. found that anti-Semitism is really part of a larger syndrome that can be called ethnocentism: it is characterized by group members being centered in their own group, belief in that group's value and rightness, and by negative attitudes toward other groups. They further found that ethnocentrism is itself part of another phenomenon called authoritarianism, and that authoritarianism describes a certain set of personality traits. Their emphasis was strongly psychological in the sense that they located ethnocentrism and authoritarianism in the individual. They were probably correct, but it is likely that both are affected by social forces and variables outside individuals. Nevertheless, *The Authoritarian Personality* is a major achievement of behavioral science and research, a distinct and important contribution to understanding prejudice, authoritarianism, and ideology, and the relations between personality and ideology.

Virtually all of this research was basic research. Its stated goal was to understand and explain prejudice, even though the researchers and their sponsors had deep convictions about the evils of prejudice and strong desires to eradicate it. No one can say for sure, of course, whether it has had any real effect on prejudice itself. I think that it probably has had such influence because, in increasing understanding of prejudice, it has given intellectual leaders and a generation of students a basis for understanding how to deal with prejudice. It has probably also helped to create a stronger sense of the necessity of egalitarianism in many more people. From the vantage point of this chapter, *The Authoritarian Personality's* authors showed not only research skill, insight, and acumen; they displayed wisdom when they chose to do basic research. A set of applied studies may have led nowhere because they would have been likely to miss the deeper relations that the authors found.[9]

A FINAL WORD: SCIENTIFIC VALUES

One of the most significant things about science is its system of values. When a scientific research tradition is strong in an institution or a society, an open atmosphere of critical inquiry is fostered. With such an atmosphere, all questions and statements that are potentially "testable" are considered open questions subject to scientific scrutiny and investigation. All other questions and statements are of no scientific interest. Questions that are in general empirically untestable may have value, but they are not relevant to science simply because they are untestable. Examples of such questions were given in Chapter 1 and elsewhere in the book. In short, two of the values of science are open and critical inquiry and insistence on

[9] There has been, as one might suspect, much criticism of and controversy about *The Authoritarian Personality*. The following references may be useful to the interested reader: Christie and Jahoda (1954) and Kirscht and Dillehay (1967).

working with questions that are empirically approachable. With all questions, however, science and scientists are always skeptical.

A third value of science is faith in science itself combined with the skepticism mentioned above. Scientists believe that with appropriate conditions and methodology limited understanding of most natural phenomena can be attained. While absolute knowledge and understanding are forever beyond reach, limited probabilistic knowledge and understanding are within reach. This faith is especially important for behavioral scientists because many people doubt that the methods of science can be used to study human behavior. For example, it is said that no one can ever know the real nature of human intelligence because it is not directly observable and thus not measurable. Similarly, human motivation is forever beyond reach, since important human motives also cannot be observed, and inferring motivation from behavior is always deceptive, even illusory. While recognizing the great difficulty of inferring intelligence, motivation, and similar phenomena, scientists maintain the faith that it can be done. The faith seems to have been justified: substantial progress has been made in the scientific study not only of intelligence and motivation but of many other "unobservable" phenomena. (Of course, many of the variables of physics and other "hard" sciences are also "unobservable.")

Fourth, science and scientists have to be completely honest—and they usually are. This has nothing to do with personal morality. The personal morality of scientists is probably no better or no worse than that of other people. Within the scientific system, however, the scientist *must* be completely honest because the system demands it. Indeed, one of its foundations is a "high morality." It is as though there were the commandments: Thou shalt not fake and thou shalt not fudge. To be sure, there have been cases of faking and fudging, and even the most scrupulous scientist may unconsciously fudge. But if dishonesty in doing and reporting research, conscious or unconscious, were to become widespread the scientific enterprise would break down.

The analogy to objectivity as a basic criterion of scientific methodology is close. Without objectivity there can be no science, as explained earlier. Similarly, without *complete* honesty, no science. There are no compromises, no in-betweens, as there are in politics and business. The ethic of science is absolute. That the ethic is observed by most scientists is shown by the shock that greets cases of cheating that have been exposed. It is also shown by the fate of the scientific cheat: he loses his status as a scientist. The case of Sir Cyril Burt, who was one of England's most distinguished and respected psychologists, may be a case in point. It has been alleged that careful scrutiny of the evidence he presented to support notions of the heredity of intelligence indicates that he must either have falsified his data or made them up. This is not the place to argue the case. The point is that a shock went through the Western behavioral scientific world. Any scientist falsifying results for whatever reason causes shock. But Burt even more so because of his status and the respect in which he was held. The question is still not settled. There are those who are convinced that Burt did what was alleged and was thus dishonest. But there are also those who do not believe it. It is unlikely that the issue will ever be completely resolved because Burt is no longer here to be questioned and because the evidence seems to be equivocal.

Another important problem that is related to the values of science and that has contributed to misunderstanding of science and research is the presumed conflict between science and the humanities. It is thought that science misses some or most of the important aspects of human experience. It is thought, for example, that the essence of music and poetry is beyond science, and that, indeed, science misses the most important of human experiences. Aesthetic and spiritual matters, among other things, elude science and scientists.

It would be nice to give an eloquent and romantic answer to such arguments. But no real answer is possible. First, the "facts" are correct: science has nothing to do with music and poetry, and science *does* miss many aspects of human experience. But that is true of any human activity. Does music somehow embrace all humanity? Literature? Painting? If there is any satisfactory answer it is that science, on the one hand, and music, art, literature, mystical experience, and so on, on the other hand, are just different. They cannot be compared in the usual sense of the word. Does one say that flowers are better than coffee?—unless, of course, one is pursuing the bizarre or comparing some single quality of each, like smell or color.

Second, to suppose a conflict between science and the humanities lacks meaning and sense. The two are simply different; they have different purposes. It is absurd to expect science to have the purpose of aesthetic satisfaction (except, maybe, to the scientist), just as it is absurd to expect science and research to solve social problems. Science is for achieving understanding. It is not for enhancing life, aesthetic experience, or the existential being of the individual. The conflict or polarity between science and the humanities, then, is a psychological conflict: it is in the minds of men and women and does not inhere in the "opposed" nature of science and the humanities. For two things to be opposed implies that there is something common between them. Science and the humanities are both human intellectual activities. But there it seems to end. Virtually nothing else is common to them. So how can they be opposed? An understanding of science requires understanding that its nature and purpose are quite different from other human activities. This means that it is not in opposition to anything, although its effect is to open up areas of human activity usually kept closed to critical and skeptical scrutiny.

We ask two final difficult questions: Has the influence of science been good or bad? If one means by "good" physical comfort and conveniences, and one grants that much or most modern technology developed from scientific knowledge, then one must answer Yes, science has been a good influence, people are better off physically than they were in the nineteenth century. If one asks questions about the quality of life that science may have enhanced or not enhanced, the answer is much more complex and ambiguous. We limit ourselves here, then, to behavioral science and behavioral research.

Contrary to what many believe, behavioral science and research have contributed a great deal in the area in which they should be judged: knowledge and understanding of human behavior. Before going further, however, let us acknowledge that any contribution is always partial, perhaps, even, only a small part of all possible contributions. It is highly doubtful that complete scientific understanding of human behavior will ever emerge. There will probably always be murky and unknown areas and aspects of economics, sociology, psychology, anthropology, and so on. Economic depressions will probably never be wholly understood, if for no other reason than that social situations constantly change and so, therefore, do economic situations. Even new phenomena and variables emerge. Complete knowledge of human motivation and human abilities will continue to elude our grasp. The complexities of social institutions and social movements are also unlikely ever to be completely understood.

One of the expectations of science held by many people is that, given enough time, maturity, and work, research will ultimately yield complete knowledge and understanding of phenomena. This expectation is misguided and unfortunate. Science and research will never yield complete knowledge and complete answers to questions. To hold this expectation is to misunderstand science and research. This is not, however, a counsel of despair. It does not mean that because complete answers cannot be given the scientific enterprise is worthless. Far from it.

A more realistic and accurate way to look at science is to conceive it as a powerful means to reduce ignorance. Take intelligence again. In 1850, say, there was no scientific evidence on the nature of intelligence. What was "known" was the result of shrewd or not so shrewd, wise or not so wise, observation and deduction. Systematic controlled investigation into intelligence was not done. In short, the state of ignorance, if not complete, was almost complete. In the 1970s, however, a great deal is known about human intelligence. There is a great deal more that is unknown, of course, but this does not mean that we know almost nothing about it. We know, for example, that human intelligence is a product of both heredity and environment. We know that it is not a single unitary thing, meaning, for instance, that a person of high intelligence is highly intelligent in all areas. Rather, it is a multifaceted function that evidently has as many manifestations as people. Certain factors, or kinds of intelligence, are now well established and well known: verbal, numerical, spatial, and so on. There is even evidence, though not as yet firm evidence, that there may be not just 6 or 7 factors of intelligence but more than 20 or 30.

One of the great scientific and technical achievements of the century, then, is the measurement of intelligence. It can be measured with high reliability and commendable validity. There are doubters, naturally. One of the causes of doubt is the suspicion that what is being measured is not the real essence of intelligence. Perhaps not. But, then, the "real essence" of intelligence will never be measured. This in no way detracts from the theoretical and practical magnitude of the achievement. Virtually complete ignorance has been cut down to what can be called partial ignorance.

Thanks to the work of social scientists, we know that social class has a pervasive influence on intelligence, achievement, and occupation. We know a good deal about the role race plays in the home, in the school, and at work. We know a good deal about how economic systems work—not enough to prevent depressions and check inflation but a great deal, nonetheless. Sociologists and economists have successfully cut down social and economic ignorance. They have also helped to dispel false beliefs and misleading mythologies about society and its working.

Some years ago, Deutsch, Platt, and Senghaas (1971) published a study of advances in the social sciences and where the advances came from. They listed 62 advances made during the period 1900–1965 that influenced research and practice. Omitting those contributions that are not scientific, we are still left with a formidable list of achievements: the sociology of bureaucracy, culture, and values, learning theory and research, intelligence tests, authoritarianism studies, attitude and opinion research, and many methodological advances, like factor analysis, content analysis, operational definitions, statistical analysis, computers, multivariate analysis, and so on. The authors say,

> Together these advances add up to unmistakable evidence of the cumulative growth of knowledge in the social sciences in the course of the century. Today, statements such as "we know no more about human psychology and politics than Aristotle did" mainly express the ignorance of those who utter them (p. 455).[10]

In sum, the contributions of behavioral science and research have been impressive in cutting down ignorance. Advances have not been as spectacular as in physics, chemistry, and biology, but considering their relative youth and great complexity, they are very impressive indeed. Our understanding of the physical world and our bodies has been enormously advanced due to science. Our understanding of ourselves and our environment, while of course not enormous, has been and is an outstanding achievement in cutting down our virtually complete ignorance of one hundred years ago.

[10] One can quarrel with the list of 62 advances in social science. For instance, a number of the advances were not science at all: Lenin's theory of one-party organization and revolution, psychoanalysis and depth psychology, national income accounting, and so on. Moreover, certain significant advances were omitted. The list is, nevertheless, still impressive and incontestable as evidence of achievement.

True, we may not know very well how to cope with depressions, inflations, unemployment, terrorism, racial and religious prejudice, and massive intellectual deprivation. We do know, however, some of the causes of these phenomena and the relations among them. We are beginning to understand them scientifically. While this does not mean ultimate solution of the problems—again, that is not the purpose of scientific research—it at least means cutting down the massive ignorance that pervades these and similar psychological and social problems. It means some measure of understanding, understanding that may provide us with the reasons, if not the remedies, for our unhappiness and our happiness, for our failures and our successes.

Types of research, observational methods, and statistical significance testing

Since the basic purpose of this book is to convey conceptual understanding of scientific behavioral research, a number of aspects and topics ordinarily important to more complete coverage of the subject were omitted. Whereas such a general conceptual approach may be valuable in aiding understanding of scientific research and its rationale, approach, and methods, a risk is run that omission of certain topics, like statistical calculations and analysis and different kinds of research, may lead to a somewhat distorted, even narrow, notion of what research is about. The purpose of this appendix is to fill in some of the gaps that were left in the text, even though superficially. The specific function of the appendix, then, is not to teach or even explain these omissions but simply to define and characterize them briefly. This will be done by considering three main areas or categories important to a more complete understanding of research and not discussed in the body of the book, or only mentioned in passing: types of research, methods of observation and data collection, and the testing of statistical significance.

TYPES OF RESEARCH

In the text, one major kind of research dominated the discussion: research in which relations between independent and dependent variables were studied. This is, of course, the most important kind of research and the ultimate goal of almost all scientific research: research to test hypothesized relations among variables. There are, however, several other kinds of research that are important. We examine two of them briefly.

Historical Inquiry

Historical research, or inquiry, is critical investigation of events, developments, and experiences of the past, careful weighing of evidence of the validity of sources of information on the past, and the interpretation of the evidence. The historical method, or *historiography,* differs from other scholarly inquiry mainly in its elusive subject matter, the past, and the difficult interpretative task imposed by the elusive nature of history. Although historical research is not scientific research—recall the earlier discussion of its idiographic nature—it is extremely important and valuable in behavioral research because the origins and roots of behavioral disciplines have to be understood if contemporary theories and research are to be understood.

But historical research is important in its own right. Its emphasis on primary and secondary sources, for instance, is a valuable contribution to behavioral research in general. A *primary source* is the original repository of an historical datum, like an eyewitness account of an event, a photograph, minutes of meetings, and an original record kept of an event. A *secondary source* is an account or source of information one or more steps removed from the original source, for example, a newspaper story about a meeting of Congress rather than the original Congressional record, or an account by another historian. In behavioral research an original research report is primary, but a textbook account of the research is secondary. A basic rule of historiography is: Use primary sources. To use secondary sources when primary sources are available is a major error in history—and in behavioral research. The reason is obvious: things get distorted in the telling.

Other canons of historiography are also important, but we leave the subject to other sources (see Borrowman, 1960, and Social Science Research Council, 1946). A significant point needs to be made, however. The rise of scientific research in the behavioral sciences in the twentieth century has had the effect of subordinating historical inquiry to a lesser position than it deserves in behavioral inquiry. All behavioral research has a past and traditions. Behavioral scientists developing theory, for instance, need to know the origins of the theory they are developing. They need the perspective of earlier roots and developments to feed their own work. They need a healthy respect for primary sources and for what historians call external and internal criticism. Science is not only theory-making and hypothesis-testing. It is also the weighing and assessing of past trends and nonquantitative evidence.

Methodological Research

Methodological research, already mentioned in Chapter 16, is a significant and important part of all scientific activity. It is the controlled investigation of the theoretical and applied aspects of mathematics, statistics, measurement, and ways of obtaining and analyzing data. The scientist or nonscientist who dismisses methodology using the expression "mere methodology" is expressing a curious understanding of science. Some of the most competent and imaginative individuals in modern psychology, sociology, and education have been and are methodologists. Moreover, it is almost impossible to do outstanding research without being something of a methodologist. So the "mere methodology" point of view is misleading.

Perhaps the largest area of methodological research is in measurement and statistics, or the combination called psychometrics. The methodologist is here preoccupied with the theory and practice of measurement instruments. Problems of scale construction and types of items and of reliability and validity require much attention. Measurement is an area in which social scientists have to be knowledgeable because almost all research needs some kind of measurement. If appropriate instruments already exist, researchers have to be able to appraise them. If they do not exist, they have to be able to construct them.

Statistics has always required the attention of methodologists. It is hard to conceive of modern behavioral research without statistics—no, it is impossible. The probabilistic approach to knowledge is so deeply ingrained that research without statistics simply cannot be conceived. As said in earlier chapters, psychological measurement and statistics are two of the great intellectual achievements of the century. The invention of analysis of variance and the development of factor analysis are two of the outstanding achievements of our times. Methodological research can indeed be important.

One more example to emphasize the point. Aspects of survey research, especially sampling and interviewing, have been areas of intensive and extensive methodological study. How can we best obtain a representative sample of a modern country? What are the relative merits of different kinds of sampling? What is the best kind of interview question? How should interviewers ask questions? The problems suggested by these and other methodological questions have been intensively investigated, and we now have an extensive body of reliable technical information to guide research practice.

METHODS OF OBSERVATION AND DATA COLLECTION

An integral part of the work of the scientist is making observations and collecting data. Making observations and collecting data must be done with great care so that researchers have assurance that the relations they are studying are not "contaminated" by variables other than the ones under study. In any case, there are a large number of methods of observation, some of which have been mentioned earlier. We now briefly characterize three of the most-used methods.

Observation is a general term meaning any sort of datum obtained by noting events, counting them, measuring them, recording them. Methods of observation are systematic and standard procedures for obtaining data. Almost all methods have the technical purpose of enabling the researcher to obtain measures of variables. The major purpose of "making observations," then, is to measure variables. In science, making observations means more than just looking at things. It also means any devices used to measure variables.

Interviewing

There are two general ways to get information from people. One way is to ask them questions. This is quite direct. The second way is to have individuals respond to some sort of structured stimuli, as discussed and illustrated in Chapter 9. This way is more indirect. Examples of direct questions are: Are you married? Do you think that your marriage is a success? What do you think of the proposed law to lift restrictions on abortion? Why do you think that? The respondent then answers the questions. He or she supplies the responses which yield information that can be converted into variable form. Such questions are used in interviews. A set of such questions is incorporated into an interview schedule. Trained interviewers then use the schedule and obtain responses from (usually) preselected respondents.

Interviewing is time-consuming and expensive. It is sometimes the only way to obtain the information necessary to a research study. And it has certain advantages that other methods do not have. For example, the interviewer can, after asking a general question, probe for reasons for given responses. One of the great advantages of interviewing, then, is depth. Researchers can go below the surface of responses, determining reasons, motives, and attitudes.

As indicated in Chapter 16, the construction of interview schedules and interviewing are high art and engineering. In competent hands, they are powerful tools for making observations. Used routinely in survey research, they are also useful in other kinds of research in which it might be difficult or impossible to use other methods.

Objective Tests and Scales

It was just said that the second general way to get information from people is to have them respond to structured stimuli. In most behavioral research the structured stimuli are objective tests and scales, which are used far more than anything else to make observations. In previous chapters, examples of such tests and scales were mentioned, and in Chapter 2 they were defined. We repeat the definitions. A *test* is a systematic procedure in which individuals being tested are presented with a set of constructed stimuli, called *items*, to which they respond in one way or another. These responses enable the researcher to assign individuals scores, which presumably indicate the degree to which the individuals possess the attribute being measured, or the degree to which they "know" whatever is being tested.

A *scale* is like a test in that it has items each of which are supposed to measure whatever is being measured. Scales, however, lack the competitive flavor of tests. They are so constructed that different numbers can be assigned to different individuals to indicate different amounts of the property or attribute being measured. Examples were given in the text. Recall, for instance, that the well-known F Scale measures authoritarianism. Recall, too, the referent scales designed to measure conservatism and liberalism. Literally hundreds of scales have been constructed and used in behavioral research: to measure attitudes, values, rigidity, prejudice, interests, introversion-extroversion, and so on.

Observation of Behavior

Another way to categorize methods of observation is as asking and watching. In essence, interviews and tests and scales ask people for information, usually about themselves. They differ in directness: the interview is more direct than tests and scales. In contrast to asking, we can observe people's behavior directly. The purpose is the same: to obtain measures of variables. Suppose we wish to measure cooperativeness in small groups. After defining cooperative behavior, we watch a group in some systematic way, say at randomly chosen periods for 10 minutes each time, and note acts of cooperative behavior. It may seem strange, but direct observations of behavior have not been used too much in behavioral research. One reason is the great difficulty of the method. To observe behavior is not nearly as simple as it sounds. Let us look at a part of the problem more closely.

Many people think that it would be better in the behavioral sciences to observe behavior directly. After all, people don't always say what they think. How can one trust interviews and tests and scales? In responding to attitude or motivation scales, for instance, people won't give valid responses. (This is not true, by the way.) So it would be better to watch their behavior. Actions speak louder than words! Not only is this argument naive; it also misses the difficulties involved in observing behavior. We do not wish to go into technical problems, but one significant difficulty with observations of behavior can be mentioned: the observer-inference problem.

This problem arises from the quite different inferences that can be made observing the same behavior. A child may be scored by one observer "aggressive" if he hits another child. Another observer may score the same behavior "playful." Similarly, observers can differ on variables like cohesiveness, friendliness, dominance, and so on. On the other hand, human observers have a strength that observer machines, if they were possible, do not have. Human observers can relate the behavior they are observing to the variables of a study—and can ignore other behaviors. They can attend to and observe one variable and one variable only—or, of course, two or three. Moreover, the agreement or lack of agreement between observers can be ascertained. Competent observers and well-made observations of behavior can help bridge the difficult gap between construct and behavior by knowing clearly what behavior reflects what construct, at least for the purpose of the study at hand.

There are other methods of observation, data collection, and analysis too numerous and complex to describe in this appendix: sociometry, Q methodology, projective methods, content analysis, and so on. The researcher in the behavioral sciences needs to know and understand these methods. They all have different purposes and special characteristics that make them suitable for obtaining certain kinds of data. For the nonresearcher, there is less need to study them. The main things to know are the broader aspects of data collection as described above. The reader interested in pursuing such methods further can consult one or more texts on the subject (Festinger & Katz, 1953; Kerlinger, 1973; Lindzey & Aronson, 1968).

STATISTICS AND ANALYSIS

One or two readers of the first manuscript of this book complained because it contained little instruction in statistics. It still contains little such instruction because of the purpose of the book—which is not to teach statistics. Nevertheless, the ubiquitous nature of statistics and its vital importance in analyzing data require more than cavalier dismissal. The subject has been far from neglected. The conceptual bases of analysis, studying relations, and testing hypotheses were given in Chapters 4, 5, 6, and occasionally elsewhere. Frequency analysis was discussed in Chapter 10. Correlation, regression, and multivariate approaches were taken up in Chapters 11, 12, and 13. A descriptive analysis and overview of statistics were not systematically discussed, however. We do so now, but in a limited way. The purpose is not to teach statistics; it is to deepen insight into behavioral research in general. We precede discussion of statistics with consideration of the nature of analysis.

Analysis is the categorizing, ordering, manipulating, and summarizing of data. Its purpose is to reduce large quantities of raw data to manageable and interpretable form so that characteristics of situations, events, and people can be succinctly described and the relations among variables studied and interpreted. Statistics, of course, is part of analysis. It was defined earlier, but we characterize it again for clarity. *Statistics* is the theory and method of analyzing data obtained from samples of observations in order to describe populations, to study and compare sources of variance, to help make decisions to accept or reject relations among phenomena, and to aid in making reliable inferences from empirical observations (Kerlinger, 1973, p. 185). We consider only how to assess statistical significance in three varied and commonly used research situations.

Statistical Significance: The *t* Test

The first and perhaps most frequent function of statistics is to test obtained results, which are expressed as statistics of one kind or another—means, differences between means, variances, correlation coefficients, and so forth—for statistical significance. As explained in Chapter 5, this means testing a statistical result for its departure from chance expectation. If such a result departs sufficiently from chance expectation, it is said to be "statistically significant."

The basic idea was illustrated earlier mainly by using means. In Table 5.1, for example, the means of 10 sets of random numbers were "checked" against the total mean. Since the numbers were random, the means of the 10 sets should not depart too much from the mean of all 100 numbers. In Table 5.2, five sets of quasi-random means of two groups and the differences between them were presented. The differences varied from −1.15 to +2.15, essentially random fluctuations. The actual experimental and control group means of the Clark and Walberg study were also given. The difference between them was +4.76, considerably greater than the random differences. Other similar examples of the principle of comparing obtained results with random expectations were also given in Chapter 5.

Statisticians invent statistical tests and then incorporate what are essentially random results—or the limits of random results—in tables for convenient reference. Each statistical test has a name and a specific purpose. Let us look at three such tests, one for continuous measures, the *t* test applied to differences between means; one for frequencies (or counting), chi square; and a third, again a *t* test, for correlation coefficients. In Chapter 14, actually, we looked at the *t* test and the Clark and Walberg results, but somewhat superficially. We now take the same example in more detail and depth. The Clark and Walberg experimental and control group means were 31.62 and 26.86. Does this 4.76 difference differ enough from chance to warrant calling it a statistically significant difference?

Instead of having gigantic tables of random means, on the model of Tables 5.2 and 5.3, statisticians work out formulas for tests of statistical significance. There is a formula for *t*. (Actually, there are several formulas for *t*, depending on what sort of test is being made.) In our case, the difference between two means is given in the numerator of the formula and a measure of the variability of random differences between means in the

TABLE A.1   Selected Values from a *t* Table

p^a	.05	.01
df^b		
10	1.81	2.76
15	1.75	2.60
25	1.71	2.49
30	1.70	2.46
.	.	.
.	.	.
108	1.66	2.36

[a] *p*: probability; .05 and .01: .05 and .01 levels of significance.
[b] *df* = total number of cases minus 2, or N − 2.

denominator, or:

$$t = \frac{\text{Mean 1} - \text{Mean 2}}{\text{Variability of Random Means}}$$

Such formulas have been neatly characterized as information versus error (Diamond, 1959). The information, in this case the difference between two means, is in the numerator. The error is in the denominator. The result is then checked against a so-called *t* table (given in any statistics text). The entries of a *t* table are *t* ratios, as above, and these *t* ratios are given for group samples of different numbers of cases in the samples and for different levels of significance (probabilities). A small part of a *t* table is given in Table A.1.

p in the table means "probability," and *df* means degrees of freedom, which need not be explained. In this case, *df* is equal to the total number of cases minus 2, or N − 2. In the Clark and Walberg study, there were 110 children; so $df = N - 2 = 110 - 2 = 108$. Two *p* or probability levels are given, .05 and .01. These are two commonly used "levels of significance." The entry for $df = 108$, 1.66, means that if a *t* yielded by the *t* formula is 1.66 or greater, then the difference between the two means is statistically significant: the difference departs significantly from chance expectation at the .05 level; it is not a result that chance alone would be likely to yield.

The *t* of the Clark and Walberg study was 3.09.[1] Suppose we accept the .05 level as our criterion. This means that we are willing to accept a 5 percent risk of being wrong. Since the obtained *t*, calculated from the data of the two groups of children, was 3.09, and this is larger than the 1.66 in the table, the difference of 4.76 is statistically significant, which means that it is probably not a chance result. Remember that the tabled entries are chance results, so to speak. If the obtained *t* had been, say, 1.54, then we would be forced to say that the difference between the means of 4.76 was one of the many differences that could have happened by chance alone.

---

[1] I calculated this *t* from the published results. How this was done is not relevant here.

Therefore, it is a result that is not statistically significant. This means, in turn, that there was really no difference in reading achievement between the experimental and control groups that could be attributed to other than chance factors, thus implying that massive reinforcement had no appreciable effect on the achievement of the experimental group children.

If we wanted to be considerably more sure of the statistical significance of the 4.76 difference, we could have selected the .01 level value of 2.36. Then the difference of 4.76 is statistically significant at the .01 level, meaning that there is only one chance in 100 of obtaining so large a difference by chance alone. The same conclusion as in the preceding paragraph would follow, except that we should be considerably more sure that the result was statistically significant.[2]

Statistical Significance: The Chi Square Test

t tests and similar tests of statistical significance are used with continuous measures. (Continuous measures, roughly speaking, are on a continuous scale of measurement. For example, 1.0, 1.5, 1.7, 2.5, 4.8 imply continuous measures.) There are many research situations, however, in which only counting is done, for example, the number of Republican Congressmen who voted for a certain measure versus those who did not vote for it, the number of middle-class mothers who weaned their children early versus the number of working-class mothers who weaned their children early. This last example is from the Miller and Swanson study described in Chapters 1 and 10. Such data are frequency data as described in Chapter 10. How do we assess the statistical significance of frequency data?

In a highly interesting study by Whiting and Child (1953), psychoanalytic hypotheses were tested using data in the so-called Yale cross-cultural files (Murdock et al., 1950). In these extensive files, varied information on different cultures is stored. In the particular substudy we wish to examine, Whiting and Child selected 39 of the cultures or societies and extracted information from the recorded information to test the hypothesis that societies fostering oral anxiety in their socialization of children would explain illness orally. Using a content analysis procedure, they classified each society in two ways: whether it was high or low on oral anxiety and whether it used or did not use oral explanations for disease. The results are given in Table A.2. The entries in the table represent numbers of societies. For example, 17 of the total of 39 societies were high on oral anxiety and also used oral explanations of illness.

---

[2] The use of *t* and similar tables will perhaps become obsolete, as indicated in Chapter 14. Computers can calculate the probabilities of obtained *t*'s. Instead of assessing a result by whether it is equal to or greater than a tabled value, the computer will yield a "more exact" value. Such calculations can even be done on the small programmable calculators mentioned in Chapter 14. For example, I calculated the *p* value of the *t* of 3.09 on such a machine. The probability was .001, which means only about one chance in 1,000 of the difference of 4.76 occurring by chance. Obviously I need no *t* table.

TABLE A.2   Relation between Oral Anxiety and Oral
Explanation of Illness, Whiting and Child (1953)
Study[a]

	SOCIETIES WITH ORAL EXPLANATION	SOCIETIES WITHOUT ORAL EXPLANATION	
SOCIETIES HIGH ON ORAL ANXIETY	17 (11.79)	3 (8.21)	20
SOCIETIES LOW ON ORAL ANXIETY	6 (11.21)	13 (7.79)	19
	23	16	39

[a] Cell entries are frequencies. Entries in parentheses are expected frequencies calculated from marginal totals, for example, (20)(23)/39 = 11.79. χ^2 = 11.49, significant at the .01 level; C = .48. (See text for explanation of χ^2 and C.)

If we calculate proportions or percentages in the manner described in Chapter 10, we will see a strong relation. But percentages are not calculated, because such analysis is not our purpose here and because calculating percentages with so few cases can be misleading. We really want to test the frequencies in the table for departure from chance expectation. To do so, we calculate a statistic called chi square (χ^2). How this is done precisely is not our concern; it is the idea we want. The marginal totals (17 + 3 = 20, 17 + 6 = 23, and so on) and the total of 39 are used to calculate the frequencies of each cell expected by chance. The expected frequency of the first cell, for example, is: (20 × 23)/39 = 11.79. The expected frequencies have been inserted into the cells of Table A.2 in parentheses. The obtained frequency of each cell is compared to the expected frequency for that cell, in effect. The larger the discrepancies, the greater the departure from chance. These discrepancies for the four cells of the table are all 5.21.

If there were no relation between the two variables, then the obtained cell frequencies would be close to the expected frequencies. If, for example, the obtained frequencies had been those of Table A.3, then the differences between the obtained and expected frequencies would be smaller. These differences are 2.21 for each of the four cells of Table A.3. Compare these differences with the differences of 5.21 for Table A.2.

TABLE A.3   Crossbreak of Table A.2 with Fictitious
"Obtained" Frequencies Close to Chance
Expectation[a]

14 (11.79)	6 (8.21)	20
9 (11.21)	10 (7.79)	19
23	16	39

[a] See footnote to Table A.2. χ^2 = 2.06, C = .22.

Like the *t* ratio, chi square is easy to calculate. If we do so, we obtain, for the data of Table A.2, 11.49. This is checked at the .05 or .01 (or other) level of significance in a chi square table (to be found in any statistics text) at the appropriate degree of freedom, in this case *df* = 1. The tabled .05 entry is 3.84; the tabled .01 entry is 6.64. The same reasoning as that outlined for the *t* test is used: if the obtained chi square is equal to or exceeds the tabled entry, then the data are statistically significant, they depart sufficiently from chance expectation to warrant belief in the non-chance nature of the relation expressed by the data. The Whiting and Child hypothesis is supported: there is a significant relation between oral anxiety and oral explanation of illness.

A chi square calculation of the fictitious obtained frequencies of Table A.3 yields 2.06. This is less than the tabled .05 level entry of 3.84. Therefore the "obtained" frequencies do not depart significantly from chance expectation. That is, they could have arisen by chance, given the same marginal frequencies of Table A.2.[3] There is thus "no relation" between oral anxiety and oral explanation of illness. It is possible to calculate measures of the approximate magnitude of the relation in crossbreaks like those of Tables A.2 and A.3. One such commonly used measure is called the *coefficient of contingency*, or *C*. *C* for Table A.2 is .48, and for Table A.3 is .22. These *C* coefficients are only rough measures of the relations. They underestimate the magnitude of relations, for example. Nevertheless, they do give some idea of the relative magnitude of the relations in the two tables.

The Statistical Significance of Correlations

In principle any statistical result can be tested for significance. In practice it may sometimes be difficult to do so, but it is always theoretically possible. The basic principle of such testing is comparison of obtained results with results expected by chance. There are two general ways to do this. One way, associated with counting or enumerating the possibilities of events, was discussed and illustrated in Chapter 5. Such questions as: What is the probability of a seven in one roll of two dice? What is the probability of getting all hearts in a hand of bridge? What is the probability, in a random sample of 500 adult citizens of Geneva, Switzerland, of obtaining between 240 and 260 men, assuming that there are equal numbers of men and women in Geneva?

Answering such questions in principle requires counting or specifying all the possibilities, counting or specifying the number of times the event in question can occur, and then calculating the probability fraction. For example, the probability of getting a seven in one roll of two dice is $6/36 = 1/6 = .17$, because there are 36 possible combinations of two dice and six possible ways for a seven to turn up. Such questions can be com-

---

[3] The "actual" probabilities associated with the two chi squares, calculated with a small programmable calculator, are: for 11.49, $p = .0007$; for 2.06, $p = .1512$.

plicated and hard to answer. The question on the numbers of men and women in a sample of Geneva citizens, for instance, is not easy because enumerating all the possibilities is difficult. (When another readily available method is used, however, the problem becomes easier.)

The second general way of comparing obtained results with chance expectation is to set up random contingencies, so to speak, and to compare the obtained results to appropriate random contingencies. We did this with the *t* test and the chi square test. Certain formulas, like those for the *t* and *F* tests, express the idea nicely. Take the formula for the *t* test of the significance of the difference between two means. It is in a little different form than given earlier:

$$t = \frac{\overline{X}_1 - \overline{X}_2}{SE_{\overline{x}_1 - \overline{x}_2}}$$

where $\overline{X}_1$ and $\overline{X}_2$ are the means of groups 1 and 2, and $SE_{\overline{x}_1 - \overline{x}_2}$ is the so-called standard error of the differences between two means. A *standard error* is a measure of chance fluctuation. In this case it is the standard error of the difference between two means. It is an estimate of the variability of differences between means, the means having been calculated from sets of two groups of random numbers. For example, suppose we draw random numbers in sets of two, with, say, 20 numbers in each group. Then we calculate the means of each set and the differences between these means. We do this a large number of times and then calculate the variability (the standard errors) of the differences. This standard error, then, is used to assess the magnitude of the obtained difference. If the obtained difference is "sufficiently larger" than the standard error, then the *t* ratio is "large" and it is considered statistically significant.

This general approach is used a great deal in the behavioral sciences. We now illustrate it with the assessment of the statistical significance of correlation coefficients. The reasoning and the method are similar. The formulas for the standard error, of course, are different. The formula for assessing the statistical significance of a correlation coefficient is:

$$t = \frac{r}{SE_r}$$

How to calculate SE_r, the standard error of r, does not concern us. The main thing to note is that we again have a *t* test, and the form of the formula is the same as that for the formula for the significance of the difference between two means: information (in the numerator) versus error (in the denominator).

Suppose we are interested in understanding attitudes toward women, and, in line with an example given in an earlier chapter, we believe that social beliefs are systematically related, and that belief in equality for women is positively related to beliefs in sexual freedom and legalized abortion. That is, individuals who believe there should be considerable sexual freedom for both sexes and that abortion should be legalized and should be done when women want it also believe in equality for women. Suppose, further, that scales have been constructed to measure, on the one hand, attitudes toward sexual freedom and legalized abortion and, on the other hand, equality of women, both scales have been administered to 20 men, and the coefficient of correlation between the two scales is .30.

Does this r of .30 support our belief that there is a positive correlation between the two sets of beliefs? As with all other statistics, we must ask whether this r is statistically significant. Or is it one of the many r's that could be calculated between sets of random numbers? If we calculate t for this r, we obtain $t = 1.33$. The tabled t at the .05 level for 18 degrees of freedom ($N - 2 = 20 - 2 = 18$), which, say, we earlier accepted as our criterion of significance, is 1.73. Our obtained t, however, is only 1.33. Since it is less than 1.73, we realize that our correlation coefficient of .30 is not statistically significant. Therefore we conclude that there is little or "no" relation between our sets of beliefs.

Suppose the obtained r had been .62 with 20 subjects who had responded to both scales. Is this statistically significant? Yes, it is. The t is then 3.35, which is greater than both the .05 and .01 entries in the t table (the .05 t is 1.73, as above, and the .01 t is 2.55). The r of .62 is therefore statistically significant, and we can then think about the magnitude of the r and its meaning. It means that there is a fairly substantial relation between the two sets of attitudes: individuals who believe in sexual freedom and legalized abortion also tend to believe in equality for women. In short, the statistical significance of a correlation coefficient is first established and then its magnitude assessed.

Note that the size of N, the sample size, affects the statistical significance of statistics. Suppose, for instance, that we had obtained an r of .30, but there were 30 subjects who responded to the two attitude instruments (instead of 20 subjects). Then $t = 1.664$. Although this is not significant according to the t table—the t-table entry at the .05 level for $df = 28$ is 1.701—it is almost significant. If we calculate the probability with a computer, as we did earlier, we find it to be $p = .054$, just slightly greater than .05. So this would be, although marginal, suggestive. We would not categorize it as clearly not significant. If we had 35 subjects and an r of .30, $t = 1.807$, which *is* significant at the .05 level. (The machine calculated probability is $p = .04$.)

There are, of course, many different kinds of tests of statistical significance. Most of them, no matter how complex their formulas, are based on the same relatively simple principle: the comparison of obtained results with results expected by chance. The reader should be aware, however, that statistical significance says little or nothing about the magnitude of a difference or of a relation. With a large number of subjects, say more than 200, most tests of significance show statistical significance even when a difference between means is quite small, perhaps trivial, or a correlation coefficient is very small and trivial. With 1,000 subjects, for example, an obtained r of only .06 is significant at the .05 level! As usual, there is no substitute for good judgment and experience. To use statistics adequately, one must understand the principles involved and be able to judge whether obtained results are statistically significant *and* whether they are meaningful in the particular research context. A correlation coefficient of .30 may be low, even trivial, with one research problem, and yet it may be substantial with another problem.

REFERENCES

Adorno, T. W., Frenkel-Brunswik, E., Levinson, D. J., & Sanford, R. N. *The authoritarian personality*. New York: Harper & Row, 1950.

American Psychological Association. *Standards for educational and psychological tests and manuals*. Washington, D.C.: American Psychological Association, 1966.

Aronson, E., & Gerard, E. Beyond Parkinson's law: The effect of excess time on subsequent performance. *Journal of Personality and Social Psychology*, 1966, 3, 336–339.

Aronson, E., & Mills, J. The effect of severity of initiation on liking for a group. *Journal of Abnormal and Social Psychology*, 1959, 59, 177–181.

Barker, R. G., Dembo, T., & Lewin, K. Frustration and regression. In R. G. Barker, J. S. Kounin, & H. F. Wright (Eds.), *Child behavior and development*. New York: McGraw-Hill, 1943.

Bennett, E. L., Diamond, M. C., Krech, D., & Rosenzweig, M. R. Chemical and anatomical plasticity of brain. *Science*, 1964, 146, 610–619.

Berelson, B., & Steiner, G. A. *Human behavior: An inventory of scientific findings*. New York: Harcourt, 1964.

Berkowitz, L. Anti-Semitism and the displacement of aggression. *Journal of Abnormal and Social Psychology*, 1959, 59, 182–187.

Berkowitz, L., & Walster, E. *Equity theory: Toward a general theory of social interaction*. New York: Academic Press, 1976.

Bock, R. D., & Bargmann, R. E. Analysis of covariance structures. *Psychometrika*, 1966, 31, 507–534.

Boneau, E. A. The effects of violations of assumptions underlying the t test. *Psychological Bulletin*, 1960, 57, 49–64.

Borrowman, M. History of education. In C. Harris (Ed.), *Encyclopedia of educational research* (3rd ed.). New York: Macmillan, 1960.

Brain, W. R. Science and antiscience. *Science*, 1965, 148, 192–198.

Braithwaite, R. B. *Scientific explanation*. Cambridge: Cambridge University Press, 1953.

Brier, A., & Robinson, I. *Computers and the social sciences*. London: Hutchinson, 1974.

Brooks, H. Can science survive in the modern age? *Science*, 1971, 174, 21–30.

Campbell, A. *White attitudes toward black people*. Ann Arbor, Mich.: Institute for Social Research, University of Michigan, 1971.

Campbell, D. T., & Stanley, J. C. *Experimental and quasi-experimental designs for research*. Chicago: Rand McNally, 1963.

Cantor, N., & Mischel, W. Traits as prototypes: Effects on recognition memory. *Journal of Personality and Social Psychology*, 1977, 35, 38–48.

Cattell, R. B. Theory of fluid and crystallized intelligence. *Journal of Educational Psychology*, 1963, 54, 1–22.

Christie, R., & Jahoda, M. (Eds.). *Studies in the scope and method of "The Authoritarian Personality."* New York: Free Press, 1954.

Citron, A., Chein, I., & Harding, J. Anti-minority remarks: A problem for action research. *Journal of Abnormal and Social Psychology*, 1950, 45, 99–126.

Clark, C. A., & Walberg, H. J. The influence of massive rewards on reading achievement in potential urban school dropouts. *American Educational Research Journal*, 1968, 5, 305–310.

320 Coleman, J. S., Campbell, E. Q., Hobson, C. J., McPartland, J., Mood, A. M.,

Weinfeld, F. D., & York, R. L. *Equality of educational opportunity*. Washington, D.C.: Government Printing Office, 1966.

Comroe, J. H., & Dripps, R. D. Scientific basis for the support of biomedical science. *Science*, 1976, 192, 105–111.

Cooley, W. W., & Lohnes, P. R. *Multivariate procedures for the behavioral sciences*. New York: Wiley, 1962.

Cooley, W. W., & Lohnes, P. R. *Multivariate data analysis*. New York: Wiley, 1971.

Cronbach, L. J., & Meehl, P. E. Construct validity in psychological tests. *Psychological Bulletin*, 1955, 52, 281–302.

Cutright, P. National political development: Measurement and analysis. *American Sociological Review*, 1963, 27, 229–245.

Deutsch, K. W., Platt, J., & Senghaas, D. Conditions favoring major advances in social science. *Science*, 1971, 171, 450–459.

Diamond, S. *Information and error*. New York: Basic Books, 1959.

Dollard, J., Doob, L. W., Miller, N. E., Mowrer, O. H., & Sears, R. R. *Frustration and aggression*. New Haven, Conn.: Yale University Press, 1939.

Dubos, R. Scientist and public. *Science*, 1961, 133, 1207–1211.

DuBridge, L. A. Science serves society. *Science*, 1969, 164, 1137–1140.

Duncan, O. D., Featherman, D. L., & Duncan, B. *Socioeconomic background and achievement*. New York: Seminar Press, 1972.

Edwards, A. L. *Statistical methods* (3rd ed.). New York: Holt, Rinehart and Winston, 1973.

Edwards, A. L. *Experimental design in psychological research* (4th ed.). New York: Holt, Rinehart and Winston, 1972.

Etzioni, A. *Modern organizations*. Englewood Cliffs, N.J.: Prentice-Hall, 1964.

Festinger, L. *A theory of cognitive dissonance*. Stanford, Calif.: Stanford University Press, 1957.

Festinger, L., & Katz, D. (Eds.). *Research methods in the behavioral sciences*. New York: Holt, Rinehart and Winston, 1953.

Flavell, J. H. *The developmental psychology of Jean Piaget*. Princeton, N.J.: Van Nostrand, 1963.

Frederiksen, N., Jensen, O., & Beaton, E. A. *Organizational climates and administrative performance*. Princeton, N.J.: Educational Testing Service, 1968.

Gates, A., & Taylor, G. An experimental study of the nature of improvement resulting from practice in a mental function. *Journal of Educational Psychology*, 1925, 16, 583–592.

Getzels, J. W., & Guba, E. G. Role, role conflict, and effectiveness. *American Sociological Review*, 1954, 19, 164–175.

Goldfarb, W. The effects of early institutional care on adolescent personality. *Journal of Experimental Education*, 1943, 12, 106–129.

Green, B. F. *Digital computers in research*. New York: McGraw-Hill, 1963.

Guilford, J. P. *Psychometric methods* (2nd ed.). New York: McGraw-Hill, 1954.

Guilford, J. P. The structure of intellect. *Psychological Bulletin*, 1956, 53, 267–293.

Guilford, J. P. Three faces of intellect. *American Psychologist*, 1959, 14, 469–479.

Guilford, J. P. *The nature of human intelligence*. New York: McGraw-Hill, 1967.

Guthrie, E. R. *The psychology of learning*. New York: Harper & Brothers, 1935.

Hartz, L. *The liberal tradition in America*. New York: Harcourt, 1955.

Harvey, J. H., Ickes, W. J., & Kidd, R. F. *New directions in attribution research* (Vol. 1). Hillsdale, N.J.: Lawrence Erlbaum Associates, 1976.

Harvey, J. H., & Kelley, H. H. Sense of own judgmental competence as a function of temporal pattern of stability-instability in judgment. *Journal of Personality and Social Psychology,* 1974, 29, 526–538.

Hays, W. L. *Statistics for the social sciences* (2nd ed.). New York: Holt, Rinehart and Winston, 1973.

Hilgard, E. R., Atkinson, R. C., & Atkinson, R. L. *Introduction to psychology* (6th ed.). New York: Harcourt, 1975.

Holtzman, W. H., & Brown, W. F. Evaluating the study habits and attitudes of high school students. *Journal of Educational Psychology,* 1968, 59, 404–409.

Howells, W. W. The importance of being human. In J. M. Tanur (Ed.), *Statistics: A guide to the unknown.* San Francisco: Holden-Day, 1972.

Hurlock, E. An evaluation of certain incentives used in schoolwork. *Journal of Educational Psychology,* 1925, 16, 145–159.

Husén, T. (Ed.). *International study of achievement in mathematics: A comparison of twelve countries* (Vols. I and II). New York: Wiley, 1967.

Hyman, H. H., Wright, C. R., & Reed, J. S. *The enduring effects of education.* Chicago: University of Chicago Press, 1975.

Jones, E. E., Kanouse, D. E., Kelley, H. H., Nisbett, R. E., Valins, S., & Weiner, B. *Attribution: Perceiving the causes of behavior.* Morristown, N.J.: General Learning Press, 1971.

Jones, E. E., Rock, L., Shaver, K. G., Goethals, G. R., & Ward, L. M. Pattern of performance and ability attribution: An unexpected primacy effect. *Journal of Personality and Social Psychology,* 1968, 10, 317–340.

Jöreskog, K. G. Analyzing psychological data by structural analysis of covariance matrices. In D. H. Krantz, R. C. Atkinson, R. D. Luce, & P. Suppes (Eds.), *Contemporary developments in mathematical psychology* (Vol. II): *Measurement, psychophysics, and information processing.* San Francisco: Freeman, 1974.

Jöreskog, K. G. Structural equation models in the social sciences: Specification, estimation and testing. Research report 76-9. Uppsala, Sweden: Uppsala University, 1976.

Katz, D., & Braly, K. W. Racial prejudice and racial stereotypes. *Journal of Abnormal and Social Psychology,* 1935, 30, 175–193.

Kemeny, J. G. *A philosopher looks at science.* Princeton, N.J.: Van Nostrand, 1959.

Kemeny, J. G., Snell, J. L., & Thompson, G. L. *Introduction to finite mathematics* (2nd ed.). Englewood Cliffs, N.J.: Prentice-Hall, 1966.

Kerlinger, F. N. Social attitudes and their criterial referents: A structural theory. *Psychological Review,* 1967, 74, 110–122.

Kerlinger, F. N. The structure and content of social attitude referents: A preliminary study. *Educational and Psychological Measurement,* 1972, 32, 613–630.

Kerlinger, F. N. The influence of research on educational practice. *Educational Researcher,* 1977, 6, 5–12.

Kerlinger, F. N. *Foundations of behavioral research* (2nd ed.). New York: Holt, Rinehart and Winston, 1973.

Kerlinger, F. N., & Pedhazur, E. J. *Multiple regression in behavioral research.* New York: Holt, Rinehart and Winston, 1973.

Kerlinger, F. N., Middendorp, C. P., & Amón, J. The structure of social attitudes in three countries: Tests of a criterial referent theory. *International Journal of Psychology,* 1976, 11, 265–279.

Kidd, C. V. Basic research—Description versus definition. *Science,* 1959, 129, 368–371.

Kirk, R. *The conservative mind* (Rev. ed.). Chicago: Henry Regnery, 1960.

Kirscht, J. P., & Dillehay, R. C. *Dimensions of authoritarianism: A review of research and theory*. Lexington, Ky.: University of Kentucky Press, 1967.

Krech, D., & Crutchfield, R. S. *Theory and problems of social psychology*. New York: McGraw-Hill, 1948.

Lee, R. S. Social attitudes and the computer revolution. *Public Opinion Quarterly*, 1970, 34, 53–59.

Likert, R., & Hayes, S. P. (Eds.). *Some applications of behavioral research*. Paris: UNESCO, 1957.

Lindsay, P. H., & Norman, D. A. *Human information processing: An introduction to psychology* (2nd ed.). New York: Academic Press, 1977.

Lindzey, G., & Aronson, E. (Eds.). *The handbook of social psychology* (Vol. 2). Reading, Mass.: Addison-Wesley, 1968.

Marjoribanks, K. Ethnic and environmental influences on mental abilities. *American Journal of Sociology*, 1972, 78, 323–337.

Markus, H. Self-schemata and processing information about the self. *Journal of Personality and Social Psychology*, 1977, 35, 63–78.

McClelland, D. C. *The achieving society*. Princeton, N.J.: Van Nostrand, 1961.

McClelland, D. C., Atkinson, J. W., Clark, R. A., & Lowell, E. L. *The achievement motive*. New York: Appleton, 1953.

McConnell, J. V., Jacobson, A. L., & Kimble, D. P. The effects of regeneration upon retention of conditioned response in the planarian. *Journal of Comparative and Physiological Psyhology*, 1959, 52, 1–5.

Milgram, S. *Obedience to authority*. New York: Harper & Row, 1974.

Miller, N. E. *Neal E. Miller: Selected papers*. Chicago: Aldine, 1971.

Miller, D. R., & Swanson, G. E. *Inner conflict and defense*. New York: Holt, Rinehart and Winston, 1960.

Morrow, J., & Smithson, B. Learning sets in an invertebrate. *Science*, 1969, 159, 850–851.

Murdock, G. et al. *Outlines of cultural materials* (3rd ed.). New Haven, Conn.: Human Relations Area Files, 1950.

Nagel, E. *The structure of science*. New York: Harcourt, 1961.

Nunnally, J. *Psychometric theory*. New York: McGraw-Hill, 1967.

Page, E. B. Teacher comments and student performance: A seventy-four classroom experiment in school motivation. *Journal of Educational Psychology*, 1958, 49, 173–181.

Parkinson, C. N. *Parkinson's law*. London: John Murray, 1957.

Platt, J. R. Strong inference. *Science*, 1964, 146, 347–353.

Report of the National Advisory Commission on Civil Disorders. Bantam Books, 1968.

Robinson, J. P., Rusk, J. G., & Head, K. B. *Measures of political attitudes*. Ann Arbor: Institute for Social Research, University of Michigan, 1968.

Robinson, J. P., & Shaver, P. R. *Measures of social psychological attitudes*. Ann Arbor: Institute for Social Research, University of Michigan, 1969.

Roe, A., & Siegelman, M. *The origin of interests*. Washington, D.C.: American Personnel and Guidance Association, 1964.

Rogers, C. R. Persons or science? A philosophical question. *American Psychologist*, 1955, 10, 267–278.

Rokeach, M. The nature and meaning of dogmatism. *Psychological Review*, 1954, 61, 194–204.

Rokeach, M. *The open and closed mind*. New York: Basic Books, 1960.

Rokeach, M. *Beliefs, attitudes, and values*. San Francisco: Jossey-Bass, 1968.

Rokeach, M. *The nature of human values*. New York: Free Press, 1973.

Rokeach, M., & Mezei, L. Race and belief as factors in social choice. *Science,* 1966, 151, 167–172.

Rosch, E. H. Natural categories. *Cognitive Psychology,* 1973, 4, 328–350.

Rosenberg, M. Factors influencing change in occupational choice. In P. Lazarsfeld & M. Rosenberg (Eds.), *The language of social research*. New York: Free Press, 1955.

Rossiter, C. *Conservatism in America* (2nd ed.). New York: Vintage, 1962.

Rozeboom, W. W. *Foundations of the theory of prediction*. Homewood, Ill.: Dorsey Press, 1966.

Schachter, S., Elertson, N., McBride, D., & Gregory, D. An experimental study of cohesiveness and productivity. *Human Relations,* 1951, 4, 229–238.

Shaver, K. G. *An introduction to attribution processes*. Cambridge, Mass.: Winthrop Publishers, 1975.

Shaw, M. E., & Wright, J. M. *Scales for the measurement of attitudes*. New York: McGraw-Hill, 1967.

Simpson, G. E., & Yinger, J. M. *Racial and cultural minorities* (3rd ed.). New York: Harper & Row, 1965.

Snedecor, G. W., & Cochran, W. C. *Statistical methods* (6th ed.). Ames, Iowa: Iowa State University Press, 1967.

Social Science Research Council. *Theory and practice in historical study: A report of the committee on historiography*. New York: Social Science Research Council, 1946.

Sontag, M. Attitudes toward education and perception of teacher behaviors. *American Educational Research Journal,* 1968, 5, 385–402.

Stephenson, W. *The study of behavior*. Chicago: University of Chicago Press, 1953.

Stevens, S. S. Mathematics, measurement and psychophysics. In S. S. Stevens (Ed.), *Handbook of experimental psychology*. New York: Wiley, 1951.

Stouffer, S. A. *Communism, conformity, and civil liberties*. Garden City, N.Y.: Doubleday, 1955.

Sullins, W. L. *Matrix algebra for statistical applications*. Danville, Ill.: Interstate Printers and Publishers, 1973.

Tatsuoka, M. M. *Discriminant analysis: The study of group differences*. Champaign, Ill.: Institute for Personality and Ability Testing, 1970.

Tatsuoka, M. M. *Multivariate analysis: Techniques for educational and psychological research*. New York: Wiley, 1971.

Thomson, G. The two aspects of science. *Science,* 1960, 132, 996–1000.

Thorndike, R. L. *Reading comprehension education in fifteen countries: International studies in evaluation* (Vol. III). New York: Wiley, 1973.

Thurstone, L. L., & Thurstone, T. G. *Factorial studies of intelligence*. Chicago: University of Chicago Press, 1941.

Townes, C. H. Quantum electronics, and surprise in development of technology. *Science,* 1968, 159, 699–703.

Turing, A. M. Can a machine think? In J. R. Newman (Ed.), *The world of mathematics* (Vol. 4). New York: Simon & Schuster, 1956.

Walster, E., Cleary, T. A., & Clifford, M. M. The effect of race and sex on college admission. *Journal of Educational Sociology,* 1971, 44, 237–244.

Walster, E., Walster, G. W., Piliavin, J., & Schmidt, L. "Playing hard to get": Understanding an elusive phenomenon. *Journal of Personality and Social Psychology,* 1973, 26, 113–121.

Waterman, A. T. Federal support of science. *Science,* 1966, 153, 1359–1361.

Weizenbaum, J. *Computer power and human reason.* San Francisco: Freeman, 1976.

Whiting, J. W. M., & Child, I. L. *Child training and personality: A cross-cultural study.* New Haven, Conn.: Yale University Press, 1953.

Wiley, D. E., Schmidt, W. H., & Bramble, W. J. Studies of a class of covariance structure models. *Journal of the American Statistical Association,* 1973, 68, 317–323.

Woodmansee, J. J., & Cook, S. W. Dimensions of verbal racial attitudes: Their identification and measurement. *Journal of Personality and Social Psychology,* 1967, 7, 240–250.

Worell, L. Level of aspiration and academic success. *Journal of Educational Psychology,* 1959, 50, 47–54.

Name index

Adorno, T. W., 55n, 62, 136, 298
Amón, J., 202–205, 225, 242
Aronson, E., 24, 71n, 84–85, 91–92, 94, 101, 117, 125, 283, 311
Atkinson, J. W., 232
Atkinson, R. C., 284n, 293n
Atkinson, R. L., 284n, 293n

Bargmann, R. E., 224n
Barker, R. G., 42
Beaton, E. A., 32
Bem, D. J., 293n
Bennett, E. L., 34, 123–124
Berelson, B., 122
Berkowitz, L., 32, 38, 104–105, 116n, 208
Bock, R. D., 224n
Boneau, E. A., 266
Borrowman, M., 307
Brain, W. R., 290
Braithwaite, R. B., 280
Braly, K. W., 298
Bramble, W. J., 224n
Brier, A., 250n
Brooks, H., 290
Brown, W. F., 43, 166–168, 170, 215
Burt, C., 301–302

Campbell, A., 286–287, 297
Campbell, D. T., 100, 125
Campbell, E. Q., 119–121
Cantor, N., 275
Cattell, R. B., 193, 224, 232, 281, 293
Chein, I., 94n
Child, I. L., 314–316
Christie, R., 300n
Citron, A., 94n

Clark, C.A., 4–5, 7, 8, 10, 24, 31, 32, 42, 66, 76, 80, 85, 125, 208, 285–286, 288–289, 290, 312–314
Clark R. A., 232
Cleary, T. A., 102–104
Clifford, M. M., 102–104
Cochran, W. C., 88n
Coleman, J. S., 119–121, 224, 286
Comroe, J. H., 115, 291–292
Cook, S. W., 195–200
Cooley, W. W., 210n, 222, 223, 229
Cronbach, L. J., 141n
Crutchfield, R. S., 298
Cutright, P., 177–178

Dembo, T., 42
Deutsch, K. W., 115, 292, 304
Dewey, J., 295
Diamond, M. C., 34, 123–124
Diamond, S., 313
Dillehay, R. C., 300n
Dollard, J., 36, 62, 104
Doob, L. W., 36
Dripps, R. D., 115, 291–292
Dubos, R., 290
Duncan, B., 275
Duncan, O. D., 275

Edwards, A. L., 54n, 100, 266
Ellertson, N., 34
Etzioni, A., 32

Featherman, D. L., 275
Festinger, L., 91n, 101, 113n, 311
Flavell, J. H., 295n
Flowerman, S. H., 298
Frederiksen, H., 32

Subject index

A

Abstractness, 13
Achievement, 7–8
  "explanation" of, 63
  and intelligence, 161–162
  need for, 232–237
  operationally defined, 43
The Achieving Society, 7–8
Agentic state, 113
Aggression, 20
Algorithm, 253–255
American Jewish Committee, 298–299
Analysis:
  definition, 311–312
  and statistics, 311–319
Analysis of covariance structures, 224–237
  compared to path analysis, 236–237
  and computer, 241
  and computer programs, 224n, 225
  theoretical example, 225–231
Analysis of variance, 72
Applied research, 102–104
  and basic research, 282–288
  definition, 283
  and discriminant analysis, 222–223
  two important studies, 286–288
Attribution theory, 293–294
The Authoritarian Personality, 298–300
Authoritarianism:
  meaning of, 140
  and prejudice, 297–300
Authority, and obedience, 108–110

B

Basic research, and applied research, 282–88
Behavior, observation of, 310–311
Behavioral research:
  characteristic features of, 7
  concepts and definitions, 19–28
  definition, 2n
  misconceptions and controversies, 261–278, 279–305
  objectivity in, 10–11
  probability and randomness, 71–74
  relations in, 50–57
Beta weights, 170–171
Bipolar conception, 202, 225

C

Calculator-computer, programmable, 249–250
Canonical correlation, 210–213
Case studies, 276
Categorical variable, 20
Causal inferences, 117n, 118, 161n, 177
Causal model, 233
Certainty, degree of, 65–66
Civil disorder, 155–156
Cluster, of factors, 191
Cognitive dissonance, theory of, 91, 101
Coleman report, 119–121, 158, 224, 286, 290
College admissions, and discrimination, 102–104

329